Grade 12

Grammar for Writing

Complete Course

C Common Core Enriched Edition

Senior Series Consultant

Beverly Ann Chin
Professor of English
University of Montana
Missoula, MT

Series Consultant

Frederick J. Panzer, Sr.
English Dept. Chair, Emeritus
Christopher Columbus High School
Miami, FL

Series Consultant

Charlotte Rosenzweig, Ed. D.
English Dept. Chairperson
Long Beach High School
Long Beach, NY

Series Editor

Phyllis Goldenberg

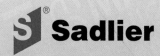

S® **Sadlier**

Reviewers

John Manear
English Dept. Chair
Seton-La Salle High
  School
Pittsburgh, PA

Cary Fuller
English Teacher
Rye Country Day
  School
Rye, NY

Galen Rosenberg
English Dept.
  Coordinator
Los Altos High
  School
Los Altos, CA

Helen Gallagher
English Dept. Chair
Maine East High
  School
Park Ridge, IL

Rose F. Schmitt
Education
  Consultant
Melbourne, FL

Carolyn Waters
Language
  Arts/Reading 7–12
  Supervisor
Cobb County School
  District
Marietta, GA

Roxanne Hoblitt
English Dept. Chair
Belgrade High School
Belgrade, MT

Dr. Muriel Harris
Former Writing Lab
  Director
English Dept.
Purdue University
West Lafayette, IN

Thomas C. Anstett
English Dept. Chair
Lincoln-Way East
  High School
Frankfort, IL

Patricia Stack
English Teacher
South Park High
  School
South Park, PA

Mel Farberman
Former Assistant
  Principal
  Supervision–English
Cardozo High School
Bayside, NY

Wanda Porter
Former English Dept.
  Head
Kamehameha
  Secondary School
Honolulu, HI

Donna Fournier
English Dept. Chair
  and Teacher
Coyle Cassidy
  Memorial High
  School
Taunton, MA

**Katherine R.
Wilson**
Secondary English
  Coordinator, K–12
North Penn School
  District
Lansdale, PA

Student Writers

Adam Andress
Clearwater, FL

Katherine Boone
Dallas, TX

Mark Boucher
Pennington, NJ

Jason Farago
Scarsdale, NY

Molly Gondek
Rocky Hill, CA

Pat Healy
Grosse Pointe
Farms, MI

Katherine Ivers
Meriden, CT

Rachel Kamins
Middletown, CT

Gene Liu
San Francisco, CA

Uthara Srinivasan
Flossmoor, IL

Anh Van Vu
Houston, TX

Lacey Waldron
El Cajon, CA

Andrew Young
Yonkers, NY

Acknowledgments

Every good faith effort has been made to locate the owners of copyrighted material to arrange permission to reprint selections. In several cases this has proved impossible.

Thanks to the following for permission to reprint copyrighted materials.

Excerpt from "Baseball's Negro Leagues," by Matthew Eisenberg. Copyright © 1994 by *The Concord Review*, 730 Boston Post Road, Suite 24, Sudbury, MA 01776. Reprinted by permission.

Excerpt from "The Fall of the Berlin Wall," by Andreas Ramos. Copyright © by Andreas Ramos. Reprinted by permission of the author.

Excerpt from "Lincoln-Douglas Debates," by David Herbert Donald. Reprinted with the permission of Simon & Schuster Adult Publishing Group. From *Lincoln*, by David Herbert Donald. Copyright © 1995 by David Herbert Donald.

"On Hardy's *The Mayor of Casterbridge*," by Dennis Potter. Copyright © 1978 by PFH (Overseas) Ltd.

"Prepared for Life: Loving the liberal arts:...," by Alan Cordova. From *Current Magazine*, Summer 2006. Copyright © 2006 by Newsweek, Inc. All rights reserved. Reprinted with permission.

"The Rural Life: A Momentary Pause," by Verlyn Klinkenborg. Copyright © 2006 by The New York Times Co. Reprinted with permission.

Excerpt from *Understanding Human Behavior: An Introduction to Psychology*, second edition, by James V. McConnell. Copyright © 1977. Reprinted with permission of Wadsworth, a division of Thomson Learning: www. thomsonrights.com

"We've Overlooked One of Our Greatest Assets," by William D. Green. From *Newsweek*, May 1, 2006. Copyright © 2006 by Newsweek, Inc. All rights reserved. Reprinted by permission.

Credits

Cover Art and Design
Quarasan, Inc.

Interior Photos
Neal Farris: 21 right, 36, 213, 265. Getty Images/John W. Banagan: 36 background; Image Source: 283; James Lauritz: 139;

M. Llorden: 303; Antonio Mo: 175; Photodisc: 119, 159 right, 159 left; Bill Reitzel: 52; Lorne Resnick: 21 background; Harald Sund: 52 background; Travel Pix: 159 background; Kari Weatherly: 229 background. Jupiter Images/ Rubberball: 229.

Puncshstock/Comstock: 195; Digital Vision: 247, 317 inset; Photodisc: 8, 317 background; Rubberball: 317. Used under license from Shutterstock.com/ Styve Beineck: 175 background; Cloki: 139 background; Dario Diament: 8 background; Colman

Lerner Garardo: 195 background; Scott Kapich: 119 background; Karen Kean: 21 left; Sean Nel: 283 background; Stuart Taylor: 265 background; Hedser van Brug: 247 background; Wizdata, Inc.: 213 background, 303 background.

As a student, you are constantly being challenged to write correctly and effectively in a variety of subjects. From homework to standardized tests, more and more assignments require you to write in a clear, correct, and persuasive way.

This new *Common Core Enriched Edition* of *Grammar for Writing* has been prepared to help you master the writing and language skills you'll need to meet the Common Core State Standards, which have been designed to ensure college and career readiness for all students.

The writing section of this book takes you through the writing process and contains **Writing Workshops** with instruction and practice in different types of writing, including the kinds of writing called for on standardized tests and the Common Core assessments.

In the grammar section, **Test-Taking Tips** appear in lessons covering the grammar and usage skills most often assessed on tests, and **grammar and usage practice** in standardized-test formats is included as well.

Of course, there are many reasons to write effectively other than to score well on standardized tests and other assessments. People judge you by the way you write and speak. Your use of English is evaluated in the writing you do in school, on job and college applications, and in many different kinds of careers.

No textbook can make writing easy. Good writers work hard and revise their work often to find just the right words to move their audience. Consequently, in *Grammar for Writing* you will find many exercises called **Write What You Think**. These exercises are designed to help guide you in developing clear, logical arguments to persuade people that your opinion is right. These exercises will sharpen your thinking as well as your writing skills.

No one has to prove that writing is important—it just *is*. But writing can always be improved, and the best way to improve it is to learn and practice the skills and strategies in this book. *Grammar for Writing* presents the rules of grammar as simply as possible; whether you are merely refreshing your memory or learning the concepts for the first time, you'll be able to understand the rules and *apply* them to your writing.

All of the skills you learn and practice in this book—grammar, writing, and thinking—will last you a lifetime.

Good Luck!
The Authors

CONTENTS

COMPOSITION

GRAMMAR

* Denotes lessons with skills most commonly assessed on standardized tests.

USAGE

* Denotes lessons with skills most commonly assessed on standardized tests.

MECHANICS

* Denotes lessons with skills most commonly assessed on standardized tests.

STANDARDIZED TEST PRACTICE

* Denotes lessons with skills most commonly assessed on standardized tests.

The Writing Process

Prewriting: Gathering Ideas

▶ **Prewriting** is all the thinking, planning, and organizing you do before you actually start writing.

Sometimes, you have a burning desire to write, and you know exactly what you want to say. More often, though, you and other writers need to take a few steps before writing. Here are five of the many strategies that writers find helpful during the prewriting stage, when they face a blank page or screen.

PREWRITING STRATEGIES

1. *What if?* **questions** One way to demonstrate creativity is to imagine what hasn't happened or what might happen in the future.

You might ask yourself imaginative questions about anything. For example, "What if I had been born in a different age?" and "What if I didn't live in this country?" Or ask *What if?* questions about a broad topic that you need to narrow, or limit. For example, if a teacher assigns you the general topic, "The Way West," you might make a list such as the following *What if?* questions; they can help you focus on a challenging but narrower topic.

> ### Writing Model
>
> *What if gold had not been discovered in 1848 in California?*
> *What if there had been railroads all the way to California in 1848—*
> *or airplanes?*
> *What if the Rocky Mountains had been impassable?*

2. **Brainstorming** Brainstorming is related to *What if?* questions because, when you brainstorm, you let your mind roam freely to create an open-ended list of words and phrases.

Begin by selecting a single word or topic, and write down everything that comes to mind regarding that word or topic. Focus on each idea as it comes without going back to fix mistakes or make changes. If you brainstorm with a group or a partner, make sure one person keeps the record of everything that is said, and be sure to add everyone's contributions to the list. When you run out of thoughts, go through the list item by item, and circle the entries that most appeal to you as topics to write about.

Enriching Your Vocabulary

A *strategy* is a plan for achieving a particular goal. The related word, *stratagem*, is a trick meant to achieve a goal through some deception. The *stratagem* of the Greeks in the war against Troy was to pretend to withdraw, leaving behind them the Trojan Horse, a giant wooden horse that concealed a powerful raiding army.

Writing Model

ASSIGNMENT: Select an aspect of law in the old West, and write three hundred words about it.

BRAINSTORMING LIST:

Cowboys	Ranchers	Tombstone & other towns
Famous gunfighters	Wyatt Earp	Saloons and card games
Stagecoach holdups	Nonviolence?	Stereotypes of lawmen in movies and TV

3. **Freewriting** This strategy for finding a topic to write about is similar to brainstorming but involves *nonstop* writing.

When you freewrite, let your writing wander. Don't worry about writing complete sentences or about grammar or spelling. If you get stuck, just write the same word over until you get a new thought. Keep moving forward, even if you make mistakes. Write without stopping for five minutes.

Writing Model

TOPIC: Cattle drives

When did cattle drives happen? For how long? Where did they start from? Texas? Where did they end? Why? How many cowboys needed for how many animals? What were the trails like? Life on the trails, life on the trails, what can I say about that? How about the dangers and pleasures of life on the trail? Or how about famous cowboys? Cow towns? Why did cattle drives happen? Huh? That's a pretty basic question. Basic is good. OK. That's what I want to focus on. What the purpose of the cattle drives was in the first place.

4. **Clustering, Mapping, or Webbing** If you already know a topic well, this strategy is helpful for gathering and organizing details or for breaking a large topic into smaller parts.

First, write your topic (or any word or phrase) in the middle of a piece of paper, and then circle it. Around the circled topic, write subtopics—related words and phrases. Circle each new word or phrase, and connect it to your original topic by drawing a line. Each new word or phrase may have subtopics, too. Keep going until you run out of thoughts. See the example on the following page.

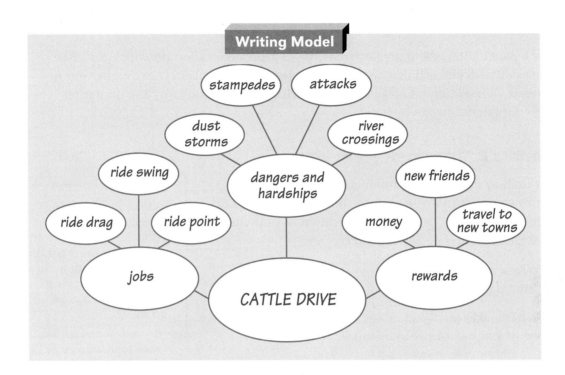

Writing Model

5. **Writer's Notebook** This prewriting strategy involves keeping a separate notebook or folder (paper or electronic) in which you jot down experiences and thoughts about anything that interests you.

Try to jot down thoughts in your writer's notebook on a regular basis. Then, when your teacher gives you an assignment to "write about something that you care about," you can convert your writer's notebook notes into effective paragraphs, essays, and short stories. Include in your notebook any quotations or thoughts you get from films, interviews, artworks, or even cartoons. Explain in your notebook why these ideas affected you.

Writing Model

Mon. 5/2.
Home sick; watched hours of TV. Saw movie about lonely, hard, but rewarding life of homesteader in the old West. Got new appreciation of value of hard work and perseverance. Life was tough then! Simple pleasures were important—still are, I think. What must life have been like for my great-grandparents when they first came to this country and struggled to get a foothold? I wonder. Ought to find out sometime.

EXERCISE 1 Maintaining a Writer's Notebook

Use a paper notebook or an electronic file to keep a quotation notebook for three consecutive days. Each day, write down at least one quotation that caught your interest—something you read or heard. Include a note about why the quotation got your attention.

EXERCISE 2 Thinking of Topic Ideas

For each of the following numbered items, come up with two topics that you could write about in a one- to three-page paper. Use at least three different prewriting strategies to generate writing topics.

1. Why a particular celebrity, politician, or artist is popular

2. What makes an object, place, activity, or event stand out in your memory

3. Something unusual that happened to you and that you're willing to share with readers

4. A school, local, or national issue you care about

EXERCISE 3 Narrowing a Topic

Choose two of the broad, general topics below. For each one you select, suggest three narrower topics that you can cover in a three-page essay.

TOO BROAD   Television

LIMITED   The fall's new sitcoms; Monday night's lineup; the best soap opera

1. Flowers   3. Civil Rights

2. Sea Travel   4. College

EXERCISE 4 Gathering Supporting Details

Choose one of the narrower topics you identified in Exercise 3. Generate ideas and details about that topic by brainstorming, clustering, or asking *What if?* questions.

WRITING HINT

Some of the prewriting strategies covered in this lesson deal with narrowing a topic. Narrowing is a key to successful writing. How can you tell if a topic is too broad, too narrow, or just right?

• If you can break down your topic into more than five subtopics, it may be too broad. Consider one of the narrower subtopics to write about.

• If you cannot break down your topic into more than two subtopics, it may be too narrow already. Think more broadly.

Organizing the Ideas and Drafting

▐▐▶ Now that you've gathered your ideas, decide on the order in which to present them. Think about whether the best way to sequence your ideas would be, for example, chronological order, order of importance, compare and contrast, or cause and effect.

▐▐▶ You may want to use your prewriting notes to create an **outline**. An outline forces you to make two important decisions about your prewriting notes: (1) which main ideas and supporting details to use in your draft and (2) in what order to present them.

The outline at right is rough. You may wish to add details or to write your outline in full sentences. Either way, your outline should help guide you as you draft your paragraph or essay.

▐▐▶ One of the most important questions to ask yourself before you write is "What should my style be?" Writing style is determined by two things: your audience and your purpose.

Your **audience** is the person or persons who will read what you write. Your **purpose** may be to describe, to explain, to tell what happened, to persuade, or to entertain. Or you may have a combination of purposes. Together, the audience and the purpose will determine your **style**—the manner in which you express your thoughts.

▐▐▶ **Drafting** is the step in the writing process in which you put your thoughts into sentences and paragraphs.

When you have narrowed your topic, generated prewriting notes, laid out an outline, and considered your audience and purpose, it's time to apply the following strategies for writing your first draft.

Writing Model

A Rough Outline: Two Controversial Home Run Races

I. The Maris/Ruth controversy

   A. Ruth's record

   B. Maris's record

   C. Nature of the 1961 controversy

II. McGwire/Sosa home run race

   A. State of the national pastime

   B. Effects on the game of baseball

   C. Nature of the 1998 controversy

DRAFTING STRATEGIES

1. **Write the Big Idea** Remember your writing audience and purpose, and draft a sentence that expresses the main idea of your paragraph or essay. As some writers do, you may want to begin your draft with this sentence. Or, as others do, you might simply keep this sentence in mind as you write.

2. **Grab Your Reader** Begin with a "hook," or a statement or question certain to catch your reader's attention.

3. **Stay Flexible** Follow the basic direction of your organizational plan, but do make appropriate changes and add or drop details if necessary. Don't concern yourself with mistakes when you draft. Just focus on getting your ideas down on paper.

4. **Create an Ending** Conclude your writing in your last paragraph by including one or more sentences that revisit your main idea. A successful conclusion is one that wraps up your writing logically and gracefully. It may contain a quote, a call to action, or a final thought on the subject.

Below is a first draft based on the outline on page 13. The writer's purpose was to inform history classmates about two controversial home run races. Remember, when you're drafting, let your ideas flow without pausing to fix mistakes. You'll have time for that during the next two steps in the writing process: revising and editing.

Writing Model

What information in the draft is redundant and can be deleted?

Remember, drafting is only one part of the writing process.

Does the writer include a memorable ending?

In 1961, there was much controversy when Roger Maris broke baseball icon Babe Ruth's longstanding home run record of 60 "round trippers." The concern was that Maris hit his 61 home runs in a 162-game season, rather than in the 154-game season of Ruth's time.

In 1998, when baseball attendance was getting less and less, another home run race rejuvenated the sport. It returned to its former status as a national pastime. Baseball was losing fans. That year just about every at-bat of Mark McGwire and Sammy Sosa was covered by the media, as both people tried to beat Maris's record. Although both players broke it by a lot, their achievements, like Maris's, were not without controversy. What was at issue this time was not the length of the season, but whether McGwire's and Sosa's awesome feats were phony. What hurt their achievements was that both players had used performance enhancers.

Critical Thinking   After reading the draft on page 14, answer the following questions.

1. What sentence in the first paragraph expresses its main idea?

2. What sentence in the second paragraph expresses its main idea?

3. How does the writer sequence her ideas in the draft?

4. Did the writer follow the general plan of her outline?

> **WRITING HINT**
>
> Be alert to what is being asked of you for each writing assignment. Pay special attention to the verbs: *analyze, judge, discuss*. Make sure you know your writing purpose.

EXERCISE 5 Making an Outline

For this assignment, your audience is your language arts class. Your purpose is to inform. Choose a topic you know something about—a hobby, an interest, or something you've recently studied. Generate prewriting notes, using any of the strategies from Lesson 1.1. Then write an outline to plan a two- or three-page paper.

EXERCISE 6 Drafting Part of a Paper

Using your outline from Exercise 5, draft two or three pages. Remember who your audience is and what your purpose is—to give information.

EXERCISE 7 Outlining and Drafting Another Paper

Use the prewriting notes you made for a limited topic in Exercise 4, page 12. First, choose and describe your audience and purpose for writing. Then create an outline. Before you begin drafting, meet with a partner or small group to discuss what you're planning to write. See if you can clearly summarize your topic, main idea(s), and supporting details. Use the drafting strategies from this lesson as you prepare your paper.

Revising

�|||▶ When you **revise**, you shape your draft into its almost-final form.

At this stage in the writing process, you try to make your draft clearer. Now is the time to add new information, to cut words or sentences, to change the order in which information appears, and to replace weak words with more effective ones. Use the revising strategies below to help you improve your first draft.

REVISING STRATEGIES

When you revise, you look for ways to eliminate problems with ideas and unity, organization and coherence, sentence variety, and word choice. To revise, try this four-step strategy. Reread your first draft four separate times, concentrating on only one of the issues below with each reading.

1. **Ideas and Unity** Can you summarize your main idea(s) or the main event of your paper? Do you have enough supporting details? Do you have too many? Will adding or cutting details improve your paper? Do you need more background information? Is everything you've written relevant?

2. **Organization and Coherence** Does the opening sentence grab the reader's attention? Can you improve your draft by rearranging paragraphs or by moving sentences? Do you present your information in an order that makes sense for your purpose and audience? Do you need to add any transitions? Do you have an effective concluding paragraph?

3. **Sentence Variety** Do your sentences read smoothly? Have you varied their structures, beginnings, and lengths? Would some sentences work better combined? In short, are you satifisfied with *how* you say *what* you say?

4. **Word Choice** Keep an eye out for vague nouns, verbs, and modifiers that you can replace with more precise words. Look for clichés or overused words that you can replace with fresh ones to enliven your descriptions. Is your choice of vocabulary appropriate for your intended audience? Should you replace any difficult words with simpler ones? Do you need to define any technical terms you've used?

Below is the first draft on baseball's home run controversies from Lesson 1.2. Notice the revisions the writer has made to it.

Writing Model

How did the writer's changes in word choice affect the quality of the writing?

In 1961, there was much controversy when Roger Maris broke baseball icon Babe Ruth's longstanding home run record of 60 "round trippers." The concern was that Maris hit his 61 home runs in a 162-game season, rather than in the 154-game season of Ruth's time.

In 1998, when baseball attendance was ~declining,~ ~~getting less and less,~~ another home run race rejuvenated the sport. ~~It returned~~ *returning it* to its former status as a national pastime. ~~Baseball was losing fans.~~ That year just about every at-bat of Mark McGwire and Sammy Sosa was covered by the media, as both *sluggers* ~~people~~ tried to beat Maris's record.

What do you notice that's different from the first draft and this revision?

Although both players ~~broke it by a lot,~~ *handily shattered it,* their achievements, like Maris's, were not without controversy. What was at issue this time was not the length of the season, but whether McGwire's and Sosa's *remarkable* ~~awesome~~ feats were *tainted* ~~phony~~. What *diminished* ~~hurt~~ their achievements was the *perception* ~~thought~~ that both players had used performance enhancers.

Does the writer create an ending?

What would Maris think about this? What would the Babe say? They might agree that these controversies are difficult to resolve.

▸ **Working with a writing partner** involves using revising strategies to give feedback to your classmates and getting help from them on your works in progress.

Exercise 8 Revising a Letter to a Government Official

Imagine you are revising a letter to your state representative. Focus on the four issues of ideas and unity, organization and coherence, sentence variety, and word choice. Your purpose is to persuade. There is no single correct way to revise this letter. Feel free to add additional details and delete sentences that stray from the main idea. Consider adding transitions, combining or breaking apart sentences, and offering examples.

Dear Representative:

[1]I'm writing to you because I wish to bring to your attention the icky state of our local park, James Park. [2]The park, once beautiful and long a cherished neighborhood gathering place, has become a pain and even a hazard. [3]It is no longer a place families can enjoy. [4]We, the concerned citizens of your district, urge you to look into ways to bring our park back.

[5]In the past, the park was the scene of picnics, concerts, and fairs. [6]And many positive community activities took place there as well as picnics. [7]Sadly, these events don't happen now because our park has become a dangerous, run-down eyesore. [8]The lighting is crummy, the benches are broken, the bicycle paths are overgrown, all the landscaping and ball fields are bad news, and all the rowboats are leaking. [9]There aren't enough workers to give our beloved park the care and attention it asks for. [10]In short, James Park is a disaster. [11]You need to act. [12]Show you care. [13]Bring our park back to life. [14]You'll quickly discover how supportive your constituency is. [15]You gotta care about stuff like this. [16]Show us the dough!

EXERCISE 9 Revising a Paper

Use the guidelines in this lesson to revise any paper you've written for this or another class.

EXERCISE 10 Work with a Writing Partner

1. Revise the paper you drafted in Lesson 1.2, Exercise 6. Use the revising strategies in this lesson to improve your draft.

2. Work with a partner to revise your paper. Allow your partner to read your paper without your input. Your partner should respond to your writing using the revising strategies on page 16 as a guide.

3. Review your writing partner's comments on your paper and incorporate those that you feel will improve your writing. Ask for his or her positive comments as well as questions and suggestions for improvement.

Editing and Proofreading

▶ When you **edit** or **proofread** (these words mean the same thing), you search for mistakes in spelling, punctuation, and capitalization.

Readers will judge your writing, to a greater or lesser extent, by your use of the conventions of standard written English. Even the most careful writers need to proofread their work! Always check your own writing for errors in spelling, punctuation, capitalization, and usage.

EDITING QUESTIONS

1. **Spelling** Are all words spelled correctly? Use a college dictionary or the spell-checker on your computer to make necessary corrections. Watch out for words that you've spelled correctly but that don't fit the sentence (*their* instead of *there* or *they're*, for example). Your spell-checker won't catch these homonyms.

2. **Capitalization** Do all proper nouns and proper adjectives begin with capital letters? Have you capitalized a word that's supposed to start with a lowercase letter? Do all your sentences or direct quotations begin with capital letters?

3. **Punctuation** Have you used commas and other punctuation marks correctly? Is dialogue correctly punctuated?

4. **Sentence Correctness** Does the passage contain any fragments, run-ons, or misplaced modifiers?

5. **Verbs** Do all present tense verbs agree with their subjects? Are verb tenses consistent and correct?

6. **Pronouns** Are pronoun references clear? Do all the pronouns agree with their antecedents?

7. **Usage** Are adjectives modifying nouns and pronouns? Are adverbs modifying verbs, adjectives, and other adverbs? Are all comparisons clear and complete? Do comparisons correctly use the *-er/more* and *-est/most* forms?

▶ **Publishing** means sharing what you've written. For example, ask friends and family to read your work, or deliver it to them in a multimedia presentation. You can also use a computer and the Internet to share your work with a wider audience. For more ideas on how to publish your writing, see the following page.

Enriching Your Vocabulary

The verb *transpose*, used in proofreading (see page 20), comes from the Latin *transponere*, which means "to change the position of." *Transpose* can also be used in the sense of "to change in nature or form." The director *transposed* the setting of *Romeo* and *Juliet* from Verona to Civil War America.

See **Mechanics**, Lesson 14.5, for more on punctuating dialogue.

Proofreading Symbols		
CORRECTION	**SYMBOL**	**EXAMPLE**
Delete (remove).	ℯ	She ate a ℯpeach.
Insert.	^	He sta^red in the movie.
Transpose (switch).	⌐⌐	I only ate one.
Capitalize.	≡	did Mayor Jones show up?
Make lowercase.	/	Were other Mayors there?
Start a new paragraph.	¶	¶"Yes," they cried.
Add space.	#	We visited New#York.
Close up space.	⌣	She loves foot ball.

Exercise 11 Proofreading a Paragraph

Find and correct every error in the following paragraph. Write the corrected paragraph on a separate piece of paper.

[1]*A Portrait of the artist as a Young Man*: by James joyce is a novel in five sections. [2]It is considered by many two be the best example of a book that shows the psychological and morale development of its mane character? [3]It includes the rich symbolic and stream-of consciousness language that characterized Joyce's later works. [4]The novel is autobiographical, portraying theearly years of Stephen Dedalus, a character who reappears in Joyce's masterpiece, *Ulysses* (1922). [5]Joyce wrote each of the Five sections of *A Portrait of the Artist as a Young Man* in a third-person voice that reflects stephens age and emotional State. [6]For example, their earliest childhood memories are written in simple, childlike language.

Publishing Suggestions
WRITTEN WORDS
Magazine of student writing
School or local paper
Local or national poetry, story, or essay contest
Class anthology
Writing portfolio
Letters/e-mail
SPOKEN WORDS
Speech
Audio podcast
Oral interpretation
Radio broadcast
Reader's theater
Interview
Debate
DIGITAL
E-mail
E-book
Web site
Blog
Podcast
Video recording

Writing Effective Paragraphs and Essays

Ideas and Unity

||||➡ A paragraph has **unity** (it is unified) when all of its sentences focus on a single main **idea**.

As you draft a paragraph, focus on one main idea. Your single focus will help your audience stay with you. Then, when you revise, you'll have another chance to improve unity by dropping any irrelevant sentences or details.

||||➡ A **topic sentence** states the paragraph's main idea.

Although a topic sentence is most often the first or second sentence, announcing what's coming in the rest of the paragraph, you can place a topic sentence in the middle or at the end of a paragraph. When a topic sentence appears at the end of a paragraph, it serves as a summary statement.

Some paragraphs—especially narrative and descriptive paragraphs—have no topic sentences. But even a paragraph without a directly stated topic sentence usually suggests, or implies, a main idea.

||||➡ A paragraph may have not only an opening topic sentence but also a **clincher sentence**, which ends the paragraph.

Use clincher sentences for the following purposes: to restate a topic, to summarize, to add persuasive power, and to create a transition to the main idea of the next paragraph.

Read the following two paragraphs about vintage baseball. Each is an example of a paragraph with unity.

Enriching Your Vocabulary

The word *converged*, used on page 23, comes from the Latin prefix *com*, meaning "together," and the root *vergere*, meaning "to turn or bend." Thus, the meaning of *converge* is "to bring together." A traffic light might be installed where Main Street *converges* with Broad Street.

Writing Model

Topic sentence stating boom in vintage baseball

Statistics that support main idea

Topic sentence about the Old Bethpage league

[1]To most people, the idea of playing baseball without a glove probably sounds like canoeing without a paddle. [2]At the Old Bethpage Village Restoration in Old Bethpage, New York, however, it's the only sporting way to play. [3]Vintage baseball is booming around the United States. [4]At least 70 programs are fielding teams that play by rules of past eras, which range from 1845 to 1924; many such clubs have appeared just in the past five years. [5]The biggest and most competitive of all is the Old Time Base Ball Program at Old Bethpage.

[6]"Ours is the only program with full-blown leagues," says Ken Balcom, the museum village's assistant site director. [7]Old-time baseball

games have been played here since 1980 as one of the village's living-history demonstrations, like quilt-making and black-smithing. [8]The program got a boost four years ago when hundreds of baseball-hungry Long Islanders, disgusted that the major leagues' millionaires were out on strike, converged on Old Bethpage to watch or to play an older, purer game. [9]Today, the program involves 130 players, all volunteers, on ten teams in two leagues, over a 60-game season.

— Doug Stewart, "The Old Ball Game"

Incident that supports main idea

Clincher sentence

SKILLS FOR MAINTAINING UNITY

1. **Topic Sentence** As with any sentence, a topic sentence can be long or short, simple or complex. Stewart may have chosen any number of ways to state the main idea of his first paragraph. For example, he may have written the following topic sentence.

   The cry "Play ball" is changing to "Play *old* ball" as vintage baseball catches on around the country.

2. **One Main Idea** Each of the model paragraphs sticks to its main idea. Notice how Stewart grabs the reader with the first sentence of the first paragraph but avoids cluttering either paragraph with unnecessary sentences.

3. **Clincher Sentence** Stewart uses a clincher sentence at the end of the second paragraph to restate—with more specifics—the idea expressed in the topic sentence of the first paragraph.

EXERCISE 1 Revising a Paragraph

1. Which of the following sentences would work in place of the topic sentence in the first paragraph by Stewart? Give reasons for your choice.

   a. Playing vintage baseball is the only way to go.

   b. Old-time baseball programs are a new sensation.

2. Which of the following sentences could serve as a clincher sentence for the first paragraph by Stewart? Explain your choice.

   a. People are streaming to old-time baseball games in Old Bethpage and all over the country.

   b. In vintage baseball games, like the real old-time baseball contests, the scores are very high.

Elaborating with Supporting Details

▐▐▐▶ **Elaboration**, or **development**, is the process of adding details to support a main idea.

You must make your paragraphs interesting, specific, and complete. To do so, develop or support each paragraph's main idea by using the following kinds of details: **facts**, **statistics**, **quotations**, **definitions**, **anecdotes** or **incidents**, **examples**, **reasons**, and **comparisons**.

Feel free to use more than one kind of supporting detail in a paragraph. Just make certain that each sentence adds something to the paragraph that helps readers to better understand your subject or to appreciate your view.

The writer of the following paragraph realized that the first draft did not contain enough specific details to support her topic sentence. Notice the details she added during revision to elaborate on her main idea and to interest her readers.

WRITING HINT

Wandering from one idea to a completely different idea is fine in freewriting but not in the paragraphs you're writing for an audience. Delete or revise sentences that do not support your main idea, or you may confuse readers.

Writing Model

[1]In ancient Greece, *from 776 B.C. to A.D. 394,* athletic games took place every four years at *sacred site of Olympia* the same place. [2]A truce ~~was always observed~~ *Warring city-states always observed* as the games approached; it lasted for the duration of the contests. [3]A ~~horse race~~ *dangerous chariot race in which drivers drove teams of horses over a treacherous course* opened each series of Olympic games. [4]But the greatest event was the pentathlon, *which included a foot race, wrestling, jumping, and throwing both the discus and the javelin* [5]In 1896, a French baron revived the games in Athens. *, Pierre de Coubertin,*

EXERCISE 2 Improving Unity and Adding Details

Revise the paragraph on the following page. Cross out any words or sentences that damage the paragraph's unity by moving away from the main idea. Then, from the list below the paragraph, select the details that you think would improve it. Write the letter of the detail where you think it belongs in the paragraph. You may want to insert some of the details as phrases or clauses. Write the fully revised paragraph on a separate piece of paper.

[1]In addition to athletics, the ancient Greeks excelled in architecture. [2]The elegant but simple buildings they designed reflected their love of balance and their appreciation of beauty. [3]No buildings meant more to them than their temples. [4]Greek artisans produced fine pottery. [5]The Parthenon, which is still standing, is a good example of the Greek belief in harmony and proportion. [6]Its carefully carved columns create the impression of height and lightness. [7]Greek sculptors also believed in perfect harmony.

Details
A. Most Greeks were farmers who used ox-drawn plows.
B. Pericles rebuilt Athens.
C. Many public buildings of our time use graceful stone columns
   modeled on those of the Greeks.
D. The Greek temples were built in honor of gods and goddesses.

Exercise 3 Improving Unity and Adding Details

Work with a partner or small group to revise the following paragraph. Cross out any words or sentences that damage the paragraph's unity by moving away from the main idea. Then write the letter of the detail where you think it belongs in the paragraph. You may want to insert some of the details as phrases or clauses. Write the fully revised paragraph on a separate piece of paper.

[1]Any discussion of written history should begin with the work of the great Greek historians Herodotus (485–424 B.C.) and Thucydides (460–395 B.C.). [2]Herodotus was the first to attempt to gather and analyze information about the past. [3]He traveled widely and learned firsthand about cultures and geography. [4]In so doing, he presented a great deal of useful information about the ancient world. [5]Egyptian scribes of an earlier era wanted only to show the deeds of the pharaohs. [6]Thucydides, who wrote *History of the Peloponnesian Wars*, improved on the methods of Herodotus. [7]He tried to present a balanced perspective on events and to include only information he could substantiate. [8]In the century

following the wars between Athens and Sparta, Alexander spread Greek

civilization across a huge empire.

Details

A. Herodotus wrote *History of the Persian Wars*.
B. Herodotus did not always distinguish fact from legend in his
   writings.
C. Athens was defeated by Sparta in the Peloponnesian Wars.
D. Thucydides set an example of impartial reporting for later
   historians.

EXERCISE 4 Writing a Paragraph from Notes

On a separate piece of paper, write a unified, well-developed paragraph based on
the information on the notecard below. You do not need to use all of the
information. Make sure your paragraph contains a clear topic sentence.

Socrates (469–399 B.C.)

One of the most influential figures in history and philosophy

Son of poor stonecutter

Championed the use of reason to challenge conventional ideas

Spent his days talking and listening to people

Left no writings of his beliefs; Plato would record his ideas later

Believed that through knowledge people could discover how to act

_His question-answer technique that used reason to examine beliefs came
to be known as the "Socratic method."_

Seen as troublemaker and dangerous corrupter of Athens's youth

Accused of not honoring the gods

Condemned to death by Athenian jury; had to drink hemlock (deadly poison)

Plato, his most famous pupil, was an aristocrat.

Plato was 28 when his mentor died.

Organization and Coherence

▐▐▐▶ Each of your paragraphs should be **coherent**; that is, its sentences should be sensibly **organized** so that your reader can follow your thoughts easily.

Another term for coherence is flow. Here are three tips for writing coherent paragraphs—paragraphs that flow well.

Strategies for Writing Coherently

1. **Be Clear** The primary goals of any paragraph are simplicity and directness. Eliminate wordiness and avoid overly long and complicated sentences.

2. **Guide the Reader** Use signposts that alert the reader to what lies ahead and the relationship among thoughts. Signposts include transitional expressions (like those on page 28) and pronouns and synonyms that refer to terms you've already used. Repeating key words and phrases emphasizes important points and also helps to connect your thoughts. Using parallel structures also improves coherence.

3. **Put Your Thoughts in Order** Arrange information so that "first things come first."

▐▐▐▶ You can choose from at least five common ways for organizing paragraphs and essays.

> See
> **Grammar,**
> Lesson 8.6, for
> more on
> parallel
> structure.

- **Chronological Order** Organizing your writing chronologically means telling about events in the order in which they occurred. Use chronological order for narrative paragraphs, for writing about a historical event, and for describing the steps in a process.

- **Spatial Order** Organize your ideas spatially when you wish to describe a person, place, or object. Provide details in an orderly way—for example, moving from left to right, top to bottom, near to far, or inside to outside.

- **Order of Importance** Organize your thoughts by degree of importance when you are writing to persuade your readers. Present your reasons and other details in order of increasing or decreasing importance.

- **Logical Order** Organize your ideas logically to give readers information in the order they need to know it. Use logic to determine which details to group together or where to provide definitions or background information.

Organization and Coherence

- **General-Specific Order** Make a general statement first, and then include the specifics that support the generalization. Or reverse your information, giving specific details first and ending with the generalization that grows out of the details.

The revisions in the following model show how one writer improved organization and coherence in response to a writing partner's notes in the margin.

Writing Model

Put in chronological order.

Eliminate repetition.

Add transition.

Add transition.

Add transition.

Add transition.
Eliminate wordiness.

Use pronoun.
Eliminate repetition.

[1]Dinosaur hunting continues today. [2]Dinosaurs inhabited North America from the Triassic time right through the rest of the Jurassic and Cretaceous periods ~~in North America~~. [3]American dinosaur discovery dates from 1818, when Anchisaurus bones were found in Connecticut. [4]*Next,* Birdlike tracks were discovered in Massachusetts. [5]*Then,* In 1856, a Philadelphia anatomist identified three dinosaurs from fossil teeth. [6]*Soon after that,* In 1858, Hadrosaurus was described from a partial skeleton. [7]*But* Dinosaur discovery really got going in the 1870s, ~~when there began~~ *with* a fierce competition to find and name the largest ~~dinosaurs~~ *ones*. [8]The fossil remains of many ~~Late Jurassic~~ giants were discovered in the Late Jurassic rocks in Colorado and Wyoming.

Some Common Transitional Words and Expressions

To show **time**		To show **examples**		To show **order of importance**		To **compare**	
after	first	for example	namely	above all	second	also	as
afterward	immediately	for instance	that is	finally	then	and	similarly
at last	later	in addition		first	last	like	too
before	soon	in other words		most important		likewise	
during	then						
finally	when	To **summarize**		To show **cause and effect**		To **contrast**	
		all in all	finally			although	but
To show **position**		as a result	therefore	as a result	since	however	still
above	inside	in conclusion	thus	because	so	in contrast (to)	yet
across	into	in summary		consequently	so that	nevertheless	
among	off			if . . . then	therefore	on the other hand	
behind	outside	To **emphasize**		for that reason			
below	there	for this reason	again				
between	through	moreover	in fact				
in front of	under	most important					

EXERCISE 5 Revising a Paragraph for Organization and Coherence

On a separate piece of paper, improve the following paragraph by putting its details into a clear spatial order. Add new details as necessary, and add transitional expressions, reorder information, and combine sentences. Make any other changes you think will improve the paragraph.

[1]You enter the natural history museum by walking up several tiers of steps to the main door. [2]You pass bronze signs with names of famous naturalists. [3]Then you find yourself in a large room. [4]There is a dome. [5]There is also an information booth. [6]That is in the center of the room. [7]From there, you can make out the Hall of North American Mammals. [8]If you look to the right, there's the Hall of African Mammals. [9]Then there's the Egyptian Wing and then the Hall of Fishes. [10]The other way has the Hall of Invertebrates, and then there's a room with huge bugs, and then there's the museum's restaurant. [11]If you're hungry, you can eat. [12]The second floor has many other exhibit halls, so does the third floor, too. [13]My favorite exhibit way up on the third floor is the Hall of Biodiversity. [14]It is a new exhibit.

EXERCISE 6 Writing a Paragraph from Notes

Write a unified, coherent, well-developed paragraph based on the information in the note card below. You do not need to use all of the information. Be sure to include a clear topic sentence.

Pericles (495–429 B.C.)

Great leader of city-state of Athens during its Golden Age (460–430 B.C.)

A nobleman; wealthy; well-liked

Supported democracy
– people making decisions for themselves
– an assembly of thousands of Athenian men met many times a year and voted on the city's business

Activities: 1) built up navy, trade by sea; 2) hired best artists to create new buildings; 3) encouraged scientists, philosophers

Died in 429 B.C. during war that Sparta (another city-state) started with Athens

Types of Paragraphs and Longer Writing

Your purpose in writing may be to describe, to tell a story, to explain or inform, or to persuade. In this lesson, you'll examine these different purposes for writing paragraphs and longer pieces.

DESCRIPTIVE

Use the following suggestions when your purpose for writing is to tell about a person, emotion, animal, place, or object.

- **Use sensory details** to appeal to the reader's five senses (sight, hearing, smell, touch, and taste) and to create a **main impression**, or **mood**.

- **Use spatial order** to present the sensory details from left to right, top to bottom, near to far, or inside to outside.

Writing Model

Spatial order— far to near

Sight detail

Taste detail

Smell detail

Sound detail

¹Just below the bare, rocky summit, we unexpectedly came upon a swimming-pool-sized pond. ²It was gray-green and tucked in amongst the weathered and gently rounded gray and green-gray boulders and jagged slabs of stone. ³We sat for a moment and rested. ⁴Moist clouds had enveloped the mountain, and we could see no more than a few hundred yards distant in any direction. ⁵The icy water had a clean, fresh, invigorating taste. ⁶Our deep breaths were rewarded with the bracing, moist mountain air, which was sweetened by the faint fragrance of the last of the pines just a few feet below us. ⁷And it was quiet up there above the timber line, completely quiet. ⁸Only the occasional harsh sounds of the hawks circling overhead intruded on the eerie silence.

Enriching Your Vocabulary

The Latin root of *exhilarated*, used on page 31, is *exhilarare*, and it means "to gladden." It can also be used to mean "to invigorate or stimulate." A brisk walk on a cool fall day can be *exhilarating* after a long study session.

NARRATIVE

When your purpose is to tell how to do something or to recount a story, either a fictional one or a true narrative, use the following suggestions.

- Break the process or story into its most critical steps or events.

- Use **chronological order** (time order) to relate the events in which they occurred. Chronological order is also useful when you explain a step-by-step process.

	Writing Model

Event A

Event B

Event C —

Event D —

Event E

¹The parking area was 4.5 miles from the traffic light, just as the ranger had said. ²We parked by a sturdy fence and put on our packs. ³After checking that all gear was in order, <u>we started out</u>. ⁴Following a short walk along a gently climbing old timber road, we spotted the trailhead on the right. ⁵<u>Now the real hike began</u>. ⁶Within a hundred yards or so, the narrow, rocky trail began to climb. ⁷Then it dipped and began to climb again, even more steeply, along the shoulder of the mountain. ⁸The challenging uphill trail made for some heavy breathing and demanded that we often stop for rest, food, and water. ⁹The views were breathtaking and becoming more so with each gain in elevation. ¹⁰Finally, after four hours of rigorous effort, <u>we sighted our destination</u>. ¹¹Within a few excited moments, we arrived at the top, thoroughly exhilarated. ¹²Our whoops and whistles could be heard for miles around.

EXPOSITORY

When your purpose is to explain or inform, you can write a comparison-contrast paragraph or essay, a cause-effect piece, a classification, or a definition—all forms of exposition. When writing any exposition, use the following suggestions.

• State your **main idea** as early and as clearly as possible.

• Use facts, examples, quotations, statistics, and definitions as supporting details to develop your main idea.

• Present details in a **logical order**—in a way that makes sense to the reader. Use transitions to help your reader follow your thinking (see page 28).

	Writing Model

Main idea

Facts —

Transition

Clincher sentence

¹<u>Using visual symbols rather than words to express information has become very popular.</u> ²One key use of visuals is in meteorology. ³Agreed-upon international weather symbols provide data that meteorologists the world over understand. ⁴For example, circles show sky coverage. ⁵An empty circle indicates a clear sky, whereas a totally shaded one means the sky is or will be overcast. ⁶A circle that is three-fourths shaded represents a very cloudy sky, and a circle that is one-fourth shaded means that the sky has only slight cloud cover. ⁷<u>Meteorologists around the globe use these and other effective symbols to indicate weather activity.</u>

PERSUASIVE

When your purpose is to convince someone that your opinion is correct or to move someone to action, use the following suggestions.

• Begin with a sentence that grabs the reader's attention.

• Include a **thesis statement,** or **claim,** that clearly expresses your view.

• Supply **reasons and other evidence** (facts, examples, statistics, anecdotes, quotations) to support your claim.

• Arrange supporting details in **order of importance**—from most to least important or the reverse.

• Include a **call to action** that tells what you want the reader to do.

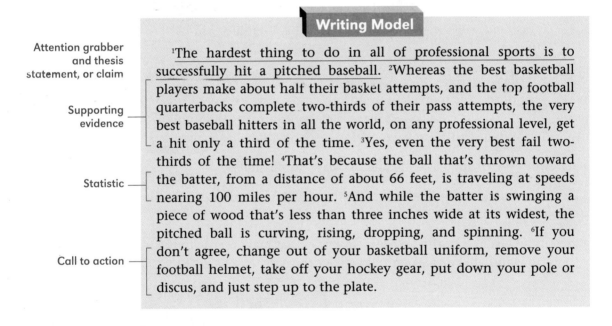

Writing Model

Attention grabber and thesis statement, or claim

Supporting evidence

Statistic

Call to action

¹The hardest thing to do in all of professional sports is to successfully hit a pitched baseball. ²Whereas the best basketball players make about half their basket attempts, and the top football quarterbacks complete two-thirds of their pass attempts, the very best baseball hitters in all the world, on any professional level, get a hit only a third of the time. ³Yes, even the very best fail two-thirds of the time! ⁴That's because the ball that's thrown toward the batter, from a distance of about 66 feet, is traveling at speeds nearing 100 miles per hour. ⁵And while the batter is swinging a piece of wood that's less than three inches wide at its widest, the pitched ball is curving, rising, dropping, and spinning. ⁶If you don't agree, change out of your basketball uniform, remove your football helmet, take off your hockey gear, put down your pole or discus, and just step up to the plate.

EXERCISE 7 Writing for Different Purposes

Write a paragraph for two of the topics suggested below.

1. A **persuasive paragraph** for or against grading students on report cards

2. A **descriptive paragraph** about your favorite place, book, or music

3. A **narrative paragraph** about an adventure, a contest, or a humorous event

4. An **expository paragraph** explaining the rules of a game or giving information about a career you are considering

Writing Essays

An **essay** is a multiparagraph piece of writing on a limited topic. An essay always has an introduction, a body, and a conclusion.

INTRODUCTION

The first paragraph of an essay accomplishes two things.

• It gets the reader interested in continuing to read.

• It presents the overall idea of the essay.

The essay's **overall idea** is presented in a sentence called a **claim**, a **controlling idea**, or a **thesis statement**.

A thesis statement is for an essay what a topic sentence is for a paragraph.

Each paragraph in the body of your essay should support your thesis statement. For instance, a paragraph about Clara Barton's nursing work during the Civil War could be part of an essay with the following thesis statement, or claim.

> In times of national crises, remarkable women stepped forward and made laudable contributions.

One effective way to begin an essay is to address the reader directly, as in the following example of a thesis statement.

> You may be generously contributing on an annual basis to the Help the Children Fund, but you may be surprised to learn that local governments are undercutting the fund's work on child labor.

An alternative for beginning an essay is to state your position directly.

> My recent interview with the executive director of the Help the Children Fund revealed troubling and disappointing developments in the organization's work on child labor.

A journalist writing a human-interest essay often builds a first paragraph around a specific example involving a particular person. Then, in the second paragraph of the essay, the journalist generalizes about a social phenomenon. The generalization is the thesis statement for the essay. Here's an example of the specifics-to-generalization essay introduction.

> It's the end of another long day at the factory for ten-year-old Ramón, and, just like yesterday, it is dark when he finally staggers home. His dinner is cold, but as always, he is too tired and hungry to notice. Before long, he will be fast asleep.

Enriching Your Vocabulary

The Latin root of *laudable* is laus, meaning "glory" or "praise." As an adjective, *laudable* means "praiseworthy" or "commendable." The World Hunger Organization has made *laudable* efforts to bring food to families in hundreds of cities.

The Help the Children Fund, which last year announced a ten-nation campaign to move children like Ramón out of factories and back into classrooms, has reported ongoing resistance to its efforts. . . .

The side column lists other ways to begin an essay.

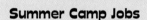

Some Ways to Begin an Essay

- anecdote • vivid image
- example • quotation
- question
- bit of dialogue
- startling statement or fact

Body

The body of an essay can include many paragraphs. This is where you write everything you have to say to support your thesis statement, or claim. Keep the following advice in mind about the body.

- **What Every Paragraph Needs** Think of the body as a series of main **ideas:** Each paragraph expresses a topic sentence and is supported by **details.**

- **Organization** Arrange your main ideas logically, in a way that makes them easy to follow. Begin with first things first—background information—and then move through your main ideas in the way readers need to know them. When you outline an essay prior to writing it, you are organizing the ideas for the body.

In a **formal outline**, you use letters, numbers, and Roman numerals to organize ideas and details.

- Place your title or a working title above the outline. It does not need to be numbered.

- Use Roman numerals to designate main ideas.

- Use capital letters to designate supporting details. (You must always have at least two or none at all.)

- Use numerals to designate further subdivisions.

A **topic outline** uses single words or short phrases.

Some teachers request a **sentence outline** in which each letter or numeral is followed by a complete sentence.

- **Importance of Coherence** Use transitional words that make your organization clear to your readers. For instance, words such as *before*, *after*, *until*, and *suddenly* indicate a time order of events. Words such as *because*,

Summer Camp Jobs

I. Counselor positions
  A. Waterfront
  B. Arts and crafts
    1. Pottery
    2. Weaving
    3. Sculpture
    4. Jewelry crafting
  C. Theater
    1. Acting and
      singing coach
    2. Costume designer
    3. Stage set designer

II. Other staff jobs
  A. Kitchen Staff
    1. Waiter
    2. Busperson
    3. Cook
  B. Bus driver
  C. Clinic work
  D. Landscaping and
    gardening

consequently, and *as a result* show a cause-effect relationship of ideas. You can also use other strategies to link your paragraphs so that your essay is coherent. For example, you can repeat key words and phrases to emphasize significant points or to connect related concepts.

• **Word Choice** Eliminate wordiness. Ask yourself, "What am I trying to say?" and then write it as clearly as you can, using precise nouns and vivid verbs and modifiers.

CONCLUSION

When you've said all you have to say on your topic, stop writing. Check the side column for ways to conclude an essay.

The most effective conclusions follow naturally from the rest of the essay and connect to the introduction.

Some Ways to End an Essay

• summary of main ideas
• comment on importance of topic
• thought-provoking question
• quotation
• prediction about the future
• call to action

EXERCISE 8 Drafting an Introduction

Assume that, for an eyewitness essay, you choose to write about the time you watched a tightrope walker cross from the roof of one tall office building to the building across the street. Despite the high winds and distractions from the busy street below, the acrobat made the journey safely. Draft an introduction that will make the reader want to read your whole essay. Make up any details you need.

EXERCISE 9 Drafting a Conclusion

Draft a concluding paragraph for a persuasive essay about proposed limits on the number of hours a teen can work during the school week. Make up any details that you need. Be sure to state your claim and the key reasons for it.

EXERCISE 10 Revising an Essay

Choose an essay that you have written in the past. Revise the essay to strengthen the introduction, body, and conclusion. Replace weak sentences with new ones that strengthen the unity of the essay. Reorganize the sentences within paragraphs, and move paragraphs, if necessary, so that information flows logically. Add details as appropriate. Revise or rewrite your conclusion to connect it to the essay's thesis statement, or claim.

Writing Effective Sentences

Combining Sentences: Using Conjunctions

Unnecessary repetition of words and grammatical structures wastes space and sounds monotonous. Instead, try to use compound subjects, compound verbs, and compound sentences.

▥➡ Learn to tell the difference between (1) a compound sentence and (2) a simple sentence with a compound subject or compound verb.

           S   S   V   V

Regular cast members **and** understudies rehearse **and** show up for every performance. [simple sentence with compound subject and compound verb]

           S   V   S

Regular cast members receive most of the glory, **but** understudies

      V

also work hard. [compound sentence made up of two simple sentences—each with its own subject and verb]

▥➡ A **compound sentence** combines two or more simple sentences into a single sentence.

SIMPLE	Actors in plays have understudies. Understudies show up for every performance.
COMPOUND	Actors in plays have understudies, and they show up for every performance.

▥➡ Use these strategies to combine sentences into a compound sentence.

1. Use a comma and a subordinating or correlative conjunction.

SIMPLE SENTENCE	Seats in the orchestra are the most expensive. Mezzanine seats usually cost less.
COMPOUND SENTENCE	Seats in the orchestra are the most expensive, **while** mezzanine seats usually cost less.

2. Use a comma and a coordinating conjunction.

COMPOUND SENTENCE	Seats in the orchestra are the most expensive, **but** mezzanine seats usually cost less.

3. Use a semicolon and a conjunctive adverb or a transitional expression to combine the sentences.

COMPOUND SENTENCE	Seats in the orchestra are expensive; **however**, mezzanine seats usually cost less. [conjunctive adverb]
COMPOUND SENTENCE	Seats in the orchestra are expensive; **on the other hand**, mezzanine seats usually cost less. [transitional expression]

WRITING HINT

Use conjunctive adverbs and transitional expressions to create compound sentences.

SOME CONJUNCTIVE ADVERBS

accordingly	moreover
also	nevertheless
besides	otherwise
consequently	still
furthermore	therefore
however	

SOME TRANSITIONAL EXPRESSIONS

as a result	in summary
for example	meanwhile
most important	
on the other hand	

For a list of subordinating, coordinating, and correlative conjunctions, see **Grammar** Lesson 5.7.

EXERCISE 1 Compound Subjects, Compound Verbs

On a separate piece of paper, combine the sentences in each numbered item into a single sentence with a compound subject or a compound verb. You may need to change or omit words. In your revised sentences, underline the subject(s) once and the verb(s) twice. Do not underline the conjunction as part of the compound.

1. Juan's first choice for college is a local school. Tom's last choice for college is a local school.
2. Rita's mother thinks highly of a college nearby. She would understand another choice by Rita.
3. Carmen dreams about Europe after graduation. Dolores dreams about Europe, too.
4. Pat spoke with the college adviser. Pat conducted research on the Internet about community colleges.
5. Jack will go to a state college. Suki will go to a state college. Elijah will go to a state college.

EXERCISE 2 Compound Sentences

On a separate piece of paper, with a partner or small group, combine the sentences in each numbered item into a single compound sentence. Choose from among the strategies discussed on page 37.

1. The school soccer team has played poorly all season. It probably won't contend for the state championship.
2. The school basketball team has played well. The coach expects an invitation to a tournament.
3. The center on the basketball team has had a great season. His performance has attracted the attention of college and professional coaches.
4. The softball team has had a disappointing season. The lead pitcher attributes the losses to her knee injury.
5. The team's top swimmer has broken school records. Her teammates are urging her to try out for the Olympics.

EXERCISE 3 Creating Compound Sentences

On a separate piece of paper, write some notes about your pet peeves and the things that annoy you. Then write as many compound sentences as you can based on your notes. Exchange papers with a partner or a small group to check that all your sentences are indeed compound sentences.

Combining Sentences: Using Subordinate Clauses

▐▶ You can combine two related sentences by turning one sentence into an adjective clause.

Change one sentence into an adjective clause that begins with *who*, *which*, *that*, or another word from the list of relative pronouns on page 179. Then place the adjective clause after a noun or pronoun in the remaining sentence. Remember to use commas to set off nonessential adjective clauses.

ORIGINAL   Ana broke the school long-jump record. Ana is Eddie's cousin.

COMBINED   Ana, **who is Eddie's cousin**, broke the school long-jump record.

ORIGINAL   Ana is an all-around athlete. College recruiters have been watching her performances.

COMBINED   Ana, **who is an all-around athlete**, has college recruiters watching her performances.

▐▶ You can combine two related sentences by turning one sentence into an adverb clause.

Use a subordinating conjunction to create an adverb clause out of one sentence. Then attach the adverb clause to the remaining sentence. Choose a subordinating conjunction that shows how the ideas in the two sentences are related. For example, *because* and *since* show a cause-effect relationship; *while*, *when*, *whenever*, *before*, *after*, and *until* show a chronological relationship; and *although* and *but* show contrast.

ORIGINAL   Storms raged along the coast. Several beach houses were damaged.

COMBINED   **When storms raged along the coast**, several beach houses were damaged.

COMBINED   Several beach houses were damaged **when storms raged along the coast**.

ORIGINAL   Some inhabitants remained. Many evacuated to safety.

COMBINED   **Although some inhabitants remained**, many evacuated to safety.

COMBINED   Many evacuated to safety, **although some inhabitants remained**.

WRITING HINT

If a paragraph contains several sentences in a row with adjective clauses, change one or more of the clauses to appositive phrases (see Lesson 7.2).

Ana, who is Eddie's cousin, broke the school long-jump record. ~~Ana, who is an~~ *An* all-around athlete, ^*she*^ has college recruiters watching her performances. She broke several other school records, which were also city records.

EXERCISE 4 Combining Sentences Using Adjective Clauses

Work with a partner to combine each pair of sentences into a single sentence by using an adjective clause. An introductory word is suggested in parentheses. Put the less important idea in the adjective clause. Write your responses on a separate piece of paper, and underline the adjective clause in your combined sentences.

> EXAMPLE   Sandra Cisneros is a critically acclaimed author. Her books have been translated into more than a dozen languages. (who)
> *Sandra Cisneros, whose books have been translated into more than a dozen languages, is a critically acclaimed author.*

> **HINT**
>
> Set off nonessential adjective clauses with commas.

1. Cisneros attended the Writers' Workshop at the University of Iowa. She learned to become a writer there. (where)

2. At the Writers' Workshop, Cisneros improved her writing skills dramatically. The Writers' Workshop has a terrific reputation. (which)

3. Her Mexican American heritage provided her with a source of ideas for her fiction. Her heritage made her stand out among other young writers. (which)

4. Cisneros wrote a group of stories about her childhood. She put them in her first book, entitled *The House on Mango Street*. (who)

5. Her next book won critical acclaim and earned her popular recognition. It was entitled *Woman Hollering Creek*. (which)

EXERCISE 5 Combining Sentences Using Adverb Clauses

Work with a partner to combine each pair of sentences into a single sentence with an adverb clause. An introductory word is suggested in parentheses. Put the less important idea in the adverb clause. Write your responses on a separate piece of paper, and underline the adverb clause in your combined sentences.

1. *Bless Me, Ultima*, by Rudolfo Anaya, won as the best novel written by a Mexican American in 1972. Anaya wrote many other books. (after)

2. Anaya became a full professor at the University of New Mexico. He taught in junior and senior high schools first. (before)

3. Anaya had taught creative writing at the university for nineteen years. He retired in 1993. (when)

> **HINT**
>
> Set off an introductory adverb clause with a comma.

4. Anaya has been described as one of the most widely read Mexican American writers. He has not published a book in several years. (although)

5. Anaya remains by nature a quiet person. His fame has given him a feeling of great satisfaction. (even though)

Combining Sentences: Inserting Phrases

▐▶ Combine related sentences by inserting a phrase from one sentence into another sentence.

Sometimes, you must alter the words from one sentence to create a phrase for another sentence. Sometimes, you can simply pick up a phrase from one sentence and move it to another sentence.

ORIGINAL   Benny was traveling through Europe. He visited several circuses.
COMBINED   **Traveling through Europe**, Benny visited several circuses. [participial phrase]

ORIGINAL   Lisa plays in a band. The band is in New York. Janet and Rebecca are the other members of her band.
COMBINED   Lisa plays **in a band in New York with Janet and Rebecca**. [prepositional phrases]

ORIGINAL   We have time. We will buy the tickets at the ticket window. The ticket window is by the third-base line.
COMBINED   We have time **to buy the tickets at the ticket window by the third-base line**. [infinitive phrase containing two prepositional phrases]

ORIGINAL   My uncle enjoys something. He enjoys walking briskly.
COMBINED   **Walking briskly** is something my uncle enjoys. [gerund phrase]

Often there is more than one way to combine sentences. Here are two other versions of the last sentence.

COMBINED   To walk briskly is something my uncle enjoys. [infinitive phrase]
COMBINED   My uncle enjoys walking briskly. [gerund phrase at end]

In addition to creating a verbal or a prepositional phrase to put in another sentence, you can convert a sentence to an appositive phrase (see Lesson 7.2) and transfer it to another sentence.

ORIGINAL   My uncle lives in St. Louis now. He is an immigrant from Russia.
COMBINED   My uncle, **a Russian immigrant**, lives in St. Louis now.

WRITING HINT

Too many prepositional phrases in sentences can make them confusing and singsongy. Avoid this problem by breaking apart and rewording sentences.
The cashmere sweaters are **on the rack next to the ties on display in front of the shirt counter.**
The cashmere sweaters are displayed **on a rack.** They're **next to the ties.** You'll find the ties displayed **in front of the shirt counter.**

EXERCISE 6 Combining Sentences by Inserting Phrases

Use phrases to combine the sentences in each numbered item. Remember to insert commas where they belong.

EXAMPLE   The SAT is a long exam. The exam is a test of reading, writing, and math abilities.

The SAT, a test of verbal and mathematical abilities, is a long exam.

1. The College Board and the Educational Testing Service are the producers of the SAT. They produce other tests, too.

2. They also produce the SAT Subject Tests. The SAT Subject Tests are achievement tests in specific content-area subjects.

3. In 1995, the College Board recalculated test takers' mean SAT score. The mean score is the average score.

4. The scale of scores runs from 200 to 800. Scores are also given as percentiles.

5. In 1941, the mean score was about 500. This score reflected the results of only ten thousand students.

6. Then more and more students took the test. This resulted in lower individual scores.

7. Students want to score well. They must prepare carefully for the test.

8. Students are better at preparing now. This means higher scores.

9. Students take practice tests. The practice tests help them gain confidence. The confidence is for the real test.

EXERCISE 7 Writing Paragraphs

The information in the table is about mean, or average, verbal and math scores of college-bound seniors from 2001 to 2010. Use the information in the table to write one or more paragraphs about trends in the Scholastic Aptitude Test (SAT) scores over that ten-year period. Exchange papers with a partner, and make suggestions for improving each other's paragraphs. Try combining related sentences by inserting phrases.

Refer to **Composition,** Lessons 4.4 and 4.5, to find strategies for writing an expository

SAT Mean Verbal and Math Scores of College-Bound Seniors										
	2001	2002	2003	2004	2005	2006	2007	2008	2009	2010
CRITICAL READING SCORES	506	504	507	508	508	503	502	502	501	501
Males	509	507	512	512	513	505	504	504	503	503
Females	502	502	503	504	505	502	502	500	498	498
MATH SCORES	514	516	519	518	520	518	515	515	515	516
Males	533	534	537	537	538	536	533	533	534	534
Females	498	500	503	501	504	502	499	500	499	500

Source: National Center for Educational Statistics

Varying Sentence Beginnings, Structures, and Lengths

▐▌▶ For variety, begin some of your sentences with a subordinate clause.

Subordinate clauses give you a tool for varying sentence beginnings. Keep clauses and noun clauses in mind as a variety of ways for expressing an idea. Here is the same idea expressed in several different ways.

ORIGINAL	Ulysses S. Grant died on July 23, 1885, less than a month after he completed his memoirs.
PREPOSITIONAL PHRASE	**On July 23, 1885**, after he completed his memoirs, Ulysses S. Grant died.
PARTICIPIAL PHRASE	**Resting after his work on his memoirs**, Ulysses S. Grant died on July 23, 1885.
ADVERB CLAUSE	**Shortly after he completed his memoirs**, Ulysses S. Grant died on July 23, 1885.
NOUN CLAUSE	**What Ulysses S. Grant did just before he died on July 23, 1885**, was complete his memoirs.

▐▌▶ When you write a paragraph or longer paper, vary the sentence structures and the lengths of sentences.

Varying the sentences helps keep readers engaged in your writing. Use phrases and clauses in some sentences but not all, and provide a mix of long and short sentences.

WRITING HINT

It never hurts to count the words in each sentence of a paragraph you write. If all the sentences are about the same length (say, twenty-two words), consider rewriting to create one very short sentence (say, eight words).

EXERCISE 8 Varying Sentence Beginnings

On a separate piece of paper, rewrite each of the following sentences to change the structure with which it begins. Be sure to preserve the meaning of the sentence.

1. Girls officially played Little League baseball, starting in 1975.

2. President Gerald Ford signed legislation on December 26, 1974, to open the Little League baseball program to girls.

3. The Little League charter was amended to replace the word *boys* with *young people.*

4. Changes in the Little League charter occurred after parents filed numerous lawsuits to open the leagues to girls.

5. Women's baseball is more popular in Europe than in the United States, even with the increase of girls in the Little League here.

Enriching Your Vocabulary

The verb *amend* means "to correct, change, or alter." From the same root, and similar in meaning, is the verb *emend. Amend* is more general in usage than *emend*, which usually refers to text.

EXERCISE 9 Revising a Report

Work with a partner to revise the following report on the history of women's basketball. Write on a separate piece of paper. Your audience is the readers of your school newspaper. In your revision, try to vary some sentences' beginnings and structures. Combine sentences, and find other ways to eliminate unnecessary repetition and monotony.

[1]Women first played basketball at Smith College in 1892. [2]Smith College is in Northampton, Massachusetts. [3]Senda Berenson introduced the game. [4]She was the director of physical education at Smith. [5]The first women's intercollegiate basketball game was between teams from Berkeley and Stanford. [6]It took place on April 4, 1896. [7]Male spectators were barred from the game.

[8]Berenson drew up the first rules for women's basketball. [9]She did so in 1899. [10]These were the sport's first official rules. [11]According to Berenson's basketball rules, players could dribble only three times. [12]They could hold the ball for three seconds or less. [13]These rules remained the standard for nearly three-quarters of a century.

EXERCISE 10 Writing a Paragraph

Use the notes below along with other ideas that you may have to write a one-paragraph school newspaper article about the opening of a new school gymnasium. Write your paragraph on a separate piece of paper. Put the ideas into a sensible order, and try to vary your sentence beginnings, structures, and lengths.

Seats 1,500 for basketball

Can serve many purposes, some simultaneously

Came in under budget

Money raised by student body and by community efforts

Can seat 2,000 for concerts

Has state-of-the-art locker rooms and other facilities

Has state-of-the-art security system

Opening day ceremony: May 25

Former student, now mayor, to speak

Eliminating Short, Choppy Sentences

Short sentences can be powerful when used occasionally, but when strung together, they can make your writing sound choppy. Add rhythm and variety to your writing by varying your sentence lengths. One way to do so is to combine short sentences.

ORIGINAL   The sailboats were in the lagoon. These boats were small. They rocked. The rocking was dangerous. The water was rough. It was rising, too.

You can combine these six sentences by inserting key words from several of them into a base sentence.

COMBINED   The **small** sailboats rocked **dangerously** in the **rough**, **rising** waters of the lagoon.

The combined sentence sounds more sophisticated because it avoids both unnecessary repetition and stops and starts. Notice that the key words inserted into the base sentence work as **modifiers**—adjectives and adverbs. Here is another example of combining.

ORIGINAL   A restaurant will open in the port. It is new. It will open soon.
COMBINED   A **new** restaurant will **soon** open in the port.

Sometimes the key words change form when you combine sentences.

ORIGINAL   The restaurant's walls are decorated with paintings. They are paintings of the region. The paintings are of the sea. They were painted by local artists.
COMBINED   The **regional seascapes** on the restaurant's walls were painted by local artists.

ORIGINAL   The port is pretty. It stands out among many scenic towns along the coast.
COMBINED   The pretty port stands out among the many scenic **coastal** towns.

STEP BY STEP

Combining Sentences

To combine a group of short sentences:
1. Find the sentence that gives the most information.
2. In the other sentences, look for single words that can be picked up and inserted into the sentence you chose in Step 1.
3. Insert the single words where they make sense. You may need to slightly change the words you're moving.
4. Read the combined sentence aloud to hear if it sounds natural.

EXERCISE 11 Combining Sentences

Combine the groups of sentences on the following page into single sentences with adjectives and adverbs. Drop some words, and change the form of others, as needed.

EXAMPLE   William I was from Normandy. William I led a successful armed invasion against England in 1066. He was ambitious.
William I was the ambitious Norman invader who conquered England in 1066.

1. William, known as William the Conqueror, achieved victory in the invasion. The victory had great importance.

2. William II was William's son. He was ruthless, too.

3. William's grandson was Stephen, also a soldier. Stephen was triumphant as a soldier.

4. In the twelfth century, King Henry II quarreled with the Archbishop of Canterbury. The quarrel was loud. The quarrel was angry.

5. King Richard I, who reigned in the last decade of the twelfth century, went on crusades. The crusades were for religion. Richard was gallant.

Working Together

EXERCISE 12 Revising a Paragraph

With a partner, improve the following paragraphs about the English king Richard III for a history report. Look for opportunities to combine sentences. Compare your new paragraphs with those of other pairs of students.

[1]Some people view King Richard III as a monster with ambition. [2]They say the ambition was unquenchable. [3]They assert that he killed all who stood in his way. [4]They count the princes in the Tower of London among the victims. [5]The victims were Richard's nephews. [6]The princes were young. [7]William Shakespeare saw Richard as evil. [8]Shakespeare saw Richard as ruthless.

[9]Others hold another view. [10]Their view is different. [11]They absolve Richard of almost every crime of which he has been accused. [12]They claim that Richard was conscientious. [13]They say that he was strong and successful. [14]They assert that he had supporters. [15]The supporters were numerous. [16]The supporters were loyal. [17]They say it is not certain that Richard had the princes killed. [18]The princes were young.

[19]Opinion about Richard III varies. [20]That is obvious.

Eliminating Wordiness

Writing is most effective when it is direct and clear and when it is not weighed down with unnecessary words and phrases. Here are ways to achieve clarity in your writing.

▶ **Eliminate padding.** Don't pad your writing with more words to make it longer. Use precise words and trim your phrases to make your writing succinct.

ORIGINAL   In my very humble opinion, "The Outcasts of Poker Flat" is the best story that Bret Harte ever produced, even though many other stories, poems, parodies, and plays that he penned certainly furthered his growing reputation.

REVISED   In my opinion, "The Outcasts of Poker Flat" is the finest piece of writing that Bret Harte ever produced, even though many other pieces he wrote enhanced his reputation.

▶ **Eliminate unnecessary repetition.** Unnecessary repetition is simply another kind of padding. Avoid redundancy.

ORIGINAL   Bret Harte had a very close, intimate knowledge of camp life in the mining camps; he knew firsthand what life in them was like.

REVISED   Bret Harte had an intimate knowledge of mining camp life, gained from firsthand experience.

▶ **Write in your own voice.** Avoid using overly difficult words and intricate, complicated sentences. Write what you mean as simply and as directly as you can.

ORIGINAL   Viewers of a recent television series about a real-life western mining town can readily gain a resolute appreciation of the hazardous existence and degradation that were common aspects of the perilous camp habitat.

REVISED   Viewers of a recent television series about a western mining town can clearly see that everyday life in those camps was both dangerous and degrading.

WRITING *HINT*

When you write an essay, you may sometimes restate your main idea in a concluding paragraph. Repetition there is acceptable. In general, though, avoid repeating the same idea in sentences that follow each other.

EXERCISE 13 Revising Sentences

On a separate piece of paper, revise the following wordy sentences.

1. Following the discovery of the mineral gold in California, people flocked there in droves seeking wealth and riches.

2. By 1852, the surface gold in California was all but gone, finished, used up, and nowhere to be found by any individual.

3. No matter how hard an individual miner put forth a laborious effort, he could no longer, alone, retrieve the gold with only a pick, pan, and shovel.

4. The gold lay there at the bottoms of rivers, hidden, unseen, in hillsides from where it needed to be blasted out of the ground in the hills.

5. I wish to point out that because colossal, Brobdingnagian, expensive, and pricey machinery was needed, California's gold fields were eventually, over time, controlled by wealthy San Francisco investors who were headquartered in that city.

EXERCISE 14 Revising a Paragraph to Eliminate Wordiness

On a separate piece of paper, revise the paragraph below to trim wordy expressions and make the writing as clear and economical as possible.

¹The former towns of Gleeson, Pearce, and Courtland are three Arizona ghost towns within easy reach of Tombstone. ²All you need to call upon these towns is a good road map, a four-wheel-drive vehicle with good clearance, such as a truck, or maybe just a car, and a spirit of adventure. ³In some of these former mining boom towns, which were once certainly overflowing with quite a lot of people and activity, all that remains are a few dilapidated ruins, and, of course, the mines themselves, whether they were gold mines, silver mines, or copper mines. ⁴Let me say that visitors to this region in southeastern Arizona are truly provided with enjoyment by obtaining a glimpse into the area's wild past. ⁵There is truly nothing else like this area in the rest of the country.

Revising and Editing Worksheet 1

Improve the following draft by revising for ideas, organization, word choice, and sentence variety. After revising, edit the draft for errors in spelling, capitalization, punctuation, and usage. Write your revised and edited version on a separate piece of paper. Compare your changes with those of a writing partner.

[1]For those with a passion for natural history, New Mexico is famous for its ancient past. [2]It is an intriguing place. [3]With its 310 days of sunshine each year, the "Land of Enchantment" is indeed an outdoors paradise. [4]It is a place where dinosaurs once roamed. [5]It is where the Anasazi built a number of their unique cliff dwellings and some of their largest settlements but the state is worth a visit simply for its natural beauty.

[6]If you like caving, then head for Carlsbad Caverns National Park. [7]It is in the southeastern corner of the state, due south of Roswell. [8]These underground caverns, formed some 250 million years ago. [9]That is when the region was an inland sea. [10]The caves feature gigantic and often weird formations. [11]Visitors to the park should be certain not to miss Lechuguilla. [12]It is the nation's deepest limestone cave. [13]It boasts an area known as the Big Room. [14]The Big Room is a chamber that is the size of eight soccer fields.

[15]If you are interested in volcanoes, New Mexico will not disappoint. [16]At El Malpais national monument, located a few miles west of Albuquerque, cinder cones, pressure ridges, and complex lava tube systems dominate an exotic landscape. [17]It is a breathtaking landscape. [18]You can walk on established trails to view these volcanic features. [19]You can hike amidst them on your own. [20]At El Malpais, you also can explore underground lava flows. [21]They formed thousands of years ago.

[22]If what you really want is to stare with your mouth open at extraordinary beauty, be sure to visit two other spots. [23]One is the Bisti Badlands, located in the high desert of the northwestern corner of the state. [24]The other is the White Sands National Monument. [25]It is situated at the northern edge of the Chihuahua Desert.

Revising and Editing Worksheet 2

Improve the following draft by revising for ideas, organization, word choice, and sentence variety. After revising, edit the draft for errors in spelling, capitalization, punctuation, and usage. Write your revised and edited version on a separate piece of paper. Compare your changes with those of a writing partner.

[1]Mammoth Cave National Park is about 85 miles south of Louisville, Kentucky. [2]It is also about 85 miles north of Nashville, Tennessee. [3]Park visitors can spot white-tailed deer and flocks of wild turkey. [4]They can see chipmunks, raccoons, and squirrels along the many miles of marked trails. [5]Beneath the ridges of the park lies its main attraction, the most extensive cave system on Earth. [6]Erosional forces formed the cave system.

[7]At least 10 miles of Mammoth Cave were explored by aboriginal peoples 4,000 years ago. [8]However, exploration of the cave ceased about 2,000 years ago. [9]It did not begin again until the cave was rediscovered in 1798. [10]Mammoth Cave now boasts 350 miles of surveyed passageways. [11]It is three times longer than any known cave.

[12]One of the first uses of Mammoth Cave in modern times was as a mine for saltpeter. [13]Saltpeter was a key ingredient in the manufacture of gunpowder. [14]Then came the onset of the War of 1812. [15]Slaves were brought in to mine large quantities of the mineral. [16]By the end of the war, the notoriety of Mammoth Cave had increased. [17]People began to visit it.

[18]In 1925, an unfortunate event took place. [19]It happened in the region. [20]Amateur caver Floyd Collins was pinned by a boulder in a cave. [21]Despite their heroic efforts, rescuers could not extricate him. [22]The failure to save Collins drew national attention. [23]The publicity led to the authorization of Mammoth Cave as a national park in the following year. [24]It led to further investigation of the cave's diverse ecosystem. [25]It led to the goal of preserving this international treasure for generations to come. [26]Perhaps that second goal is the more important one.

Revising and Editing Worksheet 3

Improve the following draft by revising for ideas, organization, word choice, and sentence variety. After revising, edit the draft for errors in spelling, capitalization, punctuation, and usage. Write your revised and edited version on a separate piece of paper. Compare your changes with those of a writing partner.

[1]In *Les Miserables*, Victor Hugo made the sewers of Paris famous. [2]His character, Jean Valjean, says that Paris has another Paris under herself. [3]Valjean says it is a city of sewers, complete with its own streets and crossings. [4]Valjean also says that it has a great amount of squares, blind alleys, and arteries. [5]Some sociologists assert the sophistication of a city can be judged by the quality of its sewer system. [6]This means, then, that Paris, the city of lights, would score quite high, without a doubt. [7]But, as one might expect, this was not always the case.

[8]In the early Middle Ages, the state of waste removal in Paris, as in other European cities, was deplorable and abominable. [9]Parisians deposited their waste in fields or right onto the unpaved streets. [10]This created a landscape of foul-smelling mud. [11]Then, in about 1200, the city's thoroughfares were paved with cobblestones. [12]Some improvements in waste removal took place over the next few hundred years. [13]But the wretched disease-spreading conditions remained essentially unchanged.

[14]During the reign of Napoleon, $18\frac{1}{2}$ miles of sewers were constructed beneath the city. [15]By 1850, when the Industrial Revolution made iron pipes and other construction equipment readily available, Baron Haussmann developed a more modern sewage system. [16]This more modern sewage system provided separate underground channels for sewage and drinking water. [17]Over the years, that system has been enlarged. [18]It has been improved. [19]Today, the network of sewers measures 1,300 miles. [20]It consists of mammoth underground passages. [21]It has four enormous principal tunnels.

Writing Workshops

Narrative Writing: Autobiographical Incident

Your life is like a book in progress. When you write about an **autobiographical incident**, you tell a true story about something that happened to you, and you communicate the importance of the incident in your life. An autobiographical incident should focus on events both that took place in a brief period of time and that helped you understand yourself and your life a little better.

In his article "The Rural Life: A Momentary Pause," the writer Verlyn Klinkenborg recalls seeing leafless trees in the woods, a sign that spring has not arrived. He also relates other incidents that reflect his thoughts about the changing seasons. As you read, think about what these experiences mean to the author. Also think about the feelings you think he hopes to convey.

The Rural Life; A Momentary Pause
by Verlyn Klinkenborg

[1]I have to keep reminding myself that it is only late March. [2]I have been so eager for spring that it feels as though time has almost stopped. [3]One reason may be that it was warm a few weeks ago and then the cold returned, putting the season on ice. [4]But there is something else going on as well. [5]Scientists say that spring comes earlier than it used to. [6]The snow cover dwindles sooner and bud break comes earlier. [7]And yet our awareness of that makes it feel as though spring comes even earlier than it is already coming. [8]Global warming accelerates faster in our heads than it does in fact. [9]March is not quite the new April yet.

The author introduces his topic; he includes vivid details to establish tone.

[10]The other day I passed at least a hundred wild turkeys in separate flocks among the cornfields that line the highway. [11]They were stooped over the stubble, somber backs perfectly rounded, except for a few that kept watch. [12]Above them, the woods were every bit as bare as they were in mid-

Uses the first-person point of view; presents the first incident

Narrative Writing:
Autobiographical Incident

December. [13]Every day I look for that first reddish flush along the tree line,

Presents a series of additional incidents — or perhaps the eruption of a willow down in the valley. [14]I passed a flock of Canada geese in the fields and had to remind myself that it was not quite time to be seeing their young. [15]When I return home from the city, I find myself testing the ground underfoot as I walk to the mud room door in the dark. [16]How much give is there? [17]How long before it is time to start spading the garden? [18]When will I start tracking mud into the house?

[19]For all this anticipation, a part of me wants to hold on to the old

Presents another incident — schedule. [20]I remember a piece I wrote for this page five years ago noting that the garden was buried under 20 inches of snow. [21]The date was April 2.

Descriptive details contribute to tone — [22]It seemed like a betrayal at the time. [23]But the wind has been blowing steadily for a month now. [24]There has been little rain. [25]The earth is chapped.

[26]Twenty inches of snow right now would bring out the curmudgeon in all of us who live here. [27]There would be grousing and grumbling everywhere.

Suggests meaning — [28]But I have learned that all that grousing and grumbling usually conceals a satisfaction with the way things are. [29]It is the wry, ironic language of the hardware store. [30]The fact is, we need the moisture.

Descriptive details contribute to tone — [31]In the country it's easy to find yourself leaning forward all through the year, always waiting on the next season, getting through your life as though you were walking into a stiff wind. [32]This is one of those days when I catch

Conclusion suggests meaning — myself in that posture—pitched forward into the gale of time. [33]So I'll try to slow down and straighten up. [34]I'll walk down to the barnyard later this morning and fix the gate on the horse corral, which has sagged since the warm weather last month. [35]It should be good for another year once I am done.

Critical Thinking   After you read the autobiographical incident, answer the questions below.

1. Choose one of the incidents Klinkenborg narrates, and pay close attention to *how* he retells it. Are there enough details to make the place and events come to life? What details does Klinkenborg include?

2. How do the details in this autobiographical incident work together to create a tone of reflection?

3. With a partner, read the narrative aloud. Then analyze the sentences for variety in length, structure, and beginnings.

Build Your Vocabulary. Which of these words from the article can you define: *accelerates* (sentence 8), *somber* (sentence 11), *eruption* (sentence 13), *spading* (sentence 17)? Look up the words you don't know in a dictionary. Add the ones you look up and their meanings to your vocabulary notebook.

Writing Strategies   The purpose of writing an autobiographical incident is to narrate a series of events. The audience can be any that you choose. For example, you might write for children, for your peers, or for a faraway friend. Use the following strategies as you write.

1. **Select a meaningful incident.** An incident, which, in effect, is a mini-story, has a **plot**, **characters**, and a **setting**.

2. **Use the first person**. You—the storyteller—are the "I," the **narrator**, using the **first-person point of view**. Remember, as a first-person narrator, you do not know what other characters think, unless they tell you.

3. **Concentrate on time order**. An incident is often defined as an experience that happens all at once, in a few hours, or in a few days. An incident may consist of several individual events that occur in **chronological order**. But make sure your reader always knows how all the events fit together.

4. **Ask and answer questions**. Your readers will want to know *Who? What? Where? When? Why?* and *How?* (the *5W-How?* questions reporters answer at the beginning of a news story). If possible, introduce suspense into your narrative.

5. **Answer, "So what?"** You've selected an incident that's important to you. Your essay should tell how the incident changed you, what you discovered, or why you remember it. Klinkenborg uses his conclusion to relate what he has learned from the incidents he shares.

6. **Reflect on your thoughts and feelings**. This piece of advice relates to Strategy 5. Try to recall—or imagine—what you thought and felt at the time the incident took place—and what you feel and think about it now. Your thoughts and feelings will tell your readers the full significance of the incident. Follow Klinkenborg's example, and include a reflection of what the incident means to you in your conclusion.

7. **Sprinkle in sensory details**. A few details about sights, sounds, smells, tastes, and sensations of touch will help the reader imagine what you remember clearly. Use precise description to paint a vivid picture of settings, characters, and events as you move the plot along.

8. **Generate some dialogue**. Some writers integrate dialogue into the incidents they describe. Dialogue can enliven your writing and help readers better imagine the event.

> **WRITING HINT**
>
> As you try to get across the importance of the event, keep in mind that it is more effective to *show* than *tell*. Klinkenborg uses descriptive details to paint a picture of rural life and to suggest the rhythm of the seasons.

EXERCISE 1 Get Started

You might, like Klinkenborg, write about something you've observed. Or you might write about a person, a place, a time, or a feeling. Use one or two of the prewriting techniques mentioned in Lesson 1.1 to get ideas for incidents to write about. **Remember:** (1) The incident must be in some way important to you. (2) You must remember the incident vividly. (3) It must have taken place in a short time period.

EXERCISE 2 Plan Your Narrative

Use a **story map** to capture all the important elements in your narrative. You won't necessarily write your narrative in the order of the map's questions and answers, but the map will keep all the data in front of you. On a separate piece of paper, write the following questions and answer them with as much detail as possible.

1. What is the **setting**?

2. Identify the main **characters**, and describe them briefly.

3. Identify the **conflict**, or problem, and briefly summarize the plot. Remember that conflict can be internal as well as external.

4. Why was the experience important to you?

EXERCISE 3 Draft the Autobiographical Incident

Use your prewriting notes to draft your incident. Be sure to reflect on your feelings about the incident as you conclude your essay.

Consider your classmates the audience for your narrative. You may also want to keep friends and relatives in mind as you write.

EXERCISE 4 Revise Your Autobiographical Incident

Read your essay aloud to yourself and then to a partner.

First, go back over your essay to find and eliminate any padding. Second, focus on the words and phrases you used to describe your characters. Keep your audience in mind, and be sure that you have provided sufficient details so that they can visualize the characters you have described. Third, check that your order of events is clear. Use transitions to link your sentences. Then work on getting the sentences to read smoothly. Replace vague, general nouns, verbs, and modifiers with more precise words.

EXERCISE 5 Proofread and Publish

Carefully proofread your revised narrative for errors in spelling, punctuation, and capitalization. Think about sharing your narrative with friends and family, especially with anyone who was present when the incident happened.

Narrative Writing: Eyewitness Report

Like a report on an autobiographical incident, an **eyewitness report** is also a firsthand account of an incident, but in contrast, it focuses more on the significance of the incident to the community or society than to the writer. In an eyewitness report, the narrator is an observer, not a participant.

An eyewitness report usually reads chronologically. It may have a first-person or third-person point of view. An effective eyewitness report includes anecdotes, sensory details, and dialogue.

from The Fall of the Berlin Wall
by Andreas Ramos

Ramos hooks readers by stating the magnitude of the incident.

Uses the first-person point of view

Proceeds chronologically

Gives vivid details. What's implied by the heavy media presence?

Builds suspense with these details

Describes setting

¹On Thursday, the 9th of November 1989, and Friday, the 10th, the TV and radio in Denmark was filled with news about the events in Berlin. ²<u>The wall was about to fall.</u> ³On Saturday morning, the 11th of November, I heard on the radio that East Germany was collapsing. ⁴[On] the spur of the moment, I suggested to Karen, my Danish wife, and two Danish friends that <u>we should go to Berlin.</u> . . .

⁵We arrived in [West] Berlin at 4:30 A.M., [the trip taking] five hours longer than usual. ⁶We drove first to Brandenburgerplatz, where the statue of Winged Victory stands atop a 50 meter column, which celebrates a military victory in the 1890s over Denmark. ⁷Cars were abandoned everywhere, wherever there was space. ⁸Over 5,000 people were there. . . . ⁹We left the car and began to walk through a village of television trucks, giant satellite dishes, emergency generators, and coils of cables and tents. ¹⁰Cameramen slept under satellite dishes. ¹¹At the wall, West German police and military [were] lined up to prevent chaos. ¹²West German military trucks were lined up against the wall to protect it from the West Germans. ¹³Hundreds of West German police stood in rows with their tall shields. ¹⁴On top of the wall, lined up at parade rest, stood East German soldiers with their rifles. ¹⁵Groups of West Germans stood around fires that they had built. ¹⁶No one knew what was going on.

¹⁷After a while, we walked to Potsdammer Platz. ¹⁸This used to be the center of Berlin. ¹⁹All traffic once passed through the Potsdammer Platz. ²⁰Now it was a large empty field, bisected by the wall. ²¹Nearby was the mound that was the remains of Hitler's bunker, from which he commanded Germany into total defeat. ²²We talked to Germans and many said that the

Tells what people are doing and saying at time of breakthrough

next break in the wall would be here. ²³It was still very dark and cold at 6 A.M. ²⁴Perhaps 7,000 people were pressed together, shouting, cheering, clapping. ²⁵We pushed through the crowd. ²⁶From the East German side, we could hear the sound of heavy machines. ²⁷With a giant drill, they were punching holes in the wall. ²⁸Every time a drill poked through, everyone cheered. ²⁹The banks of klieg lights would come on. ³⁰People shot off fireworks and emergency flares and rescue rockets. ³¹Many were using hammers to chip away at the wall. ³²There were countless holes. ³³At one place, a crowd of East German soldiers looked through a narrow hole. ³⁴We reached through and shook hands. ³⁵They couldn't see the crowd so they asked us what was going on and we described the scene for them. ³⁶Someone lent me a hammer and I knocked chunks of rubble from the wall, dropping several handfuls into my pocket. ³⁷The wall was made of cheap, brittle concrete: the Russians had used too much sand and water. . . .

Sight and sound details

³⁸By 7 A.M., everything was out of control. ³⁹Police on horses watched. ⁴⁰There was nothing they could do. ⁴¹The crowd had swollen. ⁴²People were blowing long alpine horns which made a huge noise. ⁴³There were fireworks, kites, flags and flags and flags, dogs, children. ⁴⁴The wall was finally breaking. ⁴⁵The cranes lifted slabs aside. ⁴⁶East and West German police had traded caps. ⁴⁷To get a better view, hundreds of people were climbing onto a shop on the West German side. ⁴⁸We scampered up a nine foot wall. ⁴⁹People helped each other; some lifted, others pulled. ⁵⁰All along the building, people poured up the wall. ⁵¹At the Berlin Wall itself, which is 3 meters high, people had climbed up and were sitting astride. ⁵²The final slab was moved away. ⁵³A stream of East Germans began to pour through. ⁵⁴People applauded and slapped their backs. . . . ⁵⁵Near me, a knot of people cheered as the mayors of East Berlin and West Berlin met and shook hands. ⁵⁶I stood with several East German guards, their rifles slung over their shoulders. ⁵⁷I asked them if they had bullets in those things. ⁵⁸They grinned and said no. ⁵⁹From some houses, someone had set up loudspeakers and played [the portion of] Beethoven's ninth symphony [which contains the words] *"Alle Menschen werden Bruder"* ("All people become brothers"). ⁶⁰On top of every building were thousands of people. ⁶¹Berlin was out of control. ⁶²There was no more government, neither in East nor in West. ⁶³The police and

Brings essay to close; announces meaning of the event

the army were helpless. ⁶⁴The soldiers themselves were overwhelmed by the event. ⁶⁵They were part of the crowd. ⁶⁶Their uniforms meant nothing. ⁶⁷The wall was down.

Critical Thinking After you read the eyewitness report, answer the questions below.

1. Pay close attention to how Ramos describes what he witnesses. Is the order of events clear? Are there enough details to make the people, place, and event come to life? Too many?

2. Imagine the incident reported with dialogue. What, if anything, would the dialogue add?

3. Reread sentences 59–66. Are they facts or opinions? On what are the comments based?

4. With a partner, read aloud one of the lengthy passages in the report. Then analyze the sentences for variety in length, structure, and beginnings.

Build Your Vocabulary. Underline the unfamiliar words in the selection. Use a dictionary to look up their meaning and write brief definitions in the margin or in your notebook.

Writing Strategies The purpose of writing an eyewitness report is to give an account of actual events. Your audience is made up of people who want to know about the event you describe. Use the following strategies to help.

1. **Brainstorm about incidents**. An eyewitness report is about a compelling incident, particularly one that is newsworthy. Incidents that lend themselves to eyewitness accounts include accidents, crimes, natural catastrophes, sporting events, political meetings, exciting performances, and other public gatherings. Select one to observe and report on. Although you may not have the opportunity to be present at an incident as monumental as the fall of the Berlin Wall, there's *always* something newsworthy happening.

2. **Find a beginning point**. When you retell the events of your incident, you don't have to start at the absolute beginning. Include only what readers need to know—for example, Ramos omits details about his trip *to* Berlin—and pace events to establish a particular tone and outcome, such as to build mystery or suspense.

3. **Use the first-person or third-person point of view**. Either way, make your readers feel as if they, too, are witnessing the event. Ramos puts readers in the midst of West Berlin with him as he roams around.

4. **Give sufficient details in the right order.** While your overall report will proceed chronologically, some of it may benefit if you arrange details spatially. Focus on what the scene looks like, sounds like, or even smells like. Use vivid verbs, nouns, and modifiers to describe these sensory details and all

other details with precision. Include details that lend immediacy to your report. Ramos tells readers what he sees and hears from the time he arrives in Berlin to the actual fall of the wall.

5. **Make comparisons.** If possible, help readers understand what the incident is like and how it is similar to or different from other incidents you have witnessed or heard about. Ramos comments briefly in sentence 21 about another event that took place on this site.

6. **Find human interest**. Include quotations, if possible, from participants in the incident or from local authorities. Focus on specific participants, not just the general crowd. Ramos tells readers what the soldiers, politicians, and other participants are doing, such as playing a Beethoven symphony, climbing onto building tops, and hammering away at the wall.

> **WRITING HINT**
>
> Think of an eyewitness reporter as similar to a cinematographer. Both present compelling visual images of unfolding events. Try to give readers a sense of seeing the events through the lens of a camera. Clue them in with transitional words and phrases that show time order or spatial order (see pages 27–28).

7. **Determine closure**. Let readers know where you are leaving them. Give them an idea of the significance of the event or of any long-term effects that may come from the event. Ramos lets readers know that the wall is down, the crowds are "out of control," and the authorities are helpless.

EXERCISE 6 Get Started

Brainstorm with classmates, or use one or two of the prewriting techniques in Lesson 1.1 to think of an incident that you remember or that you can cover and then write about. One source of ideas is the local newspaper or community calendar. Find events that are coming up in your area in the near future, such as a potentially heated political or civic meeting or a key ballgame.

EXERCISE 7 Plan Your Eyewitness Report

You'll need to carefully observe what goes on around you in order to collect useful information during the incident. Jot your observations and impressions in a notebook while you're at the scene. If possible, record interviews with participants, or photograph events as they unfold. Later, you may find it useful to draw a time line or series-of-events chain to which you can transfer the notes you decide to use in your draft. If your report is about a past event, write down all the details you can remember. Then talk to others who witnessed the event with you. They may help you remember additional details.

EXERCISE 8 Draft the Eyewitness Report

Draft your report in whatever way feels comfortable to you. Keep a specific audience in mind throughout. Here are some pointers.

- **Follow your organizational plan.** Make it chronological or spatial or both.

- **Grab the reader's attention.** Make readers want to find out what happens and why it happens. Figure out how to draw them into the scene right from the start.

- **Include details.** As you write, find a balance between too few and too many details.

- **Give a solid conclusion.** Try to work in the drama or significance of the event.

EXERCISE 9 Revise Your Eyewitness Report

Try reading your report aloud to yourself and then to a partner to get a sense of its impact. When revising, keep these questions in mind.

- Does my introduction draw readers into my report?

- Is the order of events clear?

- Do my details help readers visualize the event?

- Do my sentences read smoothly?

- Have I maintained a consistent point of view?

- Have I eliminated repetition or unnecessary words?

- Do I convey the significance of the incident?

When you're satisfied with your report, share it with the members of your writing group. Ask for their positive comments as well as questions and suggestions for improvement.

EXERCISE 10 Proofread and Publish

Proofread your revised report for errors in spelling, punctuation, and capitalization. Share your report with friends and family or with someone who took part in the incident you've described. Consider submitting your account for publication on a Web site or blog related to the incident.

Persuasive Writing

When your goal is to **persuade**—that is, to win over readers to your point of view—you must build an argument based on strong reasons and relevant evidence. As you read the following article by Alan Cordova, see if you can identify the reasons he uses to try to persuade students to study the liberal arts.

Prepared for Life
Loving the liberal arts: Why a broad knowledge base is more important than ever
by Alan Cordova

[1]We need the liberal arts—now more than ever. [2]While studying Márquez, Mozart, and Picasso might seem irrelevant to would-be MDs or MBAs, exposure to a wide range of ideas and disciplines provides an unparalleled foundation for addressing the challenges of the 21st century. [3]In a world where career changes are frequent and creative thinking is crucial, the flexibility and resourcefulness that remain the hallmarks of a liberal arts education are essential.

> Grabs reader's attention and states claim

> Supports claim with factual information; appeals to logic

[4]Liberal arts institutions emphasize breadth of learning and have long allowed students to experiment with different fields of study. [5]Their graduates pick up diverse skills over their four years on campus that give them a competitive advantage in many occupations. [6]Who's to say that Carl Icahn's corporate raiding strategy doesn't find some basis in his philosophical roots at Princeton? [7]Or that John Lithgow's performance in "Terms of Endearment" wasn't informed by his History and Literature training at Harvard?

> Provides more factual information to support claim

> Uses questions that provoke thought and appeal to reason

[8]Rather than scheduling their entire undergraduate careers from the start, liberal arts underclassmen are free to broaden their knowledge base. [9]It's at this point that Economics majors can learn Arabic and linguists can get their heads around budgets. [10]Moreover, because most of the courses are open to everyone, all students can benefit from this academic cross-pollination.

> Uses details to build support for claim

[11]Today's liberal arts experience is more than a set of classes; the learning environment plays a significant part in undergraduate life. [12]This is particularly true at small colleges. [13]Students' close interaction with faculty, a liberal arts trademark, creates unique opportunities for intellectual mentorship.

> Makes an emotional appeal

[14]This environment also produces highly competitive grad school applicants, and not just in Medieval French History. [15]Classes that critics dismiss as unnecessary, such as literature or sociology, help students address situations that call for creativity, empathy, and judgment. [16]Today, graduate programs look for more than MCAT, LSAT, or GMAT scores—they want their doctors and lawyers to have broad problem-solving experience.

> Makes a logical appeal

> Counters opposition with factual information

[17]With admissions more competitive than ever, this perspective can be the factor that sets the liberal arts applicant apart.

Makes an emotional appeal — [18]The benefits of a liberal arts background also yield hidden rewards in later life. [19]A common story at Williams tells of an art history graduate who excelled in dentistry because analyzing paintings had taught him how to look for details. [20]Liberal arts gives students the tools to access whatever comes their way. [21]The training in analytical and creative thinking teaches graduates to be versatile in their craft while retaining a cosmopolitan attitude outside the workplace.

Restates claim

Makes a logical appeal by pointing out the limitations of the alternatives

Reinforces claim in conclusion — [22]Although the liberal arts have been around for centuries, they are more important now than ever. [23]Only their graduates possess the range of educational experience that is increasingly valuable in an uncertain job market. [24]A pre-professional graduate faces a narrow career path, subject to myriad market forces. [25]Technical and vocational courses often teach skills that will be outdated in three years. [26]But a liberal arts education allows graduates to adapt quickly to new intellectual environments. [27]The job market may boom and collapse but being taught to think for oneself never disappears.

Critical Thinking After you read the persuasive essay, answer the questions below.

1. How does Cordova establish his position? How does he entice the reader?

2. Summarize Cordova's reasons for studying the liberal arts. Which of his reasons do you find most persuasive?

3. What does Cordova mean when, in sentence 21, he tells readers that liberal arts graduates retain a "cosmopolitan attitude outside the workplace"?

4. What is Cordova's most effective emotional appeal? Which is the best logical appeal?

5. Who are all the people that Cordova mentions? Use context clues to identify the following: Márquez, Mozart, Picasso, Carl Icahn, John Lithgow.

Build Your Vocabulary. Which of these words from the essay can you define: *unparalleled* (sentence 2), *breadth* (sentence 4), *cross-pollination* (sentence 10) *mentorship* (sentence 13), *empathy* (sentence 15)? Look up the words you don't know in a dictionary, and use the phonetic symbols to pronounce the words correctly. Add these words to your vocabulary notebook.

Writing Strategies Usually, a **letter to the editor** is only a few paragraphs long. A **persuasive essay**, such as Cordova's, gives you more room to argue your point. For both types of persuasive writing, however, most of the following strategies apply.

1. **Clearly state your claim.** State your **claim** as clearly as you can in a sentence or two. Use precise language and an objective tone to form your argument. Your claim (also called a **thesis statement**) often, but not always, belongs at the beginning of an argument.

2. **Give reasons.** Logical appeals take the form of reasons. Usually, you'll need two or three strong, distinct reasons to support your claim.

3. **Use evidence to support each reason.** A strong argument includes a variety of evidence. Some examples include credible **facts, quotations from experts**, important **definitions**, accurate **statistics**, relevant **examples**, and convincing **anecdotes**.

   A **horizontal outline** can help you connect your evidence to reasons.

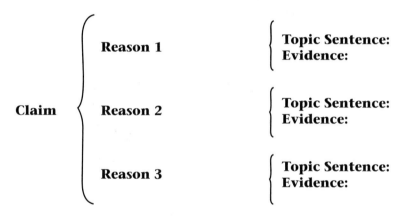

4. **Use emotional appeals wisely.** Emotional appeals argue your case by calling upon the reader's hopes fears, wishes, or sense of fairness. Most of your support should be logical. Sometimes, however, an emotional appeal can be more effective than a logical one. **Loaded words**—words that carry either positive or negative connotations, or slants—are helpful when appealing to a reader's emotions.

5. **Anticipate and refute counterclaims.** A **counterclaim**, or **counterargument**, is an opposing viewpoint. First, acknowledge a counterclaim's strengths and any weaknesses in your own argument. Then refute the counterclaim with logic and evidence to shows its limitations.

6. **Be sure your logic is sound.** As you write, look for holes in your own reasoning. Here are some common errors.

- *Stereotyping*—overlooking individual differences among members of a group

- *Using false analogies*—making weak or far-fetched comparisons

- *Overgeneralizing*—using data from a limited or unrepresentative sample

- *Oversimplifying*—not considering the multiple causes for a particular situation

- *Personalizing*—attacking the person making the argument instead of refuting the argument made

7. **Include transitions.** Use a variety of words, phrases, and clauses to link your ideas. Connect claims to reasons, link reasons to evidence, and distinguish claims from counterclaims. Transitions also connect ideas across paragraphs and help readers follow your argument.

8. **Establish a formal style and objective tone.** Tone, or attitude, and style are crucial in writing an effective argument. Maintain a formal style and a confident, objective tone to show that you are reliable and knowledgeable about your topic. Keep your tone reasonable and respectful, particularly when refuting counterarguments.

9. **End with a call to action.** End your argument with a concise conclusion that supports your claim and follows logically from the evidence presented. Sometimes, you may need more from readers than agreement. A **call to action** urges the reader to do something—donate money, vote for a candidate, or buy a product, for example.

Exercise 11 Choose a Topic

To come up with a topic for a letter to the editor or a persuasive essay, you can check the "Write What You Think" exercises throughout this book, pursue an issue or incident in the news, or survey classmates to learn what issues concern them. Once you have explored a variety of issues, select one topic to write about. Whatever topic you choose, keep in mind that it must have the following two qualities:

- It must be arguable (something people disagree about).

- It must be important to you personally.

If you plan to write a letter to the editor in response to a news article or an editorial that you've read in the newspaper, be sure to record the title of the piece, the author, and the date of publication. Keep it at hand when you write so that you can refer to it and quote from it, as needed.

EXERCISE 12 State Your Claim

Discuss with your writing group these possible claims that could be added to the first few paragraphs of Cordova's essay. Which is the strongest? Why? Which is the weakest? Why?

(a) I'd say that college students might want to study the liberal arts because doing so helps some students learn to think creatively.

(b) Studying the liberal arts contributes to a student's well-being and makes him or her more marketable in the long run.

(c) Studying the liberal arts makes both logical and emotional sense to me.

Determine what you think about the topic you selected in Exercise 11, and try to state your claim precisely and forcefully in one or two sentences. You might find it helpful to draft several versions of your claim. Review them, and then select the best one.

EXERCISE 13 Support Your Claim

While still in the prewriting stage, consider your audience. You need to keep your readers in mind in order to choose logical and emotional appeals that will have an impact on them. Determine how much background information they'll need before you launch into your argument. In preparing your notes, be specific: List specific examples, facts, and statistics from reliable sources. Avoid general expressions such as "most people" and "many states." Mention your sources; your audience will want to know that you've done careful research. Finally, stay focused. Keep your argument concise and appropriate for your audience and purpose. Include only the most relevant details.

EXERCISE 14 Draft Your Letter or Essay

As you write your first draft, remember these four elements of effective writing:

• **Unity and Ideas** The more support you give for your claim, the more persuasive you will be, as long as everything you say is **relevant**—to the point. To illustrate, which of the following items would help to strengthen Cordova's argument?

a. Quotations from college students who agree with him

b. A table or graph showing lifetime earnings of liberal arts graduates

c. A description of a typical course in the liberal arts

d. A comparison of the educational "experience" of liberal arts students and those who have elected to study other disciplines.

- **Organization and Coherence** As you organize your supporting reasons and evidence, let your readers know where your argument is headed. For example, mention the number of reasons you'll present, and as you mention each one, alert readers with appropriate transitional words and phrases, such as *first, second, more important*, and *finally*.

- **Word Choice** Concentrate on expressing every thought as clearly and succinctly as you can.

- **Tone** Try to establish an objective tone that shows that you know what you are talking about, that your information will be reliable, and that you firmly believe that your position is the right one—and that you are fair and open-minded.

EXERCISE 15 Revise, Edit, and Publish

First, revise your work for large-scale problems in ideas and organization. Check that you've accurately represented opposing arguments and have addressed those you've found unclear or incorrect. If you've appealed to your readers' emotions, check to make sure you've done so respectfully. Check that you've ended your essay by asking readers to change their minds or to take a particular course of action. Then, consider your audience and purpose, and revise your essay to eliminate unnecessary or inappropriate details. Edit for spelling, grammar, usage, and mechanics. Share your work with the members of a writing group, and ask for their comments.

Expository Writing: Compare and Contrast Essay

When you write a **compare and contrast essay**, you identify the ways two or more subjects are alike and the ways they are different. The following excerpt introduces the 1858 series of debates between Abraham Lincoln and Stephen A. Douglas, the challenger and the incumbent candidate for U.S. Senator representing Illinois. Both would run for President two years later. In the excerpt, David Herbert Donald **compares** and **contrasts** the two men.

The Lincoln–Douglas Debates
an excerpt from *Lincoln* by David Herbert Donald

[1]The seven formal debates between Lincoln and Douglas were . . . only a small part of the 1858 campaign, though they naturally attracted the greatest interest. [2]All of them followed the same format. [3]The speakers alternated in opening the debate. [4]The opening speaker was allowed an hour for his presentation; his opponent had an hour and a half for reply; and the initial speaker then had a final half hour for rebuttal. [5]Lincoln grumbled that the arrangement allowed Douglas to make four of the opening and closing statements, while he was allowed only three.

> Background information

[6]As the Republican *New York Times* observed, Illinois in 1858 was "the most interesting political battle-ground in the Union," and newspapers throughout the country offered extensive coverage of the canvass. [7]Local papers, of course, gave it great attention. [8]For the first time reporters were assigned to cover candidates throughout the long campaign season. . . .

[9]Reporters noted how sharply the candidates contrasted in appearance. [10]Douglas, so short that he came up only to Lincoln's shoulder, was a ruddy, stout man, with regular features marred only by a curious horizontal ridge that stretched across the top of his nose, while Lincoln was exceptionally tall and painfully thin, with a melancholy physiognomy and sallow skin. [11]Douglas had a booming, authoritative voice, while Lincoln spoke in a piercing tenor, which at times became shrill and sharp. [12]Douglas used graceful gestures and bowed charmingly when applauded, in contrast to Lincoln, who moved his arms and hands awkwardly and looked like a jackknife folding up when he tried to bow.

> Contrasts appearances; uses transition

> Contrasts voices, speaking styles, gestures

[13]There was also a marked contrast in the way the candidates presented themselves to the public. [14]Douglas wished to appear a commanding figure, a statesman of national reputation. [15]Accompanied by his beautiful, regal second wife, Adèle Cutts, he usually traveled by special train, splendidly fitted out for comfort and for entertaining. [16]When he stood on the platform in his handsome new blue suit with silver buttons and in his immaculate

> Contrasts public image each candidate sought

linen, he was unquestionably a great United States senator reporting to his loyal constituents. [17]Lincoln deliberately cultivated a different image. [18]When he went by train, he traveled in the regular passenger cars—a practice that afforded him endless opportunities for meeting the voters and talking about their concerns. [19]Except at the final debate in Alton, Mary Lincoln did not accompany him; it was not part of the persona he was projecting to display his elegantly dressed wife with her aristocratic bearing. [20]Lincoln took pains to wear his everyday clothes during the debates, appearing usually in what Carl Schurz, the German-American leader, who campaigned for the Republican ticket, described as "a rusty black frock-coat with sleeves that should have been longer" and black trousers that "permitted a very full view of his large feet."

Author builds on contrasts already established — [21]From time to time, Lincoln tried to capitalize on the differences between Douglas's appearance and his own. [22]The senator's followers, he said, anticipated that their leader at no distant day would become President and saw in his "round, jolly, fruitful face" promises of "postoffices, landoffices, marshalships, and cabinet appointments, chargeships and foreign missions, bursting and sprouting out in wonderful exuberance," while in Lincoln's "poor, lean, lank face" nobody ever saw "that any cabbages were sprouting out," because "nobody has ever expected me to be President." [23]There was nothing false about all this; Lincoln was in fact a homely man with simple tastes, indifferent to personal comfort. [24]It was important in this contest to present himself to the voters not as a man of considerable means and one of the most prominent lawyers in the state but as a countryman, shrewd and incorruptible.

Critical Thinking   After you read the compare and contrast essay, answer the questions below.

1. Overall, would you say that Donald emphasizes the similarities between the two statesmen or the differences? Explain.

2. The word *while* in sentence 10 is a **transition**; it indicates that a contrast will follow. List other transitional words and phrases Donald uses to help readers follow his thinking about Lincoln and Douglas. (See page 28 for a list of transitions.)

Build Your Vocabulary. Which of these words from the essay can you define from context clues or word roots: *ruddy* (sentence 10), *melancholy* (sentence 10), *physiognomy* (sentence 10), *sallow* (sentence 10), *persona* (sentence 19), *lank* (sentence 22)? Look up the words you don't know in a dictionary, and use the phonetic symbols to say them aloud. Add these terms to your vocabulary notebook.

Writing Strategies The purpose of writing a compare and contrast essay is to inform your readers about a subject or to explain a subject. It is critical, therefore, that you plan your essay carefully and that you organize your thoughts clearly. Use the following suggestions.

1. **Choose your subjects.** Pick two subjects (for example, two people, two places, two events, two objects, two points of view) that you know something about—and that you want to explore further.

2. **Conduct research and integrate information.** After you have chosen your subjects, conduct research to find multiple sources of information from print and multimedia sources that helps you answer the question, *How are these two subjects alike and different?* For example, you might research newspaper reports, audio or video recordings, photographs, and statistics and other data. As you research, evaluate the relevance of the information, and integrate information from your sources to identify features of your subjects to compare and contrast.

WRITING HINT

You may choose to write about similarities only, differences only, or both similarities and differences, perhaps emphasizing one or the other.

3. **Try a Venn diagram or a chart.** A Venn diagram is a useful prewriting graphic organizer for identifying your subjects' similarities and differences. The overlapping part of two circles contains the features that your subjects share. The outer parts of the circles contain your subjects' differences—what is unique to each. Examine the Venn diagram below, which shows the similarities and differences between Lincoln and Douglas.

DOUGLAS

1. Physical appearance: short, ruddy, stout; regular facial features, ridge

2. Public-speaking style: authoritative voice, graceful gestures, charming

3. Public image: commanding, well-dressed, regal; travels grandly; accompanied by wife

4. Expectations: to be president

Similarities (Implied)

1. Seek public office

2. Create public image

LINCOLN

1. Physical appearance: tall, thin; melancholy, sallow

2. Public-speaking style: shrill, piercing tenor; awkward movements

3. Public image: poorly dressed, homespun; travels like common people; not usually accompanied by wife

4. Expectations: not to be president

The comparison and contrast chart that follows is a different way to show the same information.

Comparison and Contrast Chart			
FEATURE	DOUGLAS	LINCOLN	SIMILAR (+) DIFFERENT (−)
Physical appearance	short, ruddy, stout; regular facial features, ridge	tall, thin; melancholy, sallow	−
Public-speaking style	booming, authoritative voice; graceful gestures, charming	shrill, piercing tenor; awkward movements	−
Public image	commanding, well-dressed, regal; travels grandly; accompanied by wife	poorly dressed, homespun; travels like common people; not usually accompanied by wife	−
Expectations	to be president	not to be president	−
Seeks public office?	yes	yes	+
Works on image	yes	yes	+

4. Organize. Use one of the two basic formats shown below and on the top of page 73 for a compare and contrast essay.

- In the **block method**, shown below, you discuss all the features of one subject. Then you discuss the features as they relate to the second subject. You should discuss the features in the same order.

- In the **point-by-point method**, shown on page 73, you first deal with one feature in both subject 1 and subject 2. You then present a second feature in both subject 1 and subject 2. Continue in this manner for the remaining features.

Block Method:
One subject at a time

All About Douglas

Feature 1: physical appearance
Feature 2: public-speaking style
Feature 3: public image
Feature 4: expectations

All About Lincoln

Feature 1: physical appearance
Feature 2: public-speaking style
Feature 3: public image
Feature 4: expectations

Point-by-Point Method:
One feature at a time

Feature 1: Physical appearance

Douglas: short, ruddy, stout;
  regular facial features, ridge

Lincoln: tall, thin; melancholy,
  sallow

**Feature 2: Public-speaking
style**

Douglas: booming, authoritative
  voice; graceful gestures, charming

Lincoln: shrill, piercing tenor;
  awkward movements

Feature 3: Public image

Douglas: commanding, well-dressed,
  regal; travels grandly; accompanied
  by wife

Lincoln: poorly dressed, homespun;
  travels like common people; not
  usually accompanied by wife

Feature 4: Expectations

Douglas: to be president

Lincoln: not to be president

5. **Use clear transitions.** Transitional words and expressions help readers follow your thinking. *Like, similarly, just as, both, also,* and *in the same way* signal similarities. *Yet, on the other hand, in contrast, however, unlike, whereas, while,* and *nevertheless* signal differences. You can also use transitions such as *first, second, finally, more importantly,* and *most significantly* to highlight each new feature.

EXERCISE 16 Choose Subjects

Use one or all of the following questions to come up with two things to compare and contrast.

- **What two things are somewhat similar but mostly different?** The subjects must have at least one feature in common. The easiest subjects to write about are specific, limited ones that you can observe directly.

- **What has changed significantly with the passage of time?** You might compare a subject in the past with the same subject in the present. For example, what was Chicago like one hundred years ago, and how is it different today? How has television changed? How have women's lives changed?

- **Which sources are available and relevant?** You may want to do some preliminary research to help narrow your subjects. Research available print and multimedia sources, and identify features that you could compare and contrast between subjects. Consider which features might be best suited to visual and other types of multimedia.

EXERCISE 17 Gather Information

Which features of your two subjects will you examine as you compare and contrast? Brainstorm features by thinking about the categories listed in item 2 on page 71— and others. Then create a Venn diagram or a chart (see pages 71 and 72). As you work, use one or more of the following techniques.

- **Inspect your subjects**. If your subjects are available for close inspection, take notes as you actually examine them. Consider using a camera or a digital recording device.

- **Conduct research.** Use encyclopedias and other reference sources to find information about subjects you don't know much about. Gather facts, examples, and specific details to back up your statements. Be sure to refer to more than one source so that you get a fuller view of your subjects. Remember to do other kinds of research, such as conducting interviews, exploring online sources, or watching relevant videos.

- **Differentiate between fact and opinion.** A fact is a statement everyone agrees is true or that you can prove. An opinion, on the other hand, is a person's idea or belief; it's not necessarily true or provable. Opinions backed up with reasons and other evidence are stronger than unsupported opinions.

EXERCISE 18 Organize Your Essay

Try these strategies for planning your comparison and contrast essay.

- **Focus on key features.** From the notes you've made about features of your subjects, choose only two or three features to focus on.

- **Pick a plan.** Some writers think that block organization works better for shorter papers but prefer to use point-by-point organization for longer ones.

- **Make a rough outline.** Jot down your subjects and features in an order that makes the most sense to you. Your rough outline may look like one of the two sets of notes on pages 72 and 73.

EXERCISE 19 Drafting Your Essay

Consider these three hints as you write.

- **Tell the reader.** In your introduction, (1) identify your subjects, (2) let your readers know whether you'll discuss the subjects' similarities or differences or both, and (3) grab your readers' attention. Draft a **thesis statement,** or **claim,** that summarizes your essay's main idea. Which of the thesis statements on the following page is strongest? Why?

a. Lincoln and Douglas wanted the same thing but were different.

b. Although Lincoln and Douglas were politicians, they were different.

c. Lincoln and Douglas sought the same political office but differed in their appearance, in their oratory style, and in their public image.

- **Begin writing.** Stick to your rough outline to explain the differences and similarities between your subjects. Be sure to use a formal style and objective tone. Use precise language and techniques, such as metaphors and analogies, to help readers understand complex ideas.

- **Wrap it up.** In your **conclusion**, summarize your findings without simply repeating the similarities and differences you've fleshed out. Are your subjects more alike or more different? Is one feature more significant than the others? Share any new insights you have gained.

EXERCISE 20 Revising

Read your essay aloud to help you listen for what content is missing and for how to improve your writing style. When revising, keep these questions in mind:

- Does my introduction draw readers into the essay?

- Does the order of features make sense?

- Have I explored the most important or the most interesting differences and similarities between my subjects? Have I given enough (or too many) examples?

- Have I used transitional words and phrases to clarify similarities and contrasts and to help readers follow my thoughts?

- Have I eliminated any unnecessary words?

When you're satisfied with your essay, share it with the members of your writing group. Ask for their positive comments as well as questions and suggestions for improvement.

EXERCISE 21 Proofread and Publish

Proofread your paper, and enlist a partner to check it, too. Once you've corrected errors in grammar, usage, mechanics, and spelling, find a way to share your paper with an audience. Your class might compile separate anthologies of comparison and contrast essays about history, ecology, literature, popular culture, and so forth. Distribute these anthologies to teachers in other departments or to the school library for future classes to use.

Expository Writing: Cause-Effect Essay

A **cause** is the condition, situation, or event that makes something occur. The result of that cause is called its **effect**. A **cause-effect essay** explores the link between one or more causes and the effect(s).

The following passage is from a case history reported in a psychology textbook. The author describes the treatments that a severely burned infant receives and the ways she responds.

from **Understanding Human Behavior**
by James V. McConnell

Background provides information to draw reader in.

[1]Their patient was a 17-month-old girl who suffered severe burns that covered 37 percent of her body. . . . [2]Medical care for the burns consisted chiefly of applying a stinging drug called silver nitrate, which was squirted over the little girl's bandages at frequent intervals by the nurses. [3]The doctors also began a series of skin grafts, but discontinued them when the infant's physical condition grew markedly worse. [4]After a month of treatment the little girl refused to eat; more than this, she became markedly upset whenever she was approached by any of the nursing staff.

[5]At this point social workers Shorkey and Taylor were called in to help. [6]They observed that the nurses, who were extremely disturbed at the child's condition, would frequently interrupt the painful treatment procedure and would attempt to soothe the little girl by talking to her, singing, and playing with her toys. [7]The more the nurses attempted to give the child love, the more violent the little girl became in her rejection of their attention and affection. [8]Indeed, it almost appeared that the staff members were making the child worse, not better.

Explains cause for girl's behavior

[9]Shorkey and Taylor reasoned that, in the infant's depressive state, <u>she simply could not discriminate between love and pain</u>. [10]To her, a nurse coming into the room had become a stimulus that too often was followed by unpleasant consequences (the silver nitrate). . . . [11]The infant had become conditioned to expect hurt rather than love whenever a nurse appeared on the scene. [12]Psychotherapy, then, should consist of helping the infant associate one set of stimuli with pain, another set with love and affection.

Description of treatment designed to establish new cause-effect relationships

[13]Shorkey and Taylor instituted the following changes: Whenever the nurses were to bathe the girl's bandages with silver nitrate, bright white lights were turned on. [14]The nursing staff wore green medical garments but were instructed not to talk or handle the infant unnecessarily, not to play with her, and not to spend one moment longer in the room than they had to. [15]Then, at other times, a set of red lights was turned on, the nursing staff wore distinctive red garments, and they spent as much time as possible play-

ing with the girl, rubbing the unburned parts of her body, talking to her, and giving her food. [16]Medication was never given during the "red light" or social-stimulation condition.

Two new
treatments
(causes) bring two
new behaviors
(effects)

[17]By the end of the second day the infant began responding differently to the two treatment situations. [18]That is, she continued to cry—but briefly—when the white lights were on and she was doused with the painful silver nitrate. [19]But when the red lights were on, her crying ceased and for the first time in several weeks she lost her fear of the staff members. [20]By the fourth day the infant began entering into little games with the staff; by the end of two weeks she was playing happily during the "red light" condition. [21]At this point the doctors

Conclusion:
further causes
and effects

resumed the skin grafts. [22]By the end of 6 weeks the little girl was well enough to be discharged from the hospital.

Critical Thinking   After you read the cause-effect essay, answer the following questions.

1. What cause-effect relationships does McConnell identify?

2. Explain how the effect stated in sentence 4 can be considered the cause for the action noted in sentence 5.

3. In your own words, explain what the social workers were trying to do in sentences 13–16. How would you rate their success?

Build Your Vocabulary. Look at the following words in context. What do you think each means: *discriminate* (sentence 9), *stimulus* (sentence 10), *stimuli* (sentence 12), *social-stimulation condition* (sentence 16)?

Writing Strategies   The purpose of a cause-effect essay is to explain an event, the result of an event, and often the reason the event came about. Use the following suggestions.

1. **Choose your topic.** Choose an issue that you genuinely wish to explore—perhaps an issue from history (for example, Why did the United States enter World War 1?); one of the *How come?* questions small children ask (for example, Why is the sky blue?); an issue you've heard on TV and radio talk shows; or a behavioral change going on around you.

2. **Be open-minded about causes and effects.** No matter what your topic is, you'll need to be careful not to make certain assumptions when you gather your information. **Consider several causes and effects.** Here's why.

- **The first cause you spot is not necessarily the only one or the most important one.** For example, a low score on a test might be the result of insufficient studying, or it might be traced to lack of sleep or illness. Furthermore, the test might have been too hard or poorly constructed, or you might not have had enough time to complete it.

- **A cause may have effects other than the one you've linked it with.** For example, switching schools in the middle of the year is not the only effect of moving to a new town.

- **Distinguish among different kinds of causes. Immediate** causes come right before an effect; **underlying** causes may be far removed from an effect and, therefore, may not be readily apparent. Some causes are part of a **cause-effect chain**, which is a series of events in which each cause creates an effect that, in turn, becomes the cause for another effect. An example of a cause-effect chain for McConnell's article is below.

CAUSE-EFFECT CHAIN

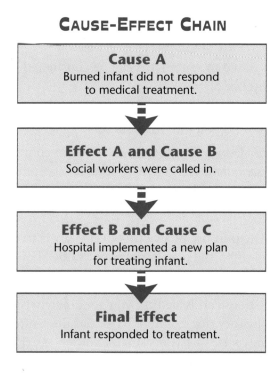

Cause A
Burned infant did not respond to medical treatment.

Effect A and Cause B
Social workers were called in.

Effect B and Cause C
Hospital implemented a new plan for treating infant.

Final Effect
Infant responded to treatment.

3. **Gather evidence.** Your writing will be more impressive and convincing if you offer credible evidence. Give your readers facts, statistical data, examples, incidents, and expert opinions. McConnell, for example, provides background information, gives descriptions of the infant's condition and her specific behaviors, and presents the expert views of social workers Shorkey and Taylor.

4. Determine an organization for your material.
You might begin with a single cause and then explore the effects that it has. Or you might state an effect and trace its cause(s). You can present your information chronologically—particularly if you are reporting on a cause-event chain. Or, when there are several causes and effects to explore, you might order information in the order of importance. The three organizers below show plans for three different cause-effect essays. You may wish to use them as models when you write your own essay.

WRITING *HINT*

Just because one event precedes another does not mean the first event necessarily causes the second one. For example, if you were to come down with a cold after standing in line for a movie on a freezing, blustery day, the weather may not be the only cause of your illness.

CAUSE-EFFECT ORGANIZERS

Single Cause → Single Effect

IF
The school parking lot is too small.

THEN
Students parking on the street might be subject to theft and vandalism.

Multiple Causes → Single Effect

IF
Football players all went to summer training camp.

AND
An energetic coach was hired this year.

THEN
This year the team might win every game.

Single Cause → Multiple Effects

IF
Travel time between classes has been shortened to three minutes.

THEN
Students have trouble making it to class on time.

AND
The shortened day allows bus drivers to deliver students before rush hour.

5. Connect ideas. Transitional words and expressions help readers follow your thinking. Transitions such as *yet, therefore, as a result, so that, consequently,* and *because* are particularly helpful for writers and readers of cause-effect essays. *Next, after that, tomorrow, just before,* and *finally* are examples that show time order. *More important, of greater value, less important,* and *most significant* signal order of importance.

EXERCISE 22 Choose Your Topic

Use one or more of the following strategies to come up with a topic for a cause-effect essay.

- **Out of the Past** Think of a key historical event that interests you, and determine its underlying and immediate causes. Or ask yourself a *What if?* question that guides you to imagine what might have occurred had the event turned out differently. For example, what if the Russians had not launched the satellite that started the space race in the 1950s?

- **In the News** Form a stimulating question based on what you come across in periodicals, on TV, and on the radio. For example, why are people avoiding a particular food? Why do people want particular changes made in the law?

- **Right Under Your Nose** Look all around yourself. Why do people act as they do? What are the causes and effects of the simple events you witness every day?

- **Outside English Class** Refer to observations you've made in other classes. In your social studies class, what issue would you like to investigate further? In your science class, what new or surprising discoveries did you make?

EXERCISE 23 Gather Your Information

To investigate cause-effect relationships, you can do research in printed or digital reference sources, locate newspaper and magazine articles, interview participants in an event, and open your eyes and ears to make original observations. You are looking for evidence (facts, statistics, examples, and so on) to support your claims about causes and effects. Take careful notes from your sources, making sure to indicate where each idea comes from.

EXERCISE 24 Organize Your Information

Copy or modify one of the graphic organizers on pages 78 and 79, and use it to arrange your notes from Exercise 23. You may have gathered a lot of information when you researched your topic. Select only the most relevant and significant details, statistics, and other information to include in your draft.

EXERCISE 25 Draft Your Essay

Consider these hints for writing about the cause-effect relationship that you've identified and outlined graphically.

- **Present your thesis statement, or claim.** In your introduction, provide one or two sentences that express your main point.

- **Keep your audience in mind.** Think about how much your readers already know about your topic and what you'll need to tell them. Use an objective tone that will make readers receptive to your ideas and conclusions.

- **Use precise, formal language.** Choose your words with care, and use techniques, such as similes, to explain complex concepts. Use a straightforward, formal style that is easy for readers to follow.

- **Wrap it up.** In your conclusion, summarize your main point, and share any new insights you have gained.

EXERCISE 26 Revise

Read your essay aloud to yourself to get a sense of whether you have succeeded at what you set out to do. If you can, set it aside overnight before revising. When you revise, keep these questions in mind:

- Does my introduction draw readers into the essay?

- Have I provided enough evidence for each cause-effect relationship I suggest?

- Have I kept my writing as straightforward as possible?

- Have I used transitions to make my writing flow and to make relationships clear?

- Have I eliminated any unnecessary words?

When you're satisfied with your essay, share it with your writing group. Ask for their positive comments as well as questions and suggestions for improvement.

EXERCISE 27 Proofread and Publish

Proofread your paper, and enlist a partner to check it, too. Once you've corrected errors in grammar, usage, mechanics, and spelling, find a way to share your paper with an audience. Consider distributing it to a club you belong to or post it on a blog or Web site that is related to your topic.

Expository Writing: Problem-Solution Essay

In a **problem-solution essay**, you identify a significant problem, analyze it, and then propose one or more workable solutions.

The following article is from an issue of *Newsweek* magazine. In it, the authors identify and describe a problem. They then review possible solutions, pointing out both benefits and current drawbacks.

We've Overlooked One of Our Greatest Assets:

I believe that our community and junior colleges can help America regain its competitive edge.

by William D. Green

The author relates a personal story to set the stage for his argument and to establish his credibility.

[1] If you had told me back in 1971—the year I graduated high school—that I'd be going off to college soon, I would have assured you that you were sorely mistaken. [2] I was the son of a plumber living in western Massachusetts, and we had all assumed that in the end I'd be a plumber, too.

[3] I spent the year after high school working in construction. [4] Then one day I went to visit some friends who were students at Dean College, a two-year residential college 45 minutes outside of Boston, and my mind-set began to change. [5] As I walked around campus and listened to my friends talk about their experiences, I realized this was an opportunity to change my path that might not come again—an opportunity to take another shot at learning. [6] So I enrolled at Dean, and I can honestly say it was a life-altering experience.

Provides factual information from a personal perspective

[7] The school's philosophy is to educate, energize and inspire. [8] In fact, it was a Dean professor, Charlie Kramer, who ignited my passion for economics and taught me how to think analytically. [9] After all these years, I still have my notes from his economics classes, and I've referred back to them from time to time—even as I went on to Babson College, where I earned my bachelor of science degree in economics and then an M.B.A. [10] I'm proud to say that today I'm a member of Dean College's board of trustees.

Relates his personal story and relevant statistics to support his argument

[11] Would I be running a global consulting company with $17 billion in revenue and 130,000 employees today if I'd followed a different path? [12] Who knows? [13] But there is no doubt that my two years at Dean College not only prepared me for advancing my education and gearing up for a career, but also transformed me as a person. [14] And that's not a bad start no matter where life takes you.

Identifies problem

¹⁵But while Americans are waking up to the idea that we need to sharpen our competitive edge in the world—President George W. Bush threw down the gauntlet in his State of the Union address earlier this year—many still overlook our system of community and junior colleges. ¹⁶The truth is, these schools can be the solution for what our K–12 programs might not be getting done.

Proposes a solution

¹⁷Whenever I get the chance to talk to young people, I urge them to consider options other than four-year schools. ¹⁸Junior and community colleges can help them become better equipped to continue their education and to face real-world challenges. ¹⁹These colleges can smooth their transition from high school to work life, provide them with core decision-making skills and teach them how to think and learn.

Supports proposed solution with facts and statistics

²⁰In the United States there are more than 1,100 community colleges, most of them publicly funded, which serve nearly 12 million students. ²¹Almost two thirds of these students attend school part time, and many of them are holding down a full-time job. ²²What's especially striking is the diversity of these schools: 47 percent of all African-American undergrads in this country attend community college, as do 56 percent of Hispanic undergraduates.

²³But what is it about these schools that make them so important to our competitive future? ²⁴For starters, I can't think of any other institutions so tuned into the needs of our communities. ²⁵The American Association of Community Colleges estimates that more than half of new health-care workers get their training at community colleges. ²⁶In 2003, 62 percent of the applicants who took the national exam to become licensed registered nurses were graduates of such programs.

Analyzes proposed solution by identifying its specific benefits

²⁷Community colleges excel at working with local businesses to identify specific needs, whether helping displaced autoworkers gain new job skills or helping local companies ensure they will have a steady supply of skilled workers. ²⁸Chances are, if there's a large manufacturing plant in your town, your community college offers technical training in conjunction with the plant. ²⁹Better skills and better pay lead to happier, more productive employees. ³⁰That boosts the economy, which gives us all a better standard of living.

Proposed solution includes a call to action

³¹I believe that since businesses benefit from these institutions, we also have an obligation to help them. ³²This is especially true as state support, which constitutes an estimated 44 percent of community colleges' financial resources, continues to decline. ³³We can show our support by donating funds, recruiting students, offering career counseling and encouraging our employees to teach classes.

Restates his main idea

³⁴An investment in your local junior or community college is a sound investment in the competitiveness of our country and the potential of our citizens.

Restates his authority

³⁵I should know.

Critical Thinking   After you read the problem-solution essay, answer the questions below.

1. How does the writer grab—and keep—the readers' attention?

2. How does the writer's personal story lend credibility to his proposed solution?

3. Which paragraphs introduce and analyze the problem? Which paragraphs discuss the proposed solution?

4. How does the writer use the concluding paragraphs?

Build Your Vocabulary. Look at the following words in context. What do you think each means: *sorely* (sentence 1), *ignited* (sentence 8), *analytically* (sentence 8), *gauntlet* (sentence 15), *displaced* (sentence 27)? Look up the meanings of the words you don't know. Add these words to your vocabulary notebook.

Writing Strategies   The purpose of a problem-solution essay is to identify and explain a problem and to explain or report on a solution. Your audience, most likely, will be people who are interested in or concerned about the problem you are discussing. Use the following suggestions.

1. **Identify a problem.** The number of problems in need of solution is endless. We face large problems and small problems every day. To identify a problem to write about, review what you've already written in your notebooks or journals; brainstorm with friends and classmates; turn to TV, radio, newspapers, and magazines for issues; or interview people active in local organizations. Try to pinpoint a problem for which possible solutions may exist. Steer clear of complicated problems that don't lend themselves to a brief essay.

2. **Explore the problem.** Think and read about the problem you chose. Pose a variety of questions such as the following: Who experiences this problem? How serious is the problem (a minor inconvenience or a major tribulation)? What proof, or evidence, supports your statement that the problem is indeed a problem? What tone should you take in discussing it? Can you break the problem into parts, each of which might have a solution?

3. **Brainstorm solutions.** Think about the whole problem or parts of the problem. What have others said about handling the problem? What new thoughts can you add?

WRITING HINT

You don't have to work on a monumental problem. Consider choosing one that is somewhat lighter or one that you can treat with humor. For example, what's wrong with your school's colors or basketball uniforms? How can you get support for a new fight song?

4. **Rank the possible solutions.** Determine which are ineffective solutions—and why. Then identify the best solution. Is it the best because it has the fewest negatives? Because it is the most practical? The cheapest? The most morally appropriate? List the evidence that proves the validity of your ranking.

5. **Address resistance.** Acknowledge arguments that some readers may raise against your proposed solution. Counter their resistance by providing additional information.

6. **Note how to implement the solution.** What step-by-step instructions can you give your readers about putting the solution into place?

7. **Organize your presentation.** Go back over your notes, and determine how much of your essay you will devote to the problem and how much to the solution. Distribute your notes onto the frame at right or a variation of it.

A Problem-Solution Frame

Statement of Problem
- Proof

Possible Solutions
- Deficiencies

Best Solution
- Justification
- Steps for Implementation

Objections to Solution
- Defense of Solution

Conclusion

EXERCISE 28 Choose Your Topic

Use one or more of the prewriting strategies in Lesson 1.1 to come up with a topic for your problem-solution essay.

EXERCISE 29 Gather Your Information

After you identify your problem, generate notes about the extent of the problem. List facts, statistics, and examples. Then start considering solutions for part or all of the problem. List the most relevant information for each solution—facts, statistics, examples, experts' opinions and quotations, and anecdotes. Which solutions pose their own problems? Note which solution you prefer and which ones you will emphasize in your essay.

EXERCISE 30 Draft Your Essay

Consider these hints for writing about the problem you have identified and the solution you will put forth. These hints supplement the problem-solution frame above.

- **Introduce the problem, and elaborate on it.** In a few sentences, present and explain the problem. Think about how much your readers already know about the problem and what additional information you'll need to tell them. Use interesting statistics, quotations, or observations to grab and hold your readers' attention. Maintain an objective tone that will make readers receptive to your thinking.

- **Organize your ideas.** Present the preferred solution in detail. Decide on an order for presenting the facts, statistics, experts' opinions and quotations, anecdotes, and examples that you have gathered. You may consider using formatting, such as headings, to clarify your organization.

- **Address your critics.** Consider drafting one or more paragraphs that answer the objections to your solution.

- **Itemize steps.** Use precise language to tell readers how to carry out the solution.

- **Restate your case.** Your **conclusion** should include a compelling statement that supports your solution. It can be a thoughtful quotation or a question or statement that invites readers to think more about your ideas and to take them seriously.

EXERCISE 31 Revise

Read your essay aloud to yourself to get a sense of whether you have succeeded at what you set out to do. If you can, set it aside overnight before revising. When you revise, keep these questions in mind:

- Does my introduction draw readers into the essay?

- Have I stated the problem clearly and fully?

- Have I presented a solution readers can understand? Have I provided a strong case for the solution, one backed by ample evidence?

- Does my conclusion give readers something to think about?

- Have I used transitional words and phrases to make my writing flow smoothly and to make relationships clear?

- Have I eliminated any unnecessary words?

- Does my conclusion summarize my solution effectively?

When you're satisfied with your essay, share it with the members of your writing group. Ask for their questions, comments, and suggestions.

EXERCISE 32 Proofread and Publish

Proofread your paper, and enlist a partner to check it, too. Once you've corrected errors in grammar, usage, mechanics, and spelling, find a way to share your paper with an audience.

- If other students tackle the same problem but offer different solutions, consider participating with them in a debate or panel discussion. Debaters can use the essays to prepare their oral arguments.

- Submit to the school or local newspaper any essays that deal with issues of concern to your peers or to the community.

Writing About Literature: Analyzing a Work

When you set out to write about a work of literature, you generally choose among three common types of essays: (1) the **personal response essay**, in which you share the thoughts and emotions that strike you as you read particular passages in the work; (2) the **evaluation essay**, in which you rate a work of literature according to established criteria, such as believability of characters or plot; and (3) the **literary analysis**, in which you comment about the work as a whole from one perspective—for example, from the perspective of history, from the perspective of a certain philosophy of life, or from the perspective of one or more of the elements of literature (characterization, plotting, imagery, setting, and so on).

The following excerpt is part of an analysis of Thomas Hardy's novel *The Mayor of Casterbridge*. The author, Dennis Potter, explains how the characters in the novel inevitably fall to the twists of fate that Thomas Hardy has in store for them.

On Hardy's *The Mayor of Casterbridge*
by Dennis Potter

[1]The story of Michael Henchard, who rose from itinerant haytrusser plodding the country roads with his young wife and child to be the richest corn merchant and chief citizen of Casterbridge and then fell back again into embittered poverty and loneliness, is the tragedy of a proud man buffeted by what Thomas Hardy calls "the persistence of the unforeseen." [2]This ominous phrase comes in the last, sad sentence of the novel when the entranced reader can at last look back at the great surge of narrative and measure the inexorable tide of fate as it swamps the central character and all that he has worked for, all that he has loved.

[3]Henchard is not idly swept aside. [4]He is tough and headstrong and passionate, a man with a tremendous will and a tenacious spirit—one of the greatest characters, indeed, in modern literature. [5]We are pulled in to the turmoil of his life almost before he opens his mouth, for there is nothing but "the voice of a weak bird singing a trite old evening song" to temper the taciturnity of the stern young man with the springless walk who takes his family and his basket of tools in the search for work. [6]The novel begins its long journey with the same slow tread along the dusty road, but we soon sense in its steady rhythm the unfolding of a vast purpose and a noble struggle for self-fulfillment. [7]And it is a journey that the reader makes, too

Enriching Your Vocabulary

The noun *taciturnity* comes from the Latin verb *tacere,* which means "to be silent." Most often, the adjective form of the word, *taciturn,* is used. A person who thought deeply, yet seldom spoke, my grandfather was known all through the county for his *taciturnity.*

Thesis statement or claim

Analysis of main character; relates to thesis

Quotation helps describe character

—one which will illuminate the shape of his or her own life and thus press upon fundamental emotions which are scarcely half engaged by so many of the impoverishments of modern fiction: I envy anyone who is reading *The Mayor of Casterbridge* for the first time.

Short plot summary — [8]Within a few pages of the opening of the story, the young Henchard, through his own foolishness, has lost his wife and child. [9]It is this event which will forever haunt him, no matter how far he rises or how real his remorse. [10]The past cannot be disowned. [11]It rises up again and strikes him down, but not before Michael Henchard seems to have repaired the hole that has been torn out of his being by his own feckless behavior.

[12]The loops and coils of the plot, where accident, coincidence, even rain and sunshine bear down on the characters at the most crucial moments, give one not only the uncomfortable dislocations of "the persistence of the unforeseen" but also a broad and vivid picture of rural England as its agriculture began to change. [13]The novel brings a whole community alive, and the things that count in it are money and work and the harvest, rumour and gossip and reputation, a complete mesh of life and circumstance in which the characters are also their own audience, their own remorseless judges. [14]Even the comical old yokels nodding their bald pates together in the pub are turned into witnesses who suddenly astound us with a long perspective of the ups and downs which bind these lives together in the streets of "Casterbridge" (Dorchester) and the barns and fields beyond.

[15]Yet no matter how pinioned by the grip of their own destinies, the people in these pages are not paper boats on the tide or, more appropriately, mere stalks to be cut down by the scythe. [16]They defend themselves. [17]They scheme and plan and pit their energies against whatever persistence it is that sharpens or drains their passions, and we are unable to remain aloof from the pathos, the expectations, the loves or the rivalries which make this such a great novel. [18]The ironies and vagaries of fortune which afflict the characters spring out at the reader, too. [19]No one who starts the book will altogether escape the tense pleasure or anxiety about "*What is going to happen*?" that pulses through the narrative. . . .

Refers back to thesis statement — [20]The book reminds us just as much of the continued certainties of our lives as of "the persistence of the unforeseen" which haunts the man in the brown corduroy jacket pacing along the country road on a summer evening long ago. [21]He is making a path into our own imaginations.

Critical Thinking After you have read the literary analysis, answer the questions below.

1. In your own words, summarize this excerpt of a literary analysis.

2. How does Potter interpret the phrase "the persistence of the unforseen" (sentence 1)?

3. From what you've read of Potter's essay, would you be interested in reading the novel? Why or why not?

4. Find examples of how Potter shows his respect for Hardy's writing.

Build Your Vocabulary. Which of these words from the essay can you define: *taciturnity* (sentence 5), *feckless* (sentence 11), *pates* (sentence 14), *pinioned* (sentence 15), *vagaries* (sentence 18)? Use context clues to help you. Then look up the words you don't know in a dictionary, and use the phonetic symbols to pronounce them correctly. Add these terms to your vocabulary notebook.

Writing Strategies You will be asked to write many book reports in your academic career. The purpose of this type of writing is to examine a work carefully and to explain your interpretation of it. Your audience will usually be a teacher or peer who is familiar with the subject of your essay. Use the following suggestions.

1. **Present a thesis statement, or claim.** Somewhere in your introductory paragraph, make clear what your essay is going to do—what piece of literature you are going to analyze, from what perspective, and to what end (that is, what are you going to prove?).

2. **Determine how much plot summary to give.** Potter does not assume that his readers know the story well. When you suspect that your intended reader is not familiar with the work you are analyzing, devote a few sentences or a paragraph in a summary. If the work you are analyzing is very well known, you can forgo most of the plot summary.

3. **Proceed by balancing general statements (your main points) with specifics in support of them.**
   • Quote from the text where appropriate.
   • Refer to details (incidents and characters) in the text without quoting.
   • Make comparisons: A comparison or contrast with another work or other characters may clarify a point you are making.
   • Quote or summarize what an expert has written, making sure to give full credit to the expert.

4. Use present tense. When you refer to characters or events in the work, cast their actions in the present tense. Here are examples from Potter's essay:

Hencherd **is** not idly swept aside.

. . . the people in these pages **are** not paper boats on the tide . . .

The book **reminds** us . . .

5. Keep your tone consistent. Adopt and maintain a formal and serious tone. Generally, contractions, sentence fragments, and slang do not belong in literary analysis. You can, however, use images of your own; notice, for example, Potter's comment about the book, "I envy anyone who is reading *The Mayor of Casterbridge* for the first time."

> **WRITING HINT**
>
> To quote from literature:
> - Make sure that you copy word for word with exact punctuation.
> - Set off as a block any quotations longer than three lines; do not enclose the block in quotation marks.
> - Use ellipsis points (. . .) to indicate that you've made a deletion from a passage.
>
> See Chapter 14 for details about quotation marks and ellipsis points.

QUESTIONS FOR LITERARY ANALYSIS

Use the following questions to get ideas for writing.

QUESTIONS FOR ANY LITERARY WORK

Characters: What do the characters want or need at the beginning of the work of literature? How do the characters change? Are the characters complex or simple? What can you say about the characters' motivations? About their speech? What does the main character learn or discover? What is that character's relationships with other characters like? How does the author reveal what the main characters are like?

Plot: What is the central conflict? Is it internal or external? How is it revealed and resolved? What larger meaning does the resolution suggest? Does the writer use foreshadowing or suspense?

Setting: How does the setting influence the action, the characters, and the outcome? How does the author describe the setting?

Point of view: Who tells the story? Why has the author selected this point of view? How would the work change if the story were told from a different point of view?

Theme: What universal insight about life or people does the work offer? Which passages or elements most clearly convey that insight? If the theme is not expressed directly, can you infer a theme from the outcome or by how the characters change?

Imagery: What effect is created by metaphor, simile, personification, and symbolism?

ADDITIONAL QUESTIONS FOR POETRY

Speaker: What can you say about the speaker of the poem? Is the speaker standing in for the poet or for another character?

Sound: What effect is created by any of the following: meter, rhythm, repetition, onomatopoeia, alliteration, consonance, rhyme scheme?

ADDITIONAL QUESTIONS FOR PLAYS

Structure: How does the division into acts and scenes underscore the theme of the play?

Stage directions: How do the stage directions help to convey the setting? How do they affect the action and the delivery of lines?

EXERCISE 33 Prewriting: Choose and Limit a Topic

Choose a piece of literature—a short story, a novel, a play, or a poem—to which you already have a strong personal response. In this workshop, you will have the opportunity to look at the work more deeply, more critically, and perhaps figure out what caused your initial response. Use the questions above and on page 90 to help you choose one literary element from the work to focus on. After choosing a literary element, consider narrowing your focus even further—perhaps to one character, one setting, or one image.

EXERCISE 34 Prewriting: Major Points and Supporting Details

As you reread the literary work, take notes on anything of relevance to the literary element you're studying. Next, form clear statements that generalize about the details of that literary element. Then, based on those statements, draft a thesis statement, or claim—one or two sentences that express what you will cover in your essay.

EXERCISE 35 Organize and Draft Your Essay

Now you have the opportunity to take the statements about major points (and their corresponding details) that you prepared for Exercise 34 and decide in what order to present them in your essay. Sit down and start writing at any point in the essay—

beginning or middle. What's important at this stage is getting your ideas down in sentences and paragraphs. Later, you can polish them. The draft stage may also be when you want to come up with a possible title for your essay. The title, ideally, should mention the work of literature and hint at your essay's claim.

EXERCISE 36 Revise Your Essay

After you've given yourself a break from your essay, take it out, and read it with the following questions in mind.

• Does the introduction identify the work?

• Is the claim of your essay clearly presented in the introduction?

• Are the general statements—the major points—clear but not wordy?

• Have you provided enough details to support each major point?

• Are all the details relevant?

• Is the organization of your essay easy to follow?

• Does the conclusion clearly and effectively wrap up your essay?

EXERCISE 37 Proofread and Publish Your Essay

When you're satisfied that you have corrected all problems in grammar, usage, mechanics, and spelling, exchange papers with a partner so that you can help each other find errors you may have missed. Then consider sharing it with others. On the Internet, you might locate a discussion group dedicated to the author of the work you wrote about. Consider joining the discussion and posting all or part of your essay to the group for response and criticism.

Expository Writing: Research Paper

Writing a research paper gives you the opportunity to become an expert on a topic. Usually, the goal of a research paper is to answer a question or solve a problem related to your topic. You will spend a lot of time doing research and writing your research paper, so select a question that intrigues you and a topic that you want to learn more about.

There are at least five kinds of research papers.

1. **Summarizing/synthesizing paper.** In the most common type of research paper, you **summarize** or explain information that you have gathered from several sources. You **synthesize** (put together to form a new whole) what other writers have reported.

2. **Evaluation paper.** This research paper is similar to the first kind but also includes evaluation, or your opinion of what your research reveals. For example, your paper might present several observers' statements about the cause of a particular effect and conclude with *your* statement about which observer seems most on target and why.

3. **Original research paper.** In this type of paper, you present and summarize your original research. For a social studies paper, you might present findings based upon surveys, questionnaires, or interviews you have conducted, drawing conclusions and making predictions from your data. In a science research paper, you might report on the results of a series of your own experiments.

4. **I-search paper.** In this type of paper, you tell the story of how you wrote your research paper. An I-search paper not only presents information you discovered about a topic but also explains why you chose that topic, how you conducted your research, and what you experienced along the way.

5. **Combination paper.** In this type of research paper, you would draw on elements from the others. You could, for instance, provide your own claim related to the research others have done.

On the following pages, you will find excerpts from a high school student's research paper, printed in *The Concord Review*. Keep in mind that MLA (Modern Language Association) style has guidelines for research paper format. Research papers should have one-half-inch margins on all sides, and the first word of every paragraph should be indented one-half inch from the left margin. Parenthetical citations and a Works Cited page are also required.

Matthew Eisenberg
Mrs. Elizabeth Devine
AP United States History
1 May 2012

Baseball's Negro Leagues

From 1898 to 1947, America's national pastime, baseball, fell prey to the racism in the country and excluded black players from white teams and leagues. Despite their acknowledged equality as players, black players were forced to play in inferior ballparks, under inferior conditions, because of their skin color. In the early years of all-black baseball, teams struggled to make money, players struggled to earn a living, and leagues struggled to stay together. By the 1930s, however, two new leagues had formed: the Negro American League and the Negro National League. It was during this period that black baseball flourished, and despite the disappointment of being left out of the major leagues, Negro ballplayers and teams made the two organizations a success.

Baseball had become a popular game during the Civil War, as bored soldiers looked for ways to spend their time in between battles (Palmer and Thorn 7). By 1872, as military governments ruled the South, the first black player, John Fowler, joined a professional league (Peterson 18). Fowler wandered from minor league to minor league, and although he played all nine positions, he never distinguished himself as a ballplayer (Peterson 21). Soon after Fowler, another black man joined the professional baseball ranks. Moses Fleetwood Walker, a student at Oberlin College, left school early to join the minor leagues with the Toledo club of the American Association. When that league was declared an official major league in 1885, Walker became the first black major leaguer. Despite threats of lynching from the Richmond club, Walker played on. Eventually too much pressure mounted against him, and Toledo released him. Walker's precedent, however, led the way for many more blacks in the following years (Peterson 21–24). In 1885, there were four blacks in white baseball, and by 1887, there were twenty (White 82).

At the same time, however, the first all-black baseball team was formed in Babylon, Long Island. This team, chosen from waiters at area hotels, began barnstorming the Northeast with the players making $12 to $18 per week. In 1886, the Cuban Giants, as they were called to make people think they were foreigners, recruited some of the finest black ballplayers from all over the country. After beating one white team after another, they won wide acclaim by beating the Eastern League (an upper-level minor-league) champion, Bridgeport (White 11–23). In 1887, they joined with other newly formed Negro teams to form the League of Colored Baseball. Although it folded after a week because it was a financial disaster, in Solomon White's

4-line heading: Name/Teacher/ Class/Due Date

Title, centered

Introductory paragraph; ends with 2-sentence claim

Background information—two paragraphs

Margins should be set to one-half inch.

Running head,
one-half inch from
top of paper

words, "The short time of its existence served to bring out the fact that colored baseball players of ability were numerous" (26). Later that year, the Cuban Giants once more distinguished themselves by nearly beating the World Champion Detroit club (White 59).

Introduces
establishment of
color barrier

Although blacks were having success in white baseball, in 1887, Jim Crow began to take blacks away from the white game. Many players competing against blacks complained, and in Syracuse, several players were suspended for refusing to play (Peterson 28). With venom and hate, baseball great Adrian "Cap" Anson led the drive to segregate the game. In his book, Solomon White charges Anson with nearly single-handedly creating the color barrier. After entire teams refused to play against blacks, the clubs which they were on slowly began to release the blacks (Peterson 31). . . .

By 1889, there were just two blacks in white baseball: Fleet Walker and Dick Johnson, who both had distinguished themselves with their off-the-field class. Walker was released after the 1890 season, however. . . . By 1898, the barrier was complete, and no black players or teams remained in white baseball (Peterson 49). . . .

Background on
early history of
black professional
baseball

In 1900, there were five black professional teams: the Cuban Giants, the Cuban X Giants, the Red Stockings, the Chicago Unions, and the Columbia Giants. Each barnstormed in a separate region of the country, and each was mildly successful playing blacks, whites, or each other (Peterson 59). In 1906 a new league formed made up of these teams, one that lasted for almost an entire year. The final game was played in front of ten thousand mostly black fans at the Philadelphia Athletics' stadium (Peterson 62–63). Between 1900 and 1920, many Negro teams were formed, most barnstormed, and a few leagues were attempted. Players would travel at night, often encountering problems, because of their race, with lodging and restaurants. They would play every day, sometimes two or three times (Peterson 63–65). Most made from $40 to $100 a month plus expenses, far below the salaries of white ballplayers (Peterson 70). It was a hard life for the ballplayers, especially those who knew they could have been superstars in white baseball. The greatest player of the era was John Lloyd, nicknamed the Black Honus Wagner. Wagner, the Hall of Fame shortstop, proudly acknowledged, "I am honored to have John Lloyd called the Black Wagner. It is a privilege to have been compared with him" (Peterson 73).

Topic sentence
introduces
"golden age" of
Negro league
baseball;
following
paragraphs
provide support.

The 1930s and 1940s—an era of racism, segregation, and hate in this country—surprisingly became the golden age of Negro league baseball. Through hardship, depression, and war, all-time great players like Satchel Paige, Josh Gibson, Buck Leonard, and Cool Papa Bell showcased their tremendous talents in the leagues that were gaining fast acceptance among

Eisenberg 3

whites and blacks alike. The Negro leagues of the era were a tremendous success for various reasons.

The quality of play and the players delighted fans and helped gain blacks acceptance, easing the eventual integration of blacks and whites. The attendance is a testament to the fact that blacks finally had a game of their own and role models to look up to, and many whites also found enjoyment by watching Negro baseball. Financially, the Negro leagues grew to a two-million-dollar-a-year enterprise, the biggest black-dominated business in the country (Peterson 93). Finally, Negro league baseball provided many blacks with the chance to do what they loved most: play the game. As Bill Wright, a Negro league player for twenty-one years said, "I think people know now that it was a mistake not to let us play in the major leagues, but we didn't ever hold a grudge. We had too much fun" (Smith 80).

Andrew "Rube" Foster, an excellent pitcher in the early twentieth century, is widely considered the father of Negro league baseball. In 1919, he proposed the first Negro National League, made up of eight teams (Peterson 80–84). The league began a new era for black baseball, as crowds of eight thousand to ten thousand were common in 1920. Attendance soon fell as Foster's death in 1923 left the league with no strong leadership, but the profit made by clubs during the four years was undeniably a source of inspiration for the next series of pioneer owners.

The year 1933 saw two strong men emerge to create the second Negro National League. Cum Posey, founder of the Homestead Grays, and Gus Greenlee, founder of the Pittsburgh Crawfords, worked together to help found the longest-lasting league in Negro baseball. Both owners had made considerable money off their talent-rich teams and saw an even greater potential in organized baseball. The Crawfords, Grays, Chicago American Giants, Indianapolis ABC's, the Detroit Stars, and Columbus Blue Birds—and later the Nashville Elite and the Baltimore Black Sox—filled out the roster in 1933. Greenlee's strong and sometimes dictatorial hand helped the Negro National League rule the East Coast (Peterson 91–103).

Soon thereafter, H. G. Hall founded the Negro American League. At first it was quite unstable, as teams rotated in and out of the league. By the late 1930s, however, both leagues were on strong financial ground (Peterson 93). There were many problems at first, though, as weak leadership hurt the play on the field. It was not unusual for a player to attack an umpire who made an unfavorable call because there was rarely punishment handed down from the league hierarchy. As players began to realize that the owners were out solely for money, many jumped from team to team, often in mid-season, and played for whoever would pay the larger salary (Peterson 94–95).

Eisenberg 4

Despite this, there was little doubt that the Negro leagues were becoming the proving ground for black baseball players in the 1930s. Each team played between thirty and forty games a year, and the winners from each league played each other in the World Series (Peterson 277). Similarly, black ballplayers were beginning to gain fame as they became household names in black families, and many sportswriters began to openly wonder how these men would fare in the white leagues. The Negro leagues were no longer laughed at by white baseball, and in the next two decades many black players proved that they were equal to if not better than any white counterpart. . . .

With the influx of talent and the new respect for the league came a boom in attendance. While the first Negro National League's World Series in 1926 drew only nine thousand fans, the famous East-West games in the 1930s and 1940s never drew fewer than twenty thousand. These games, the brainchild of Gus Greenlee, were tremendous showcases of Negro talent. At the peak of Negro league baseball success, 1943, the East-West game was played at Comiskey Park, home of the Chicago White Sox, and drew 51,723 fans. Mostly blacks attended these games, but it was not uncommon for whites to attend. Regular season games also drew well, although not nearly as well as the East-West games, and a marquee player like Paige or Gibson could always draw a large interracial crowd of spectators (Peterson 100).

The league was a financial success for the owners, and the players were compensated nicely as well. By World War II, an average Negro league player would make about $400–$500 a month plus expenses, and stars could make nearly $1,000 per month. While these numbers did not compare to the salaries of white major leaguers, they were far superior to the money made in white minor leagues or by most blacks in America (Peterson 98). . . .

The Negro leagues may not have received the respect that major league baseball earned, but they certainly enjoyed a success of their own. Constantly battling racism and doubts about their ability, the players went on the field to play their game and, in so doing, earned the admiration of blacks and many whites alike. Life was not easy for black ballplayers, but they overcame the disappointment of being left out of the white game and proved that they could do just as well. By the end of the 1940s, the Negro leagues had become so successful in showcasing black baseball talent that the white leagues were forced to question the wisdom of their decision to exclude them. They could no longer claim to have the greatest talent in the country when everyone knew that only half of baseball's superstars actually played on white teams.

Eisenberg 5

Introduces new
topic: the need to
integrate

By 1940, pressure was mounting in major league baseball to allow blacks to play. Managers and many ballplayers called for the end of the racial barrier (Peterson 177). Bill Veeck led the charge in 1943 with an idea to buy the last-place Philadelphia Phillies and fill the team completely with Negro league stars. "I had not the slightest doubt that in 1944 . . . the Phils would have leaped from seventh place to the pennant," Veeck claimed (Peterson 180). Although Veeck failed when baseball's owners learned of his idea and didn't approve the sale of the team, it was a large step in integrating baseball.

In the mid-1940s, several baseball teams held tryouts for black players. The Boston Red Sox, for example, invited several players, most notably Jackie Robinson, to a private workout. Each player showcased tremendous talent but never heard from the team again. This was a typical scenario for most of the tryouts as, for one reason or another, the players never made the team (Peterson 183–86). Branch Rickey, president of the Brooklyn Dodgers, set out to change this pattern (Dixon and Hannigan 302).

Under the pretense that he was planning to buy a Negro league team, Rickey sent out scouts to watch Negro league games. These scouts would report back to Rickey on the best players, and Rickey would personally see many of them. Realizing that it would take more than just a great ballplayer to become baseball's pioneer, Rickey had specific criteria. One name kept popping up from all his scouts: Jackie Robinson, the fleet-footed second baseman of the Kansas City Monarchs. Although Robinson was not the best player in black baseball, he was an excellent ballplayer known for his competitive fire on the field and his gentlemanly conduct off of it. Robinson was a non-drinking, non-smoking, former tri-sport star at UCLA, and an army veteran (Dixon and Hannigan 188--89). He was signed by Rickey to the Triple-A Montreal Royals of the International League (Dixon and Hannigan 190). Ordered never to fight back against any racism he encountered, Robinson held up under the media's magnifying glass and the constant taunts of spectators and quietly became the Royals' star player. The next year, on April 15, 1947, he broke the color barrier when he started at second base on opening day for the Dodgers. Rickey had carefully orchestrated his debut, and, shortly before the season started, he traded a bunch of players who had spoken out against Robinson playing on the team. Robinson went on to win the National League Rookie of the Year award (Peterson 198). . . .

It is likely that if it had not been for the success of the Negro National League and the Negro American League, black baseball players would have had to wait years longer before breaking the color barrier. Similarly, had Robinson failed to impress the Montreal crowds or the Brooklyn Dodgers' front office, or simply reacted to the prejudice he faced with any rage or hint of retribution, it would have set Rickey's effort back several years. The Negro leagues had been successful in opening the door to so many opportunities that black players had never before been confronted with, and, given the chance, they proved their equality and often superiority to white ballplayers. The Negro leagues and the courage of Robinson gave Willie Mays, Hank Aaron, and even the great black players of today the opportunity to play in the major leagues.

Background information—two paragraphs—on demise of Negro league baseball

And so, with the beginning of a new era for major league baseball, the era of the Negro leagues reached the beginning of the end. In 1947, every Negro league team lost money, and attendance plummeted (Peterson 201). As one Negro league star after another went to the major leagues, the league withered. Barnstorming once more became common, but now each team needed a gimmick. Clowns, cannibals, midgets, and many other sideshows were used to draw fans to the games. Only players with personality played on black teams because they were called upon to make jokes or humorous plays to keep the fans excited. Negro league baseball ceased to be a breeding ground for the finest black talent in America, and instead fans went to the major league parks, where they could see their black heroes play with whites for the first time in nearly sixty years (Dixon and Hannigan 302). The Negro American League and Negro National League survived on a small scale until they finally collapsed in 1960.

The Negro leagues, even with their faults, proved to the world the equality of blacks on the baseball field. At the time, every small step in the overall struggle against racism had an impact, and the fact that white baseball was forced to admit that it needed blacks lifted the spirits of many who were fighting the civil rights battle. Baseball had slammed the door on black players in the 1890s, and the blacks became such a success without whites that fifty years later many baseball executives were virtually begging to get them back. . . .

Concluding paragraph: writer's final observations

The impact of the Negro leagues has in many ways been lost among today's baseball players and fans. In a recent *Sports Illustrated* survey, several players didn't even know who Jackie Robinson was, but there is no way to tell what the game would have been like without him or without the Negro leagues. Baseball's Negro leagues, despite the tragic circumstances through which they were created, had a tremendous impact on the game of baseball and all of society, even if they are not well known today. Denied their dream, black players took the field and made that dream possible for generations to come, while winning the hearts and minds of millions of baseball fans in the process.

Centered title, 1 inch from top

Book by one author

Original interviews conducted by writer of research paper

Book by two authors

Magazine article

Eisenberg 7

Works Cited

Chadwick, Bruce. *When the Game Was Black and White*. New York: Abbeville, 1992. Print.

Craft, David. *The Negro Leagues*. New York: Crescent, 1993. Print.

Craig, Thomas. (National Baseball Hall of Fame and Museum). Telephone interview. April 8, 1994.

Dalin, David. (University of Hartford). Telephone interview. April 1, 1994.

Dixon, Phil, and Patrick J. Hannigan. *The Negro Baseball Leagues*. Mattituck: Amereon, 1992. Print.

Holway, John B. *Blackball Stars: Negro League Pioneers*. New York: Carroll, 1992. Print.

James, Bill. *The Bill James Historical Baseball Abstract*. New York: Villard, 1986. Print.

Palmer, Pete, and John Thorn. *Total Baseball*. New York: Warner, 1989. Print.

Peterson, Robert. *Only the Ball Was White*. New York: Oxford UP, 1992. Print.

Rogosin, Donn. *Invisible Men: Life in Baseball's Negro Leagues*. New York: Atheneum, 1983. Print.

Smith, Shelley. "Remembering Their Game." *Sports Illustrated* 6 July 1992: 80+. Print.

White, Solomon. *Official Baseball Guide*. Library of Baseball Classics. Columbia: Camden, 1997. Print.

Writing Strategies The purpose of a research paper is to provide in-depth information on a limited topic. Apply the following strategies.

1. **Select a general topic.** Choose a field that interests you. Within that field, you need to come up with a topic and research question limited enough so that you can address them well given the time, reference sources, and space you have. While searching for a topic, try the following ideas:

   • Skim articles in magazines and newspapers, including online archives.

   • Review your own writer's journal.

   • Visit science, art, or history museums.

   • Go to the zoo, a play, a botanical garden, a concert, an ethnic fair, or a celebration.

  - Jot down ideas as you read for pleasure.

  - Browse through your textbooks and through encyclopedias, atlases, and
    other reference sources.

  - Talk with someone who works in a field that interests you.

2. **Limit your topic further.** Be sure you pick a topic that you can cover
   sufficiently within the length assigned for the paper, and be sure you can find
   adequate information. Narrowing a topic to the right size may require
   adjustments as you go. For example, a student trying to write a paper called
   "Black Players in Baseball" in just a few pages would find the topic much too
   broad; on the other hand, "Black Players' Batting Stats in the 1920s" is
   probably too narrow.

   Check to determine if you will be able to find at least four or five useful
   sources on your library's shelves, in an electronic database, and from credible
   Web sites on the Internet.

3. **Budget your time.** Don't wait until the last minute. The list below suggests a
   sensible way to budget time for each step in the research process, given an eight-
   week time frame. Notice that you'll probably spend much more time doing research
   and taking notes than you will spend on actually writing your first draft.

Steps in Research Process	Time
Choose and limit topic	3 days
Find and evaluate sources; make bibliography cards	3 days
Read sources and take notes	1 ½ weeks
Draft thesis statement and title	2 days
Draft outline	1 week
Write first draft	1 week
Document sources	2 days
Revise	1 ½ weeks
Proofread	2 days
Prepare final manuscript	3 days

4. **Find multiple credible sources.** Chances are that you will need to consult
   both primary and secondary sources. A **primary source** is an original text or
   document, such as a literary work, a diary, a letter, a speech, an interview, or a
   historical document. A **secondary source** presents a writer's comments on a
   primary source. Reference books, biographies, literary criticism, and history
   and science textbooks are examples of secondary sources.

In many libraries, electronic databases have replaced card catalogs, the *Readers'
Guide to Periodical Literature*, and newspaper indexes. InfoTrac's General
Reference Center, available in many libraries, and other electronic indexes give
you access not only to the titles of relevant magazine articles but also to the texts
of the articles.

5. **Find Internet sources.** A contemporary researcher needs to be comfortable using
   computers and the Internet for current information. If necessary, ask a librarian to
   help you conduct an online search on your topic. You will need to work with various
   search engines, and you will need to word your searches carefully. You will have an
   opportunity to follow online links to related topics. As you proceed, you will have to
   consider whether to modify your research topic in light of productive Web sites that
   you find unexpectedly.

6. **Evaluate possible sources.** Your secondary sources must meet the
   following criteria.

   • **Are sources up-to-date?** Which is a better source for information about
     the impact of escalating salaries in Major League Baseball: a fifty-year-old
     book or last week's *Sports Illustrated*?

   • **Are sources accurate?** Don't believe everything you read. Reliable sources
     are both accurate and unbiased. You might trust a *New York Times* article more
     than a column in a sensationalistic tabloid. Be especially careful about Internet
     sources. A university-connected site or a government database is usually a
     more reliable source than a personal home page by someone who has not yet
     established credibility as a reference source.

   • **Are sources appropriate for you?** Figure out for what audience the
     printed or electronic source is intended. Materials written for experts might
     be too technical, while those intended for younger readers might simplify
     issues too much for your purposes.

   • **Are sources relevant?** Finally, the information you collect for your
     research paper must directly relate to your limited topic. If a source isn't
     pertinent, either skip that source for now, or modify your research topic
     in a way that justifies using the source.

7. **Keep track of your sources.** For every source you use, make a source card
   (sometimes called a **bibliography source card**) that contains all essential
   publishing information. Give each source a number, and write that number in the
   upper right-hand corner of the card. Then, when you take notes, instead of rewriting

all this information on each note card, you can simply place the source's number in the upper right-hand corner of your note card for identification. Or if you prefer, keep track of your sources electronically. Add a new entry for each new source.

SAMPLE SOURCE ENTRY

1	Number of source
Peterson, Robert. *Only the Ball Was White.* New York: Oxford UP, 1992. Print.	

8. **Take notes.** After you've read a source, you may quote it exactly if the writer's words perfectly express a point you want to make. Most often, though, put the information into your own words.

- You can **summarize** the information by giving only the most important ideas in your own words.

- Or you can **paraphrase** the information, restating every idea in the same order as in the original but in your own words.

For each source, write the main idea, and underline it.

SAMPLE NOTE

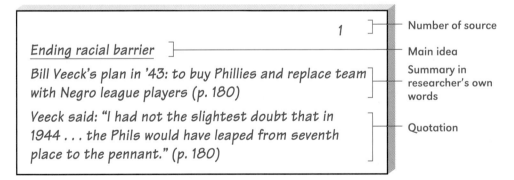

1	Number of source
Ending racial barrier	Main idea
Bill Veeck's plan in '43: to buy Phillies and replace team with Negro league players (p. 180)	Summary in researcher's own words
Veeck said: "I had not the slightest doubt that in 1944 . . . the Phils would have leaped from seventh place to the pennant." (p. 180)	Quotation

9. **Make an outline.** Sort your notes according to main ideas. You should have at least three main ideas, which you can then lay out as an outline for your paper.

10. **Draft a thesis statement, or claim.** Some researchers create the outline first; others draft a thesis statement first and then create the outline. Either sequence is acceptable. Your claim announces the controlling idea for your paper; it often comes at the end of your introduction. It tells readers what you are going to write about in the rest of your paper. You may find yourself revising the thesis statement several times in the course of applying the writing process to a research project.

11. **Give credit.** Your research paper has to show where your information comes from. You'll need to acknowledge a source whenever you (1) quote a phrase, sentence, or passage directly; (2) summarize or paraphrase another person's original ideas in your own words; or (3) report a fact that exists in just one source. The Modern Language Association (MLA) has created a system for giving credit to sources.

   • You can use **parenthetical documentation** at the point of citing each quotation or borrowed idea. The information that you put in parentheses is brief: it consists of the author's last name and the page number(s) of the book from which you took the material; if there is no author for a source, then provide within the parentheses a shortened version of the title along with the page number; finally, if you use two sources by the same author, give the author's last name and a shortened title along with the page number(s).

   • You then must provide a **Works Cited list** at the end of your paper. On this list, which gives fuller information about each source you have used, follow the MLA guidelines (see **Writing Hint** in the margin). **Note:** Some instructors prefer that students cite each source in a footnote or endnote rather than in parentheses.

> **WRITING HINT**
>
> For more information about MLA style, consult the *MLA Handbook for Writers of Research Papers*, 7th edition. An online version of the work is accessible at www.mla.org.

12. **Don't plagiarize. Plagiarism**, using someone else's words or ideas without acknowledgment, is a serious offense. High-ranking officials have lost their jobs because of plagiarism, and writers have lost their reputations and have been sued. Be especially careful when paraphrasing your sources. If you think your paraphrase may be too close to the original, revise what you wrote or quote the original text. Teachers and other readers often can detect plagiarism, which undermines a writer's credibility.

EXERCISE 38 Prewriting: Consider and Limit your Topic

A teacher may give you a highly focused research assignment such as
the following:

> Explore the role of color imagery in Shakespeare's *Macbeth*, as commented on by at
> least three critics.

Or a teacher may give you more freedom, as in the following assignment:

> For your research paper, select an aspect of Shakespeare's *Macbeth* that we did not
> discuss in class. Explain why this aspect should be part of next year's study of the
> play. Cite critics who consider this aspect of the play important.

Or a teacher may leave the door wide open for you, inviting you to conduct a
research study on anything that interests you.

In any of these cases, you have to narrow, or focus, and personalize a topic so
that it reflects your own taste and thoughts. Depending on which of the
preceding scenarios your teacher presents you with, spend some time thinking
about and limiting a topic for a research paper that will run the length that
your teacher specifies. Write a paragraph telling what research question you
have chosen (and how you have chosen it). Include a sentence that identifies
your audience and purpose in exploring this research question.

EXERCISE 39 Prewriting: Gather Information

Use the following checklist as you think about collecting and evaluating sources.

• Will I need primary sources, secondary sources, or both in order to carry out
the assignment?

• What general sources can I check to get background information on my limited topic?

• Now that I have background information, how do I proceed? Should I use
reference books, periodicals, the Internet, other media (movies, television,
radio), published interviews, or scientific studies?

• Do I need to conduct original research—through observation, interviews,
or surveys?

Write a paragraph giving and explaining your answers to the preceding
questions and others that you address during this stage.

EXERCISE 40 Prewriting: Getting to the Outline Stage

This exercise assumes that you have already proceeded through Writing Strategies 4–8 (pages 101–103). You may now be ready to arrange your notes and prepare an outline for your research paper. Begin by grouping related notes together. Then move on to sequence the grouped notes in a way that makes sense to you: What will you deal with first? Second? Which notes do you probably not even need? Here are three common problems you may face while working with your notes; here, too, are suggestions for dealing with the problems.

**Plan for
Research Paper**

Title page or heading

Introduction
Attention grabber
Thesis statement

Body
Main idea 1
   Support A
   Support B
Main idea 2
   Support A
   Support B
Main idea 3
   Support A
   Support B

Conclusion
Works Cited Page

- **Too few main ideas** If all your notes basically deal with the same one or two main ideas, your research hasn't been broad enough, and you won't have enough to say in your research paper. You probably have to go back to your sources and find other related main ideas to include in your paper.

- **Not enough supporting information** It's not uncommon for researchers to discover that they have intriguing main ideas but not enough supporting details (examples, anecdotes, quotations, and so on) to convince readers of those main ideas. If you find that you have holes to fill, try to find additional sources that you can summarize, paraphrase, or quote.

- **Too much information** It's very difficult to discard information that you have worked hard to find. Still, it's better to eliminate unnecessary notes now than bore your readers by repeating information or by using new information that may be interesting but not totally relevant. (Caution: Keep material that you now think may be unnecessary; it just may turn out that you need that information after all.)

When you've dealt with the preceding problems or others, move on to generating an outline for your paper. Use the boldfaced elements on the plan in the sidebar above as a guide for your outline. That is, substitute your specifics for the general categories in the plan. Use numerals and letters to designate elements on your outline and to keep the hierarchy, or relationship, of ideas clear in your own mind.

EXERCISE 41 Write a First Draft with Documentation

It usually makes sense for you to proceed from the beginning of the draft to the end, but if you get stuck at any point, try jumping ahead; come back to the difficult part later. One reason for generating an outline (Exercise 40) is to help you think about the research paper in distinct sections, and you may find some sections easier to write than others. Some writers prefer to write their introduction and conclusion—two critical points of the research paper—after they've written the body, but other writers write everything in sequence. Follow the approach that works for you.

As you draft, make sure you indicate in parentheses the source and page numbers from which you've taken information. Citing sources as you draft is the best way to avoid plagiarism.

Watch your tone, your use of the pronoun *I*, and your use of quotations as you write.

- Tone refers to your attitude toward your topic. Generally, a research paper requires a serious tone. You shouldn't sound stiff and formal, but you shouldn't sound overly familiar and informal either.

- An I-search paper, as noted earlier, includes your commentary on your research process, but most other research papers generally avoid the first person.

- Use your own words as much as possible. Include direct quotations and paraphrases only when necessary.

EXERCISE 42 Revise Your Draft

When you've finished your draft, set it aside for a while—ideally, overnight. Typically, getting some distance from your draft will help you revise with a fresh eye. Later, read through your draft several times, concentrating on a different issue each time—ideas and unity, organization and coherence, sentence variety, and word choice. Ask yourself questions such as the following:

- Do I have too many, not enough, or a sufficient amount of main ideas?

- Do I have too many, not enough, or a sufficient amount of support for my main ideas?

- Are my ideas in a logical, easy-to-follow order?

- Where would transitions make my sentences and paragraphs easier to follow?

- What can I do to improve my sentence structures and my word choice?

Then ask for feedback on your paper from classmates, friends, or relatives. Listen carefully to their reactions, and use their suggestions as your revise. You may find yourself revising your research paper more than once.

EXERCISE 43 Proofread Your Paper

Double-check each quotation for accuracy—and for correct capitalization and punctuation. Check each parenthetical reference and each item on your Works Cited list for correct form. When you are satisfied that you've fixed all errors in grammar, usage, mechanics, and spelling, ask someone else to review your work. Writers often can't see their own mistakes.

EXERCISE 44 Prepare the Final Copy and Publish

You will first publish your research paper by submitting it to your teacher or by otherwise following your teacher's directions. Be aware, though, that both print and electronic periodicals or other publications sometimes carry research papers by high school students. If, as suggested earlier, you have pursued a topic of genuine interest to yourself and are proud of your resulting research paper, you may want to share it with a larger community than your teacher and class.

Special Writing Tasks: Résumé and Cover Letter

Workplace writing includes memos, reports to supervisors, directions to colleagues, and business letters. Most people learn business-writing skills on the job. Two kinds of business communication you need to know about before you land a job—while you are looking for paid or volunteer work—are résumés and cover letters.

A **résumé** is an organized list of your educational background, extracurricular activities, and work experience. Usually, you send the same résumé to several businesses or organizations. A **cover letter** (also called a **letter of application**) accompanies the résumé; it must not repeat what is on the résumé, but rather, it should explain how the general facts of your résumé match the needs of the specific organization or company you are sending it to. Together, the résumé and the cover letter often determine if you get a job interview.

Cover letters can be written in two different styles. In the **full-block style**, every line of the letter is aligned at the left-hand margin and paragraphs are not indented. In a **modified-block style**, the heading and the signature are indented about halfway into the page, and the first line of every paragraph is indented. The letter on page 111 is in the full-block style. The full-block style is the most common format used for professional writing today.

Today, most businesses prefer to receive résumés and cover letters electronically via e-mail or their company Web site. In those cases, follow any guidelines the company may set out for online submissions. Otherwise, the style and format of your résumé and cover letter should match the models presented in this lesson.

The following models illustrate appropriate content and acceptable format. You may modify the order and placement of elements on your own résumé, and you may use full- or modified-block style for your own letter. Your goal for both documents is clarity.

Writer's name, address, phone number, and e-mail address

Statement of objective

Details about performance and programs outside of high school

Details about abilities; action verbs throughout; phrases rather than full sentences acceptable

Current and prior work experience, including volunteer roles

Thomas L. Vandrosky
47 Beech Lane, Baltimore, MD 21204
(555) 567-8910 <thomvan@bpm.com>

OBJECTIVE: Summer opportunity that builds on mentoring and leadership experiences

EDUCATION: Senior at Jackson High School, Baltimore, Maryland (expected graduation June 2014) G.P.A.: 3.2

National Honor Society, 2011 to present

U.S. Naval Academy Science & Engineering Seminar, Annapolis, June 2013
- Attended six-hour seminar for high school students interested in military career

ACTIVITIES AND SKILLS: President of Junior Class, Jackson High School
- Presided over weekly meetings
- Ran class recycling program

Student Council member during freshman and sophomore years

Debate Club member during junior and senior years (Maryland State Champions, 2013)

Swim Team member during sophomore, junior, and senior years
- Placed second in 100-yard breaststroke at State Championship, 2013
- Won 200-yard medley relay at State Championship, 2013

WORK EXPERIENCE: Chemistry Lab Assistant, Harper College, Baltimore, Maryland, summer 2012
- Kept inventory of all lab equipment
- Set up lab stations before classes
- Substituted as lab partner for absent students

Mentor, Big Buddy Mentoring Program, Baltimore, Maryland, 2011 to present
- Meet weekly with fifth-grader to help with reading and writing
- Designed poster to recruit more volunteers

REFERENCES: Available upon request

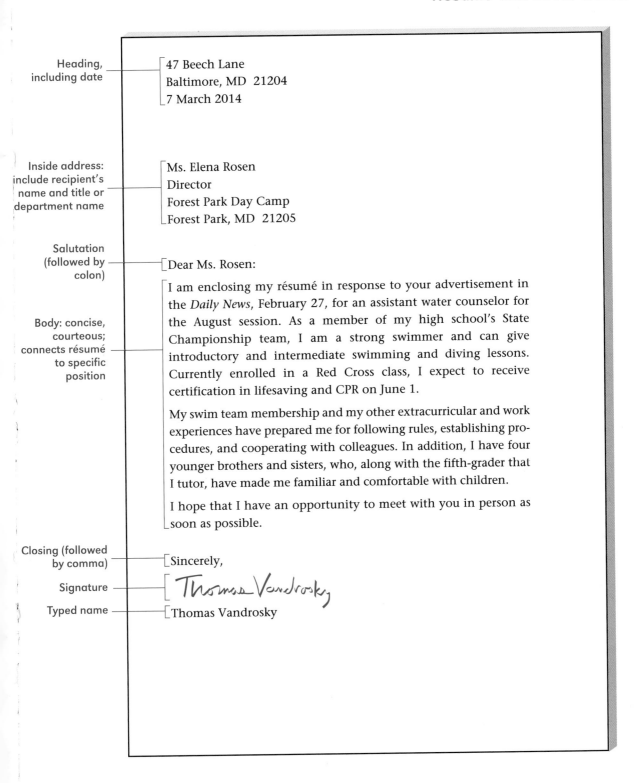

Heading, including date

47 Beech Lane
Baltimore, MD 21204
7 March 2014

Inside address: include recipient's name and title or department name

Ms. Elena Rosen
Director
Forest Park Day Camp
Forest Park, MD 21205

Salutation (followed by colon)

Dear Ms. Rosen:

Body: concise, courteous; connects résumé to specific position

I am enclosing my résumé in response to your advertisement in the *Daily News*, February 27, for an assistant water counselor for the August session. As a member of my high school's State Championship team, I am a strong swimmer and can give introductory and intermediate swimming and diving lessons. Currently enrolled in a Red Cross class, I expect to receive certification in lifesaving and CPR on June 1.

My swim team membership and my other extracurricular and work experiences have prepared me for following rules, establishing procedures, and cooperating with colleagues. In addition, I have four younger brothers and sisters, who, along with the fifth-grader that I tutor, have made me familiar and comfortable with children.

I hope that I have an opportunity to meet with you in person as soon as possible.

Closing (followed by comma)

Sincerely,

Signature

Thomas Vandrosky

Typed name

Thomas Vandrosky

Critical Thinking After you read the résumé and cover letter, answer the questions below.

1. What is the difference in form and in content between the model résumé and the model cover letter?

2. Into what parts is the résumé divided? The cover letter?

3. What do you think of Thomas's stated objective on his résumé? What role do you suppose the objective serves on a résumé?

4. If you were the director of the day camp, would you invite Thomas in for an interview to discuss his qualifications for the job? Why or why not?

SKILLS FOR WRITING A RÉSUMÉ

1. **Include all vital information.** Be sure to include phone numbers and addresses. If appropriate, tell when you are most easily available.

2. **Limit the length.** The person reviewing the résumé wants to spend only a matter of minutes with it, so it must be brief and easy to read. While you are still in high school, a résumé should not generally exceed one page.

3. **Use specific action verbs.** Be as precise as possible so that the person reviewing the résumé will know exactly what your responsibilities are or were.

4. **Be honest and accurate.** Integrity and attention to detail are among the most important qualities that an employer looks for in new employees. Careful proofreading of your résumé cannot be stressed enough.

SKILLS FOR WRITING A COVER LETTER

1. **Make all parts of your letter conform to standard business-letter format.** The full-block style shown here is the simplest to master. Pay particular attention to

   • complete and accurate addresses (yours and theirs).

   • polite salutation (ending with colon) and formal tone throughout.

   • simple, straightforward language.

   • information above and beyond what is in your résumé.

2. **Make sure the purpose of your writing is clear.** If there is indeed a job opening that you've heard about, explain how you acquired that information. Sometimes, there is no specific job opening as far as you know, but you hope

that the recipient will keep you in mind for a future opening or lead you to people who are hiring. If you are writing under those conditions, tell the recipient (a) how you heard about him or her and (b) that you are requesting an **informational meeting** to learn more about the organization or industry; make it clear that you are not expecting a job offer at this time.

3. **Remember to date and sign the letter.** Omissions of date or signature can irritate recipients.

Exercise 45 Prewriting: State an Objective; Choose a Job

- Think of what you would like to do on a part-time, full-time, short-term, or permanent basis. Write a statement that indicates that you have skills, interests, and an immediate goal. You'll be able to use that statement on your résumé for the heading "Objective" or "Job Desired."

- Identify a job that would put you on the road to meeting your stated objective. To identify a job for this exercise, check newspaper classified ads, your school's placement or guidance office, bulletin boards in your community, and adult friends who may know about job openings.

- Write two lists—one with skills required by the job you've selected; one with skills and experiences that you have. If the two lists match closely, proceed with this workshop. Otherwise, keep looking for a job that better fits your experience.

Exercise 46 Prewriting: Gather Details for Your Résumé

For each category on the model résumé (beyond "Objective"), start generating notes about the facts of your life by answering the following questions:

Education
- Where do you go to school—including city and state?

- When do you expect to graduate?

- What is unusual or exceptional about your high school experience? Do you want to share any statistics? Tell about any special course of study?

> **WRITING HINT**
>
> Appearance counts.
> - For printed résumé and cover letters, use white or ivory paper, $8\frac{1}{2}$ x 11 inches.
> - Single space with double space between elements (see models).
> - Select a simple typeface and easy-to-read type size.
> - Leave ample margins (at least an inch) at the top, bottom, and both sides of the résumé and cover letter.

- What courses or training have you had outside high school? Do you want to give that information here, or would you rather save it for "Activities and Skills"?

Activities and Skills
Which clubs, teams, and other organizations do you belong to or have you belonged to?

Work Experience
What specific jobs have you had—paying or volunteer jobs? (Some high school students list volunteer jobs with "Activities and Skills.") Wherever possible, give an exact title, the name of the business or organization, and its city and state.

EXERCISE 47 Draft Your Résumé and Cover Letter

- Based on your preceding notes and the models that appeared earlier in this lesson, organize your experience into a multipart résumé. Use strong action verbs to describe your role in the jobs, organizations, clubs, and teams that you are putting on the résumé.

- Now study again the job you found out about in Exercise 45. In what way does your résumé fall short in telling the employer that you are suited for the job? Your answer to that question should form the basis for your cover letter. There, you should announce what opening you want to fill, how you heard about the opening, and why your general skills listed in the résumé make you appropriate for this specific job. Draft that cover letter now.

EXERCISE 48 Revise Your Résumé and Cover Letter

Reread your résumé and cover letter carefully. Where do they fall short in persuading the employer to give you an interview? What does a classmate who has read your résumé and cover letter think about them? Fix your letter as necessary so that it is clear, complete, and courteous.

EXERCISE 49 Proofread and Publish

After you have carefully proofread for grammar, usage, mechanics, and spelling errors, follow the advice given in the Writing Hint on page 113 about formatting and spacing. Remember to sign hard copy versions of your cover letter.

Writing a Timed Essay

Essay questions on standardized tests measure your ability to generate ideas relevant to a specific topic and to present those ideas clearly and logically in an appealing style, while following the conventions of standard written English. You are expected to do all of this within a limited amount of time.

On a standardized test, you will find essay topics, also called "prompts," that present an issue or question and ask you to develop a thoughtful written response.

Although you will be given a limited amount of time to plan and write your essay, you will be expected to develop your ideas thoroughly. The goal of a timed essay is to produce in a short time frame clear and coherent writing that follows a well-organized structure and formal style.

Most standardized tests allot 25–30 minutes for timed writing. During that time, you should organize your ideas with an outline or cluster diagram, write your essay, and use any remaining time to revise what you wrote. Edit your finished essay and check that you use the conventions of standard English, including capitalization, punctuation, and spelling.

TEST-TAKING TIP

Most standardized test essays are scored from 6 (highest) to 1 (lowest).

The writing prompt below is similar to one you might find on a standardized test. After the prompt, you will find one writer's essay in response to it.

> In any human relationship, the most essential element is trust. This applies to relationships between individuals as well as groups, including nations. Without trust, any relationship is doomed to failure.
>
> **Assignment:** Do you agree or disagree? Write an essay in response to this issue. Develop and support your position with ideas, facts, and examples gained from your reading, observations, or personal experience.

    I believe very strongly that trust is the most important element in human relationships, as without trust, relationships crumble quickly. I'd add respect, too, but I think that respect and trust go hand in hand. If you trust someone, you respect that person; and if you respect someone, you will trust that person.

Thesis statement, or claim

Introductory paragraph—includes thesis statement

    Imagine this true-life scenario: You extract a promise from your best friend that whatever you're about to tell him will remain completely confidential. But the next day your secret or news bounces back to you from

Introduces example from personal experience

a third party, whom you haven't talked to. What can you conclude except that your friend, despite his promise, has gossiped about your secret? As a result, your friendship is damaged, perhaps broken. That really happened to me last year, and the friend I confided in isn't my best friend anymore. You have to be able to trust that people will keep their promises and that friends won't hurt or lie to you, or you cannot have lasting, meaningful relationships.

Introduces first example from literature

The importance of trust and the damaging effects of its loss—essentially betrayal—is a prevalent theme in literature. In William Shakespeare's tragedy *Othello*, for example, Othello trusts his friend Iago, who eventually insinuates that Othello's bride, Desdemona, has been unfaithful to him. So Othello, believing Iago's lies, loses trust in his wife and kills her, even though she is totally innocent. In Shakespeare's *King Lear*, the aged king of Britain turns over his kingdom to Goneril and Regan, the two daughters who profess to love him. But once they are in power, they turn against him. With this betrayal, Lear dies, mad with grief.

Introduces second example from literature

Example from history

Trust between nations is essential, too. Nations must feel confident that their neighbors will stay peacefully within their borders and cause no harm. If this confidence is destroyed, the effects can be disastrous. For instance, Japan's unprovoked bombing of Pearl Harbor, Hawaii, shocked the world and propelled the United States into World War II.

Concluding paragraph—restates main idea

Like the oil that keeps machinery moving efficiently, trust between individuals and groups is essential to keeping relationships moving along smoothly. Without trust, without our feeling confident that people will keep their word, we're all in a mess of trouble.

Critical Thinking After you read the essay on pages 115–116, answer the following questions.

1. Where in the essay does the writer make clear her position on the issue stated in the writing prompt?

2. What support does the writer give for her opinion? Briefly outline the reasons, examples, and facts in the essay.

3. Using the scoring model in the Test-Taking Tip on page 115, how would you score this sample essay? What suggestions, if any, might you make to improve it?

Writing Strategies   Use the following strategies as you write your essay.

1. **Read the prompt carefully.** Make sure you understand exactly what you are being asked to do. For example, is the purpose to inform or persuade? Then identify (underline or circle) key ideas as you read the prompt a second time.

2. **Prewrite: Narrow your focus.** Remember that you will have only a limited amount of time and space in which to write your essay. Know how many minutes and how many lines you will have, and plan accordingly. You will not be able to write everything you know about a topic, so limit your response to a manageable focus.

3. **Prewrite: Gather and organize ideas.** You might use a brief outline or a cluster diagram to generate ideas. Spend no more than two or three minutes jotting down ideas, key words, and supporting details. Number the ideas in the sequence you plan to use them.

4. **Write the main idea in a thesis statement, or claim.** Remember that this sentence usually appears early on in your essay.

5. **Start writing and stick to the point.** Begin with an introductory paragraph that includes your thesis statement and grabs the reader's attention. Use details that support your ideas in the clearest, most logical way possible. Use topic sentences and transitions to organize your writing. End with a concluding paragraph that wraps up your writing.

6. **Consider word choice and sentence variety.** Clarity is your goal, so avoid vague words and confusing sentences. Strive for vocabulary and sentence variety that fits your writing purpose and audience.

7. **Proofread your essay.** Save two or three minutes to read over your essay and *neatly* correct any errors in spelling, punctuation, or usage.

EXERCISE 50 Read the Prompt Carefully

Choose one of the prompts below, and refer to that prompt as you complete Exercises 51–54.

> More than two thousand years ago, philosophers from three different cultures (the Chinese Confucius, the ancient Greek Aristotle, and the Jewish scholar Hillel) expressed the basic principle of human interaction as some form of the Golden Rule, which is commonly stated, "Do unto others as you would have others do unto you."
>
> **Assignment:** Do you agree or disagree? Write an essay in response to this issue. Develop and support your position with ideas, facts, and details gained from your reading, observations, or personal experience.

Imagine that your local school officials are trying to come up with ways to reduce the number of high school dropouts. They have considered programs such as online courses, course credit for community service, and so on.

Assignment: Write an essay in which you propose a way to help reduce the high school dropout rate. Support your ideas with examples and details.

EXERCISE 51 Prewrite: Focus, Gather, and Organize Ideas

Decide on your position, and generate the ideas you will use as support (facts; statistics; details; personal experience or observations; examples from literature, history, and/or current events). Try using a graphic organizer or an outline. Number the ideas in the sequence you plan to use them.

EXERCISE 52 Prewrite: Thesis Statement, or Claim

Write your main idea in a thesis statement. Decide where you will use this sentence in your essay.

EXERCISE 53 Write Your Essay

Begin with an introductory paragraph that grabs the reader's attention and includes your thesis statement. Say everything as clearly and logically as you can, and develop your essay with relevant examples to support your main idea. Use topic sentences and transitions to organize your ideas. Remember to choose effective words and sentences that accomplish your writing purpose. End with a concluding paragraph that restates your main idea, poses a new question, or adds a final thought.

EXERCISE 54 Revise and Proofread Your Essay

Save two or three minutes to revise and proofread your writing. Make sure the sentences flow smoothly and are clear and succinct. Neatly cross out anything that strays from your main idea. Correct any errors in spelling, punctuation, capitalization, and usage.

Parts of Speech

STUDENT WRITING
Compare and Contrast Essay

Matisse and Picasso
Two Artists' Former Rivalry Presented at Kimbell Art Museum
by Katherine Boone
high school student, Dallas, Texas

Spending an afternoon at the Kimbell Art Museum in Fort Worth may not sound like the ideal pastime for many; however, it is time well spent.

The exhibit, which runs until May 2, outlines the "gentle rivalry" between the two masters of modern art in chronological order. Separated into acts which span the years from their introduction in 1906 to Matisse's death in 1954, the tour is augmented by a hand-held audio guide that gives specifics about the paintings on display and the interaction between the artists.

The tour begins in Act One, which displays works by the artists from 1917 through the 1920s, a period in which Matisse took a brief hiatus from his artwork, while Picasso produced paintings similar to his contemporary's in style and substance in an attempt to "tease" him back to the art world. Much of the work in this act is answer/response, with Matisse taking much of the credit for many new ideas and styles. . . .

This act also displays bronze sculptures by both artists of human forms and faces, in which the similarity between the styles is astounding. The distorted features in the image of one artist are answered with nearly identical work by the other. To see such parallel genius at work is amazing, and the Kimbell takes great pains to arrange the works so that the similarities and differences are starkly juxtaposed.

Three paintings in this act which especially exhibit their blatant similarities are Picasso's *Repose*, Matisse's *Woman with Yellow Hair*, and Matisse's *Dream*. All are portraits of women done in similar settings and in similar poses.

As Act Two opens, the styles of the artists diverge significantly, but the thematic similarities remain as Picasso becomes more abstract and cubist, while Matisse paints with flowing lines and washed-out color.

Act Three chronicles the time during World War II when the artists could no longer keep in touch and often painted from imagination what the other would be doing. Again, the similarities are striking, though [each artist] could only guess at the other's inspiration. Both unwittingly maintained a theme of rocking chairs, among others, at this time. . . .

The paragraphs above are the beginning of a compare and contrast essay that is organized in a point-by-point method. Katherine Boone leads the reader step by step through the exhibit and through important stages of both artists' lives. Look back at the essay to see how Katherine uses words and phrases to help her reader follow the progress. She also uses examples to explain each point.

In this chapter, you'll take a close look at the different kinds of work that words do—the parts of speech. As you do the writing exercises in this chapter, you will apply what you learn about the parts of speech.

Nouns

Nouns name everything you come across in life, including things you can imagine.

▶ **Nouns** are words that name persons, places, things, or ideas.

PERSONS	cousin, Hank Aaron, coach, ally, Yo-Yo Ma
PLACES	school, highway, Phoenix, Lincoln Memorial
THINGS	calculator, speech, microwave, tissue
IDEAS	ambivalence, joy, legality, gladness, fascism

▶ Names of ideas form a category of nouns known as **abstract nouns**. Names of persons, places, and things form a category known as **concrete nouns**. All concrete nouns identify objects that you can see, hear, smell, taste, or touch.

ABSTRACT	fear, cleverness, misery, civilization, honor
CONCRETE	trumpet, street, tortilla, Golden Gate Bridge

▶ When you name particular persons, places, or things, you are using **proper nouns**. Always capitalize proper nouns. Some proper nouns contain two or more words; some are titles. Because **common nouns** are general, not particular, do not capitalize them.

COMMON	city, turnpike, attorney, war, scavenger
PROPER	Sioux City, New Jersey Turnpike, Supreme Court Chief Justice Roberts, the Civil War

▶ **Collective nouns** name a group of people, animals, or things.

COLLECTIVE	squad, class, flock, club, association

▶ **Compound nouns** consist of two or more words—sometimes hyphenated, sometimes written as one word, and sometimes written as two words. Check a dictionary whenever necessary.

COMPOUND	great-aunt, one-fourth, horseradish, postal worker, junior high school

▶ A **noun phrase** is a noun and its modifiers.

NOUN	girl, children, tulip, chocolate
NOUN PHRASE	the young girl, several children, the yellow tulip, sweet as chocolate

Enriching Your Vocabulary

Scavenger is an alteration from the Middle English word *scawager*, which means "tax collector." The word *scavenger* suggests a person picking up dirt or refuse from the street. The pigeons acted like *scavengers* after the messy picnickers left the park bench.

WRITING HINT

Nouns can signal possession. When you're working with plural nouns, add either an apostrophe or 's, depending on the last letter of the plural noun. If the last letter is -s, use just an apostrophe; if the last letter is not -s, use 's.

winners' blue uniforms

the **Kennedys'** fame

the **children's** shrieks

the **mice's** cheese

EXERCISE 1 Using Nouns

Complete each sentence by inserting the type of noun indicated. Make up any details that you need.

1. The [concrete noun] _____ was filled with fans.

2. The [collective noun] _____ that planned the track meet worked hard.

3. [proper noun] _____ won the 400-meter race handily.

4. The team from [proper noun] _____ won the mile relay.

5. Tony won the [compound noun] _____.

6. One [collective noun] _____ arrived late and missed the first two events.

7. One runner showed her [abstract noun] _____ by racing despite her injury.

8. During the storm, a [collective noun] _____ met to decide what to do.

9. When the meet resumed, many runners complained about the slippery surface of the [concrete noun] _____.

10. Our coach's [abstract noun] _____ was complete when we won the overall competition.

Working Together

EXERCISE 2 Revising a Paragraph

With a partner, improve the weak paragraph below by replacing the italicized words with specific nouns or noun phrases. Also feel free to add details, drop or add words, and combine sentences. Compare your response with that made by other pairs of classmates.

¹Last year in *a certain time*, along with *some people* and their two small children *and pet*, I climbed into *a place*. ²Wanting to get a jump on the other hikers, we left our *accommodations* at 7:15 A.M., ate *food*, and hit the *trail*. ³We were feeling *a mood* because *weather* was in the forecast. ⁴But our luck held. ⁵On the way down, we spotted *animals* and *birds*. ⁶We hiked through *trees* and over *different kinds of land*. ⁷When we arrived at *our destination some time* later, we rested for *a while* and ate *what* we had brought with us. ⁸After talking about *things*, we began the *walk* back to the rim. ⁹When we finally got there, we felt *a mood* despite our *condition*. ¹⁰What *a feeling!*

Pronouns

▐▶ **Pronouns** are words that take the place of a noun or another pronoun.

Most—but not all—pronouns refer to something previously mentioned. The word or group of words to which the pronoun refers is called its **antecedent**. In the following sentences, arrows point to the antecedents of the pronouns.

> Inez and **her** friend are newspaper staff members. **They** go to an editorial meeting each Tuesday. **It** is held in Mr. Chen's office.

▐▶ The pronouns English speakers use the most are the **personal pronouns** and their **possessive forms**.
> **She** was the first to arrive because **her** train was early.

▐▶ Use **indefinite pronouns** to express an amount or to refer to an unspecified person or thing.
> **Many** came despite the rain, and **few** were disappointed.

▐▶ Use **demonstrative pronouns** to point to specific people or things.
> **This** is the reserved section; **those** seats over there are available.

▐▶ Use **relative pronouns** to introduce some subordinate clauses. (See Chapter 8 for more on subordinate clauses.)
> Suki, **who** lives farthest from the school, has never been absent.

▐▶ Use **interrogative pronouns** in questions.
> To **whom** are you speaking? **What** did you say?

▐▶ The pronouns that end in -*self* and -*selves* are either **reflexive** or **intensive**.

Use reflexive pronouns to refer to an earlier noun or pronoun. Use intensive pronouns to add emphasis.
> I love **myself**. [reflexive]
> The principal **himself** taught the class. [intensive]

Reciprocal pronouns express mutual action or relation.
> Teammates rely on **one another** for support during a game.

Personal Pronouns, Including Possessive

I	me	my	mine
we	us	our	ours
you	you	your	yours
she	her	her	hers
he	him	his	his
it	it	its	its
they	them	their	theirs

Some Indefinite Pronouns

all	another
any	anybody
anyone	anything
both	each
either	everybody
everyone	everything
few	many
most	neither
nobody	none
no one	one
others	several
some	somebody
someone	

Demonstrative Pronouns

this	these
that	those

Relative Pronouns

who	whoever	
whom	whomever	
which	that	whose

Some Interrogative Pronouns

who?	whom?	whose?
what?	which?	how?

Reflexive and Intensive Pronouns

myself	yourself
himself	herself
itself	ourselves
yourselves	themselves

EXERCISE 3 Identifying Pronouns

Underline all the pronouns in these paragraphs, including possessive pronouns. **Hint:** You'll find 18 pronouns. Not all sentences contain pronouns.

¹Today, everyone knows about the Bering Sea, which separates Asia from North America. ²But during the last Ice Age, it was not a sea. ³The sea level dropped hundreds of feet; the sea floor became a plain. ⁴Many archaeologists believe that people traveled on this plain, following their animals. ⁵Over time, temperatures gradually began to rise, causing the sea level to rise with them. ⁶The plain was slowly flooding. ⁷Families panicked. ⁸They found themselves needing to move to higher ground. ⁹Many headed eastward into the regions we know today as Alaska and Canada. ¹⁰Some then went southward into the area that is now Montana, Wyoming, and Colorado. ¹¹Others walked farther south into present-day Mexico and Central and South America. ¹²This happened about 17,000 years ago. ¹³It may have been the first great migration from the land we call Asia into the Americas. ¹⁴What did the newcomers find? ¹⁵How did they lead their lives? ¹⁶Archaeologists still seek answers.

EXERCISE 4 Writing with Pronouns

Write ten engaging, complete sentences about a personal interest of yours, such as a hobby, a sport, or a kind of music. When you finish writing, underline all the pronouns in your sentences.

CONNECTING
Writing & Grammar

Write What You Think

A friend of yours plans to go to college. But she has an opportunity to spend a year overseas as an exchange student in either Japan, Italy, or Chile before college. Write a persuasive letter to her explaining why you think being a foreign exchange student for a year is or is not a good idea. If you do think it is an opportunity not to be missed, help her choose the country she should go to. When you've finished revising and editing your letter, underline all the pronouns that you've used.

For more on persuasive writing, refer to **Composition,** Lesson 4.3.

Verbs

All verbs help to make statements. You can't make a sentence without one.

▶ **Verbs** are words that express an action or a state of being. Every sentence has at least one action verb or one linking verb.

Some **action verbs** communicate an observable action; for example, they describe what people *do—glide, laugh, applaud*. But other action verbs tell us what people *feel—appreciate, love, dread*.

> Frank Lloyd Wright **designed** and **built** homes and other structures. His clients **admired** his style.

Verbs take a variety of forms to communicate time. (For more about verb tenses, see Lesson 9.4.)

> The hiker **shivers**. The hiker **shivered**. The hiker **was shivering**.

Some but not all action verbs take direct and indirect objects. (See Lesson 6.6.)

▶ **Linking verbs** do what their name says: They link the subject of a sentence with a word that tells more about it. (For more about subjects and predicates, see Lesson 6.2.)

> The surgeon **appeared** confident. The surgeon **is** an innovator.

Some words that can be action verbs in one context can be linking verbs in another context. If a form of *be* can substitute for the verb, then the verb is functioning as a linking verb.

> ACTION VERB The performer **looked** nervously at the audience.
> LINKING VERB The performer **looked** nervous.

▶ A **verb phrase** is a verb form preceded by one or more **helping** (or **auxiliary**) verbs. *Not* (*n't* in a contraction) is never part of the verb phrase.

> **Has**n't anyone here **seen** the remote? I **have been looking** for it for half an hour.

Generally, the more vivid a verb, the better.

> BLAND John **is** on his way to work.
> VIVID John **is dashing** to work.

Linking Verbs: Some Forms of *Be*

am	is	was	were
are	be	being	
can be	is being		
will be	could be		
should be	would be		
could have been			
might have been			

Some Other Linking Verbs

appear	seem
become	smell
feel	sound
grow	stay
look	taste
remain	turn

Some Helping Verbs

be (is, am, are, was, were, been)
have (has, had)
do (does, did)

can	may	could
must	might	shall
will	would	should

EDITING TIP

To write complete sentences rather than sentence fragments, use verbs or verb phrases, not just **verbals**. Although a verbal is formed from a verb, it is a part of speech that functions as a noun, adjective, or adverb, not as a verb. (For more about verbals, see Lesson 7.3.)

> *enjoyed*
> People ~~enjoying~~ the play.

EXERCISE 5 Identifying Verbs

Underline every verb and verb phrase in the sentences. **Hint:** There are 20.

1. Anyone can create music with the natural instrument we call the voice.

2. As musical expression developed, people joined voice groups.

3. Gregorian chant, or plainsong, which arose in the early Middle Ages, was one early form of choral performance.

4. In chant, all participants sing or hum one melody in unison; the technical term for this is monophony.

5. In the late Middle Ages, composers experimented and gave different voices different musical lines within the same piece of music.

6. Soon, variations in rhythm and harmony led to the diverse polyphonic music we are familiar with today.

7. If you have ever participated in a chorus, you know about different voice parts.

8. We classify women's voices as soprano (high), mezzo-soprano (middle), or alto (low).

9. A man might sing tenor (high), baritone (middle), or bass (low).

10. Choral music produces a rich blanket of sound, which either stimulates or soothes listeners.

EXERCISE 6 Revising a Paragraph

Strengthen the following weak paragraph by adding vivid verbs and precise nouns. Feel free to add details, delete or add words, and combine sentences. Compare your revision with that of other pairs.

¹One day, I went to a choral concert. ²The program had music. ³The place where the music was was big and had many decorations. ⁴The place was packed. ⁵My seat was off to the side. ⁶I sat down and looked at the program that a person gave me. ⁷It had all the words to the songs. ⁸It also had stuff about the people who sang the music and the people who wrote the music and the people who played the music. ⁹I read some of it, and I guess that it helped me to like the music better. ¹⁰I had never heard any music like it before. ¹¹Different singers sang different things and sang some things over and over again. ¹²At the end, the people made a lot of noise to say how much they liked it, and I did too.

Adjectives

Adjectives can make nouns and pronouns come into focus.

▷ **Adjectives** are modifiers. They give information about the nouns and pronouns they modify.

WHAT KIND?	**red** flower, **straight** road, **high-altitude** climb, **surprise** visit, calamitous fire
HOW MANY?	**four** days, **few** entries
HOW MUCH?	**more** space, **some** effort
WHICH ONE?	**third** response, **that** shirt, **worst** joke, **last** month

Writers sometimes use two or more adjectives to modify a single noun.

The **long, steep, strenuous** climb back to the rim loomed before them.

Her serves are **powerful** and **accurate**.

▷ *A* and *an* are adjectives but are also called **indefinite articles**. They refer to any one member of a group and so are indefinite. Similarly, *the* is an adjective but is also called the **definite article**. It points out a particular noun.

▷ **Proper adjectives** derive from proper nouns. Proper adjectives always begin with a capital letter.

Japanese food **Confederate** troops **Jacksonian** democracy

▷ Most of the adjectives in the examples on this page come right before the word they modify. But adjectives can also follow a linking verb to modify the subject of a sentence; in this position, the modifier is called a **predicate adjective**.

The smoked salmon tastes **salty**.

The manager is **stern** but **fair**.

When a noun or a possessive pronoun modifies another noun, it sometimes is called an adjective.

motel room	**school** auditorium
mother's pie	**her** uniform
corn pudding	**its** melody

Enriching Your Vocabulary

Calamity stems from the Latin root *calamitas* meaning "destruction." The word *calamitous* describes an extraordinarily grave event. *Calamitous* floods in the Midwest left thousands of people homeless.

WRITING HINT

Sometimes, for stylistic reasons, you may wish to use adjectives after the word they modify.

The stage set, **gloomy** and **mysterious**, made the audience gasp.

The cowboy, **dusty** and **exhausted**, straggled into town.

Refer to **Grammar,** Lesson 6.7, for more on predicate adjectives.

EXERCISE 7 Identifying Adjectives

Underline the adjectives, including all proper adjectives and articles, in the following paragraph. In this exercise, count nouns and possessives before nouns as adjectives. **Hint:** There are 39 adjectives.

¹To detect movement, an alarm's sensors use radar. ²Radar is a device or system that emits radio waves to detect objects and determine their direction, distance, height, or speed. ³The echoes produced when those waves bounce off the object provide data on the object's precise location. ⁴The earliest extensive application of radar was as a defense system. ⁵During World War II, the British used radar effectively to detect German aircraft. ⁶But the waves, in experimental form, had caught scientists' attention much earlier. ⁷In 1887, Heinrich Hertz produced and detected the first ones on a homemade apparatus. ⁸His work led to new communications and provided the framework for the eventual invention of radar. ⁹Today, radar has many uses, from heating soup in a microwave to determining the speed of a fastball to figuring out whether a weather disturbance is a tornado or a hurricane. ¹⁰How effective would air-traffic controllers be without radar?

EXERCISE 8 Revising Sentences to Give More Information

Revise the sentences below to give the readers more information and to create more interesting sentences. You may add details and drop or add words. Underline all of the adjectives you add.

EXAMPLE   The boy ate the meal.
The hungry boy grabbed the full plate and devoured every morsel .

1. The woman wore a coat.
2. A car sped by.
3. It was a clear night.
4. The sea was rough.
5. I sat under a tree and read.
6. Claire made a piece of pottery.
7. The team practiced on the field.
8. Alfred lives on that block.
9. The group waited in line to buy tickets.
10. The outcome of the tournament was in doubt.

Adverbs

Like adjectives, adverbs add clarity to sentences.

▶ **Adverbs** modify, or tell more about, verbs, adjectives, and other adverbs by answering *when*, *where*, and *how* questions. **Intensifiers** are adverbs that answer the question *to what extent* or *how much*.

WHEN?	**Today**, we began rehearsals for the play.
WHERE?	They walked **here** from the station.
HOW?	The actor spoke **clearly** and **loudly**.
TO WHAT EXTENT?	We **thoroughly** enjoyed the performance.

Many adverbs, sometimes called **adverbs of manner**, end with the suffix *-ly*. However, many frequently used adverbs do not end in *-ly*.

Adverbs can modify prepositions and prepositional phrases. (See Lesson 5.6 for more on prepositions.)

> They arrived **just** *after dinner*.
> Her hand reached **almost** *to the top*.

Adverbs can also modify subordinate clauses and complete sentences.

> I'll play the tape again **only** *if you want me to*.
> **Surely** he didn't mean to put the car in reverse.

Many negatives—for example, *not, n't, barely,* and *never*—are adverbs; they can interrupt parts of a verb phrase.

> He *should* **not** *have* moved backward.

Some Common Adverbs That Do Not End in *-ly*

about	just	today
almost	late	tomorrow
already	more	too
also	never	well
always	seldom	why
around	still	yesterday
fast	then	yet
here	there	

Some Common Intensifiers

exceptionally	most	
really		somewhat
extraordinarily	nearly	
hardly	only	so
least	quite	truly
less	rather	very

EDITING TIP

Not all words that end in *–ly* are adverbs. For example, *ugly, lonely,* and *lovely* are adjectives; *comply* and *supply* are verbs.

EXERCISE 9 Identifying Adverbs

Underline all the adverbs in each sentence below. **Hint:** One sentence has no adverbs.

1. A Greek mathematician named Philon traveled about and then wrote a paper in which he listed seven wonders of the ancient world.

2. Philon's paper was circulated widely.

3. Each structure was still standing or partially standing in 150 B.C., the date of Philon's trip.

4. The only wonder that survives today—the Great Pyramid—is located near Cairo, Egypt.

5. The Hanging Gardens of Babylon were not hanging gardens.

6. The Temple of Diana at Ephesus, Turkey, was permanently destroyed by the Goths in A.D. 262.

7. After eleven years of digging, a British archaeologist finally unearthed fragments of that temple's original columns in 1874.

8. Name some physical wonders of the twenty-first century.

9. Rising to a height of four hundred feet, the marble lighthouse on the Isle of Pharos was truly a remarkable sight.

10. The Colossus of Rhodes was suddenly toppled by an earthquake, and it lay in ruins for almost nine hundred years.

EXERCISE 10 Choosing the Correct Modifier

Underline the modifier in each set of parentheses that correctly completes each sentence.

1. Whales glide (graceful, gracefully) through the water.

2. When the police got the call, they moved (quick, quickly).

3. The time capsule was buried (near, nearly) one hundred years ago.

4. She hadn't slept, so she performed (bad, badly) on the test.

5. Sick for most of the night, she looked (bad, badly) in the morning.

6. Stand (correct, correctly) on the stage.

7. Chocolate chips on pizza taste (terrible, terribly).

8. The young child spoke (polite, politely) to the guest.

9. If you continue to walk so (slow, slowly), we'll be late.

10. The (exceptional, exceptionally) graceful elephant rose on one foot.

EXERCISE 11 Revising Sentences to Add Adjectives and Adverbs

Work with a partner to add adjectives and adverbs to the following sentences. (Ask yourself: *which one, what kind, how many, how much, when, where, how,* and *to what extent.*) In addition, replace vague or general nouns and verbs, and add other details to create interesting sentences. Compare your revisions with those of other pairs of students.

EXAMPLE   The cat stalked its prey.
The jaguar stealthily stalked the mouse, which was busily devouring its last meal.

1. The athlete ran.

2. The girl smelled something.

3. A truck drove by.

4. The storm damaged the roof.

5. The train was crowded.

Prepositions

Prepositions link key words in your sentences; they never stand alone.

➠ **Prepositions** connect a noun or pronoun (and its modifiers, if any) to another word in the sentence to form a prepositional phrase. (For more information about prepositional phrases, see Lesson 7.1.)

    The crowd stood **along** the aisles.

    I spoke **on behalf of** the class.

    They dared to answer their cell phones right **under** the teacher's nose.

➠ Some prepositions contain several words. They are **compound prepositions**.

    In spite of the snowstorm, we drove to the movies.

    I had to pay for the popcorn **in addition to** the movie.

A word that you may first identify as a preposition is actually an adverb *if it is not part of a prepositional phrase.*

    ADVERB   The bully bragged, "I've been **around**."

    PREPOSITION   We strolled **around the block**.

EXERCISE 12 Revising Sentences

Expand the sentences below by adding prepositional phrases. Use no more than four in each sentence. Make up all the details you need to create interesting sentences. Underline all the prepositions you've added to the sentences. Compare your sentences with those of other groups of students.

    EXAMPLE   Benny lost his gloves.

            At the football game, Benny lost his gloves by accident, probably under his bleacher seat.

1. Andrew walked to school.

2. The dog barked.

3. Maria passed the baton.

4. Somebody was in the room.

5. She saw a dog's toy.

6. It's early.

7. Is the weather different?

8. The tree swayed.

9. Can you reach the pencil?

10. The chalk squeaked.

11. The polar bear yawned.

12. The bus stops here.

13. Bats hang upside down.

14. My tuba is heavy.

15. The cinema closed early.

Some Commonly Used Prepositions

about	above	across
after	against	along
around	at	before
below	beside	between
beyond	but (meaning *except*)	
by	down	during
except	for	from
in	inside	into
like	near	of
on	out	outside
over	past	since
through	throughout	
to	toward	under
underneath		until
up	upon	within
with/without		

Some Common Compound Prepositions

according to	in addition to
along with	in front of
apart from	in place of
aside from	in spite of
as to	instead of
because of	next to
behind	on behalf of
due to	out of
in the middle of	

See Lesson 5.5 for more on adverbs.

EXERCISE 13 Choosing Prepositions

Underline all the prepositions in the parentheses below that make sense for each sentence. Notice how the meanings of the sentences change, depending on which preposition you choose.

1. We climbed steadily (down, up, around, across) the mountain.
2. (Before, Until, After, Beneath) our arrival at the top, we stopped to rest.
3. Upon reaching the pinnacle, we walked (up, to, across, over, beside, with, down, around) a spot where we could pitch our tents.
4. We placed our packs on the ground, opened them, and spread our things (over, under, around, beyond, in) the immediate vicinity.
5. (Since, After, Before, In the middle of) pitching our tents, we had lunch.
6. While eating, we noticed a bighorn sheep standing (near, behind, in front of, next to, between, beside) a huge boulder.
7. "What a magnificent animal!" we all thought (for, to, from, upon) ourselves.
8. Then we spotted two other sheep (near, apart from, behind, without, beyond) the first one we saw.
9. We had really come here to observe wolves (in, under, throughout, in addition to) the park.
10. We had heard about wolf watching (from, in, past, along) a newspaper.

EXERCISE 14 Distinguishing Prepositions from Adverbs

Fill in the blank with *PREP* if the underlined word is functioning as a preposition and with *ADV* if the underlined word is functioning as an adverb.

———— 1. Why not seize the pleasure <u>at</u> once? —Jane Austen
———— 2. Good painters imitate nature; bad ones spew it <u>up</u>. —Cervantes
———— 3. Patriotism is the last refuge <u>of</u> a scoundrel. —Samuel Johnson
———— 4. Peace is when time doesn't matter as it passes <u>by</u>. —Maria Schell
———— 5. The best way <u>out</u> is always through. —Robert Frost
———— 6. The darkest hour is that <u>before</u> the dawn. —Proverb
———— 7. We trifle <u>with</u>, make sport of, and despise those who are attached to us, and follow those that fly from us. —William Hazlitt
———— 8. A verbal art like poetry is reflective. Music is immediate; it goes <u>on</u> to become. —W. H. Auden
———— 9. Prejudice is being down <u>on</u> something you're not up on. —Anonymous
————10. Blest is the bride the sun shines <u>on</u>. —Old English Proverb

Conjunctions and Interjections

||||➤ Conjunctions join words or groups of words.

Coordinating conjunctions join words or groups of words that are equal in importance.

> I like the taste of asparagus **and** broccoli. I enjoy cauliflower **but** not spinach. In a choice between carrots **or** beets, I'd pick beets.

Correlative conjunctions function in the same way as coordinating conjunctions, but they always appear as pairs.

> **Either** a National League team **or** an American League team will win the World Series. I don't care **whether** one **or** the other wins, as long as the games are close.

Subordinating conjunctions connect adverb clauses to main clauses. (For more about adverb clauses, see Lesson 8.3.)

> The parade took place, **although** it rained the whole time.
> **Because** I had an umbrella, the wet weather didn't bother me.

||||➤ **Interjections** express mild or strong emotion.

Interjections have no grammatical connection to the rest of the sentence. They are set off by a comma or by an exclamation point.

> **Ouch!** That hurt!
> They have three pets: a dog, a parrot, and, **ugh!**, an iguana!

Coordinating Conjunctions

and	but	or	nor
so	yet		

Correlative Conjunctions

both . . . and
not . . . but
either . . . or
not only . . . but also
just as . . . so
whether . . . or
neither . . . nor

Some Common Subordinating Conjunctions

after	in order that
although	provided that
as far as	since
as long as	so that
as soon as	unless
as though	until
because	when
before	where
for	whereas
if	while

Some Common Interjections

aha	ouch	wow
hey	yo	ugh
oh	nah	well

EXERCISE 15 Identifying and Classifying Conjunctions

Underline all the conjunctions and interjections in the sentences below. On a separate piece of paper classify the conjunctions as a coordinating, correlative, subordinating, or interjection.

1. My room at home needs either a paint job or new wallpaper.

2. Because I prefer the look of paint, I'll go with paint, not wallpaper.

3. I'll choose among the colors periwinkle, taupe, and butter yellow.

4. My parents don't know whether to hire someone or to ask me to do the work myself.

5. They'll hire a painter provided that he or she comes well recommended.

6. Not only would a painter do a better job than I would, but he or she would also do the job faster.

TEST-TAKING TIP

A test item may contain a subordinating conjunction, such as *although*, that does not reflect the correct meaning or intent of a sentence. See the Example on page 334.

7. She can paint away while I'm at school.

8. Although a good paint job is expensive, it's worth it to my parents.

9. They'll ask her fee for painting both my room and theirs.

10. Whoa! Unless the painter's price is negotiable, my parents will ask me to do the painting after all.

EXERCISE 16 Using Conjunctions and Interjections

From the choices in parentheses, select and underline the conjunction or interjection that makes the most sense in the sentence.

1. Before 1975, women had served in the military; _____ in that year, Congress ended the tradition of male-only service academies. (for, since, but)

2. _____ women qualified, they now would be able to become officers. (Provided that, Or, Either)

3. The first women to make it into the U.S. Military Academy entered in 1976, _____ sixty-one graduated in 1980. (if, and, since)

4. The U.S. Merchant Marine had been the first academy to admit women _____ fifteen joined in July 1974. (but, when, either . . . or)

5. The Air Force Academy accepted women as cadets starting in 1976, _____ women were barred from combat until 1980. (so, as though, but)

6. "_____," contend supporters, "women can be trained to perform any duties men can." (Until, Ugh!, Well)

7. "_____" say opponents of women in the military. (Aha!, Nah!, Well)

8. The opponents claim that women _____ upset morale _____ compromise safety. (neither . . . nor, not only . . . but also, whether . . . or)

9. Movies _____ television shows have featured women in the military. (nor, yet, and)

10. _____ women should participate in combat _____ not will remain a controversial issue. (Either . . . or, Whether . . . or, Both . . . and)

Refer to **Composition,** Lesson 4.3, for more on writing persuasively.

Write What You Think

What is your opinion of the role of women in the military? Do you think female cadets should have the same training regimen and the same responsibilities and opportunities as male cadets? Write what you think. Support your opinions with a claim, valid reasons, and relevant evidence. Make sure to revise and edit your work.

Determining a Word's Part of Speech

||||▶ A word's part of speech is determined by how the word is used in the sentence. Consider the word *round*.

NOUN	After the first **round**, the home team had the lead.
VERB	The students **round** the numbers to the nearest tenth.
ADJECTIVE	The **round** shape of the theater made all seats good seats.
ADVERB	He sent **round** for the veterinarian when his dog got sick.
PREPOSITION	We walked **round** the lake.

EXERCISE 17 Identifying Parts of Speech

Identify the part of speech of each underlined word as it is used in the sentence. You may use these abbreviations:

N = noun	ADJ = adjective	CONJ = conjunction
P = pronoun	ADV = adverb	INT = interjection
V = verb	PREP = preposition	

1. The fluent members of the Linguistic Society of America meet <u>annually</u>.

2. Language development entails close study <u>and</u> hard work.

3. Would you consider a <u>major</u> in anthropology with a focus on language?

4. Francis E. Sommer, a linguist, was fluent <u>in</u> ninety-four languages.

5. He learned Swedish, Sanskrit, <u>and</u> Persian <u>while</u> he was a schoolboy.

6. He would <u>while</u> away his time by learning languages.

7. Harold Williams, who spoke fifty-eight languages, was another <u>master</u> linguist.

8. Williams could master conversation with every U.N. delegate in <u>his</u> or <u>her</u> native tongue.

9. Linguistics professors say <u>language</u> skill is like musical talent.

10. One professor, who knows forty-eight languages, claims that one language spoken in Papua New Guinea is the <u>world's</u> toughest to master.

> **Enriching Your Vocabulary**
>
> The word *entail* comes from the prefix *en-* meaning "in" and the Old French word *taillier* meaning "to limit." In English the verb has come to mean "to involve." The castle restoration will *entail* considerable expense.

Revising and Editing Worksheet

Improve the following draft by revising for ideas, organization, word choice, and sentence variety. After revising, edit the draft for errors in spelling, capitalization, punctuation, and usage. Write your revised and edited version on a separate piece of paper. Compare your changes with those of a writing partner.

[1]It has been absent for nearly four hundred years. [2]Now Shakespeares' Globe Theatre has been resurrected. [3]Drawing on lots of scholarly research and archaeological evidence. [4]Using Elizabethan building techniques, they have re-created the Globe. [5]They've done it authentic. [6]The process has been an adventure from the start. [7]They had fund-raising nightmares, lawsuits, and scholarly arguments. [8]They had other disasters, too. [9]But the result is a new Globe Theatre. [10]It would make Shakespeare hisself proud.

[11]A brewery is where the original Globe Theatre once was. [12]That spot is on the bank of the Thames River in London. [13]The bank is on the south. [14]Today's version is two hundred yards away. [15]Like the original, it has no roof. [16]Within its partial timbered walls, there are three tiers of wooden benches. [17]These going around an open yard and a platform stage. [18]On the stage, plays are performed as they were back then.

[19]All fifteen hundred seats were filled when a performance of Shakespeare's *Henry V* opened the Globe's first season. [20]The first season was 1997. [21]Richard Olivier directed. [22]He is the son of Sir Laurence Olivier. [23]Sir Laurence Olivier was famous. [24]The Globe production was pure Elizabethan: All the roles were performed by men wearing costumes from that time.

[25]The new Globe is the focus of a big-deal center that will eventually include a multimedia resource library, a bunch of buildings for education, places to eat and shop, and a three-hundred-seat indoor theater that is a copy of a 1617 design. [26]The cost of the entire project is about $45 million. [27]It cost about $900 to build the Globe in 1599.

Chapter Review

EXERCISE A Identifying Parts of Speech

Identify the part of speech of each underlined word as it is used in the sentence. You may use these abbreviations:

N = noun   ADV = adverb
P = pronoun   PREP = preposition
V = verb   CONJ = conjunction
ADJ = adjective   INT = interjection

adj   1. In the <u>last</u> half of the twentieth century, jumbo passenger jets shrank the globe.

prep   2. Today's sophisticated giants evolved <u>from</u> smaller passenger airplanes.

n   3. In 1926, the <u>Ford 4-AT Tin Goose</u> carried thirteen passengers at a speed of 100 mph.

v   4. The Boeing 247, which <u>appeared</u> in 1933, was a marvel of engineering.

adj   5. Although it held <u>only</u> ten passengers, the 247 could cruise at 155 mph.

conj   6. The Douglas DC-3 was an immediate success <u>when</u> it appeared in 1936.

adj   7. The DC-3, which is still in use today, could reach speeds of <u>nearly</u> 200 mph.

v   8. The first airliner with a pressurized cabin <u>was</u> the 1940 Boeing Stratoliner.

prep   9. The 1946 Lockheed Constellation sped its fifty-two passengers along <u>at</u> a speed of 300 mph.

adj   10. The <u>swept-back</u> wing, which appeared in a 1952 German plane, made speeds of 500 mph possible.

EXERCISE B Using Parts of Speech

Add a word or words to complete each of the following sentences. Also identify the part of speech of the words you add.

1. American eating habits are changing because of the influence of <u>*many* (*adj*)</u> cultures.

2. New restaurants <u>*incorporate*</u> *(v)* ingredients from many countries and cultures.

3. For example, salsa has replaced ketchup as one of America's most *Common* (adj)
condiments. (v)

4. Many cities *contain* more Asian or Mexican restaurants than steakhouses.

5. How would you like some chicken noodle soup flavored *exotically* with Thai
lemongrass? (adv)

Exercise C Choosing the Correct Modifier

Underline the modifier within each set of parentheses that correctly completes the
sentence.

1. We visited the Mustard Museum in Wisconsin (near, <u>nearly</u>) twenty years ago.

2. One (recent, <u>recently</u>) refurbished room in the Tenement Museum on New
York's Lower East Side illustrates the life of a single mother who toiled as a
seamstress.

3. They take their spuds (serious, <u>seriously</u>) at the Potato Museum in Albuquerque.

4. The Nut Museum in Old Lyme, Connecticut, is surrounded, (appropriate,
<u>appropriately</u>), by chestnut, walnut, and hazelnut trees.

5. The food I ate after visiting the Cockroach Hall of Fame tasted (<u>terrible</u>,
terribly).

6. I, for one, would prefer to walk (quick, <u>quickly</u>) through the U. S. National Tick
Collection in Statesboro, Georgia.

7. We felt (<u>bad</u>, ~~badly~~) when we learned that the Museum of Questionable Medical
Devices was closed.

8. I would (sure, <u>surely</u>) be sorry to miss the International Bowling Museum when
I visit St. Louis.

9. Not (surprising, <u>surprisingly</u>), the one-of-a-kind Mütter Museum at the College
of Physicians of Philadelphia has a collection of body parts of famous people.

10. The rancher found (<u>instant</u>, instantly) happiness among the thousands of types
of patented wire at the Barbed Wire Museum in LaCrosse, Kansas.

Parts of a Sentence

STUDENT WRITING
Narrative Essay

Working Pride
by Lacey Waldron
high school student, El Cajon, California

As I drove to my job interview on a sunny Saturday afternoon, my palms began to sweat. This was my first job interview, and I wanted to make sure I did everything perfectly. I thought to myself, "What should I say? How should I act?" As I came up to a white duplex that read "DR. McDONALD'S OFFICE," I started to panic. Looking at the clock, I realized I had ten minutes until I had to be in the office. I kept reminding myself that everything would be okay, but that was very hard to believe as my stomach began to turn in circles. After parking my car and fixing myself up, I slowly walked up to the office. Turning the knob of the large, oak door, it was time—time to suck up my fear and put my best foot forward. The first person that I met as I walked through the door was a lady named Mary. Mary seemed like she was a very kind hearted woman. She made me feel at home instantly. Before I knew it, a man who was skinny and had gray hair came walking out; it was Dr. McDonald.

I walked over and met him halfway, and he said, "You must be Lacey." I shook his hand firmly and remembered to make eye contact. I also remembered what my mom had advised me minutes earlier and told myself to relax. After a short interview, Dr. McDonald finished by saying, "I will call you and tell you when I want you to start working." I thanked him, shook his hand again, and walked out to my car.

"I GOT IT!" I said, "I GOT THE JOB!!" I couldn't wait to tell my mom the good news!

Getting my first job has really affected my life; it teaches me responsibility and gives me something to do rather than to get into trouble. My parents also seem to look at me as more responsible, and that's enough of a reward for me. Having money of my own has its ups and downs at times. But having the job that I am proud of is a valuable achievement that can never be forgotten.

Lacey Waldron organizes her personal narrative chronologically—in the order the events happened. She uses transition words and expressions such as *after* and *earlier*. She also includes dialogue to make the reader feel close to the action. In the last paragraph, Lacey explains the significance of the event—what the incident meant to her.

Reread Lacey's essay, and notice that each sentence is a little different from the one before. As you work on sentences in this chapter, think about how you can manipulate them to communicate your ideas in an interesting way.

Complete Sentences

▥▶ A **sentence** is a grammatically complete group of words that expresses a thought.

A sentence must perform two functions: (1) tell you the person, animal, or thing that the sentence is about and (2) tell you what that person, animal, or thing does or is.

Every sentence begins with a capital letter and ends with an end punctuation mark—a period, a question mark, or an exclamation point. (See Lesson 13.1.)

▥▶ A **sentence fragment** is a group of words that is not grammatically complete. Avoid sentence fragments when you write.

Don't let a fragment slip by just because it starts with a capital letter and ends with an end punctuation mark.

FRAGMENT   Enjoyed the concert enormously. [Who enjoyed it?]

FRAGMENT   We before. [What did "we" do "before"?]

FRAGMENT   Although we had heard the group before and enjoyed the concert enormously. [This thought is incomplete.]

SENTENCE   Although we had heard the group before and enjoyed the concert enormously, we still thought that the tickets were expensive.

A sentence always has one of four purposes.

▥▶ **Declarative sentences** make a statement. They end with a period.
The show lasted three hours.

▥▶ **Imperative sentences** make a command or a request. They end with either a period or (if the command shows strong feeling) an exclamation point.
Please sing "I Love My Sneakers More Than Her" again.

▥▶ **Interrogative sentences** ask a question. They end with a question mark.
Which is your favorite song?

▥▶ **Exclamatory sentences** express strong feeling. They end with an exclamation point.
Hey! That's my lap you're spilling soda on!

WRITING HINT

Most sentences begin with a subject followed by a verb and add modifiers and complements at the end.

A frog leaped from behind the flowerpot on the stoop.

You can vary sentences by occasionally beginning with modifiers and withholding the subject and the verb until the end.

From behind the flowerpot on the stoop, a frog leaped.

EXERCISE 1 Identifying Sentences and Eliminating Sentence Fragments

Circle the number before each group of words that forms a complete sentence. Turn each sentence fragment into a complete sentence.

1. A new kind of basketball sneaker has arrived on the scene, and everyone is buying a pair.

2. There is nothing the wearer of this shoe will not be able to do.

3. Dribbling easily, which is something that many want, in these shoes.

4. To be able to dunk a basketball whenever they try.

5. According to the manufacturer, kids' dreams will come true simply by wearing these new sneakers.

6. Wearing them every day.

7. Some even want to wear them while sleeping.

8. Kids who desire success in one thing or another.

9. Wearing the sneakers, played the best basketball game of her life! Wow!

10. Just as the manufacturer claimed.

EXERCISE 2 Editing Fragments

Edit the paragraph below. If the numbered group of words is not a sentence, add or delete words to make it one. Be sure to add capital letters and end punctuation marks where necessary.

¹From New York to Los Angeles, in recreation centers and on the streets, tap dancing is making itself heard. ²From small children to senior citizens. ³Tying up their shoes and clicking to the beat. ⁴Americans are packing dance classes at studios and in senior centers. ⁵Filling the seats on Broadway and in theaters everywhere. ⁶Watching performances of shows such as *Tap Dogs*, *Riverdance*, and *Bring in 'Da Noise, Bring in 'Da Funk*. ⁷In Manhattan, New Yorkers fill the avenues for Tap-O-Mania. ⁸In 1989, the United States Congress set May 25 as National Tap Dance Day. ⁹Which celebrated the birthday of Bill "Bojangles" Robinson. ¹⁰Who was a masterful tap dancer. ¹¹In that year, only the nation's capital honored the occasion. ¹²Today, twelve countries and more than forty cities. ¹³Have joined in the festivity.

Subject and Predicate

Every sentence must have two parts: a subject and a predicate. The **subject** of a sentence names the person, thing, or idea that the sentence is about. The **predicate** of a sentence tells what the subject does, what the subject is, or what happens to the subject. A subject and a predicate may be a single word or a group of words.

SUBJECTS	PREDICATES
Joe	studies.
The president of the senior class	will study architecture in college.
The vice president	will study engineering.

▶ The **simple subject** is the key word or words in the subject. (When a proper noun or a compound noun is the simple subject, it may be more than one word.) The **complete subject** is made up of the simple subject and all of its modifiers (such as adjectives and prepositional phrases).

▶ The **simple predicate** is always one or more verbs or verb phrases that tell something about the subject. The **complete predicate** contains the verb or verbs and all modifiers (such as adverbs and prepositional phrases), objects, and complements.

From here on, when this book uses only the term *subject*, that word refers to the simple subject; similarly, the term *verb* will refer to the simple predicate. In the examples below, the highlighted words are the simple subject and the simple predicate.

SUBJECT	PREDICATE
Pizza at Vinnie's	**tastes** better these days.
Mushrooms or **onions**	**are** extra and **cost** more.
Vinnie	now **charges** ten dollars for a pie.
That low **price**	**will** not **last** long.

For more on objects and object complements, see Lessons 6.6 and 6.8.

EXERCISE 3 Identifying Subjects and Verbs

In each sentence, underline the subject (the simple subject) once and the verb (the simple predicate) twice. **Remember:** A sentence may have more than one subject and more than one verb.

EXAMPLE   Volleyball is a team sport.

1. A volleyball team fields six players at a time.

2. The left forward, right forward, and center forward stand closest to the net.

3. Each forward can play in the attack zone or in the back zone.

4. The server stands in the 3-meter square service area.

5. The center back stands to the server's left.

6. The left back is the third player in the back row.

7. The server plays the position of right back.

8. A volleyball court measures 18 meters long and 9 meters wide.

9. The net is 2.43 meters off the ground.

10. A referee sits atop a high chair to the side of the net.

11. A linesman stands in the clear space behind the end line.

12. Players rotate in a clockwise direction.

13. In other words, the players move to their right and back.

14. Or do I mean to their left and forward?

15. The term *clockwise* sometimes confuses and frustrates me.

Working Together **EXERCISE 4 Writing Complete Sentences**

On a separate piece of paper, with a partner or small group, rewrite the following notes (which are fragments) as complete sentences to form a brief biography of V. S. Naipaul. Compare your sentences with those of other pairs or groups.

> Born 1932 in Trinidad (island in West Indies)
> Family came earlier from India
> As youth: exposed to Asian & West Indian culture
> Scholarship to Oxford University; then stayed in England
> 1957: The Mystic Masseur (novel); 1959: Miguel Street (short stories)
> Both about West Indian life
> Both impress critics
> Then trips to India—to learn about heritage
> Rest of life: fiction, nonfiction (example of nonfiction—India: A Wounded Civilization, 1977)
> Won Nobel Prize in Literature in 2001

Finding the Subject

Learning to identify the subject in every sentence you write helps you to select the right verb form so that you create subject–verb agreement.

▐▶ In an **inverted sentence**, the verb (V) comes before the subject (S). You can use inverted order for poetic reasons or to build suspense.

V   S
Over the castle's walls stormed the **knights**.

V   S
Into the valley rode the **raiders**.

▐▶ The words *here* and *there* are very seldom the subject of a sentence. In a sentence beginning with *here* or *there*, look for the subject after the verb.

V   S
Here is the front-door **key**.

V   S   S
There are two **doors** on the side and **one** around back.

▐▶ The subject of a sentence is never part of a prepositional phrase.

S   V
The **areas** of most geometric figures are simple to calculate.
[The subject is not *figures*. *Of most geometric figures* is a prepositional phrase modifying the word *areas*, the subject.]

S   V
Neither of those two figures is a parallelogram.

▐▶ To find the subject of a question, turn the question into a statement.

V S   V   S   V
Have **you** chosen your dress for the prom? [**You** have chosen your dress for the prom.]

V   S   S V
What color is your **dress**? [Your **dress** is what color.]

▐▶ In a command or request (an imperative sentence), the subject is always *you* (the person being spoken to).

[**You**] Renounce your claim to the throne!
[**You**] Please leave the kingdom.

Even when you mention the name of the person being spoken to, the subject is still understood to be *you*. Do not confuse a **noun of direct address** with the subject of a sentence.

S
Alex, [**you**] stop that this minute! [The word *you* is the understood subject of the verb *stop*. *Alex* is the noun of direct address.]

Chapter 10 takes up subject–verb agreement in detail.

WRITING HINT

Avoid beginning too many sentences with *there are, there is,* or *it is.*

WEAK	There is no one here.
STRONGER	No one is here.
WEAK	It is unlikely that she will vote.
STRONGER	She probably won't vote.

Enriching Your Vocabulary

The word *renounce* is made from the Latin prefix *re-*, meaning "back," and the Latin root *nuntiare*, meaning "to tell." To *renounce* something is to give it up. Julia *renounced* chocolate during Lent.

EXERCISE 5 Identifying Subjects and Verbs

In each sentence, underline the subject (simple subject) once and the verb twice. If the subject is understood to be *you*, write the word *you* after the sentence. If the subject is a proper noun, underline the entire proper noun. **Remember:** A subject and a verb may be compound.

1. In the Caribbean, bananas appear in many dishes.

2. Casseroles, soups, and desserts feature this common fruit.

3. A favorite recipe is for banana fish.

4. It serves from six to eight people.

5. First, carefully read and collect the list of ingredients.

6. There are two pounds of flounder, cod, or perch in this dish.

7. Two garlic cloves and two tablespoons of butter are necessary.

8. You will need a garlic press, too.

9. Sam, beat two eggs well.

10. Also important is the juice of one lime.

11. A cup of diced tomatoes is essential.

12. The recipe also calls for a teaspoon of fresh thyme and a cup of cheddar cheese.

13. Four or five cups of salted water are also critical.

14. Above and beyond all this are the three plantains.

15. The instructions are straightforward and yield a delicious casserole.

16. Once in the oven, the dish takes thirty minutes.

17. The casserole must remain uncovered for ten to twenty minutes.

18. Only then should you cut into it.

19. Would your guests like it for lunch?

20. Guests for dinner appreciate it, too.

CONNECTING
Writing & Grammar

Write What You Think

Refer to **Composition**, Lesson 4.3, for more on writing persuasively.

In many cultures, the traditional view is that the kitchen is a woman's domain. However, many of the world's most skilled and renowned chefs are men. Whose responsibility do you think it is to cook for a family? How do you account for the great number of leading male chefs? Write a persuasive paragraph putting forth your views. Support them with reasons and evidence. When you finish revising and editing, underline all the subjects of your sentences once and the verbs twice.

Correcting Fragments

As noted in Lesson 6.1, you should avoid sentence fragments. You can use the following three strategies to correct fragments while revising and editing.

▶ **Attach it.** Join the fragment to a complete sentence before or after it.

FRAGMENT   Located along the Nile south of Egypt. Nubia was largely unknown to the ancient Greeks and Romans.

REVISED   Located along the Nile south of Egypt, Nubia was largely unknown to the ancient Greeks and Romans.

▶ **Add some words.** Introduce the missing subject, verb, or whatever other words are necessary to make the group of words grammatically complete.

FRAGMENT   The wealthy region. Wondrous goods such as ebony, ivory, panther skins traveled north in abundance.

REVISED   The wealthy region offered wondrous goods such as ebony, ivory, and panther skins that traveled north in abundance.

▶ **Drop or replace some words**. Drop the relative pronoun or subordinating conjunction that creates a fragment. (See Lesson 5.7 for more on subordinating conjunctions.)

FRAGMENT   The Nubian warriors who were very skilled with the bow and arrow.

REVISED   The Nubian warriors were very skilled with the bow and arrow.

TEST-TAKING TIP

Be alert for sentence fragments, which appear in many guises on standardized tests. Remember that an independent clause must have a subject *and* a predicate. See item 4 on page 339.

STEP BY STEP

The Sentence Test

The answer to the following three questions must be *yes* for a group of words to be a sentence.

1. Does the group have a subject?
2. Does the group have a verb?
3. Does the group of words express a complete thought?

EXERCISE 6 Correcting Sentence Fragments

On a separate piece of paper, revise each numbered item to correct all sentence fragments. Use the three strategies just presented.

1. Nubia was an African empire. Rich in gold and emeralds.

2. In the Bible, its name is Kush. One of the many different names by which it was known.

3. The ancient Greeks called it Ethiopia. Which was what the Romans called it.

4. Nubia was located along the Nile. Stretching from Khartoum in Sudan north to present-day Aswan in Egypt.

5. Its land was extraordinarily hot and dry. Was an unlikely location for an empire.

6. Because Nubia had much less fertile land than Egypt.

7. Archaeologists have identified at least six different Nubian cultures. That existed from 3800 B.C. through A.D. 600.

8. A rival to its northern neighbor, Egypt. Nubia conquered Egypt in about 730 B.C.

9. Nubian kings ruling Egypt for about sixty years.

10. The Nubian civilization reached the height of its political and economic power in about 200 B.C. Which lasted longer than the civilizations of ancient Greece and Rome.

EXERCISE 7 Eliminating Fragments

Improve the paragraph below. If the numbered group is not a sentence, add words or take away words to make it one. Be sure to add capital letters and end punctuation marks where necessary.

¹Nubia was an ancient civilization once neglected by academics. ²No longer the case. ³In recent years, people beginning to recognize the many achievements of the Nubians, or Kushites. ⁴This interest was signaled by several museum exhibits across North America in the 1990s. ⁵Which celebrated the rich heritage of that neglected civilization. ⁶There were exhibits at the Boston Museum of Fine Arts and at the Royal Ontario Museum in Toronto. ⁷Among others. ⁸In 1993, an exhibit called "Vanished Kingdoms of the Nile: The Rediscovery of Ancient Nubia" was hosted by the Oriental Institute in Chicago. ⁹Been to any of these?

¹⁰The Nubians built great temples. ¹¹They created beautiful pottery. ¹²Decorating it with drawings of animals and plants. ¹³Some thin-walled pots were designed with geometric patterns and crosshatching. ¹⁴On tombstones and altars, carved inscriptions using Egyptian hieroglyphics. ¹⁵They made tools, pottery, and jewelry. ¹⁶From clay, gold, ebony, and ivory. ¹⁷Thanks in part to the exhibitions. ¹⁸Awareness of the contributions of Nubian civilizations has grown.

Correcting Run-on Sentences

▐▐▶ A **run-on** sentence is made up of two or more sentences that are incorrectly run together as a single sentence. A run-on with no punctuation separating its sentences is called a **fused sentence**; a run-on with only a comma separating its sentences is called a **comma splice**.

Here are five strategies that effective writers use to avoid or to correct run-on sentences.

1. **Separate them**. Add end punctuation and a capital letter to separate the sentences.

   RUN-ON   Corals are invertebrates, they are related to jellyfish.

   CORRECTED Corals are invertebrates. They are related to jellyfish.

2. **Use a conjunction.** Use a coordinating or correlative conjunction preceded by a comma.

   RUN-ON   Corals form colonies that cover more than 200,000 square miles of sea floor, Australia's 1,250-mile-long Great Barrier Reef is one of their creations.

   CORRECTED Corals form colonies that cover more than 200,000 square miles of sea floor, **and** Australia's 1,250-mile-long Great Barrier Reef is one of their creations.

3. **Insert a semicolon.** Use a semicolon to separate the two sentences.

   RUN-ON   Modern species of corals evolved about 230 million years ago they have changed little since then.

   CORRECTED Modern species of corals evolved about 230 million years ago; they have changed little since then.

4. **Add a conjunctive adverb.** Use a semicolon together with either a conjunctive adverb or a transitional expression. Be sure to put a comma after the conjunctive adverb.

   RUN-ON   Coral reefs provide food for fish, they are home to starfish, crabs, eels, sea slugs, and sponges.

   CORRECTED Coral reefs provide food for fish; **in addition,** they are home to starfish, crabs, eels, sea slugs, and sponges.

5. **Create a clause.** Turn one of the sentences into a subordinate clause.

   RUN-ON   Individual corals are the size of chocolate chips, they can build some of the largest solid structures on Earth.

   CORRECTED **Although individual corals are the size of chocolate chips,** they can build some of the largest solid structures on Earth.

WRITING HINT

Four or more simple sentences in a row may *sound* like a run-on sentence even when, technically, they're not. To avoid this problem, use alternative structures.

ORIGINAL

The sky is gray. It's going to rain. I'm miserable. My new shoes will get soaked.

REVISED

The gray sky suggests rain. I'm miserable because my new shoes will get soaked.

Some Conjunctive Adverbs

anyway	next
in addition	nonetheless
incidentally	soon
indeed	then
likewise	thus

Some Transitional Expressions

after all	for example
at any rate	for instance
by the way	in addition
even so	in fact
on the other hand	

See Lessons 3.2 and 8.1 for more information on subordinate clauses.

EXERCISE 8 Editing Run-on Sentences

On a separate piece of paper, correct the run-on sentences below. Use a variety of strategies.

1. A fragile layer of tissue coats coral reefs, this tissue is susceptible to diseases.

2. These diseases are old, in recent years they have intensified.

3. One ailment is called black-band disease it affects brain and star corals.

4. There are two types of white-band disease both threaten Caribbean coral.

5. Yellow-band disease is also known as yellow-blotch disease it attacks coral in the Caribbean too.

6. White pox gives some coral a white rash it was first identified in 1996 in the Florida Keys.

7. White plague was first noted in 1977 in 1995, a deadlier strain appeared.

8. Natural events, such as El Niño, have played a role in the destruction of coral reefs, increased tourism has played a role.

9. The coral in the Caribbean beckons me now I may stay on land I may watch underwater movies instead.

10. People should stay away maybe scientists can control the diseases.

EXERCISE 9 Editing a Friendly E-mail

Work with a partner or small group to correct all the run-on sentences in the following e-mail to a friend. Use a variety of strategies. Compare your version with that of other pairs or groups.

[1]Dear Max,

[2]Our senior class trip was a blast it was unique, too. [3]We went on a snorkeling excursion off the Florida Keys. [4]Whoa! [5]Did we ever see corals. [6]We swam all along the reef we saw corals of every color, we saw fish too. [7]Most fish were spectacular specimens, some were a little scary. [8]I think I saw a barracuda. [9]Mario spotted an octopus he didn't stick around to count all eight tentacles.

[10]The best part of the trip was that it was free Irma discovered a treasure chest full of jewels and pieces of gold, it was right there under a star coral. [11]We are all millionaires, none of us will have to worry about money so we'll simply spend the rest of our lives lying on the beach and snorkeling along the coral reefs. [12]Send suntan lotion!

Direct and Indirect Objects

Besides a subject and a verb, many sentences include a **complement**, which completes the meaning of the sentence. This lesson reviews two kinds of complements: direct objects and indirect objects.

A **direct object** is a noun or pronoun that receives the action of an action verb. A direct object (DO) answers the question *whom* or *what* following the verb.

Jerome carried his **backpack** (DO) to school. [He carried—*what*?—a backpack. *Backpack* is the direct object.]

We spotted the **ranger** (DO) and the **horse** (DO) by the falls. [We spotted—*whom* or *what*?—the ranger and the horse. *Ranger* and *horse* are the direct objects.]

When an action verb is followed by an object, the verb is called **transitive**. When an action verb stands without an object, the verb is called **intransitive**.

The pitcher threw a **curveball** (DO) and then a **slider** (DO). [Here, *threw* is a transitive verb.]
He threw more powerfully than ever before. [Here, *threw* is an intransitive verb.]

Some sentences have not only a direct object but also an indirect object.

An **indirect object** (IO) is a noun or pronoun that answers the question *to whom* or *for whom* or *to what* or *for what* following an action verb.

She gave **me** (IO) the **assignment** (DO). [She gave the assignment—*to whom*?—to me. *Me* is the indirect object; *assignment* is the direct object.]

I gave the **wall** (IO) and **ceiling** (IO) one more **coat** (DO) of paint. [I gave one more coat—*to what*?—to the wall and ceiling. *Wall* and *ceiling* are indirect objects; *coat* is the direct object.]

The following sentences have the same meaning, but only the first sentence has an indirect object—*Jack*. The second sentence includes *to Jack*, a prepositional phrase, not an indirect object.

Please show **Jack** (IO) the test **scores** (DO). Please show the test **scores** (DO) to Jack.

TEST-TAKING TIP

You may be asked on a standardized test to decide whether *who* or *whom* is the correct choice in a given sentence. Try rearranging the order of the words in the sentence to find whether the pronoun is serving as a subject, in which case *who* is the correct choice, or as a direct object, in which case the correct choice is *whom*. See item 3 on page 334.

EDITING TIP

Most people don't begin a question with *whom* when they write or speak informally. But in formal writing and speaking, begin a question with *whom* if that word is the object in a sentence.

INFORMAL **Who** are you calling?

FORMAL **Whom** (DO) are you calling?

EXERCISE 10 Identifying Direct and Indirect Objects

Underline every direct object and indirect object. Label them *DO* for direct object and *IO* for indirect object.

1. Some of these companies financed British colonies.

2. In 1607, the Virginia Company started a colony in Virginia and called it Jamestown.

3. The company sent 144 men there and promised them wealth.

4. Only 104 of the men survived the voyage.

5. The survivors settled swampy and inhospitable land.

6. About seventy more men lost their lives within a year.

7. They had expected wealth.

8. The environment caused settlers malnutrition and disease instead.

9. Captain John Smith's military discipline could not prevent the bad conditions and starvation.

10. Nevertheless, Britain kept sending Jamestown more settlers.

HiNT

Objects may be compound, and a compound sentence may have an object after each subject and verb.

EXERCISE 11 Identifying Direct and Indirect Objects

In the paragraphs below, underline every direct and indirect object, and label each one as *DO* or *IO*.

¹The Jamestown colonists selected a region that was home to Algonquian tribes. ²These Native Americans helped the struggling colonists. ³Powhatan, the tribal leader, gave them assistance. ⁴The colonists received corn and other foods from Powhatan's confederacy in exchange for tools, guns, and knives. ⁵In 1614, Powhatan signed a treaty with the settlers. ⁶He cemented the arrangement with the marriage of his daughter, Pocahontas, to John Rolfe.

⁷However, the relationship between the Algonquians and the settlers was not a smooth one. ⁸Huge cultural differences caused the neighbors stress. ⁹The confederacy attacked the settlers in 1622 and killed more than three hundred of them. ¹⁰The Jamestown colony survived the attack and fought back.

HiNT

Not every sentence has an object, and there are only two indirect objects.

Predicate Nominatives and Predicate Adjectives

Some action verbs take complements called direct and indirect objects (Lesson 6.6). This lesson reviews complements that follow *linking* verbs. These words are called subject complements.

▐▐▶ A linking verb needs a **subject complement**—a noun, pronoun, or adjective—after it in order to express a complete thought.

> The woman standing next to the car is its **owner**.
> Yes, the owner is **she**.
> She appears **lost**.

▐▐▶ A subject complement that is a noun or pronoun is called a predicate nominative (PN). A **predicate nominative** is a noun or pronoun that follows a linking verb (LV) and renames or identifies the subjects (S).

>   S   LV   PN   PN
> My favorite teams are the **Dodgers** and the **Mets**. [*Dodgers* and *Mets* are nouns that rename the subject, *teams*.]
>
>   S   LV PN
> The grand slam was **his**. [*His* is a pronoun that identifies the subject, *grand slam*.]

▐▐▶ A subject complement that is an adjective is called a predicate adjective (PA). A **predicate adjective** is an adjective that follows a linking verb and modifies, or describes, the subject.

>   S   LV   PA   PA
> The speech was **brief** but **powerful**. [*Brief* and *powerful* are adjectives that modify the subject, *speech*.]
>
>   LV   S   S   PA
> Were Juan and Lisa **angry**? [The adjective *angry* modifies the subjects, *Juan* and *Lisa*.]

EXERCISE 12 Identifying Predicate Nominatives and Predicate Adjectives

Underline every predicate nominative and predicate adjective in the sentences below. In the space provided, write *PN* for predicate nominative and *PA* for predicate adjective.

EXAMPLE   ___*PA*___ The movie was <u>scary</u>.

_____ 1. My radio is my companion each morning.

Common Linking Verbs

All the forms of *be* are linking verbs: *am, is, are, was, were, have been,* and so on. These other verbs can also be linking verbs:

appear	seem
become	smell
feel	sound
grow	taste
look	turn
remain	

Enriching Your Vocabulary

The Latin noun *opus*, used on page 154, means a "work" and is commonly used in reference to musical compositions. *Opus* numbers often don't tell much about the date of composition of a piece of music.

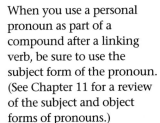

EDITING TIP

When you use a personal pronoun as part of a compound after a linking verb, be sure to use the subject form of the pronoun. (See Chapter 11 for a review of the subject and object forms of pronouns.)

                        she
The winners are Li and ~~her~~.

_____ 2. Did you ever notice how quickly the sky becomes light in the morning?

_____ 3. Does the sky turn black as quickly after sunset?

_____ 4. That's not a raven; it's an ordinary pigeon.

_____ 5. My uncle and aunt are biologists who study marine life.

_____ 6. The composer's final opus was her best.

_____ 7. On the menu, the dishes with a pepper symbol taste hot and spicy.

_____ 8. With awkwardness, I asked, "Are you angry with me?"

_____ 9. The hiker suddenly felt weak; then she became dizzy.

_____ 10. Kevin is one of the best singers in the tenor section.

Working Together

EXERCISE 13 Writing a Description

Imagine that you have won a contest sponsored by a leading architectural firm. As the winner, you have the opportunity to design the ideal small city. Work with a partner to generate ideas. Then write an essay proposing your plans for this place. When you've finished writing, underline and label all the predicate adjectives and predicate nominatives in your sentences.

• Where would your city be?

• What would it look like?

• What services, amusements, and cultural activities and spaces would it offer its citizens?

• What problems would your ideal city solve that your actual community presently has?

Object Complements

The rarest complement is called an object complement.

▐▶ An **object complement** (OC) is a noun, pronoun, or adjective that follows the direct object (DO) and identifies or describes it.

               DO   OC
The class elected me **president**.

                       S   V   DO   OC
Because of her tone, she made the committee **hers**.

               DO   OC   OC
The news made him **upset** and **frantic**.

The following verbs (and any of their synonyms) can take object complements:

appoint	consider	find	paint
call	cut	make	sweep
choose	elect	name	think

WRITING HINT

Since object complements follow only a few verbs, you probably won't use them often. Don't try to write sentences with object complements. They'll come naturally when you need them.

P.S. It's more important to know how to use the five complements mentioned in this chapter than to memorize their names.

EXERCISE 14 Identifying Object Complements

Underline the direct objects once and the object complements twice in each sentence below.

1. The student council president considers my help useful.

2. They have elected Roberta Sanchez class treasurer for the second time.

3. Doctors consider the accident victim's situation hopeless.

4. The decorator said, "Paint the walls any color, but make the trim silver."

5. A team of volunteers swept the gym clean before the big party.

6. His attitude made the college adviser suspicious.

7. I consider the idea mine, and you should identify me in your research paper.

8. He saw my test score and called me brilliant.

9. I called him kind and generous.

10. Not everybody considers the cafeteria food tasteless.

Revising and Editing Worksheet

Improve the following draft by revising for ideas, organization, word choice, and sentence variety. After revising, edit the draft for errors in spelling, capitalization, punctuation, and usage. Write your revised and edited version on a separate piece of paper. Compare your changes with those of a writing partner.

[1]The late 1500s in England were a golden age. [2]England had a grate navy. [3]England became a sea power. [4]It was London that was the city where Queen Elizabeth I had her court. [5]And London could sparkle. [6]It had wealth. [7]It had energy. [8]And it had William Shakespeare.

[9]During her rain, Queen Elizabeth I considered literature important. [10]There were many writers in England then. [11]The most famous writer of the time was Shakespeare. [12]His lyric poetry became famous. [13]Many of his poems were sonnets. [14]His poetic dramas became famous, too. [15]For example, *Romeo and Juliet*, *Macbeth*, and *Hamlet*.

[16]Many people today think Shakespeare was the best. [17]But lots of people think he is too hard. [18]Too many big words and long lines. [19]But every year still people put the plays on television and the movies. [20]And many life performances. [21]If they're too many big words and long lines, how come they put the plays on still today?

[22]All during the five hundred year since Shakespeares time, sometimes directors make the setting of his plays the day the audience is in. [23]For example, recently a movie director put *Romeo and Juliet* in the late twentieth century. [24]The movie director of this *Romeo and Juliet* made his young actors superstars. [25]This proves that Shakespeare and his language still speak to us.

Chapter Review

EXERCISE A Parts of a Sentence: Identifying Subjects and Verbs

In each sentence, underline the subject (simple subject) once and the verb twice. If the subject is understood to be *you*, write *you* following the sentence.

1. Fifty thousand fans filled the stadium.

2. The hot sun beat down on both the players and those in attendance.

3. Throughout the game, the fans cheered and booed equally loudly.

4. A sudden, unexpected downpour soaked the field and stopped play.

5. Players and fans alike headed for cover; the fans amused themselves at the food and souvenir stands.

6. Bring me a hot dog, please.

7. Finally, the game resumed, and a cheer went up.

8. The final three innings were nail-biters; players and fans were tense.

9. The game went into extra innings.

10. The final score, 7 to 6, left the crowd disappointed.

EXERCISE B Identifying Complements

In each sentence, identify the italicized word(s). Above each word, write *DO* (direct object), *IO* (indirect object), *PA* (predicate adjective), *PN* (predicate nominative), or *OC* (object complement).

1. The following sentences give *information* about the 1950s.

2. The person who invented the polio vaccine in 1952 was *Jonas Salk*.

3. Americans used *credit cards* for the first time in 1950.

4. Some people were very *upset* when the Dodgers left Brooklyn in 1958.

5. In 1958, toy makers gave *us* the *Hula Hoop* and made *kids competitive*.

6. Elvis Presley sang his first hit *song* in 1954 and soon became *famous*.

7. One key invention of 1953 was the radial *tire*.

8. People ate *TV dinners* for the first time in 1954.

9. Some of us remained *calm* when the Soviets launched *Sputnik* in 1957.

10. A key discovery of the 1950s was *DNA*.

EXERCISE C Editing Sentence Fragments and Run-on Sentences

On a separate piece of paper, correct the fragments and run-on sentences below. Use a variety of strategies.

1. Located on the west bank of the Missouri River.
2. The Amazon is the second-longest river in the world, it is by far the world's largest river.
3. More than half a million people living in the country of Djibouti in Africa.
4. With land routes to the riches of Asia becoming too dangerous and costly, Portugal seeking a water route to the East by going around Africa.
5. In 1991, Mount Pinatubo violently erupted on the Philippine island of Luzon, the blast, the third largest of the twentieth century, forced the evacuation of thousands of Filipinos.
6. South Island measuring 58,000 square miles.
7. Mexico is composed of thirty-one states and a federal district it has more than 100 million people.
8. In 1493 Pope Alexander VI drew a north-south line to divide South America into land that was Spanish territory and land that belonged to the Portuguese, a year later the Treaty of Tordesillas modified the line.
9. Good borders are made by rivers, they are made by mountain ranges, also a line between two spoken languages makes a good border.
10. Tunisia's capital and largest city, Tunis, with a population of more than one million.

EXERCISE D Writing Complete Sentences

On a separate sheet of paper, with a partner or small group, rewrite the following high school sports reporter's notes (which are fragments) as complete sentences. Be sure to begin each sentence with a capital letter and add the appropriate end punctuation mark. Compare your sentences with those of other pairs or groups.

Big game, two undefeated teams
Small gym—packed and noisy; tense atmosphere; much at stake
Early lead by Jackson so Lincoln home crowd quiet
Sudden comeback by Lincoln, which awakens fans
Tie game = overtime, much excitement
Amazing show of sportsmanship when lights go out, no problems
How game ends—last-second shot for Lincoln victory

Phrases

7

Grammar

STUDENT WRITING
Expository Essay

The Specialist
by Pat Healy
high school student, Grosse Pointe Farms, Michigan

The most important thing you can know about me is that I had polio when I was a child. The least important thing you can know about me is that I had polio when I was a child. It explains everything; it explains nothing. —Scott Roberts

Library Media Specialist Scott Roberts is disabled. His legs do not function, so he gets around with crutches or a wheelchair. He will never be able to walk or run. The rest of life, however, is fair game.

In the muffled silence of the library, the humming of Roberts's motorized wheelchair cuts through the whispers of students who turn their heads toward the sound. Roberts speeds through the rows of books, as students curiously wonder who the man in the wheelchair is.

Today, Roberts wears a neatly pressed navy suit and a crisp white shirt. His red striped tie doesn't have one wrinkle, and his polished glasses don't quite hide the sparkle in his eyes. In many ways, Roberts instantly blends into a crowd. In others, he could not be more noticeable. "I'm completely different from everyone else, but I'm also exactly the same," Roberts said. "When people first meet me, I get a sense that they're either attracted to me, or they're really uncomfortable and would rather get away.". . .

From kindergarten through ninth grade, Roberts attended a school for physically disabled students. He said he has mixed feelings about the experience. "It was sometimes good, sometimes bad," he said. "It was good because I couldn't feel sorry for myself, but bad because I didn't get to go to school with my brothers and sisters."

Everything changed for Roberts in tenth grade when he began going to Osborn High School. He describes his reaction to the new school with a line from Shakespeare's play, *The Tempest:* "A brave new world with such people in't!"

Every day, Roberts started school in a special classroom for disabled students. There, they could receive counseling or extra help.

"I got out of that room as quickly as I could," Roberts laughed. "It was 'brave new world' time for me. I went exploring every day."

And explore he did. Roberts was active with student government and the Intra-Metropolitan School Sportsmanship Council. He eventually became student president of both. . . .

Roberts has been a librarian for the Grosse Pointe Schools for fifteen years, four of them at Parcells Middle School, and eleven at North. His colleagues at South have known him for years and are happy he's here. . . .

> The opening quotation of Pat Healy's expository essay grabs the reader's attention. Pat supplies a physical description of Roberts, some background information, and quotations. Each specific detail helps create an effective essay.
>
> Pat's essay is also effective because he uses phrases to describe, to explain, and to combine sentences. As you work on the exercises in this chapter, you will learn to use phrases to improve your own writing.

Adjective and Adverb Phrases

▶ A **prepositional phrase** always begins with a preposition (PREP) and ends with a single object (a noun or pronoun) or a compound object (OBJ). It may also include adjectives (ADJ).

PREP OBJ   OBJ
for him and me

PREP   ADJ ADJ   OBJ
on the old leather chair

Note: In some sentences, the object of the preposition actually falls before the preposition; as a writer, you have to decide which way a sentence sounds better. For example, which of the following two sentences do you prefer?

Use this red **pen** to write the note **with**.
Write the note **with** this red **pen**.

▶ An **adjective phrase** is a prepositional phrase that modifies a noun or a pronoun in the sentence.

Adjective phrases (like adjectives) answer these questions: *which one, what kind.*

A car **in the parking lot** has its lights on.
It is one **of the cars** in the first row.

▶ An **adverb phrase** is a prepositional phrase that modifies a verb, an adjective, or another adverb.

Adverb phrases (like adverbs) answer these questions: *when, how, where, to what extent.*

She arrived **before the performance**.
Her seat was the closest **of all the available seats**.

More than one prepositional phrase may modify the same word.
At once the crowd showed its approval **with a loud howl**.
[Both phrases modify the verb *showed*.]

Remember: Some words function as either an adverb or a preposition depending on the sentence. If the word is part of a prepositional phrase, it is a preposition. If the word is alone, then it is an adverb. (See Lessons 5.5 and 5.6.)

Before doing the following exercises, you may wish to review the lists of prepositions and compound prepositions on page 131.

Enriching Your Vocabulary

The word *undulating*, used in Exercise 2, means "moving as if in waves." It comes from the Latin word *unda*, which means "wave." The *undulating* motion of the boat made it difficult to get a steady read of the compass.

EDITING TIP

It's never *wrong* to use a comma after one introductory prepositional phrase, but it's not always *necessary*.

COMMA OR NO COMMA OKAY
By late morning, the sky brightened.

By late morning the sky brightened.

Do *not* use a comma when a verb immediately follows an introductory prepositional phrase.

NO COMMA
From the kitchen came the pleasant aroma of bread baking.

EXERCISE 1 Identifying Adjective and Adverb Phrases

Underline every prepositional phrase in the sentences below, and draw an arrow to the word each phrase modifies. Label the adjective phrases *ADJ* and the adverb phrases *ADV*. **Hint:** Some sentences have more than one prepositional phrase.

EXAMPLE   Many foreign words have moved into the English language. *ADV*

1. A faux pas is a blunder of a social nature.
2. An ad hoc committee meets for a particular purpose.
3. We say an act is bona fide when we perform the act in good faith.
4. When someone acts with chutzpah, we mean that he or she acts with a certain amount of nerve.
5. If you gather en masse, you gather in a large body.
6. When you take office in accordance with procedures, you are an officer de jure.
7. When strained relations between countries ease, these countries experience détente.
8. When you are standing on terra firma, you stand on firm ground.
9. When I am president pro tempore, I act only for the time being.
10. A person with a temperamental nature is a prima donna.

EXERCISE 2 Revising and Editing a Paragraph

Improve the following draft of a reporter's notes. The report will be televised with footage that shows what's happening, where and when it's happening, to whom it's happening, and how and why it's happening. Make up details for the report, and on a separate piece of paper, see how many prepositional phrases you can add. When finished, underline every prepositional phrase.

[1]Parade progresses normally, marching bands play, elaborate floats. [2]What!

[3]No! [4]Huge balloon breaks from its mooring. [5]Undulating wildly, strikes lamppost, and stoplight.

[6]No! [7]Lamppost falls, and another. [8]People scurry frantically. [9]Is anyone hurt?

[10]Police sirens, distant, coming closer. [11]Parade marshals bark orders, calm onlookers. [12]Camera operators from TV stations are aiming left, right, up, down.

[13]Balloon hits building and bounces off it toward church steeple across street.

[14]Whoa! [15]It pops with a loud bang like a cannon's fire!

Appositives and Appositive Phrases

▕▌▶ An **appositive** is a noun or pronoun that identifies or explains the noun or pronoun that precedes it. An **appositive phrase** is an appositive plus all of its modifiers.

> His wife, **Kathy**, is an attorney.
> His wife, **a successful attorney**, is Kathy Stern.

If an appositive or an appositive phrase is *not* essential to the meaning of the sentence, it is called **nonessential**, or **nonrestrictive**. Set off nonessential appositives and appositive phrases with commas.

> Alex, **the tallest boy in the class**, is my closest friend.
> London, **the capital of England**, is on the Thames River.

If an appositive phrase is **essential** (**restrictive**) to the sentence's meaning, do not set it off with commas.

> My friend **Megan** is here. [I have other friends; Megan is the one I mean in this sentence.]
>
> The writer **Charles Dickens** also lectured. [The reader needs to know which writer.]

Notice how converting a sentence to an appositive phrase allows you to combine sentences, save words, and introduce a new structure, which can give your writing variety.

> ORIGINAL   I like poems by Wislawa Szymborska.
>   Szymborska is a winner of the Nobel Prize.
> COMBINED   I like poems by Wislawa Szymborska,
>   a winner of the Nobel Prize.

WRITING HINT

Appositives and appositive phrases sometimes precede the noun or pronoun they modify. This placement emphasizes the appositive.

A talented pianist, Zack began taking lessons when he was seven.

A nonessential appositive that begins a sentence takes only one comma; a nonessential appositive within a sentence needs two commas.

EXERCISE 3 Identifying Appositives

Underline the appositives or appositive phrases in the following sentences. **Hint:** Some sentences contain more than one.

1. The writer William Sydney Porter is better known as O. Henry.
2. George Eliot was the pen name of the writer Mary Ann Evans.
3. Mark Twain, my favorite writer, once worked on riverboats.
4. Frederick Dannay and Manfred B. Lee, two men, wrote together as Ellery Queen.
5. The writer Charles Lutwidge Dodgson used the pen name Lewis Carroll.
6. The American statesman Benjamin Franklin sometimes used Poor Richard as a name.

7. Maxim Gorky, a shorter name, helped the Russian writer Aleksei Maksimovich Peshkov gain fame.

8. An English novelist, Alan Sillitoe writes about the hard lives of the working classes.

9. The great novelist Joseph Conrad wrote *Lord Jim*.

10. George Orwell was the pen name that the English writer Eric Arthur Blair gave himself.

EXERCISE 4 Writing Sentences with Appositives

On a separate piece of paper, rewrite the following sentences. Take the appositive or appositive phrase out of parentheses, and insert it at the caret (∧).

EXAMPLE   Chicago, ∧ is known as the Paris of the Prairie. (a city on Lake Michigan)
Chicago, a city on Lake Michigan, is known as the Paris of the Prairie.

1. In the 1970s, ∧ Hank Aaron broke Babe Ruth's home run record. (the decade of disco)

2. In 1974, Richard Nixon ∧ resigned from office. (the thirty-seventh American president)

3. In 1986, the space shuttle ∧ exploded after liftoff. (*Challenger*)

4. The world was very upset at news of the 1986 nuclear accident ∧ . (the Chernobyl fires and explosions)

5. The year 1991 witnessed the breakup of the U.S.S.R. ∧ . (the huge Communist group of nations)

EXERCISE 5 Combining Sentences with Appositives

On a separate piece of paper, combine the sentences in each numbered item with an appositive or an appositive phrase. Don't use commas for essential appositives; use them only for those that are nonessential. **Hint:** Clues tell you if the appositive provides essential information.

1. I watched my favorite television program tonight. *Nerds on the Run* is my favorite program.

2. Greg studied hard for Tuesday's test. The test is a science midterm.

3. I'm glad Ollie's is open again. Ollie's is the closest Chinese restaurant.

4. I received an e-mail from my friend in Thailand. Suki sent me the e-mail. (I have several friends living in Thailand.)

5. My sister's bird can laugh. Her bird is named Shakespeare. (She has only one bird.)

Participles and Participial Phrases; Absolute Phrases

A **verbal** is a verb form that functions as a different part of speech. Three types of verbals are participles, gerunds, and infinitives.

▶ A **participle** is a verb form that acts as an adjective, modifying a noun or a pronoun. Like adjectives, a participle can come before or after the word it modifies.

Present participles end in *-ing*; **past participles** usually end in *-d* or *-ed*, but the past participles of irregular verbs have other endings.

> The **laughing** children clamored for more jokes.
> [present participle before the noun it modifies]
> The apples, **washed** and **polished**, are ready for the party. [two past participles after the noun they modify]

▶ A **participial phrase** is made up of a participle and all of its modifiers and complements. The whole phrase acts as an adjective.

> **Singing at the top of her lungs**, Tanya impressed the judges. [present participial phrase before the noun it modifies]
> The violinist played an instrument **made by an expert craftsperson**. [past participial phrase after the noun it modifies]

When the present participle of *have* is followed by a past participle, a **present perfect participle** is formed.

> **Having eaten his fill**, William got up from the table.
> **Having been late often**, Mary lost her job.

▶ An **absolute phrase** consists of a noun and either a participle or a participial phrase. It stands absolutely by itself— part of neither the subject nor the verb. Because absolute phrases are nonessential, they are always set off by commas. Use them to open your sentences, to conclude them, or to interrupt them.

> **Its paw broken**, the dog now limped along. [The participle *broken* modifies the subject of the phrase, paw, not *dog*, the subject of the independent clause.]
> Inez came in second, **first place going to the girl from Douglass**.

> For more on irregular verb forms, see **Usage**, Lessons 9.2 and 9.3.

STEP BY STEP

Commas with a Participial Phrase

1. Identify the phrase.

   The dog **sitting in the corner** is sick.
   Fido **sitting in the corner** is sick.

2. Decide if the phrase is essential to the meaning of the sentence. In the first example, *sitting in the corner* is essential; it tells *which* dog is sick.

   In the second example, *sitting in the corner* is not essential; the dog has been identified by name.

3. If the phrase is not essential, set it off with commas.

   Fido, **sitting in the corner**, is sick.

EXERCISE 6 Identifying Participial or Absolute Phrases

Underline the participial or absolute phrases in the following sentences.

1. Beginning in 1660, Samuel Pepys, an Englishman, kept diaries.
2. Pepys, pronounced "peeps," was twenty-seven at the time.
3. Pepys made daily entries for nine years, keeping the entries private.
4. Using a secret code, he privately recorded events of his daily life.
5. At his death, the diaries were sitting on his bookshelf, each volume neatly tied.
6. The diaries, left alone on the shelf for years, eventually found their way to Magdalene College, Cambridge.
7. A student named John Smith deciphered Pepys's code.
8. Pepys's diaries, proving very informative, contained much information about life and customs in the seventeenth century.
9. One set of entries, treasured by historians, is a description of the great London fire of 1666, a disaster not widely recorded.
10. The diary is a useful source of information on the hundreds of buildings destroyed in the fire.

EXERCISE 7 Writing Sentences with Participial Phrases

On a separate piece of paper, write a complete sentence, using each of the numbered items as a participial phrase.

EXAMPLE   organized by professionals
The Himalayan trek, organized by professionals, was both safe and exhilarating.

1. breaking into laughter
2. leaning against the wall
3. removing his hat
4. shocked by the news
5. having entered the contest
6. announced in the morning
7. spread across the ground
8. having stopped by the fence
9. stretching across the field
10. known as a reliable worker

Write What You Think

Write a paragraph in which you give your opinion about the following statement. Support your opinion with reasons and examples. Use participial phrases and absolute phrases to begin, interrupt, and end sentences.

> Under no conditions should the public ever read a diary written as a private record unless the writer has given his or her permission.

When you finish revising and editing, go back over your paragraph, and underline any participial or absolute phrases you may have used.

Gerunds and Gerund Phrases

▌▶ A **gerund**, a verb form ending in *-ing*, functions as a noun.

In a sentence, gerunds can be used in every way that nouns can be used.
Jogging is his favorite form of exercise. [subject]
Her least favorite pastime is **jogging**. [predicate nominative]
Do you enjoy **jogging**? [direct object]
Give **jogging** a try. [indirect object]
Some people call fast walking **jogging**. [objective complement]
I saw a video on the benefits of **jogging**. [object of a preposition]

▌▶ A **gerund phrase** is made up of a gerund and all of its modifiers and complements. The entire phrase functions as a noun.

Adjectives, adverbs, nouns, pronouns, and prepositional phrases can occur with a gerund to form a gerund phrase.
Watching movies is his favorite activity. [subject]
At the movies, he dislikes the **talking all around him**. [predicate nominative]
He has tried **staring at talkers**. [direct object]
Then he gives **tapping them on the shoulder** a try. [indirect object]
He calls talking at the movies **disturbing the peace**. [objective complement]
He even bought a self-help video about **quieting one's neighbors**. [object of a preposition]

> **EDITING TIP**
>
> Certain English verbs can't be followed by a gerund. Verbs such as *expect*, *plan*, *promise*, and *refuse* require an infinitive (see Lesson 7.5).
>
> We **plan** to camp this summer.
>
> We **promise** to behave ourselves.

EXERCISE 8 Identifying Gerunds and Gerund Phrases

Underline every gerund and gerund phrase in the sentences below. A gerund phrase may contain one or more prepositional phrases. Count these as part of the gerund phrase in this exercise. **Remember:** Not every *-ing* word is a gerund. A gerund functions as a noun in the sentence. **Hint:** A sentence may have more than one gerund or gerund phrase.

1. Eduardo likes getting into his sleeping bag and telling ghost stories to his tentmates.

> **Enriching Your Vocabulary**
>
> The word *sequester*, used on page 168, means "to set apart" or "to withdraw." It comes from the Latin *sequestrare*, meaning "to entrust." The jury was *sequestered* to deliberate the verdict of the murder trial.

2. Sequestering himself in the country always makes him feel independent and far from civilization.

3. He loves the strong smells of a cooking breakfast in the great outdoors.

4. He brings his binoculars for watching birds.

5. Being in the woods, according to Eduardo, is ideal for communicating with friends.

6. Talking, listening, and sharing are all easier outdoors.

7. Climbing mountain trails is another thrilling experience he relishes.

8. In fact, he loves everything about camping.

9. He even likes the buzzing of the mosquitoes.

10. His least favorite part of the trip is breaking camp.

Exercise 9 Distinguishing Between Participles and Gerunds

On the line, write *PART* if the sentence contains a participle or participial phrase; write *GER* if it contains a gerund or gerund phrase. Then underline the word or phrase that you are identifying.

1. _____ Using a computer confounds many otherwise intelligent adults.

2. _____ Why does dealing with machines stump so many people?

3. _____ Younger people have much less trouble in working with technology.

4. _____ Why are young people interested in technology?

5. _____ Growing up with computers in every household gadget makes young people comfortable around technology.

6. _____ Not intimidated by digital music players, they prepare personal music menus.

7. _____ Some young people are patient with technologically challenged adults.

8. _____ Teenagers help a parent with e-mail in exchange for getting more time on the computer for themselves.

9. _____ This phenomenon of adults needing help is temporary.

10. _____ After all, the future generations of adults will be people raised with electronics.

Infinitives and Infinitive Phrases

▐▐▶ An **infinitive** is a verb form that is almost always preceded by the word *to*. In a sentence, an infinitive can act as a noun, an adjective, or an adverb.

> His grandfather likes **to complain**. [infinitive as noun]
> At a family gathering, Grandfather is always the first one **to arrive**. [infinitive as adjective]
> He is quick **to argue** with Uncle Sam. [infinitive as adverb]

We call the word *to* the **sign**, or **marker**, **of the infinitive**. *To* is part of an infinitive if it's followed by a verb. If it starts a prepositional phrase, then *to* is a preposition.

INFINITIVE	PREPOSITIONAL PHRASE
Maria really loves *to dance*.	Maria went *to the dance*.
We tried hard *to win*.	Give the trophy *to the winner*.

Sometimes the *to* of an infinitive is omitted but understood.

> Jerome helped **[to] cook**.

▐▐▶ An **infinitive phrase** is made up of an infinitive and all of its modifiers and complements.

> **To play the guitar in a band** is Karen's dream.
> It is fun **to play volleyball on the beach**.

> **WRITING HINT**
>
> When a modifier comes between *to* and the *verb*, the infinitive is said to be **split**. Avoid split infinitives unless, by doing so, the result is awkward or sounds unnatural.
>
> *To boldly go* where no one has ever gone before

> **HINT**
>
> Not every phrase beginning with *to* is an infinitive phrase. Some sentences contain no infinitives.

EXERCISE 10 Identifying Infinitives and Infinitive Phrases

Underline every infinitive and infinitive phrase in the following lines from literature.

Hint: Not every sentence contains an infinitive or infinitive phrase.

1. I only ask to be free.—*Barnaby Rudge*
2. I believe, Sir, that you desire to look at these apartments.—*Bleak House*
3. He was very good to me.—*Bleak House*
4. 'Orses and dogs is some men's fancy. They're wittles and drink to me.—*David Copperfield*
5. The name of those fabulous animals (pagan, I regret to say) who used to sing in the water has quite escaped me.—*Martin Chuzzlewit*
6. All the wickedness of the world is print to him.—*Martin Chuzzlewit*
7. Oh! They're too beautiful to live, much too beautiful!—*Nicholas Nickleby*

8. Only when one has lost all curiosity about the future has one reached the age to write an autobiography.—Evelyn Waugh

9. Beauty is truth, truth beauty,—that is all/Ye know on earth, and all ye need to know.—John Keats

10. We have no more right to consume happiness without producing it than to consume wealth without producing it.—George Bernard Shaw

EXERCISE 11 Revising and Editing a Biography

Underline the infinitives and infinitive phrases in the paragraphs below. Then work with a partner to correct sentence fragments and run-ons and to make any other changes you think will improve this biography of Charles Dickens.

[1]When you try to think of a writer, next to Shakespeare, who occupies the most important place in popular culture, you might name Charles Dickens. [2]His works appeal to nearly everybody. [3]With their unforgettable characters. [4]Dickens's novels have already become plays and movies, and there are probably many more to come.

[5]Born to poor parents in Portsmouth on the southern coast of England in 1812. [6]When his father was sent to debtor's prison. [7]Young Charles was to spend time working in a factory. [8]He worked there pasting labels. [9]When he wasn't in the factory, he liked to wander, he walked through the streets of London. [10]He saw bleakness and poverty all around him. [11]From his unhappy childhood experiences, Dickens learned to appreciate the plight of the poor.

[12]He became a law clerk when he was fifteen. [13]He taught himself to write better, and he became a court reporter. [14]He learned to observe things around him. [15]He soon began to write sketches of everyday life. [16]Which he contributed to several periodicals. [17]He began to receive attention for his clever writing. [18]In 1836, he published his first novel, *Sketches by Boz*. [19]In the flurry of novels that followed, he showed a unique ability to express his passion for reform. [20]And to use humor and satire. [21]Few writers since have been able to match his ability to portray modern industrial conditions. [22]As he did. [23]He did it so passionately. [24]He did it so poetically.

Revising and Editing Worksheet 1

Improve the following draft by revising for ideas, organization, word choice, and sentence variety. After revising, edit the draft for errors in spelling, capitalization, punctuation, and usage. Write your revised and edited version on a separate piece of paper. Compare your changes with those of a writing partner.

[1]The giant lizard lives on a group of four small islands in central Indonesia. [2]The islands are named Komodo, Rinca, Gili Motang, and Flores. [3]The lizzard is known as a Komodo dragon. [4]The origin of its name is uncertain. [5]Probably, the origin is a result of imagination. [6]And exaggeration.

[7]It can grow to a length of nine feet or more. [8]It can weigh up to two hundred pounds. [9]It is a powerful predator. [10]A predator is a hunter of other animals. [11]Then eating them. [12]With its sharp teeth, strong and powerful claws, and unexpected agility. [13]It has quickness, too. [14]The Komodo dragon has a long, yellow, forked tongue. [15]It uses it to sense the presence of prey. [16]Prey can include large mammals. [17]Like dear.

[18]There are many tales about the giant lizard. [19]Tales about people-eating have been common. [20]The creatures have been blamed for several human deaths. [21]These accounts may or may not be reliable. [22]However, researchers claim that the lizards are not likely to attack humans. [23]Humans are not the main item on their menus. [24]They prefer birds, deer, pigs, and water buffalo. [25]They also find other dragons tasty, they also enjoy a nice dish of poisonous snake. [26]Komodo dragons are scavengers, to. [27]Scavengers eat dead animals.

[28]Today, the dragons are classified as an endangered species. [29]Indonesia protects their habitat. [30]By making much of it a national park. [31]There are an estimated two hundred of these lizards living in zoos. [32]There are another three to five thousand loose in the wild. [33]According to zookeepers, these giants are surprisingly intelligent. [34]They possess an intelligence above any other reptile's.

Revising and Editing Worksheet 2

Improve the following draft by revising for ideas, organization, word choice, and sentence variety. After revising, edit the draft for errors in spelling, capitalization, punctuation, and usage. Write your revised and edited version on a separate piece of paper. Compare your changes with those of a writing partner.

[1]Paper reached Europe. [2]It was a thousand years after its invention in China. [3]It took a long time to get to Europe. [4]Because the process of papermaking was kept secret. [5]Knowledge of the process slowly made it's way west. [6]The Middle Eastern countries introduced paper to Europe and to India. [7]They did so in the twelfth century. [8]They brought the paper to Sicily. [9]Spain too.

[10]Until the nineteenth century in the West, rags were the most important ingredient in the papermaking process. [11]By the nineteenth century, the demand for paper increased greatly, more people were reading and writing. [12]Papermakers began to substitute wood for the rags. [13]Using wood lessened the quality of the paper. [14]Using wood made the paper less durable.

[15]The availability of large amounts of cheap paper had an enormous influence on Western civilization. [16]It caused the rapidly spread of printing. [17]It popularized education. [18]It proved essential to the administration of government. [19]But is paper here to stay, it once seemed so? [20]Until now. [21]Computers have begun to shake our faith in paper. [22]Computer technology makes it possible for a whole new approach to information storage. [23]Computers have challenged the supremacy of paper. [24]Will we have a bookless, magazineless, and newspaperless society some day? [25]It isn't here yet.

Chapter Review

EXERCISE A Identifying Phrases

Underline each phrase in the following sentences. Then write one of these abbreviations above the phrase:

PREP = prepositional phrase

PART = participial phrase

GER = gerund phrase

INF = infinitive phrase

APP = appositive phrase

ABS = absolute phrase

Remember: When a prepositional phrase is part of another kind of phrase, you don't have to label the prepositional phrase separately.

1. Pancho Barnes made a name for herself as the first woman stunt pilot in motion pictures.

2. Barnes tried setting new airspeed records.

3. In 1910, Blanche Scott became the first woman to fly solo.

4. In 1912, Scott made her first cross-country flight, a trip taking sixty-nine days.

5. Known as "the flying schoolgirl," Katherine Stinson was the first woman to skywrite.

6. Stinson was the fourth woman in the world to qualify for a pilot's license.

7. The first woman to fly nonstop from the East to the West across North America was Laura Ingalls.

8. When Ruth Nichols graduated from Miss Masters' School, she got an airplane as a graduation present.

9. Breaking the women's speed record in both directions was Nichols's accomplishment for transcontinental flights in 1929.

10. Becoming the first woman to fly solo around the world was Jerrie Mock's claim to fame.

EXERCISE B Using Phrases

On a separate piece of paper, write a complete, correct sentence using each phrase given. Make each the kind of phrase indicated in parentheses.

1. with her eyes closed   (adjective)
2. a successful filmmaker   (appositive)
3. disturbing others in the audience   (gerund)
4. to make a feature film   (infinitive)
5. in front of the theater   (adjective)
6. renting movies   (gerund)
7. after the play   (adverbial)
8. the only student in the school   (appositive)
9. having seen all the nominated films   (participial)
10. to visit a movie set   (infinitive)
11. watching old cartoons   (gerund)
12. to sit quietly   (infinitive)
13. laughing the whole time   (participial)
14. in the credits   (adjective)
15. her seat taken   (absolute)
16. eating popcorn   (gerund)
17. written by a student   (participial)
18. before the movie started   (adverbial)
19. to stay in my seat   (infinitive)
20. third place going to the student from UCLA   (absolute)

Write What You Think

CONNECTING
Writing & Grammar

Over the years, Hollywood has made many films based on historical events and real people. For many moviegoers, the view presented by these films is the only one they have about the event or people depicted. Since the filmmakers use dramatic license when telling their stories, they may distort the truth in order to make a more effective movie. Does this situation produce a problem?

Write a paragraph or two about whether or not you value movies made about real people and events. Try to use prepositional, verbal, appositive, and absolute phrases to express your ideas clearly. When you finish revising and editing, underline all of the phrases you've used.

Clauses

STUDENT WRITING
Expository Essay

What I Learned About Life from Selling Shoes
by Katherine Ivers

high school student, Meriden, Connecticut

I know you're asking, "What could you possibly learn from selling shoes?" But the vast knowledge I have acquired from this minimum-wage job will last a lifetime.

Hired right before Christmas, I was about to receive a crash course in responsibility. Amid the decorations, elevator music, and hordes of customers, I learned my first lesson—patience. This virtue, unbeknownst to the six million crazed customers waving and shoving shoes in my face, is the only reason many of them were not bludgeoned to death by a high heel.

Another very important lesson is stress management. I faced the triple necessity of balancing honors courses at school, holding down a part-time job, and retaining a social life. . . .

I also learned to master quickly the art of budgeting time. I eat dinner, talk to my boss, and study for a trig quiz in fifteen minutes. Going to the bathroom can wait. In the shoe department, I learned something else that surprised me: Men and women are different! I never saw a man try on a pair of shoes and inquire whether they made his ankles look fat. On the other hand, I never saw a woman so anxious to get out of the mall that she purchased any shoe without trying it on. I learned to appreciate and adapt to these differences.

I learned, too, that physical fitness plays an important role. How many people get to do 8,432 knee squats a day? And, of course, there are the ever-present ladders and the constant reaching. From carrying sixteen boxes of size-twelve men's work boots over my head, I have developed biceps that even Arnold Schwarzenegger would envy.

Perhaps the most important lesson of all concerns responsibility. To choose between going to my job (that I love so much) or attending a party was a difficult decision. But I always try to make the right one. Who needs fun anyway?

My job in the shoe department has taught me, finally, a deep appreciation for the people who make a living by dealing with an often cranky—but always demanding—public. If we could all take the responsibility to understand and communicate with a positive attitude, we could have a more peaceful world.

In her essay, Katherine Ivers explains what she has learned from her personal experience. As you reread the essay, notice how she organizes her essay: she presents her least important lesson first and her most important lesson last. This careful organization encourages her audience to keep reading.

Katherine uses a noun clause as the title of her essay. She uses other kinds of clauses in her essay, adding variety to her sentences and connecting related ideas. In this chapter, you'll practice using clauses to express ideas clearly and to vary your sentences.

Independent Clauses and Subordinate Clauses

⫸ An **independent** (or **main**) **clause** has a subject (s) and a verb (v) and expresses a complete thought.

An independent clause can function all by itself as a **simple sentence**. Because of this power, the clause is called *independent*.

                                    S   V
INDEPENDENT CLAUSE   They stayed for dinner.
                                    S   S   V
INDEPENDENT CLAUSE   Dave and Joanne came, too.

When you put two or more independent clauses together and join them with a conjunction (CONJ) or a semicolon, you have a **compound sentence**.

                                    CONJ
I ate the lamb chop, **but** I left the asparagus on the plate.
                                    CONJ   CONJ
I'd better clean my plate, **for** chocolate cake comes next, **and** I want a big slice.

⫸ A **subordinate** (or **dependent**) **clause** has a subject and a verb but doesn't express a complete thought.

    S   V   S   V
as we drove home   that gives instructions
    S   V   S   V
if they are coming   because it was snowing

A subordinate clause can't stand alone. You must attach it to or insert it into an independent clause. Alternatively, you can drop the word that makes the word group subordinate. For example, if you take off the word *as* in the first word group above, what's left is an independent clause, or simple sentence.

You can place a subordinate clause at the beginning, middle, or end of a sentence.

            S   V   S   V
Because she knew the words, Donna joined in. [Here, the subordinate clause comes before the independent clause.]
            S   S   V   V
The Marx Brothers, **who made several movies,** have had a significant impact on American humor. [The subordinate clause falls between the subject and verb of an independent clause.]
            S   V   S   V
Many people are partial to Harpo Marx, **who was the silent one**. [The subordinate clause comes after the independent clause.]

Enriching Your Vocabulary

The Latin word *minimus*, or "smallest," is the root of *minimize*, which is used in Exercise 2, and means "to reduce" or "to make smaller." You can *minimize* your interest payments by paying off your credit card every month.

WRITING HINT

Be sure to put the more important idea of a sentence in an independent clause, where it will stand out.

Jackie, **who now swims faster and with less effort**, practiced every day.

To focus on Jackie's results, the following rewrite is more effective.

Jackie, who practiced every day, **now swims faster and with less effort**.

EXERCISE 1 Identifying Independent and Subordinate Clauses

On the blank for each numbered item, write *I* for an independent clause or *S* for a subordinate clause. On a separate piece of paper, revise every subordinate clause to make it a complete sentence.

_____ 1. Trace gases and water vapor that affect atmospheric temperature.

_____ 2. Which is a phenomenon known as the greenhouse effect.

_____ 3. The greenhouse effect is essential to life.

_____ 4. It is what keeps Earth's temperatures within a reasonable range.

_____ 5. What we've been hearing and reading about the greenhouse effect in recent years.

_____ 6. That there is significant evidence that the world is getting warmer.

_____ 7. Because of the greenhouse effect.

_____ 8. Some causes of these increases are human products and activities.

EXERCISE 2 Editing Paragraphs

Edit the following paragraphs. Look for any subordinate clauses that incorrectly stand alone as sentences. Then check for spelling errors.

¹The greenhouse effect, the destruction of the ozone layer, the pollution of the seas, and the loss of diversity among living things, which are problems that affect everyone on Earth. ²What's more, these problems are interconnected. ³Since it's clear that we're all in this together. ⁴But, for many reasons, the concept is a tough one to act on.

⁵One reason has to do with the differences between wealthy and poor nations. ⁶Because in poorer countries people care most about the basics of life—food, clothing, and shelter; they're survival is at stake, and survival comes first. ⁷That is why they aren't as concerned as we are in the United States with the chemicals that help grow their foods. ⁸Or with how to minimize industrial pollution from factories. ⁹Even here in the United States, when jobs are at stake. ¹⁰People put environmental issues second to economic ones.

Adjective Clauses

▶ An **adjective clause** is a subordinate clause that functions as an adjective. It modifies a noun or pronoun.

Put an adjective clause directly after the word it modifies.

Mike, **who is seven feet tall**, is the team's starting center.
He is the player **whom the NBA scouts are watching closely**.
They've come to watch him at our gym, **where he plays**.

The words in the side column often (but not always) signal the start of an adjective clause. These words are generally called **relative pronouns** and **relative adverbs**. (Most of these introductory words also function as other parts of speech.)

You can omit an introductory relative pronoun from a sentence if the sentence makes sense and sounds natural without one. Read aloud the sentences below to see for yourself how each sounds without the bracketed word.

Where is the magazine **[that] I left on the table**?
The college advisor is the person **[whom] you should call**.

If an adjective clause adds information that's necessary to the meaning that the writer intends, it is called an **essential clause**. When a sentence has the same meaning without an adjective clause, that clause is a **nonessential clause**. An essential clause does not need commas; a nonessential clause does.

ESSENTIAL CLAUSE (No commas)	NONESSENTIAL CLAUSE (Set off with commas)
Every player **who misses a free throw in practice** runs a lap.	Erin, **who missed two shots in practice**, ran two laps.
Arturo is looking for a lucky towel **that his mother gave him**.	The lucky towel, **which no one has seen**, has been missing for days.
Jackson is the team **that beat us twice last year**.	We are ready for the Jackson players, **who beat us twice last year**.

P.S. You learned about essential and nonessential clauses when you studied appositives in Lesson 7.2. The same rules about commas apply to adjective clauses. In other textbooks, you may hear the term *nonrestrictive* used for *nonessential* and *restrictive* used for *essential*. These terms are synonyms.

Some Words That Introduce Adjective Clauses

Relative Pronouns

that	which
who	whom
whose	whoever

Relative Adverbs

when	where

TEST-TAKING TIP

If you recognize an adjective clause in a test item, ask yourself if the phrase or clause is essential to the meaning of the sentence. If it is not, the correct answer will use commas to set off the nonessential structure. See item 7 on page 340.

EXERCISE 3 Identifying Adjective Clauses

Underline the adjective clauses in the sentences below. **Hint:** Not every sentence has an adjective clause. Write *None* if the sentence does not have an adjective clause.

1. The calabash, which grows on a vine, is an oddly shaped gourd.

2. The gourd, which comes in a variety of colors and textures, has a hard rind.

3. East African women, whose gardens produce calabashes, make several useful household items out of them.

4. From calabashes, they make eating utensils, toys, and musical instruments.

5. The women scoop out a calabash's insides and leave it in the sun, where it dries and hardens.

6. The next step is to decorate the calabash.

7. The decorator, whoever she is, has several choices to make.

8. She may simply stain the outer skin with vegetable dyes and then polish it to create a rich sheen.

9. Some women turn the gourd over to a craftsperson, who carves or burns decorations into its surface.

10. The designs may be purely geometric patterns, or they may show figures that represent familiar stories or proverbs.

EXERCISE 4 Writing Sentences with Adjective Clauses

Can you see into the future? Picture yourself—or perhaps a friend or classmate—ten years from now. What will you be doing? Where and how will you be living? On a separate piece of paper, write a descriptive paragraph that contains your predictions (or your hopes) for what your life will be like in ten years. In your paragraph, include at least three adjective clauses, and underline them.

Adverb Clauses

▐▐▐▶ An **adverb clause** is a subordinate clause that functions as an adverb. It modifies a verb, an adjective, or another adverb.

Adverb clauses, like adverbs, tell *how, how much, when, where, why, to what extent,* or *under what circumstances.* A comma always follows an introductory adverb clause.

> **Whenever he has time**, he practices the piano. [The clause modifies the verb *practices*; it tells *when* or *to what extent*.]

> He'll practice daily **unless there are too many other things to do**. [The clause modifies the adverb *daily*; it tells *under what circumstances*.]

> He was completely satisfied with his progress **after he'd played the piece several times**. [The clause modifies the adjective *satisfied*; it tells *when*.]

When the words in the side column signal the beginning of an adverb clause, they are called **subordinating conjunctions**.

An **elliptical adverb clause** omits some words. In the following examples, the bracketed words can be left out.

> Juan is younger **than Maria [is]**.
> I'm more concerned about the essay part of the test **than you are [worried about the essay part]**.
> Have you ever met anyone as funny **as Laura [is]**?

Some Words That Introduce Adverb Clauses (Subordinating Conjunctions)

after	so that
although	than
as	though
as long as	unless
as soon as	until
as though	when
because	whenever
before	where
even though	wherever
if	whether
since	while

TEST-TAKING TIP

Pay special attention to elliptical adverb clauses when they appear in test items, especially when they contain the comparisons *better than, more than,* or *as large as.* Ask yourself if the adverb clause makes better sense with the addition of a subject or verb. See item 7 on page 335.

EXERCISE 5 Identifying Adverb Clauses

Underline each adverb clause in the sentences below. Be sure to insert a comma after each introductory adverb clause. **Hint:** Not every sentence has an adverb clause. Write *None* if the sentence does not have an adverb clause.

1. When Sojourner Truth was enslaved her name was

   Isabella Baumfree.

2. One day, she took her youngest son and escaped to freedom.

3. After she changed her name she began her campaign against slavery.

4. She chose the name Sojourner Truth because she wanted to become a

   traveler spreading the truth.

5. Although Sojourner Truth was never taught to read or write she expressed her wisdom powerfully in her speeches.

6. She encouraged other formerly enslaved people when she heard them give gloomy speeches.

7. Wherever she spoke she had a profound effect on her audience.

8. Even though she was mistreated and often beaten Sojourner Truth kept up her fight.

9. While she worked as a nurse during the Civil War she urged President Lincoln to enlist free African Americans to fight in the Union Army.

10. Sojourner Truth continued to fight for equality and for women's rights after the Civil War ended.

Working Together

EXERCISE 6 Writing Sentences with Adverb Clauses

Work with a partner or small group to write a brief biography of Harriet Tubman based on the notes provided below. Your audience is seventh graders. Use adverb clauses to enrich your writing. Add details if you know them. When you have finished your draft, underline all of the adverb clauses you have used.

> Called Black Moses; born enslaved on plantation in Maryland
> Born in 1820; died in 1913
> Escaped before being sent farther south
> Returned several times to help other family members escape
> Used safe houses and hiding places of "Underground Railroad" to make 19 rescue trips
> Led more than 300 African Americans to freedom as "railroad conductor"
> $40,000 offered by slave owners for her capture; was never caught
> Received many honors, including medal from Queen Victoria of England
> Given a modest government pension for Civil War nursing services; used it to help establish home for destitute freed African Americans

Noun Clauses

▶ A **noun clause** is a subordinate clause that functions as a noun.

A noun clause, like a noun, can function as a subject, predicate nominative, direct object, indirect object, or object of a preposition. In the following examples, notice that noun clauses can have modifiers and complements. Like nouns, noun clauses can appear at the beginning, middle, or end of a sentence.

Some Words That Introduce Noun Clauses

how	which
if	who
that	whoever
what	whom
whatever	whomever
when	whose
where	why
whether	

> **Whatever you do** will be appreciated. [subject]
> This is exactly **what I was looking for**. [predicate nominative]
> I understood **why the play closed**. [direct object]
> He will tell **whoever will listen** stories about his pet pig. [indirect object]
> The committee gave a prize to **whomever entered the contest**. [object of preposition]

See the side column for a list of words that can introduce a noun clause. Sometimes, a noun clause's introductory word is understood.

> Some listeners said **[that] Lincoln had a high voice**.
> Lincoln did not think **[that] his Gettysburg Address would be so successful**.

EXERCISE 7 Writing Sentences with Noun Clauses

On a separate piece of paper, write a sentence using each group of words as a noun clause. Exchange papers with a partner to check that you have written a noun clause, not an adjective or an adverb clause.

1. that the hardest part of the test was over
2. what we have been shown
3. what I mean
4. whether we'll get to the game on time
5. whom the critics praise
6. whoever wins the World Series
7. how to program a DVD player
8. why electric cars are in our future
9. that she is a soprano
10. whoever visits the site

EDITING TIP

Make sure that omitting an introductory word won't lead to a misreading.

Do people believe **that** the government has their best interests at heart?

Without the word *that*, a reader might think that *the government* is an object of *believe* when it really is a subject of a clause.

Working Together

EXERCISE 8 Revising a Biology Report

Work with a partner to revise the following report. Express the ideas as clearly and directly as possible. Eliminate wordiness and repetition. When you finish, underline all the noun clauses that remain or that you've added. Compare your response with those made by other pairs.

Ponds and Lakes

¹What I have learned is that the study of inland waters is called *limnology*. ²Limnology is a division of the broader science of ecology, which is the study of how animals and plants coexist in an environment. ³Limnologists concern themselves with the factors that affect the inland water environment, that create and maintain the conditions that support life in that environment of inland waters. ⁴Limnologists would say to whoever would be interested that they focus not only on biology but also on geography, chemistry, weather, and climate.

⁵According to the science of limnology, a pond is different from a lake. ⁶What a pond is is a quiet, shallow body of water that sustains the growth of rooted plants on its bottom and along its shore. ⁷Ponds have uniform water temperatures from their wave-free tops to their mud-filled bottoms. ⁸Pond temperatures change with changes in the air temperature.

⁹Lakes are different from ponds. ¹⁰Lakes are larger than ponds. ¹¹Lakes have water. ¹²The water is too deep for plant growth, except around the shore. ¹³That is what limnologists say. ¹⁴Water temperatures in lakes stay relatively stable from day to day. ¹⁵Lakes that are where there are often low temperatures have what limnologists call "temperature layering" in the summer. ¹⁶Whoever knows their lakes knows that when such a large expanse of water is exposed to the wind, the shores downwind are washed with waves, unlike ponds.

Four Types of Sentence Structure

We classify sentences according to the number and kind of clauses they have. You need to know about the four types of sentence structures so that your paragraphs and longer papers offer variety to the reader.

▶ A **simple sentence** has one independent clause and no subordinate clauses.

Simple sentences are not necessarily short and uncomplicated. A simple sentence may have a compound subject (s), a compound verb (v), and many different phrases.

>   S
> The origin of the word *patsy*, like the origin of many English words and
>   V
> phrases, is not clear.

▶ A **compound sentence** has two or more independent clauses and no subordinate clauses.

>   S   V   S
> Some dictionaries list the source of *patsy* as "origin unknown"; it
>   V
> comes from the Italian word *pazzo*, or "fool."

▶ A **complex sentence** has one independent clause and at least one subordinate clause.

>   S   V   S   V   S
> The term *slapstick* comes from *slapsticks*, which were two sticks that
>   V
> could create a loud noise.

▶ A **compound-complex sentence** has two or more independent clauses and at least one subordinate clause.

>   S   V   S V
> Hubbard Keary invented the word *smog*, which is a blend of *smoke*
>   S
> and *fog*, during a winter of pollution in Des Moines, and it first
>   V
> appeared in a newspaper headline.

WRITING HINT

A complex sentence with the same subordinator before and after a main clause sounds bogged down. Try to add variety.

If you keep trying, your writing will improve ~~if you~~ , so make a special effort.

EXERCISE 9 Identifying Sentence Structure

The sentences on the following page are about word and phrase origins. Identify the sentence structure of each sentence. On the blank before each numbered item, write *S* for simple, *Cd* for compound, *Cx* for complex, and *Cd-Cx* for compound-complex.

_____ 1. Since *ante* means "before" in Latin and *bellum* means "war," *antebellum* simply means "before war."

_____ 2. *Antebellum*, in the United States, refers to the pre–Civil War period; in Great Britain, it refers to periods before the Boer War and both world wars.

_____ 3. *Apartheid*, which was the South African policy of segregation, derived from two Dutch words—*apart*, meaning the same as the English word, and *heid*, meaning "hood."

_____ 4. Theories about the origin of April Fool's Day, the day for pranks, abound.

_____ 5. One account traces April Fool's Day to Roman mythology; another links it to the time when the Gregorian calendar, which is the one we use today, replaced the Julian one.

_____ 6. Abraham Lincoln, who attended a *blab school*, learned his lessons by reciting them over and over, in unison, with his classmates.

_____ 7. The expression *bite the bullet* comes from the medical profession.

_____ 8. During surgery, when no anesthesia was available, wounded soldiers bit on bullets to deal with their pain.

_____ 9. The first *blazers* belonged to some Cambridge students in England in the nineteenth century and were of a bright, blazing red color.

_____ 10. *Levis* derive their name from Levi Strauss, the gold rush clothing merchant; he added rivets to the corners of pockets to prevent tearing when the miners filled them with ore.

EXERCISE 10 Expanding Sentences

Expand each of the following simple sentences by making up interesting details. After each new sentence you write, identify its structure by adding *S* for simple, *Cd* for compound, *Cx* for complex, and *Cd-Cx* for compound-complex sentence structure. Compare your expanded sentences with those of a partner or small group.

EXAMPLE   Jerome is seven years old.
            Jerome, who is seven years old, can stand on his head and recite poetry. Cx

1. Tamika enjoys poetry.

2. Walt Whitman is her favorite poet.

3. Carlos prefers comics.

4. He has a collection of comic books.

5. Patrick is a couch potato.

6. He watches TV programs.

7. Patrick likes watching commercials.

8. Margaret listens to music.

9. She wears her new headphones.

10. She can't hear her friends.

Effective Sentences: Parallel Structure

▐▌▶ To achieve parallel structure, use the same grammatical structure for two or more similar ideas.

NOT PARALLEL   I enjoy **beef**, **chicken**, and **eating fish**. [After the verb, the first two items are nouns, but the third is a gerund phrase.]

PARALLEL   I enjoy **beef**, **chicken**, and **fish**. [All three items are nouns.]

The principle of parallelism applies to clauses.

NOT PARALLEL   The teacher said **that I should write more** and **to talk less**.

PARALLEL   The teacher said **that I should write more** and **that I should talk less**.

PARALLEL   The teacher said **to write more** and **to talk less**.

▐▌▶ Use parallel structure with correlative constructions such as *both . . . and*, *either . . . or*, and *not only . . . but also*.

NOT PARALLEL   It was *both* **a hot day** *and* **humid**. [The first complement is a noun phrase; the second is an adjective.]

PARALLEL   The day was *both* **hot** *and* **humid**. [two adjectives]

NOT PARALLEL   I want to explain *both* **who I am** *and* **my beliefs**.

PARALLEL   I want to explain *both* **who I am** *and* **what I believe**.

To make your meaning clear in a parallel construction, repeat articles, prepositions, or pronouns whenever necessary.

After the game, I spoke with the coach and team captain.
[Are they the same person?]
After the game, I spoke **with** the coach and **with** the team captain.
[Now it is clear that the coach and captain are two different people.]

TEST-TAKING TIP

Examples of faulty parallelism often appear on standardized tests. When a sentence has a series of subjects, verbs or verb phrases, or other related structures, make sure they each have the same grammatical form. See item 8 on page 335.

EDITING TIP

Readers have trouble with lists—especially a list of instructions—if the items aren't parallel.

Directions for Grandparents' Day at my school:

1. Take bus #3 uptown to 75th St.

2. Walk 2 blocks east. *Ring bell*
3. ~~Bell~~ on main door of building with flag (on right side of street).

EXERCISE 11 Editing Sentences to Create Parallel Structure

On a separate piece of paper, edit each of the following sentences so that it has parallel structure. **Hint:** There is more than one way to edit each one.

1. The landscape of the Middle East shows evidence that humans, over thousands of years, dug canals, created and cultivated fields, and that excavation of materials for building construction took place.

2. Morocco has both Atlantic and Mediterranean coastlines, rugged mountains, and has developed a culture that is a combination of Arab, European, and African influences.

3. Jordan borders Saudi Arabia, Iraq, and it is also a neighbor of Syria.

4. In Egypt, you can see pyramids, you can ride along the Nile, and explore the streets of Cairo.

5. On Israel's Mediterranean beaches, you can try snorkeling and to swim.

6. Aqaba's reef in Jordan is alive with coral, fish, and there is also unique fauna.

7. In Israel, people live in modern cities, in small towns, and they have farms.

8. In Saudi Arabia, you can find schools for the children of American workers and where other students can go, too.

9. Some Americans like to work for oil companies in the Middle East for the high salaries and because they like the lifestyle.

10. Visitors to Middle Eastern countries can visit communities that haven't changed much over time, and ever-changing ones.

Write What You Think

Refer to **Composition**, Lesson 4.3, for strategies for writing persuasively.

Do you agree or disagree with the following statement? Respond by writing a paragraph that not only states your opinion but also offers the reasons you hold your opinion. Make sure to revise and edit your work.

The United States should always do whatever it takes to bring peace to troubled regions of the world.

EXERCISE 12 Parallel Structure

On a separate piece of paper, respond to each question below by giving a three-part answer. Then exchange papers with a partner, and check each other's answers for three parallel structures.

EXAMPLE   What did you wash last weekend?
Last weekend, I washed the car that went through many storms, the dog that played in a puddle, and the laundry that had piled up in my room.

1. What do you see when you look around the room you are now in?

2. What do you hear when you listen to the sounds in the room?

3. What are your goals?

4. What would you like to learn more about?

5. What would you consider a good summer job?

6. Why do you go to school?

7. Why do you or don't you look forward to your birthday?

8. Why are holidays important?

Revising and Editing Worksheet 1

Improve the following draft by revising for ideas, organization, word choice, and sentence variety. After revising, edit the draft for errors in spelling, capitalization, punctuation, and usage. Write your revised and edited version on a separate piece of paper. Compare your changes with those of a writing partner.

[1]The two boys had been in Nova Scotia. [2]They were camping there. [3]It was the summer following their senior year. [4]Before they were to pack their bags, go away to college, and seeing less of each other. [5]Ben and Tony had borrowed Ben's father's car. [6]They were lucky to have the car. [7]They filled it with all the camping gear that anyone who went camping where it gets cold which is not unusual in the summer would need. [8]But they didn't know Ben would get sick. [9]He had a fever. [10]While Tony drove them back home. [11]Which was far. [12]Ben simply stayed asleep or half asleep in the backseat.

[13]Late one evening is when they found themselves in a small town in New Brunswick, Canada. [14]Niether had been there before. [15]It was raining. [16]It was cold. [17]It would be too much trouble to set up their tent. [18]Because Ben was sick, they decided to spend some of their remaining money on a hotel room. [19]They found an old one. [20]It was a little shabby. [21]Also it was small.

[22]Late that night, while Tony slept like a baby. [23]Ben was up and down. [24]At about two in the morning, he was up. [25]He was standing at the sink. [26]The sink was in the room. [27]He was soaking his tea shirt in cold water. [28]He planed to hold it against his forehead that felt like it was on fire. [29]Then, suddenly, there was a loud rapping at the door.

[30]"Open up. Its the police." [31]That woke Tony.

[32]"The police!" Ben said. [33]"What do they want?"

[34]He opened the door and let the two officers in. [35]He still had the wet T-shirt in his hands. [36]Tony stood up, too.

[37]"Which one of you is Ben Anker?" [38]The boys looked at each other. [39]They had puzzled looks on their faces.

Revising and Editing Worksheet 2

Improve the following draft by revising for ideas, organization, word choice, and sentence variety. After revising, edit the draft for errors in spelling, capitalization, punctuation, and usage. Write your revised and edited version on a separate piece of paper. Compare your changes with those of a writing partner.

[1]From northern California to southeast Alaska lies an ancient forest. [2]It carpets the land. [3]It is a forest of Douglas fir, red cedars, Sitka spruce, and hemlock. [4]Which are huge trees of spectacular proportions. [5]It rivals any forest on Earth in size and grandeur. [6]It is cool. [7]It is wet. [8]It is forever green. [9]The North American temperate rain forest is where we have treasure that may be in trouble.

[10]You read alot about the severe difficulties facing rain forests that are in tropical parts of the world, which include Central and South America, which you know humankind can not afford to lose. [11]Losing them can jeopardize life on the planet. [12]But the rain forests right here in North America also have significant value. [13]The trees alone are an extraordinary resource. [14]They are a treasure, too. [15]And under the canopy of these great trees lie immense biological resources. [16]For example, their is the wild Pacific yew that, some claim, has been demonstrated to cure certain kinds of cancer. [17]Who knows what else in the way of untapped medical value the forests contain?

[18]Unfortunately, some policies in the United States and Canada have put this region in danjer. [19]Nearly 90 percent of the original forest is gone. [20]Since they explored the forest in the nineteenth century, timber barons have been logging it. [21]Cutting down trees. [22]Eroding and depleting the soil. [23]There has been a disappearance of natural habitat. [24]It has been wholesale. [25]In some parts, industry has protected the forests. [26]But more needs to be done. [27]America's temperate rain forests deserve better.

Chapter Review

EXERCISE A Identifying Independent and Subordinate Clauses

On the blank for each numbered item, write *I* for an independent clause or *S* for a subordinate clause. On a separate sheet of paper, revise every subordinate clause to make it a complete sentence.

EXAMPLE   __*S*__   When someone invented the ballpoint pen.
                       When someone invented the ballpoint pen, sales of fountain pens decreased.

_____ 1. When Pluto was discovered in 1930.

_____ 2. When color cartoon film showed up for the first time in 1932.

_____ 3. In 1933, people first played the game Monopoly.

_____ 4. Because the first mass-market paperback books came out in 1935.

_____ 5. The helicopter, which was a key invention in 1936.

EXERCISE B Identifying Types of Clauses

On the blank for each numbered item, identify the underlined clause in the sentence by writing *ADJ* for adjective clause, *ADV* for adverb clause, or *N* for noun clause.

EXAMPLE   __*ADJ*__   Kathy Waller, who holds the record for the length of an apple peeling, took 11¹/₂ hours to create her peeling.

_____ 1. The record for apple peeling, 172 ft. 4 in., which is held by Kathy Waller, was achieved in 1976.

_____ 2. Greg Mutton must have been extremely tired after he broke the bathtub-racing record in 1987.

_____ 3. When a team from Scotland wheeled a hospital bed 3,233 miles, it broke the bed-pushing record.

_____ 4. The record for brick balancing, which involves balancing bricks on one's head, is seventy-five bricks for nineteen seconds.

_____ 5. After students from a Washington high school had worked eight hours, they had washed a total of 3,844 cars—a record.

_____ 6. What made him do it is a mystery, but V. Jeyaraman clapped his hands for more than fifty-eight hours without stopping.

_____ 7. Tell whomever has a sense of humor that the record for jokes told in one hour is 345.

_____ 8. Even though he may not have liked eating oysters, Mike Racz opened a hundred of them in 2 minutes, 20.07 seconds.

Exercise C Identifying Sentence Structure

Identify the sentence structure of each. On the blank before each number, write *S* for simple, *Cd* for compound, *Cx* for complex, and *Cd-Cx* for compound-complex.

———— 1. If you enjoy listening to the blues, you may know that Jelly Roll Morton first published a blues tune in 1905.

———— 2. Some say that the expression *bring home the bacon* derives from contests for catching greased pigs.

———— 3. The word *brunch* is a blend word; Lewis Carroll's *slithy*, a combination of *slimy* and *lithe*, is another example.

———— 4. Some sources report that *buddy*, meaning "friend," is more than a century old; but other dictionaries, which disagree, claim that it is probably baby talk for "brother."

———— 5. The expression *by the skin of my teeth* comes from the Book of Job in the Bible.

———— 6. When you call someone *every name in the book*, that book is neither the Bible nor the phone book; it is the dictionary.

———— 7. A *can of worms*, which has long been an expression used by people in the advertising business, refers to a problem that is complicated and hard to solve.

———— 8. A person *who can't see the forest for the trees* is concerned with insignificant issues and is unable to grasp the larger problems.

Exercise D Editing to Create Parallel Structure

On a separate piece of paper, edit each sentence so that it has parallel structure.

1. The historical period between the ninth and thirteenth centuries is called the Middle Ages, sometimes the Dark Ages, and it's the Medieval Period.

2. Some scholars describe the period as scientifically undeveloped, backward when it comes to art, and infested by the Black Plague.

3. Other scholars describe the Middle Ages as teeming with ideas, it had exploded with energy, and flowering with regard to economic growth.

4. Gothic cathedrals, originating in the Middle Ages, are both astonishingly tall and brilliant in lighting.

5. Students at the universities in Paris that began during the Middle Ages learned what the great philosophers wrote, to recite the Church teachings, and arguing for their ideas.

Cumulative Review

EXERCISE A Identifying Parts of Speech

On the blank before each number, identify the part of speech of each underlined word as it is used in the sentence. Use these abbreviations:

N = noun   ADJ = adjective   CONJ = conjunction
PRON = pronoun   ADV = adverb   INTER = interjection
V = verb   PREP = preposition

_____ 1. In the world of <u>camping</u>, there are several kinds of tents.

_____ 2. The largest is the <u>family</u> tent.

_____ 3. Several tents come <u>with</u> canopies.

_____ 4. <u>Some</u> even have windows.

_____ 5. Guy ropes attached to stakes <u>stabilize</u> the tents.

_____ 6. The guy ropes <u>attach</u> to the grommets on the tent roofs.

_____ 7. Some tents have mud walls and sewn-in <u>floors</u>.

_____ 8. Have you ever slept <u>peacefully</u> in a pup tent?

_____ 9. A dome tent looks like but is <u>not</u> a pop-up tent.

_____ 10. Other types of tents include Baker tents, tourist tents, wall tents, <u>and</u> wagon tents.

EXERCISE B Identifying Phrases

On the blank before each numbered item, identify the underlined phrase by writing one of these abbreviations in the space provided:

PREP = prepositional phrase   INF = infinitive phrase
PART = participial phrase   APP = appositive phrase
GER = gerund phrase

_____ 1. Ms. Miller, <u>the French teacher</u>, is a gourmet cook.

_____ 2. Mr. Ruben tried <u>playing the bagpipes</u>.

_____ 3. Mr. Angelos, <u>the soccer coach</u>, has a pilot's license.

_____ 4. <u>In the summer of 1998</u>, Ms. Scott hiked on the Appalachian Trail for thirty-nine days.

_____ 5. The science teacher, <u>Ms. Jackson</u>, has a tree farm <u>in Vermont</u>.

_____ 6. Mr. Wong, the art teacher, was the first person from our school <u>to display his artwork</u> at the museum.

_____ 7. The new social studies teacher was immediately a favorite <u>with her students</u>.

_____ 8. When you get a compliment <u>from Ms. Feldstein</u>, you never forget it.

_____ 9. <u>Working through the weekend</u>, Mr. Gonzales and Ms. Reilly got everything ready for the science fair.

_____ 10. This spring, Ms. Mann plans on <u>accompanying the senior class</u> to Italy.

EXERCISE C Identifying Clauses

On the blank before each numbered item, identify the underlined clause in each sentence by writing _ADJ_ for adjective clause, _ADV_ for adverb clause, or _N_ for noun clause.

_____ 1. The Negro baseball leagues, <u>which were founded in 1920</u>, came to an end when the major leagues were integrated.

_____ 2. <u>Before these leagues were formed</u>, independent teams made up of black players competed with one another.

_____ 3. For the most part, <u>wherever the Negro baseball leagues played</u>, crowds showed enthusiasm.

_____ 4. Players such as Josh Gibson, Oscar Charleston, and Buck Leonard, <u>who were Negro league stars</u>, never played in the major leagues.

_____ 5. <u>Whatever went on in Negro league baseball</u> was largely ignored by the white communities.

_____ 6. <u>Although it was ignored by the white community</u>, Negro league baseball was a major attraction in the black communities.

_____ 7. The Eastern Colored League, <u>which lasted from 1923 to 1928</u>, was one of several Negro baseball leagues.

_____ 8. Any fan could see <u>how some of the black ballplayers excelled</u>.

_____ 9. Jackie Robinson, <u>who was the first person to break the color barrier</u>, soon had black colleagues in the majors.

_____ 10. <u>After the best Negro league players joined Major League teams in the early 1950s</u>, all the Negro leagues began to fold.

Using Verbs

STUDENT WRITING
Persuasive Essay

Refugees Still Wait for Change
by Gene Liu
high school student, San Francisco, California

The Universal Declaration of Human Rights, hailed as the "Magna Carta for humanity," turns fifty this year, at a time when Americans seem to have strayed from its objective of achieving worldwide freedom and liberty.

In December, I attended the commemoration of the original document—the first comprehensive agreement among nations on the specific freedoms and rights of all human beings. The document included freedom from torture and slavery and freedom of religion, expression, and assembly, as well as the right to education, medical care, and fair trials.

Speakers at the ceremony relayed gruesome accounts of situations overseas where such liberties were absolutely unavailable. The most moving story was about a Bosnian refugee couple captured by ethnic-cleansing Serbian troops in the early 1990s and sent to a concentration camp.

In 1993, the pair escaped with a wave of fugitives to Germany. When their German refugee visas expired . . . the couple came to the United States in hopes of obtaining citizenship here. However, by December, the United States had reached its limit on the number of refugees it accepts per year. The couple faced the daunting reality of deportation.

This case clearly illustrates how the challenges the Declaration addressed fifty years ago have not been met today. Governments continue to persecute, torture, and murder individuals because of religion and ethnicity. At the center of the human rights dilemma is the problem of refugees, who suffer significant abuse to their natural human rights. They are forced to abandon their homes, communities, and countries in fear of persecution and abuse. . . .

[S]tatistics from Amnesty International indicate that most refugees eventually become economically self-sufficient. The human rights organization has found that most refugees do not become lifelong welfare recipients. Finances aside, the bottom line remains: helping refugees escape turmoil and affliction is simply the only humane thing to do. Americans must not turn their backs to the persecuted nor force them to leave because of an inhumane technical detail like a quota.

On this, the Declaration's fiftieth anniversary, I say the most fitting celebration of it would be a public and vigorous renewal of the commitment to the Declaration by the nations that signed it. And we should rededicate ourselves to turning that commitment into reality by doing our part to alleviate the world's refugee problem.

> Gene Liu places the claim for his persuasive essay in his first paragraph. He supports it with specific examples, facts, statistics, and a call to action.
>
> As you reread the essay, notice how Gene changes verb tenses as he shifts from his opinion today to his experiences in the past. Using verb tenses precisely helps your reader understand the progression of your thoughts. As you complete the exercises in this chapter, you'll practice using verbs and verb tenses correctly.

Regular Verbs

||||► All verbs have four basic forms, or **principal parts**: the present, the present participle, the past, and the past participle.

Depending on how a verb forms its past and past participle, it is a regular verb or an irregular verb.

||||► **Regular verbs** add -*d* or -*ed* to the present to form the past and past participle.

Principal Parts of Verbs			
PRESENT	PRESENT PARTICIPLE (Use with *am, is, are, was, were.*)	PAST	PAST PARTICIPLE (Use with *has, had, have.*)
talk	(is) talking	talked	(had) talked
swallow	(is) swallowing	swallowed	(had) swallowed
care	(is) caring	cared	(had) cared

The **present participle** works with a helping verb, a form of the verb *be* (*am, is, are, was,* or *were*), to make a verb phrase.

I **am learning** Greek. Ralph **was learning** French last year.

The **past participle** works with a helping verb, a form of the helping verb *have* (*has, have,* or *had*), to make a verb phrase.

I **have requested** a transfer. Ralph **had requested** one earlier.

Spelling rules require you to drop the final -*e*, change -*y* to *i*, and double consonants under certain conditions: *cope, coping, coped; hurry, hurried; drop, dropping, dropped.* (For more about spelling rules, see Lesson 16.2.)

A few regular verbs have alternate past and past participle forms: *dreamed/has dreamed* or **dreamt/has dreamt**; *burned/has burned* or **burnt/has burnt**; *has proven* or **has proved**.

Exercise 1 Using the Principal Parts of Regular Verbs

To complete each sentence, write on the blank the correct past form or past participle form of the verb in parentheses. Some sentences have more than one verb in parentheses. **Remember:** After a form of the helping verb *have,* use the past participle.

EXAMPLE   In 1900, the Boxers (rebel) _rebelled_ against the Europeans in China, and many other events of interest (occur) **occurred** that year.

Enriching Your Vocabulary

Etymologists think that the verb *taunt,* which is used on the following page and means "to ridicule," comes from the French expression *tant pour tant* which can be translated as "tit for tat." The overconfident boys *taunted* the visiting team until they saw the size of the defensive lineup.

EDITING *TIP*

Remember to use -*d* or -*ed* endings with *used* and *supposed* before an infinitive.

She **used to be** in our class.

Were you **supposed to get** the cake?

1. In 1900, Americans once again (elect)_____ William McKinley as president.

2. Meanwhile, in South Africa, the British and Boers (clash) _____, and war (rage) _____.

3. In 1900, Conrad's novel *Lord Jim* (appear) _____, and so did Chekhov's *Uncle Vanya*.

4. In that same year, American writer Stephen Crane (die) _____.

5. In 1900, Sigmund Freud and Bertrand Russell (introduce) _____ new written works.

6. That year, Picasso (paint) _____ *Le Moulin de la Galette*, and Gauguin (report) _____ on his travels through Tahiti.

7. The births of American composer Aaron Copland and German composer Kurt Weill also (mark) _____ 1900.

8. In 1900, many people had (learn) _____ to dance the cakewalk.

9. It was also the year that F. E. Dorn (discover) _____ radon and R. A. Fessenden first (transmit) _____ human speech using radio waves.

10. During excavations in Crete in 1900, archaeologists (uncover) _____ evidence of an ancient Minoan culture.

 Working Together

Exercise 2 Revising a Story Beginning

Revise the story beginning so that it describes an event that happened in the past. Use the past form and past participle form of the italicized verbs. Compare the original version and your version. Does the story sound better to you in the present tense or in the past tense? Work with a partner or small group to finish the story.

¹The old green Ford *pulls* into the elevated parking area and into a spot right along the edge. ²It *is* all alone; there *are* no other vehicles there. ³Then the car's front doors *open*, and two men in lab coats *appear*. ⁴They slowly *walk* to the edge of the bluff and *look* down at the old covered bridge that *arches* over the swiftly moving stream. ⁵No sounds *disturb* them; nothing *interrupts* their concentration. ⁶A silent breeze *tickles* the leaves. ⁷Then one of the men *points* to a spot on the other side of the stream, just to the left of the bridge. ⁸There, next to the dying elm, they *spot* it. ⁹It *waits* for them, *taunts* them. ¹⁰They *stare* at one another for a moment and then *stroll* down the path to the bridge and across it to the other bank.

Irregular Verbs 1

Irregular verbs do not form their past or past participle by adding *-d* or *-ed* to the present form the way regular verbs do. (See Lesson 9.1.) In some cases, the irregular past and past participle are the same—but not always. This lesson and the next one cover sixty-six irregular verbs that are often used incorrectly.

▆▆▆▶ Use the principal parts of these common irregular verbs correctly when you write or speak.

The most irregular English verb is *be* because it has singular and plural forms in both the present and the past tenses. Notice that the word *be* itself is not one of its principal parts.

Principal Parts of Common Irregular Verbs			
PRESENT	**PRESENT PARTICIPLE** (Use with *am, is, are, was, were*.)	**PAST**	**PAST PARTICIPLE** (Use with *has, had, have*.)
[be] is, are	(is) being	was, were	(had) been
become	(is) becoming	became	(had) become
begin	(is) beginning	began	(had) begun
bite	(is) biting	bit	(had) bitten
blow	(is) blowing	blew	(had) blown
break	(is) breaking	broke	(had) broken
bring	(is) bringing	brought	(had) brought
build	(is) building	built	(had) built
burst	(is) bursting	burst	(had) burst
buy	(is) buying	bought	(had) bought
catch	(is) catching	caught	(had) caught
choose	(is) choosing	chose	(had) chosen
come	(is) coming	came	(had) come
cost	(is) costing	cost	(had) cost
do	(is) doing	did	(had) done
draw	(is) drawing	drew	(had) drawn
drink	(is) drinking	drank	(had) drunk
drive	(is) driving	drove	(had) driven
eat	(is) eating	ate	(had) eaten
fall	(is) falling	fell	(had) fallen
feel	(is) feeling	felt	(had) felt
find	(is) finding	found	(had) found
forget	(is) forgetting	forgot	(had) forgotten; (had) forgot
freeze	(is) freezing	froze	(had) frozen
get	(is) getting	got	(had) gotten; (had) got

▆▆▆▶ Remember that irregular verbs don't end with *-d* or *-ed*.

INCORRECT   The book costed ten dollars at last week's sale.

CORRECT   The book cost ten dollars at last week's sale.

> ## WRITING HINT
>
> When you prepare a résumé or business letter, or when you fill out a job application, check your verbs. Then check them again. People in the business world expect the standard English forms of irregular verbs. They develop negative opinions about people who don't use them.
>
> **RESPONSIBILITIES**
> *brought*
> ~~brung~~ eight-year-olds to camp by bus
>
> *drew*
> ~~drawed~~ the daily schedule on the board

P.S. All dictionaries list the principal parts of irregular verbs. The entry word is in its present form, and the past, past participle, and present participle are listed after the pronunciation or part of speech.

catch (kach) vb **caught, catching**

You can be sure that the verb is a regular verb if only the present verb form appears in a dictionary entry.

EXERCISE 3 Using Irregular Verbs

For each verb in parentheses, write the past form or past participle form as required by the sentence.

HINT

With a form of the helping word *have*, use the past participle.

1. Have the players (bring) ———— their uniforms with them today?

2. Greg thawed the pizza that he had (freeze) ————.

3. Have you (break) ———— the new vase I (buy) ———— yesterday?

4. She had (forget) ———— the steps for parallel parking.

5. Before the hike, we had (drink) ———— our fill.

6. At the car dealer, they (choose) ———— a red convertible.

7. After the beaver had (build) ———— its dam, the wind (blow) ———— a tree down on top of it.

8. The dam (burst) ————, and the water (begin) ———— to flow through it.

9. Have you ever (eat) ———— a flower salad?

10. He was quite surprised when he (bite)———— into the burrito and (feel) ———— something very hard.

11. She had (draw) ———— a map to show where she had (fall)————.

12. Jack had (be) ———— the first in line for the play-off tickets.

13. He (get) ———— four tickets for his efforts.

14. Sherman had (drive) ———— ten miles before he realized that he had (choose) ———— the wrong direction.

15. Larry (catch) ———— a cold just before the performance.

16. Once a tenor, Larry (become) ———— a baritone.

17. As soon as I (come) ———— into the room, Li (find) ———— an excuse to leave.

18. The wind had (blow) ———— over the scarecrow, and the crows were devouring the crop.

19. Julie had (do) ———— her best, but Toni (get) ———— the role.

20. Cal (find) ———— the place where all the lost socks were hiding.

Irregular Verbs 2

To the twenty-five irregular verbs in Lesson 9.2, this lesson adds forty-one more.

IIII▶ Use the principal parts of these common irregular verbs correctly.

Principal Parts of Common Irregular Verbs			
PRESENT	PRESENT PARTICIPLE (Use with *am, is, are, was, were.*)	PAST	PAST PARTICIPLE (Use with *has, had, have.*)
give	(is) giving	gave	(had) given
go	(is) going	went	(had) gone
grow	(is) growing	grew	(had) grown
hold	(is) holding	held	(had) held
hurt	(is) hurting	hurt	(had) hurt
keep	(is) keeping	kept	(had) kept
know	(is) knowing	knew	(had) known
lay [to put or place]	(is) laying	laid	(had) laid
lead	(is) leading	led	(had) led
lend	(is) lending	lent	(had) lent
lie [to rest or recline]	(is) lying	lay	(had) lain
lose	(is) losing	lost	(had) lost
make	(is) making	made	(had) made
meet	(is) meeting	met	(had) met
put	(is) putting	put	(had) put
ride	(is) riding	rode	(had) ridden
ring	(is) ringing	rang	(had) rung
rise	(is) rising	rose	(had) risen
run	(is) running	ran	(had) run
say	(is) saying	said	(had) said
see	(is) seeing	saw	(had) seen
sell	(is) selling	sold	(had) sold
send	(is) sending	sent	(had) sent
set	(is) setting	set	(had) set
show	(is) showing	showed	(had) shown
shrink	(is) shrinking	shrank, shrunk	(had) shrunk, shrunken
sing	(is) singing	sang	(had) sung
sink	(is) sinking	sank, sunk	(had) sunk
sit	(is) sitting	sat	(had) sat
speak	(is) speaking	spoke	(had) spoken
stand	(is) standing	stood	(had) stood
steal	(is) stealing	stole	(had) stolen
swim	(is) swimming	swam	(had) swum
swing	(is) swinging	swung	(had) swung
take	(is) taking	took	(had) taken
tell	(is) telling	told	(had) told
think	(is) thinking	thought	(had) thought
throw	(is) throwing	threw	(had) thrown
wear	(is) wearing	wore	(had) worn
win	(is) winning	won	(had) won
write	(is) writing	wrote	(had) written

EDITING TIP

Watch out for three troublesome pairs of verbs: *lay, lie; raise, rise;* and *sit, set.* The direct object test below can help.

WITH DIRECT OBJECTS
The chicken **lays** an egg.

I **raise** my hand.

I **set** the table.

WITHOUT DIRECT OBJECTS
I **lie** down.

I **rise** early.

I **sit** down.

EXERCISE 4 Using Irregular Verbs

On a separate piece of paper, write the past form or past participle form for each verb in parentheses as required by the sentence.

1. People in southern Louisiana and other places have (grow) used to the taste of hot pepper sauces.
2. Hot sauce sales have (rise) to $180 million yearly.
3. Vendors have (show) as many as twenty hot sauces at the national food festival.
4. Inez (ride) twenty miles just to buy a particular hot sauce.
5. When Gordon tried a red savina, the hottest pepper on Earth, the hair (stand) up on his head.

EXERCISE 5 Revising and Editing a Paragraph

Cross out any incorrect verb, and write the correct one above it. Make any other changes you think will improve the letter.

[1]As president of the senior class, I have speaked to you often of my concern that not enough of us are fluent in a second language. [2]I regret that we have fell short of my goal to be the first totally bilingual graduating class.

[3]You know why I'm pushing language study. [4]The world has shrinked. [5]The pendulum has swinged. [6]The economies of the world have became one global economy, and we have feeled the results of other countries' politics.

[7]Many young people in the world have meeted the challenge of speaking two or more languages. [8]Too many of us up until now have throwed away an opportunity to study languages. [9]My older friends in this state and others have tell me of trouble in getting jobs because of their language handicap.

[10]They originally sayed, "English has become a universal language, so everyone can understand me." [11]But then they comed to see that young Americans with two languages have took the better full-time and part-time jobs. [12]If you have hurted yourself up to now, it's not too late to sign up for summer language school.

Verb Tense

A **verb tense** expresses the time an action was performed.

Verbs have three **simple tenses** (present, past, and future) and three **perfect tenses** (present perfect, past perfect, and future perfect).

The Six Verb Tenses		
TENSE	WHAT IT SHOWS	EXAMPLE
Present	action happening in the present; action that happens repeatedly	I **start**. The tide **rises** and **falls**.
Past	action completed in the past	I **started**.
Future	action that will happen in the future	I **shall start**. I **will start**.
Present perfect	action completed recently or in indefinite past	I **have started.**
Past perfect	action that happened before another action	I **had started** before they arrived.
Future perfect	action that will happen before a future action or time	By the time you return, I **will have started**.

Each verb tense also has a **progressive form**, to show ongoing action.

The Progressive Forms for the Six Tenses	
PROGRESSIVE FORM	EXAMPLE
Present progressive	(**am**, **is**, **are**) **starting**
Past progressive	(**was**, **were**) **starting**
Future progressive	**will be starting**; **shall be starting**
Present perfect progressive	(**has**, **have**) **been starting**
Past perfect progressive	**had been starting**
Future perfect progressive	**will have been starting; shall have been starting**

One more verb form is the **emphatic form**, which takes the word *do*:

I **do** start on time every day. He **does** start on time.
She **did** start on time.

Keep verb tenses consistent whenever possible.

ORIGINAL Ed walked into the strange room. He has no idea what he is looking at.

CONSISTENT Ed **walked** into the strange room. He **had** no idea what he **was looking** at.

WRITING HINT

Professional writers in the humanities follow the style of the Modern Language Association and use the present tense when reporting research.

In his 1998 book, Harold Bloom **credits** Shakespeare with teaching us human behavior.

Writers in the sciences follow the style of the American Psychological Association and use the past or present perfect.

Jones **studied** and **wrote** about the effect of peers on teenagers.

EDITING TIP

Avoid awkward or complicated verb forms by looking for simpler ways to express yourself.

They had wanted ~~to have surprised~~ *to surprise* their dad.

If I ~~would have~~ *had* slept more, I'd be less cranky.

Of course, sometimes the meaning requires you to shift tenses.

> Erin **left** late for work this morning; her boss **will return** tomorrow.
> None of us **have been** to the new mall, but everyone **wants** to go.

EXERCISE 6 Using Verb Tenses

Replace the italicized verbs with the past or past perfect forms to show actions completed in the past.

¹In 1868, the plastic industry *begins* in America. ²Plastic *substitutes* for ivory, which *is* in short supply. ³A billiard ball manufacturer *offers* a huge cash award for a substitute material for ivory, from which he *makes* billiard balls. ⁴John Wesley Hyatt, a printer from Albany, New York, *comes up* with a product he *calls* "celluloid." ⁵Actually, Hyatt *doesn't invent* the product himself; he *produces* it from a compound that a British professor *invents* about eighteen years earlier. ⁶Hyatt *buys* the patent rights to the professor's product and *manufactures* it in the United States. ⁷Celluloid, the world's first plastic, *becomes* a household word in America by 1890.

EXERCISE 7 Using Progressive Verb Forms

Replace the italicized verbs in the paragraph to show ongoing action. Use the clues in the parentheses after each sentence.

¹Look at Luis over there; he *eats* a bag of potato chips. (present progressive) ²In fact he *polished off* the bag the last time I looked. (past progressive) ³If he hasn't already finished, he *finishes* very soon. (future progressive) ⁴I'll bet that while he *munches* those chips, he is not aware that the potato chip is America's favorite snack food. (present progressive) ⁵I'll bet also that Luis, who *was eating* potato chips nearly all his life, is unaware that the chip was invented by accident by a chef in Saratoga, New York. (present perfect progressive) ⁶The chef, who *had made* a batch of French fries for customers at his restaurant, purposely made them too thin for one difficult diner. (past perfect progressive) ⁷But the diner loved them, and millions of others *have loved* them since! (present perfect progressive)

Using the Active Voice

Verbs have voice—either the active voice or the passive voice.

▮▮▮▶ When a verb is in the **active voice**, the subject of the sentence performs an action. When a verb is in the **passive voice**, the subject receives an action.

A verb in the passive voice always involves a form of the helping verb *be*.

ACTIVE	Corrine **collected** the mail.
PASSIVE	The mail **was collected** by Corrine.
ACTIVE	Corrine **collects** the mail in the morning.
PASSIVE	The mail **is collected** in the morning by Corrine.
ACTIVE	Corrine **has thrown** out the junk mail.
PASSIVE	The junk mail **has been thrown** out by Corrine.

▮▮▮▶ When you write, use the active voice whenever you can.

Effective writers prefer the active voice because it is stronger and more economical. Writers use the passive voice, however, when they don't know the performer of the action or when they want to emphasize the action, not the performer.

The stadium **was filled** to capacity with excited fans. [The receiver of the action, not the performer, is emphasized.]
The murder **was committed** on the deserted island after dark. [The performer of the action is unknown.]

WRITING HINT

Readers can see through attempts to spare performers of the action from blame by not naming them—as in the famous phrase "Mistakes were made." Try to restrict passive voice to instances when it's fair *not* to focus on the performer. Here's an example from science writing:

Ideas taken as truths **have been put** to rest by new findings about dinosaurs. For example, evidence **has been** found that contradicts earlier theories about dinosaurs' locomotion.

EXERCISE 8 Using the Active Voice

On a separate piece of paper, rewrite the sentences to use the active voice whenever possible. If the passive voice is acceptable, explain why.

EXAMPLES   The novel *Silas Marner* was written by George Eliot.
George Eliot wrote the novel Silas Marner.

The archaeopteryx, an extinct bird, was discovered in Germany.
Keep the passive voice. The performer is not as important as the discovery itself.

1. In 1861, the state of Kansas was formed.

2. *Great Expectations* was written by Charles Dickens in 1861.

3. The Opera House in Paris was designed by Charles Garnier.

4. Daily weather forecasts were begun in Great Britain.

5. In 1862, Forts Henry and Donelson were captured by Union forces under Grant.

6. In that same year, *Les Misérables* was penned by Victor Hugo.

7. In London, the Albert Memorial was designed by Gilbert Scott.

8. In 1863, Mexico City was captured by the French.

9. New Zealand's first railroad was opened.

10. Pasteurization was invented by Louis Pasteur in 1864.

EXERCISE 9 Revising a Paragraph

On a separate piece of paper, improve the following paragraph by changing as many verbs as possible into the active voice. If you leave some examples of passive voice, be ready to explain why. Combine sentences, creating subordinate clauses or phrases as you revise.

[1]A comeback has been made by the moose. [2]According to the *New York Times*, in 1900 in America, "Moose had been all but wiped out in much of their range by hunting and by conversion of their forest habitat to farms. [3]Now hunting is tightly controlled, and many of the farms have reverted to forest." [4]The newspaper report goes on to say, "Natural predators like wolves have been eliminated from much of the north woods." [5]But the most important reason for the comeback is that logged forests have been replaced by young second-growth forests. [6]The moose have been provided a bountiful food supply by the new forests. [7]The population of moose in the northern part of the continent has been tripled in the last fifty years. [8]In northern Maine alone, the number of moose has been increased fifteen times from the number a hundred years ago. [9]Moose sighting is now popular, and moose have a reputation for tolerating humans near them. [10]But they should be approached with caution at all times.

Mood

▥▶ The **mood** of a verb shows the speaker's or writer's *intent*—whether to state a fact, opinion, or inquiry; to make a request or to command; or to state a wish, requirement, or condition contrary to fact.

Most speakers and writers have no problem with two of the three moods—the indicative and the imperative—which account for most of the verbs used in everyday communication.

▥▶ The **indicative mood** states a fact, an opinion, or a question.
The baseball team **practices** during spring training.
She **believes** the team's manager **does** not **get** enough credit.
What **does** she **think** of the Yankees?

▥▶ The **imperative mood** gives a direct command or request.
Practice bunting and hitting to the opposite field.
Please **pick** me up at six for the game.

Using the third mood—the subjunctive—can cause problems, perhaps because it occurs in English relatively infrequently, usually only in formal speaking and writing.

▥▶ The **subjunctive mood** states a wish, requirement, or condition contrary to fact.

In a *that* clause expressing a requirement, necessity, or wish, the subjunctive calls for using the infinitive form of a verb without the word *to*. Use this form whether the subject is singular or plural.
It is necessary **that** the batter **improve** his statistics.
The manager insists **that** the batter **practice** bunts.
The manager requests **that** the pitcher **be** on time.
My goal is **that** he **become** a better pitcher.

In a wish or a contrary-to-fact clause beginning with the word *if*, the subjunctive calls for using *were* instead of *was* whether the subject is singular or plural.
I wish I **were** a better catcher.
If he **were** a better pitcher, I'd be a better catcher. [This is an example of a contrary-to-fact clause; he is *not* a better pitcher.]

P.S. Don't let these terms—*indicative, imperative,* and *subjunctive*—intimidate you. With a little practice, you'll learn to use the subjunctive as easily as the other two moods.

Enriching Your Vocabulary

The Latin word *imperare* means "to command" and is the root of the word *imperative*, meaning "necessary or commanding." It is *imperative* that the driver's ed teacher know how to change a tire.

EDITING TiP

Not all *if* clauses deal with contrary-to-fact matters; some *if* clauses deal with facts and so require the indicative mood, not the subjunctive mood.

If that cake **was** fattening, the french fries were even more so.

EXERCISE 10 Using the Indicative and the Subjunctive

Based on the contexts that sentences 1–5 provide, fill in the blank with an indicative or subjunctive form of a verb of your own choice. For sentences 6–10, choose between *were* and *was*.

EXAMPLE   Ed's parents suggested that she ___*hire*___ a tutor.

1. Her parents urged that she _____ a part-time job.

2. The teacher suggested that the student _____ a computer.

3. The coach recommends that the captain _____ his attitude.

4. The coach thinks the captain _____ self-centered.

5. The teacher's goal is that the student _____ better.

6. If I _____ a billionaire, I'd give money to charity.

7. If he _____ a friend, he'd help me out.

8. If the movie _____ so bad, maybe you'll trust reviews from now on.

9. If the movie _____ available, I'd rent it.

10. At noon I heard that he _____ in the school building.

EXERCISE 11 Editing a Paragraph

On a separate piece of paper, improve the following paragraph by changing, as necessary, some indicative forms of verbs to subjunctive forms.

   [1]Whether she's dreaming or not, my friend claims that she has been granted two wishes that will come true. [2]First of all, she wishes that each individual stops bickering with others. [3]Then her goal is that each person picks a non-profit organization to help. [4]She thinks it is necessary that each of us takes an active role in making our own piece of the world better. [5]If she was able to improve the whole world with her two wishes, she would.

EXERCISE 12 Writing Sentences with the Subjunctive

Write a paragraph telling what a friend wishes for himself or herself or for the world. Make sure the sentences are related to one another so that they make a sensible paragraph. Limit yourself to the following sentence structures, and use the subjunctive mood:

   My friend wishes that _____.

   He (*or* She) insists that _____.

   For him (*or* her), it is necessary that _____.

   His (*or* her) goal is that _____.

Revising and Editing Worksheet 1

Improve the following draft by revising for ideas, organization, word choice, and sentence variety. After revising, edit the draft for errors in spelling, capitalization, punctuation, and usage. Write your revised and edited version on a separate piece of paper. Compare your changes with those of a writing partner.

[1]On the ceiling of the Sistine Chapel in rome, the Italian artist Michelangelo has painted in the early sixteenth century a handshake. [2]The handshake, a custom of greeting, has originated nearly five thousand years ago. [3]It begun in ancient egypt. [4]Where it was symbolizing the transfer of authority from a god to a king. [5]In fact, the Egyptian hieroglyph for the verb "to give" had been a picture of an extended hand.

[6]About four thousand years ago, in Babylonia, kings were required to grasp the hands of a statue of Marduk. [7]Marduk was being that civilizations chief god. [8]This act was taken place every year during the New Year's festivities. [9]It serves to provide that king with power for another year. [10]This practice catched on. [11]When the Assyrians conquered Babylonia, their kings, to, were adopting that ritual. [12]They have no interest in offending any gods.

[13]Some folklorists claim that the handshake has far earlier origins. [14]They say that the right hand, the one used in a handshake, was traditionally the one in which men holded there weapons. [15]When strangers are content that they were in no danger, they put away their weapons and will have extended their right hands as a symbol of good will. [16]This explanation is making sense for another reason. [17]It explains why women, who were rarely the warriors, never, until recently, have been developing the custom of shakeing hands.

Revising and Editing Worksheet 2

Improve the following draft by revising for ideas, organization, word choice, and sentence variety. After revising, edit the draft for errors in spelling, capitalization, punctuation, and usage. Write your revised and edited version on a separate piece of paper. Compare your changes with those of a writing partner.

¹Throughout the decade of the twenties, one dance craze after another taked the country by storm. ²The most popular of those dances was the Charleston.

³Music scholars have traced the origins of the Charleston back to Africa, where the dances of the Ashanti people have featured similar movements in their dances. ⁴In the American South, a dance known as the Jay-Bird and the Juba dances of plantation times had been similar to the Charleston. ⁵Charleston steps were done in Haiti, to, according to anthropologists. ⁶Judging from it's name, its likely that the version of the dance that arrived in New York had came by way of Charleston, South Carolina.

⁷The Charleston was first introduced in the musical *Lisa*. ⁸But it didn't gain popularity until the hit song "Charleston" was wrote for the 1923 musical *Runnin' Wild*. ⁹The Charleston will have featured whole-body shimmying movements, forward and backward fast-kicking steps, and slapping hands on the knees. ¹⁰Audiences never saw these complex rhythms danced before. ¹¹The Charleston had been causeing a sensation.

¹²People raced to learn the Charleston. ¹³Dance studios couldnt keep up with the demand for lessons. ¹⁴People from all walks of life, including the Duke of Windsor, learn the dance. ¹⁵In fact, one lingering image of the Roaring Twenties is that of young women with short "bobbed" haircuts, wearing fringed skirts, dancing the Charleston. ¹⁶Because the dance has required the birdlike flapping of all four limbs, these women become known as flappers.

¹⁷There were other dance crazes at that time, both in the United States and in Europe. ¹⁸But none equaled the popularity of the Charleston.

Chapter Review

EXERCISE A Using Irregular Verbs

Write the form of the verb in parentheses that correctly completes the sentence.

EXAMPLE   The debate (*begin*) on time. **began**

1. When Jana (bite) into the pie, she found a surprise.
2. Have you (eat) lunch yet?
3. I (feel) bad when there were no more chocolates left.
4. Alfredo (buy) that tennis racquet at a yard sale.
5. Len hit the ball right at her; she should have (catch) it.
6. Yesterday, we (drive) the whole way home without stopping.
7. The bagels had been (freeze) and had to thaw.
8. He lived nearby and (be) the first to arrive.
9. I (find) the earring I thought I had lost.
10. When the skyscraper was (build), it was the tallest structure in the city.
11. Have you (choose) the outfit you're going to wear?
12. Barbara (give) it her best shot.
13. The plant (grow) best when we placed it on the windowsill.
14. We (know) that no one would eat the cauliflower dip.
15. She (lend) her tape recorder to Iris.
16. He (lie) on the couch and finished his book.
17. Then he (lay) the book on the coffee table.
18. The fortunes of the team (sink) when the pitcher got injured.
19. Have you (speak) to Ben since Monday?
20. I (wear) my lucky sweater to the finals last week.

EXERCISE B Using Verb Tenses

Change the italicized verb to the verb tense specified in parentheses. You may refer to the charts in Lesson 9.4. Write your answers on a separate piece of paper.

1. James *eat* all his vegetables before he started in on his beef. (past perfect)
2. Sheila *finish* her homework and now can begin calling her friends. (present perfect)

3. The two girls were dismayed when they noticed that they *wear* the same dress. (past progressive)

4. Next week, all students *take* the achievement tests. (future)

5. We *sit* right behind two people with big hair. (past)

6. While we *wait* impatiently, he *take* his time. (past progressive)

7. Although she *write* all along, the letters never arrived. (past perfect progressive)

8. By next Tuesday, I *show* my paintings to all the art teachers. (future perfect)

9. Alex *run* the marathon for ten years. (present perfect progressive)

10. Alex *lose* last year's race to a future Olympian. (past)

EXERCISE C Revising and Editing a Paragraph

Improve the paragraph below on a separate piece of paper. Decide on a tense to use, and make the verbs consistent throughout. Use the active voice whenever possible, and make any other verb changes you think will improve the paragraph.

¹Have computers becoming too hard to use? ²This is what some psychologists think. ³They believe the home computer is too complicated because it is trying to do too many things: word process, manage e-mail, surf the Internet, and so on. ⁴To have gotten their point across, the psychologists ask us to have imagined a kitchen in which one appliance opens cans, made coffee, and is beating eggs. ⁵Surely, they say, all three jobs won't be done well by the one appliance. ⁶Furthermore, low cost, performance, and simplicity are cared about by consumers, they say. ⁷So the psychologists were suggesting replacing the one home computer with several smart electronic devices. ⁸They insist that each smart device performs only one task and each such device was simple to use. ⁹Maybe there would be something to this theory about simplicity. ¹⁰If the typical home computer was simpler now, maybe more technophobes would buy one.

Write What You Think

Write a paragraph or two in which you agree or disagree with the following statement. Give your opinion clearly, and support it with reasons and evidence.

The public, the government, and private industry must work together to make sure that anyone in the United States who wants one would be able to get an up-to-date computer.

After revising, edit for correct verb usage.

Subject-Verb Agreement

STUDENT WRITING
Narrative Essay

My Piano Recital
by Anh Van Vu
high school student, Houston, Texas

The soothing melody of Beethoven's *Moonlight Sonata* soared through my ears. It was so relaxing, yet my body tensed with anxiety. I stood nervously behind the dense, maroon curtains and glanced out across the stage. An elegantly dressed girl about my age sat at a grand piano; I could see her fingertips gliding over the black and white keys in front of her.

"She makes it seem so easy," I whispered to myself. "I wonder if I'll look and sound that way."

As the last chords of the music echoed, my body froze. The girl stood up from the bench and bowed deeply as the audience applauded. It was finally my turn. A part of me wanted to run home and hide under my bed. I didn't have to be here, I didn't have to come, I didn't have to say yes, but I knew I had chosen to perform. Now wasn't the time to chicken out. As the applause died down, the girl onstage walked toward me. I could hear my heart drumming loudly, and butterflies began to rise in my stomach. The girl had a proud smile pasted on her face, and when she passed me, I heard her say two words of encouragement: "Good luck!"

"Well, here goes nothing," I said to myself.

I stepped onto the stage and walked slowly toward the piano. My footsteps echoed softly. The bright lights nearly blinded me, making it difficult to see the audience. When I reached the piano, I automatically slid onto the bench and into position. The sounds of whispering and people shuffling around gave way to complete silence. I stared at my trembling fingers, and, for a moment, my mind went blank. Finally, I took a deep breath and began to play Chopin's *Nocturne in E-flat Major*. The rich tones of the piano rang out. One by one, each muscle in my body loosened and relaxed. I sat with ease on the bench, and my fingertips danced over the row of black and white keys as if they had a mind of their own. They glided over the keys while my mind drifted into the music.

When I reached the end of the piece, the audience started clapping. I rose from the bench and gave a deep bow. My mouth curled into a proud smile. Inside, I felt relieved that it was over and happy I had done so well. As the applause died down, I pivoted and glided to the other side of the stage. I saw a young boy standing nervously behind the dense, maroon curtains staring fearfully out at the stage. When I walked by, I passed to him the two words that were given to me for encouragement: "Good luck!"

> Anh Van Vu organizes her narrative essay chronologically. She includes dialogue to grab the reader's attention. The sensory details about the audience and about her nervousness draw the reader into her essay and add suspense.
>
> Because she wrote her essay in the first person, the subject of most of Anh's sentences is I. Her verbs are, therefore, first-person singular, agreeing with her subjects. You will learn more about subject-verb agreement as you do the lessons and exercises in this chapter.

Agreement with Intervening Phrases and Clauses

In talking about grammar, we say there are three **persons**. The subjects *I* and *we* are **first person**. The subject *you* is **second person**. A noun subject or *he, she, it,* or *they* is **third person**.

⮕ A third-person *singular subject* takes a *singular verb*. A third-person *plural subject* takes a *plural verb*.

TENSE	PERSON	NUMBER	
		SINGULAR SUBJECT	PLURAL SUBJECT
Present	1ˢᵗ	I swim and splash.	We swim and splash.
	2ⁿᵈ	You swim and splash.	You swim and splash.
	3ʳᵈ	She **swims** and **splashes**. Henry **swims** and **splashes**.	They **swim** and **splash**. The boys **swim** and **splash**.
Present Perfect	3ʳᵈ	She **has swum**.	They **have swum**.
Present Progressive	3ʳᵈ	Henry **is swimming**. **Is** Henry **swimming**?	The boys **are swimming**. **Are** the boys **swimming**?

Table title: Subject-Verb Agreement

The verb *be* is more complicated. The verb *be* must agree with first-, second-, *and* third-person subjects not only in the present tense but also in the past tense.

⮕ A prepositional phrase that comes between the subject and verb is called an **intervening phrase**. The subject of a verb never appears in an intervening phrase.

Make sure the verb (v) agrees with the subject (s), not with the object of a preposition.

    S   PREP. PHRASE   V
One of my teachers **is leaving** this year.

    S   PREP. PHRASE   V
The other **teachers** at the high school **are staying**.

⮕ A clause that comes between the subject and verb is called an **intervening clause**. The subject of a sentence is never within an intervening clause.

    S   INTERVENING CLAUSE   V
Jawann, who is my teacher and my friend, **is** the first to arrive.

A negative construction following the subject doesn't affect the number of the subject.

    S   V
This **book**, not those, **is** a mystery.

**Forms of *Be*
Singular**
I **am** late.
I **was** late.
You **are** late.
You **were** late.
He **is** late.
He **was** late.

Plural
We **are** late.
We **were** late.
You **are** late.
You **were** late.
They **are** late.
They **were** late.

EDITING TIP

Many speakers say *don't* when standard English grammar calls for *doesn't*. In school and business, remember that a third-person singular subject, *he* or *she*, needs the third-person singular form of the verb *do*, which is *does* + *n't*.

    doesn't
She ~~don't~~ know a thing about cooking.

EXERCISE 1 Choosing the Correct Verb

Underline the subject of each sentence and the verb in parentheses that agrees with the subject.

1. Toothbrushes (has, have) a long history.

2. The "chew stick," which was used by Egyptians more than five thousand years ago, (is, are) the earliest toothbrush we know about.

3. Some tribes in Africa (uses, use) it even today.

4. Members of a tribe (chooses, choose) their sticks only from certain trees, known as "toothbrush trees."

5. The American Dental Association, which studied these ancient tools still in use, (has found, have found) that these frayed sticks are used today in parts of the United States, too.

6. People who live in the South (calls, call) them twig brushes.

7. Dentists in the study (says, say) that these twig brushes can be every bit as effective as modern nylon-bristle brushes.

8. Bristled toothbrushes, like the one in your bathroom, (has been, have been) around for five hundred years.

9. These, not the chew stick, (traces, trace) their origin to China, where hog bristles fastened onto bamboo shoots were early tooth-cleaning tools.

EXERCISE 2 Editing a Paragraph

For each mistake in subject-verb agreement in the following paragraph, cross out the incorrect verb, and write the correct one above it.

¹Is our high schools adequately preparing students for the work world? ²Opinions on this subject varies. ³Some schools in the nation focuses their attention on the needs of their college-bound students. ⁴Those in this camp offers enriched programs to prepare graduates for college studies and professional careers. ⁵Other schools, on the other hand, emphasizes courses geared to preparing graduates for the rigorous and ever-changing demands of jobs in industry. ⁶But manufacturers who employ these graduates claims that new workers is unprepared for using the machinery and technology. ⁷These supervisors in industry says that a student comes to them not only without the necessary skills in computing but also without basic writing and math skills.

Agreement with Indefinite Pronouns

An **indefinite pronoun** expresses an amount or refers to an unspecified person or thing. When used as a subject, some indefinite pronouns are always singular, some are always plural, and some can be singular or plural, depending on their context.

Always Singular

anybody	neither
anyone	nobody
each	no one
either	one
everybody	somebody
everyone	someone
much	such

Always Plural

both	many
few	several

▶ In the present tense, the present perfect tense, and the present progressive form, use a singular verb when the subject is a singular indefinite pronoun. Use a plural verb when the subject is a plural indefinite pronoun.

SINGULAR **Much** of the audience **is expecting** to win a small prize.

SINGULAR But **somebody walks** away with a grand prize.

PLURAL **Few** of the entrants **expect** to win.

▶ The following indefinite pronouns can be either singular or plural, depending on the word they refer to: *all, any, enough, more, most, none,* and *some*.

   S   V
All of her free time **has gone** into piano practice. [singular]

   S   V
All of his performances **include** Mozart. [plural]

   S   V
Any of the food **tastes** delicious. [singular]

   S   V
Any of the tennis courts **are** available. [plural]

   S   V
Enough of the work **is** easy. [singular]

   S   V
Enough of the workers **are** union members. [plural]

   S   V
Some of the rainfall **is** heavy. [singular]

   S   V
Some of the storms **are** coming this way. [plural]

EDITING TIP

The pronoun *none* is especially tricky. Use a singular verb only when you can think of the subject as "none of it." Use a plural verb when you can substitute "none of them."

None of the story **sounds** believable. [None of *it* sounds believable.]

None of the stories **sound** believable. [None of *them* sound believable.]

P.S. Most of the time, choosing the correct verb for an indefinite pronoun will occur to you naturally. But when you need to look up a rule, check this page.

EXERCISE 3 Writing Complete Sentences

On a separate piece of paper, write a complete sentence for each numbered item, using the group of words as the subject of the sentence. Use present tense, present perfect, or present progressive verbs. Then check your sentences for correct subject-verb agreement. Read your sentence aloud to yourself for extra practice in hearing how correct agreement sounds.

EXAMPLE   Some of the actors
Some of the actors are terrific!

1. Several of the students
2. All of my teachers
3. None of the questions
4. Much of the concert
5. One of the best movies

6. More of the kids
7. Few of the events
8. Nobody in the building
9. Many of the players
10. No one in the audience

EXERCISE 4 Choosing the Correct Verb

Underline the subject of each sentence and the verb in parentheses that agrees in number with the subject. Then, with a partner, write five more sentences that practice subject-verb agreement. For each, give a choice of two present tense, present perfect, or present progressive verbs in parentheses. Exchange sentences with another pair of students.

1. Many of the countries in the world (is sending, are sending) athletes to the summer Olympics.
2. Not all of the athletes (has been, have been) professionals.
3. Some of the events (takes, take) place in a swimming pool.
4. Most of the participants (trains, train) hard for their events.
5. Each of the athletes (has, have) world-class skills.
6. Every one of them (marches, march) in the opening ceremonies.
7. Many of the viewers (prefers, prefer) the track-and-field events.
8. Few of the American viewers (is, are) familiar with the rules of team handball.
9. All of it (seems, seem) simple to the players.
10. All of the water polo players (is, are) good swimmers.
11. Everybody in the arena (has enjoyed, have enjoyed) the spectacle.
12. Some of the runners (had been, have been) injured while racing.
13. Nobody in the races (wants, want) to risk injury.

Agreement with Compound Subjects

A **compound subject** can have singular subjects, plural subjects, or a combination of singular and plural subjects.

▶ When singular subjects are joined by *and*, they take a plural verb.
   The giant armadillo, the cheetah, **and** the red wolf **are** endangered species.
   Have both the wild yak **and** the California condor **made** the list as well?

▶ When singular subjects are joined by *or* or *nor*, they take a singular verb.
   Neither the African lion **nor** the llama **is** an endangered species.
   Has either Ted **or** Elise **written** a report on endangered animals in America?

▶ When a singular subject and a plural subject are joined by *or* or *nor*, the verb agrees in number with the subject closer to it.
   Neither pythons **nor** the painted frog **is** found in North America.
   Does either the giant panda **or** camels **live** in North America outside of zoos?
   Do either camels **or** the giant panda **live** here?

P.S. Newspaper reporters and editors don't always follow this rule about *or* and *nor*. Try to be consistent in *your* writing.

▶ When *many a(n)*, *every*, or *each* precedes a single or compound subject, the subject takes a singular verb.
   Every zoologist **cares** about endangered species of plants and animals.
   Many a plant and animal **is** in danger in our rain forests.

EXERCISE 5 Choosing the Correct Verb

Underline the simple subject(s) of each sentence and the appropriate verb in parentheses. **Hint:** Not every sentence has a compound subject.
   EXAMPLE   Neither <u>you</u> nor <u>he</u> (<u>wants</u>, want) the forests to disappear.

1. Shortsighted government policies, burning, and chain saws (is, are) causing our rain forests to disappear.

2. Biological extinction and annihilation of traditional native lifestyles (is, are) two results of tropical deforestation.

3. The lush, fertile forest and the tropical climate (supports, support) more species of plants and animals than all other regions of Earth combined.

EDITING TIP

A compound subject that names only one thing or person takes a singular verb.

Peas and carrots **is** Fran's least favorite vegetable dish.

My teammate and best friend **is** also my roommate.

Enriching Your Vocabulary

The verb *annihilate* comes from the Latin prefix *ad*, meaning "to," and the root *nihil*, meaning "nothing." It is used to mean "demolish" or "to bring to nothing." When the enemy was *annihilated*, the soldiers staked their claim.

4. At least 545 species of birds, 792 kinds of butterflies, and 100 types of dragonflies (lives, live) in one Peruvian wildlife preserve.

5. Many a plant and animal (have, has) yet to be named.

6. Cancer and leukemia (is, are) diseases for which certain tropical plants provide medication.

7. Unfortunately, neither rain forests nor tropical vegetation (is, are) being protected from destruction.

Working Together

EXERCISE 6 Writing a Passage

On a separate piece of paper, write a passage about recess in elementary schools. Base your passage on the following notes and some of your own ideas. Use present tense, present perfect, or present progressive verbs. Then get together in a small group to read your paragraphs aloud and check one another's subject-verb agreement.

> *Recess under fire: a waste of time?*
>
> *Child's play—important or not?*
>
> *Some schools eliminating recess*
>
> *Pressures to increase academic performance; more time needed for core subjects*
>
> *Fear of accidents*
>
> *Fear of strangers appearing in school yards*
>
> *Many child development experts disagree. Cite importance of recess time for exercise, social interaction.*
>
> *Some cite need for kids to gain sense of independence.*

Write What You Think

On a separate piece of paper, write a paragraph (in the present tense, present perfect tense, or using the present progressive form) that expresses your view on this statement.

Use the suggestions in **Composition,** Lesson 2.1, to help you write a clear and unified paragraph.

> Students in kindergarten through sixth grade need recess only once a week. This compromise provides more time for studies as well as some opportunity for exercise.

Support your position with reasons and evidence. After revising, edit for complete sentences and for subject-verb agreement.

Agreement with Collective Nouns and Inverted Subjects

Sometimes, verbs follow subjects in sentences—for example, in sentences that are questions and in sentences beginning with *here* and *there*.

▶ A verb (V) must agree with the subject (S) even when the subject follows the verb. Be careful, *here* and *there* are never the subject in a sentence.

          V   S
Where **are** the **sleeping bags** I brought up from the basement?

      V   S
Here **are** Tami's favorite **dolls**.

     V   S
Here**'s** one **doll**. [*Here's* is a contraction involving the singular verb *is*.]

                        V   S
On the back porch by the grill **are** the old **newspapers**.

▶ A verb agrees with the subject of a sentence, *not* with the predicate nominative (PN).

                    S   V PN
The toddler's favorite **toy is** blocks.

        S   V   PN
The **films** by the new director **were** the winners.

▶ **A collective noun**, which names a group of people or things, may be either singular or plural depending on how you are using it.

Use a singular verb when you think of a collective noun as one single unit. Use a plural verb when you think of a collective noun as multiple members.

The **team is** on a winning streak. [*Team* refers to a single unit and takes a singular verb.]

The high school varsity **team are** going to five different colleges next year. [*Team* here refers to multiple members in the group and takes a plural verb.]

Grammar conventions, or practices, regarding some collective nouns, such as the ones featured in the box on the right, can change depending on common usage.

Some Common Collective Nouns

army	flock
audience	group
class	herd
club	orchestra
committee	(the) press
crowd	(the) public
family	team

WRITING HINT

Technically, *data* and *media* are plural words. However, in common usage, *data* can be used as a singular word when it refers to a pool of information and *media* can be singular when it refers to the media industry. In other cases, think of *data* and *media* as only plural.

Data on heart disease **is** impressive.

Data from many schools **are** in.

The **media loves** scandals.

My favorite **media are** TV and the Web.

EXERCISE 7 Choosing the Correct Verb

Underline the verb in parentheses that agrees with the subject.

1. Where (is, are) those copies I made?

2. There (is, are) a particular group of stores I like to visit.

3. The army (helps, help) during times of natural disasters.

4. This audience (is, are) one of the most enthusiastic we've had.

5. The orchestra (performs, perform) tonight at the hall.

6. In a small house along the river (lives, live) an elderly woman.

7. The audience (is, are) entering the theater through three doors now.

8. The media (pools, pool) their resources at times.

9. Under the stairs (is, are) the gift that I hid.

10. At the sound of the lion's roar, the herd of wildebeests (leaps, leap) away in all directions.

11. All the data (proves, prove) I'm right.

12. (Has, Have) the data come in from China and from Taiwan?

13. The final act (is, are) the jugglers and clowns.

14. The group (holds, hold) its meeting in the community center.

15. When (is, are) your brothers, sisters, and cousins coming?

Working Together

EXERCISE 8 Writing Complete Sentences

On a separate piece of paper, write a complete sentence for each numbered item, using the collective noun given as the subject of the sentence. Use present tense, present perfect, or present progressive verbs. Then check your sentences with others in your group for correct subject-verb agreement. Read your sentences aloud to one another for extra practice in hearing the sound of correct agreement.

EXAMPLE jury

The jury consists of twelve members.

1. audience
2. class
3. crowd
4. committee
5. group

6. flock
7. team
8. family
9. club
10. (the) public

Other Problems in Agreement

You must watch subject-verb agreement in both independent clauses and in subordinate clauses.

▥▶ In an adjective clause, the verb agrees with the word to which the relative pronoun refers.

In the following examples, the arrows show which word the relative pronoun refers to. When the relative pronoun refers to a singular noun or pronoun, use a singular verb in the adjective clause. When the relative pronoun refers to a plural noun or pronoun, use a plural verb in the adjective clause.

> The **story**, **which is** hard to believe, **comes** from a reliable source.
> The **stories**, **which are** hard to believe, **come** from a reliable source.

▥▶ A noun that ends in *-s* and refers to two parts working together is plural, like most nouns that end in *-s*. But some nouns ending in *-s* are singular. Other nouns ending in *-s* can be singular or plural depending on context.

> **Mumps is** a common childhood disease.
> Her **pants are** on the chair next to the bed.
> The **acoustics** in Carnegie Hall **are** superb.
> **Acoustics is** a science of interest to musicians.

▥▶ The title of a work of art (painting, literature, music, and so on) is always a singular subject and takes a singular verb.

> ***Hannah and Her Sisters* is** a film by Woody Allen.
> Calder's ***Horizontal Spines***, which **is** a sculpture, **makes** me smile.

▥▶ Use a singular verb with a subject that names an amount or time thought of as a unit. Use a plural verb when the amount or time refers to multiple items.

> Twenty **dollars is** the price of the ticket. [a single amount]
> The twenty **dollars weigh** down my pocket. [multiple bills]
> Two **weeks makes** a fortnight. [a single time period]
> These two **weeks are going** to be busy. [multiple items]

P.S. You can always check problematic nouns in a dictionary to find a note about when they're singular and when they're plural.

Singular Nouns

mathematics	news
measles	physics
mumps	

Plural Nouns

binoculars	scissors
eyeglasses	slacks
pants	

Singular or Plural

acoustics	statistics
economics	tactics
politics	

TEST-TAKING TiP

Errors in subject-verb agreement are very common and appear in many forms on standardized tests. Always identify the simple subject and ask yourself if it is singular or plural. See item 3 on page 339.

EXERCISE 9 Choosing the Correct Verb

Underline the verb in parentheses that agrees with the subject.

1. Geoffrey Chaucer, who lived and wrote in the medieval period, (is, are) best known for *The Canterbury Tales*.

2. Christopher Marlowe is one of the writers who (was, were) alive in Shakespeare's day.

3. Alan Sillitoe is one of those twentieth-century writers who (crafts, craft) stories about the English working class.

4. "Intimations of Immortality" (is, are) the short title of a Wordsworth poem.

5. Politics (has, have) been on the minds of many British authors.

6. The fourteen years at the beginning of the twentieth century (is, are) commonly known as the Edwardian Age.

7. Military tactics in World War I (is, are) the topic of poems by several British poets.

8. The poets Byron, Shelley, and Keats, who (appears, appear) in high school literature texts, (has, have) loyal followings.

9. The only one of Keats's poems that (affects, affect) me (is, are) "To Autumn."

10. Fifty dollars (is, are) a very reasonable price for a first edition of a Graham Greene novel.

EXERCISE 10 Writing Complete Sentences

On a separate piece of paper, write a complete sentence for each numbered item, using the word or group of words given as the subject of the sentence. Use present tense, present perfect, or present progressive verbs, and check your sentences for correct subject-verb agreement. Read your sentences aloud to yourself for extra practice in hearing the sound of correct agreement.

EXAMPLE scissors
> *The scissors are on the desk.*

1. measles

2. pants

3. six months

4. *Friends* (the TV series of the 1990s)

5. ten pounds

6. three inches

7. acoustics

8. two gallons

9. Geoffrey Chaucer's *The Canterbury Tales*

10. physics

Revising and Editing Worksheet 1

Improve the following draft by revising for ideas, organization, word choice, and sentence variety. After revising, edit the draft for errors in spelling, capitalization, punctuation, and usage. Write your revised and edited version on a separate piece of paper. Compare your changes with those of a writing partner.

[1]*Gulliver's Travels*, published in 1728, are the Irish writer Jonathan Swift's fictional masterpiece. [2]In the first part of the story, Lemuel Gulliver, one of the men who is traveling on a merchant ship, tell about his shipwreck on the island of Lilliput, which are the home of people only a few inches tall. [3]All of the other items on the island is one-twelfth the size Swift's readers expect. [4]Here, on Lilliput, is opportunities for Swift to satirize English politics. [5](Politics, of course, are the art and science of government.) [6]For example, a group argues among themselves about whether to break eggs at the big end or the small end.

[7]In the next part of the story, Gulliver find hisself in Brobdingnag, where everone he meets are as big as the Lilliputians are small. [8]The king, after learning about life where Gulliver come from, conclude that the life their must be awful. [9]He says that all of the English people seems hateful.

[10]In the third part of the book, Gulliver visits the island of Laputa. [11]Here, neither the philosopher nor the scientist escape Swift's satire. [12]Gulliver finds that the wise men of Laputa is so wrapped up in contemplation that they can't accomplish the simplest practical tasks. [13]Some of these men tries the dumbest projects, such as extracting sunshine from cucumbers.

[14]The last pages of the book tells about the Houyhnhnms and the Yahoos. [15]Houyhnhnms is horses, whose society are rational and clean. [16]The Yahoos, beasts in human form, is filthy and acts brutally. [17]Gulliver sadly recognizes these Yahoos as similar to the English people. [18]He is disgusted. [19]When he finally return home. [20]Gulliver withdraw from his family.

Revising and Editing Worksheet 2

Improve the following draft by revising for ideas, organization, word choice, and sentence variety. After revising, edit the draft for errors in spelling, capitalization, punctuation, and usage. Write your revised and edited version on a separate piece of paper. Compare your changes with those of a writing partner.

[1]*Frankenstein*, a tale of intrigue and terror, come from the pen of Mary Wollstonecraft Shelley, who were a nineteenth-century English author. [2]Everyone from countries all around the world have heard of this story. [3]Which has inspired several film versions. [4]The seeds for this tail of the supernatural was a nightmare that Shelley had.

[5]In the book, a man named Walton, one of the men who is exploring the Arctic, have written letters. [6]The letters by Walton relates the story of an idealistic student, Frankenstein, who has discovered how to give life to inanimate matter. [7]From bones he collects, Frankenstein creates the form of a human being and give it life. [8]The creature is strange-looking, huge, and very strong. [9]Every man and woman who come across the creature fear it.

[10]As a result, the creature is lonely and unhappy. [11]It wants a female counterpart. [12]Fails to persuade Frankenstein to create a bride for him. [13]The creature vows to hurt Frankenstein. [14]Indeed, Frankenstein's brother, friend, and fiancée dies by the creature's hand. [15]Consequently, Frankenstein along with others, pursue the creature to the Arctic in order to destroy it. [16]But after telling his story to Walton, Frankenstein dies. [17]The creature claims that Frankenstein is it's final victim. [18]Then the creature end it's own existence.

[19]*Frankenstein* is considered by some as the begining of modern science fiction. [20]Others see it as one of the noble-savage myths, which maintains that bad treatment can corrupt an essentially good nature.

[21]Have you seen any of the Frankenstein movies that is available on DVD?

Chapter Review

EXERCISE A Choosing the Correct Verb

Choose the verb in parentheses that agrees with the subject.

1. None of the content in these ten sentences (is, are) familiar to all Americans.

2. Morning television news (goes, go) back to at least 1947, the year of the premiere of the *Today* show.

3. One of the first American newspapers that (was, were) created by and for African Americans was first published on March 16.

4. (Doesn't, Don't) Bruce Willis or Glenn Close have a birthday on March 19?

5. From December 26 to January 1, many an African American (observes, observe) the festival of Kwanzaa.

6. The word *kwanzaa* comes from one of the languages that (is, are) prominent in Africa.

7. The unity of African American families (is, are) celebrated during Kwanzaa.

8. The formerly enslaved person and evangelist Sojourner Truth (is, are) remembered on November 26.

9. Tampa's Big Guava Festival, the Mount Rushmore Completion Anniversary, and the anniversary of the first time an African American athlete played in the National Basketball Association (falls, fall) on October 31.

10. (Does, Do) a Walt Disney show or *Seinfeld* claim October 27 as the date of its premiere?

EXERCISE B Editing for Subject-Verb Agreement

For each mistake in subject-verb agreement in the following paragraphs, cross out the incorrect verb, and write the correct one above it. Correct all spelling errors as well.

¹Is visits to the dentist a painful experience? ²Thanks to new laser technology, this situashion may not prevail. ³The nature of visits to dentists' offices are changing. ⁴However, neither the patient nor the dentist are complaining. ⁵The forty million in the country who hasen't been to the dentist in ages is getting ready to return. ⁶High-tech developments, including the laser, is the reason. ⁷To the rescue come the laser.

[8]Using lasers, every dentist are soon going to zap pockets of decay without damageing the surrounding tooth. [9]Here are more great news: When dentists in the modern age uses lasers, painkillers of any kind is unnecessary. [10]In other words, shots with a long hypodermic needle is on the way out. [11]Don't it sound as if families will flock to the dentist? [12]Many a dentist hope so. [13]Are "Many Pleasant Visits to Dentists" a good title for an article about these changes?

Exercise C Writing Complete Sentences

On a separate piece of paper, write a complete sentence for each numbered item, beginning your sentence with the given word or group of words. Use present tense, present perfect, or present progressive verbs, and check your sentences for correct subject-verb agreement.

1. One of the reasons
2. Every member of the group
3. The only one of the parents who
4. A flock of pigeons
5. The press
6. Everybody who was there
7. The clowns in the circus
8. Some of the people
9. Pat, not Luis,
10. The media

11. One of the players who
12. Either Ed or his sisters
13. Below the window
14. The acoustics
15. Neither Jo nor Mei
16. The film *The Ten Commandments*
17. Both he and I
18. None of the players
19. Six gallons of paint
20. Three dollars

Exercise D Writing a Summary

Using present tense verbs, on a separate piece of paper, write a summary of a movie or TV program you've seen, or of a book, short story, or play you've read. Assume your audience has *not* seen or read the work. Include key descriptive details. When you've completed your summary, review it carefully to make sure that the subjects and verbs agree.

Using Pronouns

STUDENT WRITING
Expository Essay

Crew's . . . Fun!

by Rachel Kamins *high school student, Middletown, Connecticut*

I was sitting in a boat on the Connecticut River one afternoon, bundled in six layers of clothing, contemplating my doom. My knees were squinched up to the level of my shoulders, my back was sore from being repeatedly slammed into the stern, and my gloves were still in the locker room on land. Every now and then, the arctic waters which were leaping around me jumped the gunwhales and spattered me with frigid drops.

Breaking this pleasant reverie came this question from the mouth of one of the eight bodies grunting and straining before me: "Why do we like doing this?"

To tell the truth, I have often wondered the same thing myself. What in heaven's name about the sport of crew actually attracts thinking people?

As one of these walking anomalies, I think I can actually explain the attraction of crew. At least I can explain why I like it—and that's not just because as a coxswain I get to sit around and watch people kill themselves all afternoon. Well, not entirely.

The initial attraction for me was the idea of a river. Even though it's the vile, sewage-filled Connecticut, it still looks great on a sunny day. And the scenic view from the middle of the river, especially up in Cromwell and down past Portland, is nature at its best. Tree-covered islands, boat-filled marinas, craggy rocks, and rolling hills—that's what keeps me coming back.

I also like how the sport itself looks. First of all, the equipment is downright smooth. A brand new Vespoli racing shell is like St. Patrick's Cathedral to me. Secondly, there's no athlete like a crew athlete.

The best is when all of the elements of crew come together—the boats, the rowers, and rowing. The motion of the stroke is a complex combination of pushing, sliding, pulling, and leaning, but it just looks like a beautiful, ritualistic, fluid cycle. And to see eight people doing it at once, in sync, is just mesmerizing. I often find myself staring at the river during regattas, hypnotized by the swing of the crews as they pass.

I think the most wonderful opportunity provided by crew is the chance to overcome [the physical pain of the sport]. The knowledge that one has pushed one's body to the limit and beyond—creating, in fact, new limits—is wonderfully triumphant. Accomplishing the previously impossible. One has such supreme control over the body that one can make it work when it no longer has the ability. These are awesome feelings.

Of course, athletes can get this sensation from more sports than crew, such as running and swimming. But the unique aspect of crew is that one can accomplish this simultaneously with seven other athletes and friends. When a team has come together to follow through on a commitment against all adversity, the members of that team have a connection that can't be produced by any other activity.

The purpose of Rachel Kamins's essay is to explain the reasons she enjoys her sport. Notice the transition words she uses to lead you through her explanation.

Reread the essay and pay particular attention to Rachel's pronouns. How many can you find? You'll get many opportunities to use pronouns in the exercises in this chapter.

Using Subject Pronouns

Subject Pronouns	
SINGULAR	**PLURAL**
I, you, he, she, it	we, you, they

▻ Use a **subject pronoun** when the pronoun functions as the subject (S) of a sentence or a clause.

    S   S
Marjorie and **I** are scheduling the performances.

    S
We have considered several plans.

▻ Use a subject pronoun when the pronoun functions as the predicate nominative (PN) of a sentence or clause.

Remember: A **predicate nominative** is a noun or pronoun that follows a form of the verb *be* and renames or identifies the subject.

                       PN   PN   PN
The students handling the props are Warren, Crystal, and **I**.

                    PN   PN
The teacher advisors are Mr. Li and **she**.

EXERCISE 1 Choosing the Correct Pronoun

Underline the pronoun in parentheses that correctly completes each sentence.

EXAMPLE   The people who planned our trip are Ms. Chan and (him, <u>he</u>).

1. My friend Michelle and (me, I) will visit England this summer.

2. (Us, We) are going with seniors interested in British history.

3. The person who made all the arrangements for the trip is (her, she).

4. Our faculty chaperones for the trip are Mr. Gomez and (she, her).

5. (Them, They) will take some students to visit the universities in Cambridge and Oxford.

6. Michelle and (me, I) will stay in London.

WRITING HINT

Most people answer "It's me" when someone asks, "Who's there?" But the preferred response for speeches, essays, and grammar tests is "It's I." Use a subject pronoun after a form of the verb *be*. "It is **I**." "It is **we**."

STEP BY STEP

Here's how to choose the pronoun for a compound predicate nominative.

The winners will be Al and (me, I).

1. Reword the sentence, using the pronoun as the subject.

   (Me, I) will be the winner.

2. Say the sentence with just the pronoun.

   Me will be the winner. [sounds wrong]

   I will be the winner. [sounds right]

3. Place the pronoun that sounds right in the sentence.

   The winners will be Al and **I**.

7. (Her and me, She and I) plan to visit several sights.

8. Who will get to the Tower of London first—Michelle or (me, I)?

9. It will be Mr. Gomez and (her, she) who will be responsible for us.

10. I dreamt that the English prince was (me, I).

EXERCISE 2 Editing a Paragraph

Edit the following paragraph to correct all errors in pronoun usage.

¹Michelle, Gabriel, and me visited Hampton Court on Tuesday. ²We pretended that the residents of the castle, twelve miles up the Thames River from London, were Michelle's family and her. ³We learned about Cardinal Thomas Wolsey; in 1514, the owner of Hampton Court was him. ⁴Over the years, him and other owners made many changes to the palace and grounds. ⁵Gabriel and me examined the tennis court built in about 1625. ⁶Meanwhile, Michelle explored on her own, imagining how she would redecorate if the owner really were her. ⁷Then Michelle, Gabriel, and me marveled at the gardens, at the Great Gatehouse, and at the paintings above the King's Staircase.

⁸On Wednesday, Chui and me went to Brighton, a seaside town, to see the Royal Pavilion. ⁹Her and me were astonished by this fantasy palace, with its domes, pinnacles, and minarets. ¹⁰The builder, George IV, was a regent with unique tastes, wasn't him? ¹¹Chui and me liked the music room best. ¹²Her and me especially enjoyed its Chinese landscapes and water-lily chandeliers.

Write What You Think

Refer to Composition, Lesson 4.3, to find suggestions for writing persuasively.

People have many different opinions about travel and sightseeing. Think about one of the following statements. Then, on a separate piece of paper, write a paragraph or two expressing your opinion about the statement. Support your opinion with examples and reasons. After revising, edit to see that you have used subject pronouns appropriately.

• Teenagers who live in the United States should travel to Europe, Asia, Australia, or Africa before they graduate from high school.

• Teenagers who live in the United States should explore other cities and states.

Using Object Pronouns

Object Pronouns	
SINGULAR	**PLURAL**
me, you, him, her, it	us, you, them

▶ Use an **object pronoun** when the pronoun functions as the direct object (**DO**), indirect object (**IO**), or object complement (**OC**) of a sentence or a clause.

>   **IO**   **IO**   **DO**
> My father gave Dolores and **me** the keys to the car.
>
>   **DO**
> We thanked **him** for the keys.
>
>   **DO**   **DO OC**
> The family counselor made **you** and **me us**.

▶ Use an object pronoun when the pronoun functions as the object of a preposition (**OP**) in a sentence or clause.

>   **OP**   **OP**
> Dad handed the keys to Dolores and **me**.
>
>   **OP**   **OP**
> For both of **us**, driving Dad's car was a big responsibility.

P.S. Don't become discouraged by the many terms that include the word *object*. Just get a general sense of how an object differs from a subject.

See **Grammar**, Lesson 6.6, for more on direct and indirect objects and Lesson 6.8 for more on object complements.

EDITING TIP

Avoid this common error: "between you and I." Always say or write, "between you and me."

EXERCISE 3 Choosing the Correct Pronoun

Underline the pronoun in parentheses that correctly completes each sentence.

1. Every actor in his heart believes everything bad that's printed about (he, him). —Orson Welles

2. There is nothing which (we, us) receive with so much reluctance as advice. —Joseph Addison

3. Everything intercepts (we, us) from ourselves. —Ralph Waldo Emerson

4. A man in passion rides a horse that runs away with (he, him). —Thomas Fuller

5. We shape our buildings; thereafter, they shape (we, us). —Winston Churchill

STEP BY STEP

To decide whether to use a subject pronoun or an object pronoun:

1. Decide what function the pronoun performs in the sentence.

2. If the pronoun is a subject or a predicate nominative, use the subject pronoun.

3. If the pronoun is a direct object, an indirect object, an object complement, or the object of a preposition, use the object pronoun.

6. Audiences are the same all over the world, and if you entertain (they, them), they will respond. —Liza Minnelli

7. Woe to (he, him) inside a nonconformist clique who does not conform to nonconformity. —Eric Hoffer

8. We cannot despair of humanity since (we, us) ourselves are human beings. —Albert Einstein

9. Happy are (them, they) that hear their detractions and can put them to mending. —William Shakespeare

10. (Him, He) who hesitates is sometimes saved. —James Thurber

Exercise 4 Editing Sentences

Improve the following sentences. Look carefully at subject pronouns and object pronouns. Cross out each pronoun that is used incorrectly, and write the correct pronoun above it. If a sentence is correct, write *C* after it.

> EXAMPLE   Specialists have studied what economic principles high school graduates
>   *they*
>   need to understand; ~~them~~ have identified twenty principles.

HINT

First, check to see what function the pronoun performs in the sentence.

1. Edina knows that people can't have all the goods and services them want.

2. James and her have learned that they must make choices.

3. For she and he, making choices means weighing costs and benefits.

4. Thinking in terms of more and less, not in terms of everything or nothing, is a new idea to she and her friends.

5. When positive and negative incentives are presented to people, they respond predictably to them.

6. People trade products and services when they expect some benefit.

7. Her, him, and me know that people and nations should concentrate on what they do best and then trade with others.

8. Kim and them have learned that, when buyers and sellers form a market, they determine prices.

9. You and me know that prices reflect supply and demand in the market.

10. When sellers compete, prices drop; that pattern is what Suki and I now understand.

11. Him and us also know that when buyers compete, the prices go up.

12. Carl and me understand that institutions affect markets. Among they are banks, corporations, and labor unions.

13. With money, you and me borrow, trade, invest, and save; we also use money to compare the value of goods and services.

Who or Whom?

Deciding between *who* and *whom* is the same as deciding between *he* and *him* or between *she* and *her*.

Subject Pronoun	Object Pronoun
who	whom

||||▶ Use the subject pronoun *who* when the pronoun functions as a subject or predicate nominative in a sentence or in a clause.

Who will represent the school in the debate?
[*Who* is the subject of the sentence.]
The winner is **who**? [*Who* is the predicate nominative.]

Let your ear help you decide between *who* and *whom*. Consider replacing the pronoun in a question with *he* or *him*. If *he* sounds right in the sentence, use the subject pronoun *who*. If *him* sounds right, choose the object pronoun *whom*.

If you have to choose between *who* and *whom* in a subordinate clause, ignore the rest of the sentence. Focus only on how *who* or *whom* functions within the subordinate clause. If you need to, reverse the word order in the clause to determine what function the pronoun performs.

The student **who** was chosen to go into space is in my class. [*Who* is the subject of the adjective clause.]
Do you know **who** their second choice was? [*Who* is the predicate nominative of the noun clause.]

||||▶ Use the object pronoun *whom* when the pronoun functions as the direct object, indirect object, or object of a preposition in a sentence or in a clause.

Whom did Sarah choose as her partner? [*Whom* is the direct object of *did choose*.]
For **whom** did you buy this shirt? [*Whom* is the object of the preposition *For*.]

Sometimes, a pronoun is both the object of a preposition in the main clause of a sentence and the subject or predicate nominative in a subordinate clause in the sentence. In such a case, always use the pronoun *who*, not *whom*.

Before the ball game, the pitcher and the catcher talk about who the other team's best hitters are.

WRITING HINT

Most people don't use *whom* at the beginning of a question.
Who did you see?

In formal writing and speaking, use *whom* whenever the pronoun functions as an object.
Whom did you see?

Consult this lesson or a grammar Web site if you are unsure whether to use *who* or *whom*.

STEP BY STEP

When you need to choose between *who* and *whom*:

1. Decide what function the pronoun performs in the sentence.

2. Use *who* if the pronoun functions as a subject or a predicate nominative (even if the pronoun is *also* the object of a preposition).

3. Use *whom* if the pronoun functions as a direct or indirect object or as the object of a preposition.

EXERCISE 5 Choosing the Correct Pronoun

Underline the pronoun in parentheses that correctly completes each sentence.

EXAMPLE   Jackie Robinson was an athlete (<u>who</u>, whom) inspired millions.

1. Robinson, (who, whom) was the first African American athlete to play in the major leagues, played second base and other positions.

2. Robinson, (who, whom) teammates praised, was feared by opponents for his hard work.

3. Some players (who, whom) Robinson came across in his career were less than friendly to him.

4. Robinson, (who, whom) had been a football, basketball, and track star at UCLA, eventually made his mark on the baseball diamond.

5. Scouts thought that there were other baseball stars of the Negro leagues (who, whom) were equal in talent to Robinson.

6. Brooklyn Dodgers owner Branch Rickey, (who, whom) other baseball executives criticized, brought Robinson to the major leagues in 1947.

7. Other Negro league players, many of (who, whom) were past their playing primes, eventually made it to the major leagues.

8. The African American player (who, whom) was the first to compete in the American League was Larry Doby.

9. Doby, (who, whom) played for the Cleveland Indians, also experienced both support and prejudice.

10. Today, reporters write about (who, whom) plays well without regard to race.

EXERCISE 6 Editing a Paragraph

Correct all errors in pronoun usage in the following paragraph about Maya Angelou. **Hint:** One sentence contains no errors.

[1]When you think of people who have succeeded against all odds, whom comes to mind? [2]Consider Maya Angelou, a poet who has earned international respect for her insightful work. [3]Angelou, whom is a writer, director, and educator, has also had a successful career as a singer, actress, and dancer. [4]Angelou, whom is the great-granddaughter of an enslaved person, has written several volumes of poetry that explore the themes of economic, racial, and sexual oppression. [5]Her writing captures the aspirations of other African American women, who she celebrates in her work.

Pronoun Problems

An appositive (see Lesson 7.2) can be a pronoun referring to a noun or a noun referring to a pronoun. In both instances, you must choose the correct form of the pronoun—either a subject pronoun or an object pronoun.

▶ For a pronoun appositive, use a subject pronoun if the word the appositive refers to is a subject or a predicate nominative. Use an object pronoun if the word the appositive refers to is a direct object, an indirect object, or the object of a preposition.

The best actors, Elaine and **he**, have the lead roles.
[*He* refers to *actors*, the subject of the sentence.]
The leads are the best actors, Elaine and **he**. [*Actors* is now a predicate nominative.]
The director gave the leads to the best actors, Elaine and **him**.
[*Actors* is the object of the preposition *to*.]
The director gave the best actors, Elaine and **him**, the leads.
[*Actors* is the indirect object of the sentence.]

▶ When the pronoun *we* or *us* is followed by a noun appositive, choose the pronoun form you would use if the pronoun were alone in the sentence.

We actors found the endless rehearsals tedious.
[You would say, "**We** found the endless. . . ."]

▶ In an **incomplete construction** (also called an elliptical construction), choose the pronoun form (subject or object) you would use if the sentence were completed.

Usually, an incomplete construction is a comparison, one that comes at the end of a sentence and starts with the word *than* or *as*. In the following examples, the omitted words appear in brackets. When you write an incomplete construction, say the missing words to yourself as a check for pronoun choice.

Yan is two inches shorter than **she** [is].
My aunt likes my cousin more than [she likes] **me**.

▶ Reserve pronouns ending in *-self* or *-selves* for referring to or intensifying another word in the sentence. By itself, a pronoun ending in *-self* or *-selves* cannot be a subject or an object of a sentence.

Kendra and ~~myself~~ are in the band.
I

The prize goes to the team from Adams and to ~~ourselves~~.
us

Enriching Your Vocabulary

The Latin root of *tedious*, *taediosus*, means "disgusting" or "offensive." The English word, not quite as strong, means simply "boring" or "tiresome." The *tedious* lecture on using the spell-check feature lasted far too long.

EDITING TIP

Remember to use pronouns consistently in a sentence.

One must prepare for tests
one
as thoroughly as ~~you~~ can.

I want to be a writer, but
I
~~you~~ need more confidence.

EXERCISE 7 Choosing the Correct Pronoun

Underline the pronoun in parentheses that correctly completes each sentence.

EXAMPLE   The judges gave the prize to the cleverest dog, (<u>him</u>, he).

1. (Us, We) dog owners love to show off our pets' new tricks.

2. I think my spaniel is smarter than (him himself, he himself) thinks.

3. The smartest dogs, Alexander and (her, she), make Lassie look like a dolt.

4. I prefer loyal and calm dogs such as beagles. Yes, I prefer (they, them) and retrievers.

5. The things that a mutt can do sometimes astound (us, we) judges.

6. I can't take my dog Lucy and her pup on vacation, but the dog camp will please even the most ornery campers, (her, she) and Baby Lucy.

7. Three dogs—Sam, Dottie, and (him, he)—play together all day.

8. The camp gave a special treat to the quietest dogs, (her, she) and (him, he).

9. The two dogs that bark the most, Baby Lucy and (her, she), are only puppies.

10. Do you think Lucy and her pup would like a postcard from (myself, me)?

EXERCISE 8 Editing Sentences

The following sentences contain errors with pronouns. Cross out a pronoun that is incorrect, and write the correct pronoun above it. **Hint:** Watch for incomplete constructions, unnecessary shifts, and other pronoun misuses.

1. We don't trust Amelia, but we trust Willie less than she.

2. Darnell and myself are the newest players on the team.

3. Us tenors think we have the best voices in the choir.

4. Not only Margaret but also Fatima and her performed in recitals.

5. As you go through life, you learn that one's plans often go astray.

6. The boys predicted the winners, Tina and she.

7. My male hamster is smarter than your female hamster; my hamster knows more tricks than her.

8. One never finishes cleaning up as early as she thinks she will.

9. The team from Greeley or ourselves will get the highest marks in the band contest.

10. Jonathan has played the violin longer than me.

Agreement with Antecedent

The word that a pronoun refers to is its **antecedent**. Pronouns and antecedents must agree in **gender** (male, female, or neuter) and in **number** (singular or plural).

▐▐▶ Use a plural pronoun to refer to two or more antecedents joined by the word *and*.

> *Mary, Ruth*, and *Helen* were the most popular female names in the United States in 1900. **Their** counterparts in England that year were *Florence, Mary*, and *Alice*.

▐▐▶ Use a singular pronoun to refer to two or more singular antecedents joined by *or* or *nor*. When a singular antecedent and a plural antecedent are joined by *or* or *nor*, use a pronoun that agrees with the nearer antecedent.

> In 1900, a John, a Robert, **or** a Joseph found **his** name to be very popular.
> Will the name *Jennifer* **or** other popular names lose **their** appeal one day?

▐▐▶ Use a singular pronoun when the antecedent is a singular indefinite pronoun: *anybody, anyone, each, either, everybody, everyone, much, neither, nobody, no one, one, somebody, someone, such*.

> **Anyone** with the name Robert can say that **his** name was the most popular boy's name in the United States in 1925, 1940, and 1950.

When a singular indefinite pronoun refers to both males and females, use the expression "his or her."

> **Everybody** is interested in where **his or her** name came from.

In an adjective clause, the personal pronoun agrees with the word to which the relative pronoun refers.

> **Some who** give **their** children an unusual name later apologize.
> **One who** gives **his or her** child an original name is proud.

EXERCISE 9 Choosing the Correct Pronoun

Underline the pronoun in parentheses that agrees with its antecedent. **Hint:** First, find the antecedent(s).

> EXAMPLE   Kristen, Stacey, and Courtney use (her, <u>their</u>) calculators to do the assignment.

1. Damon and his girlfriend Felicia always eat (his, their) favorite foods.

2. Neither of the girls taking the swim test finished (her, their) lunch.

WRITING HiNT

Sometimes, in a formal situation, *his or her* sounds awkward, but you can't use *their* with a singular antecedent. Avoid this problem by rewording your sentence. One way is to make the sentence plural.

~~Each student~~ *Students* must pick up

~~his or her~~ *their* bus passes

tomorrow.

Each student must pick up

~~his or her~~ *a* bus pass

tomorrow.

3. Either the twins or James will bring (his, their) football.

4. Did Tanisha or Jessica remember (her, their) homework?

5. Someone named Lee, whom I don't know, picked me for (his or her, their) team.

6. Miguel, Dave, and Naseem sent (his, their) gift by an overnight service.

7. Many a parent helps (his or her, their) child fill out a college- or job-application form.

8. Did the dancers or the soprano, Lena, practice (her, their) part?

9. Somebody has left (his or her, their) cell phone at my house.

10. Antoine, Sean, and Jermaine know (his, their) roles.

11. Several members of the club and its president will present (his or her, their) views at the next meeting.

12. Neither Mr. Wilson nor Mr. Johnson will be in town to watch (his, their) son graduate.

13. Each of the members of the band dressed in (his or her, their) best for the performance.

14. Everyone who donates to the clothing drive will receive thanks for (his or her, their) gesture.

15. Tom, Steve, or Fiona will read (their, his or her, her) story at the ceremony.

Working Together

EXERCISE 10 Writing an Opinion About a Name

Think about your first name, the first name of a friend or relative, or any first name. Write one or more paragraphs in response to the following question.

What do you like or dislike about the name you've chosen to explore? Consider writing about the meaning of the name, where it may have come from, and what it makes you think of.

Support your opinion with examples and reasons. To do so, you may have to conduct some research in books about names. When you have finished, give your writing to a partner for his or her comments. Do not give your writing to someone with the name you wrote about.

Clear Pronoun Reference

Pronouns are helpful only if your readers or listeners can figure out their meanings.

▶ Avoid an ambiguous reference, which occurs when a pronoun appears to refer to either of two antecedents.

Rewrite the sentence to make your meaning clear.

UNCLEAR	When the Millers greeted their visiting relatives, **they** smiled and laughed. [Who did?]
CLEAR	The Millers smiled and laughed when they greeted their visiting relatives.
CLEAR	The Millers greeted their smiling and laughing visitors.

TEST-TAKING TIP

Always check test items for ambiguous pronoun reference. To clarify an ambiguity, you may have to reword the sentence. See item 6 on page 340.

▶ Avoid using the words *it, this, that,* and *which* without a clearly stated antecedent.

Replace the pronoun with a noun, or make sure the pronoun points clearly to a noun.

UNCLEAR	Not many people showed up to watch the game, **which** was disappointing. [What was disappointing, the game or the low turnout?]
UNCLEAR	Not many people showed up to watch the game. **This** was disappointing. [same problem as before]
UNCLEAR	Not many people showed up to watch the game. **It** was disappointing. [same problem as before]
CLEAR	Not many people showed up to watch the game. The low attendance was disappointing.
CLEAR	The game drew low attendance. **It** was a disappointing game.

▶ Except in very informal writing, avoid using *you* or *they* without saying what the word refers to.

UNCLEAR	Math can be practical. For example, they say that a straight line is the shortest distance between two points. [Who says?]
CLEAR	Math can be practical. For example, **mathematicians** say that a straight line is the shortest distance between two points.
UNCLEAR	They are advertising a new headache pill. You don't want to take it on an empty stomach. [very informal]
CLEAR	An **advertisement** for a new headache pill is running. A **patient** should not take the pill on an empty stomach. [clearer subjects]

EXERCISE 11 Editing Sentences

The following sentences contain unclear pronouns. On a separate piece of paper, rewrite the sentences to avoid these errors. **Hint:** Multiple corrections for each sentence are possible.

EXAMPLE   They say that Bright toothpaste works best.
Dentists say that Bright toothpaste works best.

1. He tried to explain to his father how to prove a theorem, which was difficult.

2. At circuses, they expect the audience to howl with laughter.

3. Mr. Rosen separated the altos from the sopranos and practiced with them.

4. In some places, they never know when the next tornado will suddenly appear.

5. He does not believe that I broke the record. This is a fact.

6. They say that you should change the oil in a car every six months.

7. First the politicians passed, then the floats, and then three bands. It was loud.

8. I took a sheet of paper out of the envelope and then folded it.

9. When I read my friends' postcard about the Rocky Mountains, I wished they were here.

10. At many hotels, they want you to check out by noon.

EXERCISE 12 Creating Your Own Exercise

On a separate piece of paper, write ten sentences that have unclear pronouns. Include at least two of each of the following:

- sentences in which a pronoun refers to either of two antecedents
- sentences in which *it, this, that,* or *which* lacks a clearly stated antecedent
- sentences in which *you* or *they* has no antecedent

Swap papers with a partner, and rewrite each other's sentences so that their meanings are clear. Check each other's answers.

Revising and Editing Worksheet 1

Improve the following draft by revising for ideas, organization, word choice, and sentence variety. After revising, edit the draft for errors in spelling, capitalization, punctuation, and usage. Write your revised and edited version on a separate piece of paper. Compare your changes with those of a writing partner.

[1]Although many countries have wonderful food markets, they say that the vast one in Ho Chi Minh City in Vietnam is superior for their varied, attractive, and fresh products. [2]Everywhere you look, vendors are washing, cutting, peeling, and selling food, and shoppers are enjoying them. [3]When me and Brian were their, we saw fruits neither of we had ever heard of. [4]Like durian, dragon fruit, and jackfruit. [5]Brian spotted even more unusual foods than me.

[6]There was much for you to notice at this market, which was already getting crowded by 7:30 in the morning. [7]Brian and myself saw ducks and chickens, squawking in there cages, and vendors whom were squatting and eating their *pho*, a meat soup, for breakfast. [8]Nearby were jars of herbs and spices. [9]Us tourists were dazzled by the fragrances. [10]It was amazing. [11]And huge, too. [12]The market, with its many blocks of stalls and canvas storefronts, began to thin out by midmorning. [13]The vendors, for who the workday was winding down, were cleaning their stalls.

[14]Equally amazing to we tourists was the fact that they didn't use refrigerators in the market. [15]Despite the fact that temperatures never dipped below 90 degrees. [16]Foods were stocked, covered, or layered so that it all stayed cool. [17]There was, however, ice for the squid and some other fragile items. [18]They kept the fish in pools of water, and they kept changing them. [19]They slaughtered only enough poultry to sell that day. [20]Anyone who visits a market like this one will never forget their experience. [21]The memory will live for myself for the rest of my life.

Revising and Editing Worksheet 2

Improve the following draft by revising for ideas, organization, word choice, and sentence variety. After revising, edit the draft for errors in spelling, capitalization, punctuation, and usage. Write your revised and edited version on a separate piece of paper. Compare your changes with those of a writing partner.

[1]The film *Chariots of Fire* came out in 1981. [2]They gave it three Academy Awards, including one for best picture. [3]It introduced you to it's stars—Ben Cross, Ian Charleson, and Nigel Havers. [4]Several well-known actors appeared in the film, which was a key factor. [5]It was director Hugh Hudson's first film.

[6]*Chariots of Fire* tell the absorbing and unusual true tale of two runners, Eric Liddell and Harold Abrahams. [7]Both of who competed successfully in the 1924 Olympics games in Paris. [8]This compelling drama of the struggles the two faced leading up to it. [9]Liddell was a devout Scottish missionary. [10]Abrahams, a Jewish student at Cambridge University. [11]Liddell stuck to their principles when confronted with the choice of whether or not to race on Sunday, his holy day. [12]Abrahams, who anti-, Semitic forces targeted, was determined to compete on his own terms, despite the university's disapproval of himself. [13]Both overcame his crises to run and win there races.

[14]You'll love this compelling story. [15]The sets and costumes seem real, as do the running scenes. [16]They put considerable effort into it. [17]More authentic than other films. [18]And the music, which is by now familiar to ourselves. [19]Next time your in the mood for a good movie, watch it.

Chapter Review

EXERCISE A Choosing the Correct Pronoun

Underline the pronoun in parentheses that correctly completes each sentence.

1. Sarah Josepha Hale, (who, whom) the publisher appointed in 1828, was the first woman to edit a major publication for women.

2. The publisher of *Ladies' Magazine* and (she, her) worked in Boston.

3. Hale probably enjoyed saying, "The editor is not a man but (I, me)."

4. Hale believed education was important for a man and for (her, herself) too.

5. Hale, to (who, whom) education was very important, had received her own schooling at home.

6. In 1837, Louis Godey, after (who, whom) another women's magazine was named, became the owner of the magazine Hale worked for.

7. *Godey's Lady's Book* was the magazine named for (himself, him).

8. A theme that Godey and (she, her) promoted was that women, through "secret, silent influence," could affect the lives of men and children.

9. If you could meet Hale and Godey today, what would you say to (he and she, her and him)?

10. Between (she and he, her and him), they brought out an important publication.

EXERCISE B Correcting Pronoun Errors

Correct all pronoun errors in the following sentences. Cross out the incorrect pronouns, and write the correct ones in the space above each sentence. If a sentence is correct, write *C*.

1. Evan and me are meeting our friends later.

2. Helen, who a community college admitted, will also work for her father.

3. I suggest that George and her meet at the car dealership.

4. We asked Gloria and them about having us over.

5. Him and his brother were the first to start using that expression.

6. My father says the argument is between my sister and himself.

7. Who do we send the bill to?

8. Sherry, Tamisha, and her made the track team.

9. Do you know who the prime minister of England is?

10. Us guys were the last to find out about the changes.

EXERCISE C Agreement with Antecedents

Fill in each blank with a pronoun that agrees with its antecedent(s).

1. Either Tyrone or Felix will bring _____ extra racquet to the courts.

2. The four friends have _____ own opinions on things.

3. Neither the two Gong sisters nor Lucy brought _____ lunch today.

4. Either Lola or Nola gave up _____ seat on the bus.

5. Nick, Paul, and Tony called in _____ orders at the same time.

6. The woman who gave _____ account of the fire was articulate.

7. Each of the participants brought _____ own instrument.

8. Neither Chuck nor Ted drove _____ car to the beach.

9. Every entrant must send in _____ name to the committee by Tuesday.

10. Jake and Lydia rehearsed _____ parts together.

EXERCISE D Revising Sentences

Each of the following items lacks clear pronoun reference. On a separate piece of paper, rewrite the sentences to avoid these errors of ambiguity. **Hint:** Multiple revisions for each are possible.

1. The evening was a hot and sticky August night. It was uncomfortable.

2. In zoos, they expect the animals to be in suitable environments.

3. Ms. Walker removed the book from the shelf and wiped it.

4. In the mountans, they always know when the first snow will come.

5. When the World Series winners paraded past their fans, they waved enthusiastically.

6. She tried the door to the store, which was closed.

7. I took my telescope, went to the window, and looked through it.

8. I took the place mats off the tables and cleaned them.

9. When I met her new friend in her big house, I wished I had one.

10. At basketball games, they ask for time-outs.

Using Modifiers

STUDENT WRITING
Narrative Essay

Thank You
by Molly Gondek
high school student, Rocky Hill, California

Did I miss something? Why were these people so motivated to do this? My stomach turned as the leader of my youth group read us a flyer about Habitat for Humanity. The idea of waking up at seven o'clock on the first Saturday of summer vacation for a day of hammering and a night of nursing the resulting blisters did not appeal to me. I am not a fan of being dirty. Needless to say, after hearing, "Come on, Molly, it will be fun!" I reluctantly volunteered.

By no means was I counting down the days to that dreaded Saturday. My panic reached its peak as we drove to the site. The horror began when I heard, "Move the stripped roofing shingles that surround the house."

My morning included many worries. "Will I step on a nail and be rushed to the hospital? Will these directors leave us alone and stop instructing the most 'productive' method of completing the task? Is there a place to wash up a little?"

Amazingly, I made it to lunch break which came and went much too fast. Soon I returned to the grueling work. I was in dire need of a break when a thirteen-year-old boy (a member of the family moving into the house) brought me a cup of water. After I said a polite thank-you, he responded, "No, thank *you.*" In three words, my whole viewpoint changed. After introductions, we started talking about his future home. His face lit up as he told me his decorating plans for his very first room. He told me of his mother's death and of living with his aunt and cousins in a car. Not once did a tear flow from this boy's eyes as he related his misfortune and his missed opportunities. Pure joy radiated from him.

I can barely remember any more about the day. I cannot even remember the boy's name. But his beaming face is vivid in my mind. His innocence shocked me. He helped me be more appreciative. How could I complain about the dirt and the nails?

That night, soaking my sore feet, I looked around. I had gained a greater appreciation and a clearer view of life's important matters.

> From the very first sentences, Molly Gondek's narrative essay has a lively tone. She uses humor, dialogue, and sensory details to tell her story. Molly ends her essay by explaining the significance of the event.
>
> As you reread the essay, pay attention to the modifiers—the adjectives and adverbs. Modifiers add color and freshness to your writing. As you do the exercises in this chapter, you'll practice adding modifiers to your writing—and using them correctly.

Degrees of Comparison

Suppose you attended the Jumping Frog Jubilee at the Calaveras County Fair and you wanted to compare the leaps of three competing frogs. To express yourself, you would need the three **degrees of comparison**: **positive**, **comparative**, and **superlative**.

POSITIVE	Frog One's jump is **long**.
COMPARATIVE	Frog Two's jump is even **longer**. [Use the comparative to compare two items.]
SUPERLATIVE	Frog Three's jump is the **longest**. [Use the superlative to compare three or more items.]

Here are the rules for forming the comparative and superlative degrees.

▶ **One- and two-syllable modifiers** Add *-er* and *-est* to most one- and two-syllable modifiers. A dictionary will alert you to spelling changes.

old, old**er**, old**est**	fast, fast**er**, fast**est**
quick, quick**er**, quick**est**	hard, hard**er**, hard**est**
shallow, shallow**er**, shallow**est**	lazy, lazi**er**, lazi**est**

If an *-er* or *-est* modifier sounds strange, use *more* and *most* before the positive degree.

earnest, **more** earnest, **most** earnest

▶ **-ly adverbs** Use *more* and *most* for all adverbs that end in *-ly*.

slowly, **more** slowly, **most** slowly

▶ **More than two syllables** For modifiers of three syllables or more, use *more* and *most* to form the comparative and superlative degrees.

delightful, **more** delightful, **most** delightful
terrible, **more** terrible, **most** terrible

▶ **Decreasing degrees** For all modifiers (regardless of number of syllables), use *less* and *least* for decreasing degrees of comparison.

strong, **less** strong, **least** strong
urgently, **less** urgently, **least** urgently

▶ **Irregular modifiers** A few modifiers form their degrees of comparison irregularly. See the side column above for a list of these modifiers.

P.S. Most of the time the correct forms of comparative and superlative modifiers will occur to you automatically.

Irregular Degrees of Comparison

good	better	best
well	better	best
bad	worse	worst
ill	worse	worst
many	more	most
much	more	most
little	less *or* lesser	least
far	farther [*for physical distances*]	farthest
far	further [*for nonphysical advancement*]	furthest

WRITING HINT

Since *good* is always an adjective—never an adverb—do not use *good* to modify an action verb.

Sammy bats ~~good~~ *well*.

Besides working as an adverb, *well* is also an adjective that means "in good health."

The dog didn't look good. [attractive]

The dog didn't look well. [healthy]

EDITING TIP

A double comparison incorrectly uses both *-er* or *-est* and *more* or *most*. Avoid double comparisons. Use either the word *more* (or *most*) or the suffix *-er* (or *-est*).

This mountain is ~~more~~ higher than the other one.

Exercise 1 Editing Sentences

Cross out any incorrect modifiers, and write the correct form in the space above or at the end of the line.

1. We just took the most hardest test in art history class, but I think I did good.

2. The essay part was the most long of all the parts.

3. The exam was so difficult that all of us worked quietlier than on any previous test.

4. The difficultest questions were the ones about modern architecture.

5. I had forgotten that, of all architects, Louis Sullivan was more responsible for pioneering the design of skyscrapers.

6. I'd read about Frank Lloyd Wright, Le Corbusier, and Mies van der Rohe, but I couldn't tell you who was the talentedest architect of the three.

7. All I knew was that Wright, Le Corbusier, and Mies were importanter architects than their contemporaries.

8. Our teacher suggested that those three architects designed especially good and were artisticker than all the others.

9. She said that all three had a poetic vision of the world, so they advanced more further with their designs than most.

10. She also pointed out their faults, including the fact that, in Wright's most early houses, the flat roofs leaked.

Exercise 2 Forming the Comparative and Superlative

Write the comparative and superlative degrees for each of the following modifiers on a separate piece of paper.

1. formidable

2. modest

3. agile

4. good

5. curious

6. busy

7. generous

8. far [distance]

9. fearful

10. convincing

Exercise 3 Writing an Advertisement

Imagine that you are a realtor, someone who sells houses and apartments. You are writing an ad for a house or apartment that you have been hired to sell. On a separate piece of paper, write a description that will persuade prospective home buyers that your property is the best they'll see. Use at least five comparative or superlative modifiers in your ad.

Using the Degrees of Comparison

▐▶ Use the **comparative degree** to compare two things. Use the **superlative degree** to compare three or more things.

COMPARATIVE Maria's hair is **longer** than Bonita's.

SUPERLATIVE Sol's route is the **longest** of all ten ice-cream truck routes.

In dialogue and in casual conversation, you may hear someone use the superlative form when comparing only two things.

Of the two flavors, the chocolate fudge is the **best**.

When you write standard English, however, use the comparative form.

Of the two flavors, the chocolate fudge is **better**.

▐▶ **Avoid illogical comparisons** Use the word *other* or *else* to compare something with others in its group.

ILLOGICAL The Willis Tower is taller than any building in Chicago. [The Willis Tower cannot be taller than itself too!]

LOGICAL The Willis Tower is taller than any **other** building in Chicago.

ILLOGICAL Alex studies harder than anyone in the class.

LOGICAL Alex studies harder than anyone **else** in the class.

▐▶ **Avoid unclear comparisons** Add whatever words are necessary to make a comparison clear.

UNCLEAR Ken is more interested in hiking than Fiona.

CLEAR Ken is more interested in hiking than Fiona is.

CLEAR Ken is more interested in hiking than in Fiona.

UNCLEAR The temperature in Miami is usually higher than Maine.

CLEAR The temperature in Miami is usually higher than the temperature in Maine.

> **EDITING TIP**
>
> Use *fewer*, not *less*, when referring to plural nouns.
>
> I've noticed ~~less~~ *fewer* eagles than last year.
>
> Some regions have ~~less~~ *fewer* people than livestock.

EXERCISE 4 Correcting Modifiers

Review these sentences for use of modifiers. Write the sentence correctly on a separate piece of paper.

EXAMPLE Is the accident rate among teenage drivers higher than adults?

Is the accident rate among teenage drivers higher than that of adult drivers?

1. Lauren likes drag racing more than her brothers.

2. Of the five siblings, Lauren is the more accomplished racer.

3. She is the younger of the five children, all of whom love cars.

4. Of her two oldest brothers, Jim is the best mechanic.

5. But Lauren has more interest in cars than all the members of her family.

6. Lauren is one of a growing number of young women who are becoming more interested in cars than young men.

7. Until very recently, the auto business has been more a man's business than a woman.

8. Car manufacturers have aimed their advertising more directly at men than at anyone.

9. In the past, less women than men were interested in car shopping.

10. Today's women are most likely than women in the past to purchase a car.

Write What You Think

Some commentators claim that the automobile reshaped the world in the twentieth century. In a paragraph or two, answer one of the following questions. Support your opinion with reasons and evidence.

• What will be the most important law about automobiles in the twenty-first century?

• How would you feel about raising the driving-license age to nineteen?

When you have finished, give your writing to a partner for his or her revising suggestions. Both of you should edit the paragraphs for the correct use of modifiers.

EXERCISE 5 Writing a Paragraph

You may wish to refer to the strategies for writing a compare and contrast essay in **Composition,** Lesson 4.4.

Write a paragraph in which you compare two or more objects, people, animals, or places. Here are some possible topics, but feel free to choose your own.

two athletes	two musicians	two schools
three movies	three magazines	three friends
three cars	three vacations	three part-time jobs

As you draft and revise, include at least four comparative or superlative forms in your paragraph, and underline them.

Double Negatives and Absolute Adjectives

▶ Using two negative words together when one will do results in the error called a **double negative**.

Usually, only one negative word is necessary to express a negative idea. Count the contraction *-n't* (for the word *not*) as a negative word.

You can usually correct a double negative in more than one way.

INCORRECT	I couldn't never have done it without your support.
CORRECT	I could never have done it without your support.
CORRECT	I couldn't ever have done it without your support.

INCORRECT	Didn't nobody agree to clean up?
CORRECT	Didn't anybody agree to clean up?
CORRECT	Did nobody agree to clean up?

INCORRECT	I haven't got no time for nothing except studying.
CORRECT	I have no time for anything except studying.
CORRECT	I haven't got any time for anything except studying.

As shown above, in eliminating a negative, you often replace a word—for example, replace *never* with *ever*, and *nobody* with *anybody*.

▶ Some adjectives—such as *excellent, perfect, faultless, flawless, ideal, immaculate,* and *unique*—don't take comparative or superlative forms. These are **absolute adjectives**. They are already "the most" they can be. For example, if something is *flawless* ("without a flaw"), it can't be "more flawless"; if something is *unique* ("one of a kind"), it can't be "most unique."

> Her description of the event was flawless. She made it clear that the moment was unique.

EXERCISE 6 Editing Sentences

Review these sentences for their use of modifiers. Watch for double negatives and for the incorrect use of absolute adjectives. If you find an error, rewrite the sentence correctly. If a sentence is correct, write *C*.

1. In the Verde Valley in central Arizona are remnants of two distinct Native American cultures that once flourished there.

Some Negative Words

barely	none
hardly	no one
never	not (-n't)
no	nothing
nobody	scarcely

EDITING TIP

When it is essential to your meaning, two *not's* in a row are acceptable in standard English; likewise, *not* followed by a negative prefix is sometimes permitted.

I won't *not* give in, but I need time to think about the matter.
He's not unattractive.

Enriching Your Vocabulary

The noun *inkling* in Exercise 6 comes from the Middle English word *ingkiling*. The word and its root both mean "a hint" or "a suspicion." The detective had an *inkling* that the heiress was murdered by the butler.

2. The first of these very unique cultures, the Hohokam, was made up of farmers, who moved into the valley in the seventh century.

3. The Sinagua, who didn't know no Hohokam, lived in pit houses in the nearby foothills and on the plateau beyond them.

4. None of the Hohokam didn't stay in the valley; they migrated north to lands made fertile by the eruptions of a volcano.

5. At that point, the Sinagua, who wouldn't never miss such an opportunity, began using the irrigation system the Hohokam had left behind.

6. You can't hardly blame them.

7. Then the Sinagua began constructing above-ground dwellings, much like those way super perfect "apartment houses" that the Anasazi had built.

8. Anthropologists don't have no inkling why the Sinagua abandoned their sites in the early 1400s.

9. If you ever visit this area, you wouldn't never want to miss the Sinaguan sites, including Montezuma Castle, a five-story cliff dwelling.

10. Montezuma Castle is an odd name for the ruin, since the building doesn't have nothing to do with Montezuma, and it's not no castle.

EXERCISE 7 Editing a Paragraph

Correct all double negatives in the paragraph below as well as any errors with other modifiers.

[1]The saguaro cactus doesn't grow nowhere except in the Sonoran Desert of Arizona and Mexico and in the Baja Peninsula. [2]You can't hardly miss them; they're the ones with the arms. [3]It is not unexpected for these giants to reach heights of sixty feet and to live for more than 150 years. [4]These cacti survive in the desert because of their very unique ability to retain moisture. [5]Through a most flawless system of expanding pleats, the saguaro can store as much as eight tons of moisture after a rainy season. [6]That statement ain't no lie. [7]These sturdy, majestic giants couldn't hardly live without this uncanny ability.

Misplaced Modifiers

A **misplaced modifier** is a word, phrase, or clause that's in the wrong place. It modifies a word that is different from the one it's meant to modify.

Misplaced modifiers may be confusing and misleading; they may force a reader to reread the sentence to understand its meaning. Also, misplaced modifiers may unintentionally make humorous interpretations possible.

> The weary traveler boarded the train with a long face.
> At the meeting, we discussed filling swampland with local politicians.

||||▶ Correct a misplaced modifier by moving it as close as possible to the word it is meant to modify or by changing some words.

MISPLACED	Passing over the stadium, the pitcher saw an airplane.
CORRECTED	The pitcher saw an airplane passing over the stadium.
MISPLACED	The manager screamed at the umpire in the dugout.
CORRECTED	The manager in the dugout screamed at the umpire.
CORRECTED	The manager screamed at the umpire from the dugout.
MISPLACED	Modern and yet traditional, everyone loves the new ballpark.
CORRECTED	Everyone loves the modern, yet traditional, new ballpark.

Notice that in the two preceding examples, the correction involves new constructions altogether.

WRITING HINT

Make sure that the adverb *only* modifies the word you mean it to modify. Place *only* directly before the word or phrase it modifies.

MISPLACED
I only practice in the morning. [This implies that you don't do anything else in the morning.]

CORRECTED
I practice only in the morning. [Now it's clear that when you practice, you do so in the morning.]

TEST-TAKING TIP

Be alert for misplaced modifiers in standardized-test items. A modifier that is placed too far from the word it modifies causes misunderstanding. The correction will position the misplaced word, phrase, or clause closer to the noun or nouns it describes. See item 14 on page 343.

EXERCISE 8 Editing Headlines

Rewrite each of the following newspaper headlines so that it makes sense.

1. VALUABLE COIN FOUND BY BUS DRIVER WITH TWO HEADS

2. CAR CRASHES INTO LAMPPOST GOING 50 MILES PER HOUR

3. CHILD STAR BUYS MANSION ALONG WITH HIS MOTHER

4. PHILANTHROPIST DIES IN HOUSE IN WHICH SHE WAS BORN AT AGE OF 97

5. HUNGRY AND SICK, PLANE DELIVERS FOOD AND MEDICINE NEEDED BY VILLAGERS

6. AS BOSS, SMITH'S BEHAVIOR CONDEMNED

7. MAN FINDS COMPLETE MASTODON SKELETON CRAWLING UNDER PORCH

8. FOUND GUILTY OF PERJURY, JUDGE SENDS POLITICIAN TO PRISON

9. WOMAN DONATES ARTIFACT TO MUSEUM FOUND IN BACKYARD

10. MAJOR DISCOVERY OF LOST CITY LEAKED TO PRESS FROM 12TH CENTURY

EXERCISE 9 Editing a Story Beginning

Work with a partner to correct misplaced modifiers in this story beginning. Compare your changes with those made by other pairs.

¹I told my friends about how I got the game-winning hit during our social studies class. ²As a good storyteller, my friends listened intently. ³I told them how I saw teammates on all three bases stepping up to the plate. ⁴I only missed the first pitch by a hair. ⁵After two swings and misses, the pitcher eyed me menacingly, leaning forward from the pitching-mound rubber. ⁶He threw a fastball right down the middle of the plate which I was awaiting. ⁷Luckily, I remembered all the hitting hints that I was taught in that moment.

EXERCISE 10 Continuing a Story

On a separate piece of paper, continue the story started in Exercise 9. Use your imagination. You should work with a partner, but neither one of you needs to know much about baseball to pick up where the story leaves off. Then exchange papers with another pair. Check each other's work for misplaced modifiers, double negatives, and absolute adjectives.

Dangling Modifiers

A **dangling modifier** is a word, phrase, or clause that doesn't clearly and logically modify any word in the sentence.

> While watching TV, the cable went out.

In the sentence above, the introductory phrase is a dangling modifier because it appears to modify the word *cable*. Since a cable cannot watch television, the modifier is not misplaced; it simply doesn't make sense.

BETTER   While **we** were watching TV, the cable went out.

▶ Correct a dangling modifier by rewording the sentence to add a word or words that the modifier can modify.

DANGLING   While chatting with friends, the subject of college came up.
CORRECTED While chatting with friends, I brought up the subject of college.

DANGLING   Riding in the plane, many towns could be seen far below.
CORRECTED From the plane, passengers could see many towns far below.
CORRECTED Riding in the plane, we could see many towns far below.

DANGLING   To understand events today, a knowledge of American history is essential.
CORRECTED To understand events today, one must have a knowledge of American history.
CORRECTED A knowledge of American history helps a person to understand events today.

You may sometimes correct a dangling modifier in more than one way, as the two preceding examples show.

WRITING HINT

Some dangling modifiers turn up so frequently that they are widely considered acceptable in most contexts. Examples include *generally speaking, strictly speaking, to tell the truth, to be perfectly honest*, and *considering the alternative*.

To tell the truth, that car doesn't measure up.

Generally speaking, the prices go up each year.

EXERCISE 11 Editing Sentences

On a separate piece of paper, write each sentence to correct all dangling modifiers. If a sentence is correct, write *C*.

1. Lying still in bed, the loud storm outside scared her.

2. To get ready for guests, the party preparations began early.

3. While talking with teammates, the topic of college coaches came up.

4. If you want to understand the rules of rugby, you should watch several games.

5. Carrying grocery bags home, his hat blew off.

6. While trying to do my math homework, someone in the next room began to play the drums.

7. Having promised to return after dinner, my friends were made anxious when I didn't show up until much later.

8. After driving in the rainstorm for hours, the rain stopped, and visibility got much better.

9. Anticipating very tough questions, she was relieved at how easy the biology test was.

10. Annoyed by his constant complaints, the manager got tossed out of the game.

 EXERCISE 12 Editing an Anecdote

Work with a partner to correct dangling modifiers in this anecdote. Compare your changes with those made by another pair.

[1]Entering the small, dimly lit restaurant, many of the tables were empty.
[2]While hanging up our coats our table was prepared. [3]Despite the fact that other tables offered privacy, we were seated right next to a table of three. [4]After a long day of walking all over the big city, little energy remained for conversation. [5]We sat silently and looked at our menus. [6]Then, looking around the room, a chill ran down my back.

[7]Sitting at the table next to us, not more than five feet away, could be seen two celebrities. [8]Holding my breath, my sister had to be told. [9]I kicked her under the table and nodded in their direction. [10]She gasped. [11]Having clued her in to our famous neighbors, my mother wondered what we two were pretending not to stare at.

[12]"What are you two gawking at? . . . Oh, my!"

[13]I guess she figured it out. [14]They were *major* celebrities. [15]Soon the whole family was in the know. [16]While pretending to read the menu and even to carry on our own little conversation, all attention was focused on the discussion at the next table. [17]After going on with this charade for what seemed like hours, the waiter arrived and took our order. [18]I don't think I tasted any of my food that night, but I now know that I am a good listener.

Revising and Editing Worksheet 1

Improve the following draft by revising for ideas, organization, word choice, and sentence variety. After revising, edit the draft for errors in spelling, capitalization, punctuation, and usage. Write your revised and edited version on a separate piece of paper. Compare your changes with those of a writing partner.

[1]Agatha Mary Clarissa Christie, more better known as Dame Agatha Christie, was not only a writter of English detective novels but also of plays. [2]Although *The Mousetrap* (1952) set a world record for its continuous run at the Ambassador Theatre in London, she is best known for writing novels good. [3]Writing over a period of many years, her detective novels have sold more than one hundred million copies. [4]Many feature the egotistical detective Hercule Poirot or the elderly Miss Jane Marple.

[5]Appearing first in *The Mysterious Affair at Styles* (1920), people were introduced to Poirot. [6]Nobody didn't know nothing about Miss Jane Marple until she made her first appearance in *Murder at the Vicarage* (1930). [7]With *The Murder of Roger Ackroyd* (1926), considered by some to be a most perfect novel, Christie achieved recognition. [8]Following that book, she wrote dozens more, many of which sold extremely good. [9]Translated into one hundred languages, the whole world has read her books.

[10]Several of Christie's novels has been made into films. [11]Perhaps the better of them is *Witness for the Prosecution*. [12]Nobody who has saw this movie will never forget it's many unexpected twists and turns. [13]While recalling this film, other movie versions of her novels come to mind. [14]Like *Murder on the Orient Express* and *Murder on the Nile*. [15]Christie was made a Dame of the British Empire before her death in 1976, in 1971. [16]Appearing after her death in 1977, Dame Agatha Christie wrote her autobiography.

Revising and Editing Worksheet 2

Improve the following draft by revising for ideas, organization, word choice, and sentence variety. After revising, edit the draft for errors in spelling, capitalization, punctuation, and usage. Write your revised and edited version on a separate piece of paper. Compare your changes with those of a writing partner.

[1]When discussing famous British mystery writers, the names of Dorothy Sayers and P. D. James inevitably come up. [2]If it weren't for these novelists, we wouldn't never have heard of the two exceptional (but fictional) sleuths Lord Peter Wimsey, of London, and Inspector Adam Dalgleish, of Scotland Yard. [3]Its challenging to determine which sleuth is best.

[4]Sayers, who earned a degree in medieval literature from Oxford University, was among the most earliest women to have graduated from there. [5]After introducing Wimsey, the dashing gentleman scholar, in 1923, he appears in one or two Sayers mysteries each year for the next fifteen years. [6]In *Strong Poison*, Sayers introduces Lord Peter to the most perfect woman for him, Harriet Vane.

[7]Wimsey is an aristocrat who only became a detective after he discovered after graduation that he had a gift for crime detection. [8]This Oxford graduate with a private income is charming, witty, and a lover of books. [9]His servant, Bunter, who aids him in his investigative efforts. [10]While solving crimes, the assistance of Inspector Parker is helpful.

[11]P. D. James wrote the first of her mystery novels in 1962. [12]Her books are noted for their most unique characterizations and their vivid sense of atmosphere. [13]Her detective hero, Adam Dalgleish, is actually one of two of this writer's protagonists; Cordelia Gray, a private sleuth, is the other. [14]Dalgleish, in contrast to Wimsey, has climbed up the ladder in Scotland yard, no aristocrat. [15]Whereas Lord Peter is cool and detached, Dalgleish is an emotional poet. [16]But, like Lord Peter, Dalgleish's investigative methods are thoughtful and most flawless.

Chapter Review

EXERCISE A Using the Degrees of Comparison

Review the following sentences for the correct use of modifiers. If you find an error, cross out the word or phrase, and rewrite it correctly in the space above. If a sentence contains no errors, write *C*.

1. In Seattle in 1998, a competition took place for the world's smallest kite.

2. Seattle is the most largest city in Washington.

3. Kites in the competition had to soar either at a ten-degree angle of flight or more steeplier.

4. One kite was no bigger than a mosquito.

5. There were no less than twenty kites in the competition.

6. Most of the miniature kites flew good.

7. One of the most prettiest kites looked like a birch leaf.

8. All of the kites, from the most tiniest to the largest, had to be small enough to fit in the palm of the hand.

9. The judges included a test pilot, a mechanical engineer, and an administrator. Which one was the stricter?

10. The winner, although not the smaller of all the kites, may get a mention in the *Guinness Book of World Records*.

EXERCISE B Editing Sentences

On a separate piece of paper, rewrite each sentence to correct all misplaced modifiers and dangling modifiers.

1. Hanging from a hook in his locker, the pitcher took his cap.

2. The player's shoes hurt his feet, which were too small.

3. The slumping batter learned a new trick from an instructor that would help him.

4. Practicing in the batting cage, it began to rain.

5. Overweight and slow, the coach says our team needs to shape up.

6. As manager, Reilly's desk was always piled with scouting reports.

7. The rookie got on the bus with a big smile.

8. To keep the field in good condition, the grass needs lots of attention.

9. Leaving at 7 P.M., management will have a plane for the players.

10. The team was only bought by Mrs. Leary.

11. While running after a fly ball, there was some commotion in the stands.

12. In the sports magazine's editorial, they applauded the team for trading players.

13. Young but talented and aggressive, all sportswriters like our team's chances of winning.

14. Being young and inexperienced, people think we will make crucial mistakes.

15. Generally speaking, only mature teams win championships.

EXERCISE C Editing Sentences

Review these sentences for the correct use of modifiers. If you find an error, rewrite the sentence correctly on a separate piece of paper. If a sentence is correct, write C.

1. So you think there isn't nothing about money you don't know?

2. The most oldest written records of money are from ancient Mesopotamia (now southern Iraq).

3. Describing payments in silver, historians have discovered inscribed Mesopotamian tablets.

4. The most earliest coins date from the seventh century B.C. in what is now Turkey.

5. Measuring precious metals, ancient Egyptian wall paintings show the weights that were used.

6. Money in eighteenth-century Burma was pancake-shaped disks called "flower silver."

7. The people of Yap, an island in the Pacific, paid their debts with enormous, most round stone disks.

8. Made from tiny red feathers glued together and tied to coils of vegetable fiber, the islanders of Santa Cruz, in the Pacific, used these huge coils as money.

9. From the fifteenth century to 1948 in Nigeria, they had used copper rings as money called *manillas*.

10. Known as wampum, some North American Indians used belts of beads as payment.

EXERCISE D Creating Your Own Exercise

Misplaced and dangling modifiers can be funny. Work with a partner or small group to create a paragraph or at least ten newspaper headlines or sentences with misplaced and dangling modifiers. Then exchange your efforts with another group. Correct each other's deliberate errors.

CHAPTER REVIEW

Cumulative Review

EXERCISE A Using Verbs Correctly

On a separate piece of paper, correct all of the errors in verb usage in the following sentences. Look for incorrect verbs and verb forms, unnecessary shifts in verb tense, and unnecessary use of the passive voice.

1. When he bite into the sandwich, he found a surprise.

2. Have you ate your lunch yet?

3. I would feel bad if I was you.

4. She bought something every time she goes to a yard sale.

5. The ball was thrown right to her; she should have catched it.

6. The principal requests that Ms. Smith teaches usage of verbs.

7. The earring I thought I had lose was then finded by me.

8. When the bridge was builded, it would be the longest one in the city.

9. Have you choosed what you're going to wear?

10. She loaned her sweatshirt to me, which I then had gave to my cousin.

EXERCISE B Subject-Verb Agreement

Underline the verb in parentheses that agrees with the subject.

1. May 1, which is Cartoon Appreciation Day and International Tuba Day, (is, are) the beginning of quite a month.

2. On May 2, Italy honors the anniversary of the death of Leonardo da Vinci—the artist, scientist, and inventor—(doesn't, don't) it?

3. I know someone who (observes, observe) Be Kind to Animals Week.

4. On May 5, which is Cinco de Mayo, one of my friends (celebrates, celebrate) the 1862 victory of Mexican troops over France's Napoleon III.

5. (Does, Do) your Dutch mother or Dutch aunts celebrate the 1945 liberation of the Netherlands from Nazi forces on May 5?

6. Either actor George Clooney or Tony Blair, the former prime minister of Great Britain, (claims, claim) to share his birthday, May 6, with baseball great Willie Mays.

7. May 7 (is, are) the anniversary of the birth of composer Johannes Brahms and of the premiere of Beethoven's Ninth Symphony.

8. Mother's Day and my birthday (occurs, occur) on May 8 this year.

9. No Socks Day or the Poke Salad Festival (is, are) celebrated in Blanchard, Louisiana, on May 8 every year.

10. Sentence 9 is the only one of these facts that (surprises, surprise) me.

EXERCISE C Correcting Pronoun Usage

On a separate piece of paper, rewrite correctly each sentence that contains an error in pronoun usage. If a sentence is correct, write C.

1. Maria gave Celia the sweater she loved.

2. The band teacher gave we musicians the schedule for this semester's concerts.

3. Not many people came to last year's concert. It was too bad.

4. Either Angela or Raymond has college in their plans.

5. Do you know whom is going to buy a car?

6. Why don't you like the singer who I tell everyone to listen to?

7. The two best-liked seniors, Meg and her, are coming to the party.

8. Did you see where they gave the debating team high marks?

9. Everyone in the boys club who volunteers gets a medal.

10. Us members of the track team work out nearly every day.

EXERCISE D Using Modifiers Correctly

On a separate piece of paper, correct the sentences that contain errors in the use of modifiers. If a sentence is correct, write C.

1. Researchers found that in 1999 less teenagers had access to the Internet than originally thought.

2. Estimating that soon over ninety-three percent of the nation's teens will be online, a lot of kids use the Internet.

3. Compared with all other age groups, soon teens will be using the Internet in a higher proportion.

4. Some teens think that browsing the Internet on their computer or phone is the most wonderfulest thing they can do.

5. Many think that carrying on conversations with several other kids by computer is more better than carrying home stuff from the mall.

6. Expensive and controversial, some parents worry about online communication.

7. Some teens only use computers for homework.

8. The computer may be more popular than any other invention.

9. As a substitute for television, some kids turn to cyberspace.

10. For some teens, the most ideal use of cyberspace is socializing.

Punctuation: End Marks and Commas

S T U D E N T   W R I T I N G

Expository Essay

Food Committee Takes Another Stab
by Mark Boucher
high school student, Pennington, New Jersey

The Food Committee met for the first time Tuesday to evaluate menus, food preparation, fat/caloric content of meals, and food service in general.

The group is composed of Dean of Students Martin Doggett, Food Service Director and Executive Chef Roland Young, and eight students.

The students made several suggestions to improve the quality and variety of the menus. They proposed more nonsugared cereals in the Abbott Dining Center, the prompt refilling of the drink dispensers, a reinstitution of the yogurt bar, and better replenishment of the deli bar during meals. They also recommended a reduction in the number of fried foods served. Many asked for menu adjustments, and the executive chef plans to review the current menu cycles.

In addition, the company in charge of food service has promised to work toward a labeling system for all entrees. This would give students and faculty a variety of health information, including calories, carbohydrates, and fat content; it would allow them to make better-informed choices about the food they eat.

The students also proposed a series of nutrition workshops in the houses. These workshops would be geared toward specific groups, such as athletes or people trying to lose weight. In general, the students are pleased with the food service, and the meeting was very productive and organized, according to Doggett. "The students made several reasonable suggestions," he said. "It was not just bashing the [food service company]." They praised the service at the Tuesday sit-down dinners and Friday sit-down lunches.

> As you reread Mark Boucher's expository essay, notice how often he gives examples to support his general statements. When he gives more than two examples in a row (a series), he separates them with a comma. You'll get practice using commas in a series and in lots of other ways as you do the exercises in this chapter.

End Marks and Abbreviations

▊▶ Use a **period** at the end of a statement (declarative sentence).

The Beatles might have worked together again if John Lennon had lived**.**

▊▶ Use a **question mark** at the end of a direct question (interrogative sentence). An indirect question ends with a period.

DIRECT   Who was the band's first drummer**?**

INDIRECT   Inez asked me who the band's first drummer was**.**

▊▶ Use an **exclamation point** at the end of an exclamation (exclamatory sentence).

Wow**!** That woman can sing**!** or Wow, that woman can sing**!**

▊▶ Use either a **period** or an **exclamation point** at the end of a command (imperative sentence).

Call to find out where she's performing next**.**
Don't be late for the concert**!**

▊▶ Use a **period** after many abbreviations.

Papers and reports for school or work should, in general, not contain abbreviations. **Exceptions:** You may use abbreviations of time (such as A.M. and B.C.) and of certain titles before and after names (such as *Ms.* and *M.D.*)

Abbreviations and Periods				
CATEGORY	**EXAMPLE**			
Initials and Titles	Mr. D. T. Williams, Jr. Harriet C. Gomez, Ph.D. Dr. Kyle E. Tang Mrs. Elena Hart Jo Keen, M.D.			
Times	A.M. P.M. B.C. B.C.E. A.D.			
Others	Inc. Co. Assn. etc. vs.			

Don't use periods with acronyms. An **acronym** is a word formed from the first letter(s) of several words, such as *laser* (from "*l*ight *a*mplification by *s*timulated *e*mission of *r*adiation").

The modern tendency is to omit the period following common abbreviations such as *ft* (foot *or* feet) and *lb* (pound), metric measures such as *cm* (centimeter) and *kg* (kilogram), and chemical elements such as *He* (helium). Some other abbreviations that don't take periods include *mph* (miles per hour), *AM* and *FM* radio, *FBI*, *IRS*, and postal abbreviations for states (*ME*, *AZ*, *NJ*).

Use punctuation correctly in bibliographies.

Parks**,** Rosa. *My Story***.** New York**:** Penguin**,** 1992**.** Print**.**

WRITING HINT

When you use an unfamiliar abbreviation, first give the full name or expression followed by the abbreviation in parentheses.

In 1816, African American Methodist ministers organized the African Methodist Episcopal (AME) church. The AME took a leading role in the struggle to end slavery.

EDITING TIP

Use only one period with an abbreviation at the end of a sentence. However, don't omit a comma, question mark, or exclamation point following an abbreviation.

The play ended at 11 P.M.

What happened in Crete in 1200 B.C.**?**

Exercise 1 Punctuating Sentences

Proofread the following sentences to add missing punctuation and to replace abbreviations that do not belong in a school report. **Hint:** Some sentences require more than one punctuation mark.

1. The first Doric and Ionic columns appeared in Greece in the first century bc
2. D H Lawrence wrote poignant short stories
3. A majority of the srs. will take the Scholastic Aptitude Test (SAT) in Nov.
4. Besides "Mr. Pym Passes By," what did A A Milne write
5. A plague took its toll on Athens from 430 to 423 bc
6. Oh, no I've forgotten who won in 1988 Who was it
7. In 1705, young composer J S Bach walked 200 mi to attend a concert
8. In 1967, the musical *Cabaret*—by J Masteroff, J Kanter, and F Ebb—opened in New York
9. She asked if I know what K F Gauss and Wilhelm E Weber invented in 1833
10. Don't forget periods after bk. titles in your bibliography

Exercise 2 Punctuating a Paragraph

Review the following paragraph to add end marks and other periods as needed. If you're not sure whether an abbreviation takes a period, check a dictionary.

[1]The Web site for the Modern Language Association (MLA) is worth visiting [2]M.LA is perhaps best known as the authority on documentation. [3]Its Web site provides up-to-date directions and examples of how to cite sources in a research paper? [4]The most basic citation is for a book by one author, an example of which follows

[5]Peterson, Robert *Only the Ball Was White* (New York: Oxford, 1992) Print.

[6]The site also provides guidelines for citing online documents as well as movies and TV. and radio shows.

[7]The MLA style guide is also available in print [8]One advantage the Web site has over the print version of the style guide is that the former is always there, be it 6 a.m. or 10 p.m! [9]Students don't have to ask themselves, "Where did I put that book?" [10]To explore what the MLA Web site offers, go to www.mla.org.

Commas in a Series

Commas, the most frequently used punctuation mark, signal a slight hesitation but not a complete stop. Mainly, their purpose is to prevent misreading. In the next few lessons, you'll review the most important rules for using commas.

▶ Use commas to separate items in a series.

A **series** contains three or more similar items in a row.
> New York, Detroit, and Chicago have professional teams in baseball, football, basketball, and hockey.

When a coordinating conjunction (such as *and* or *but*) connects items, don't insert commas unless the items are independent clauses.
> I took the ice cream out to defrost **and** left it on the counter **but** forgot about it.
> I took the ice cream out to defrost, **but** my brother put it back, **and** it froze again.

▶ Use a comma to separate two or more adjectives that precede and modify the same noun.
> Visiting the Holocaust Memorial Museum in Washington is a powerful, memorable experience.

Don't use a comma when the last adjective in a series is really part of a compound noun.
> Which new digital music player did you get? [*Digital music player* is a compound noun, so don't use a comma after *new*.]

To decide whether to put a comma between two adjectives preceding a noun, try *and* between the two adjectives. If *and* makes sense, use a comma.
> He gave a quick *and* dismissive answer. [makes sense]
> He gave a quick, dismissive answer. [use comma]

If *and* doesn't make sense, don't use a comma.
> He walked some *and* large dogs. [doesn't make sense]
> He walked some large dogs. [no comma]

> See also
> **Mechanics**, Lesson 14.2, which explains when to use semicolons rather than commas for a series.

WRITING *HINT*

Some publications omit the comma after the next-to-last item in a series.

She hates broccoli, beans and asparagus.

This book advises *always* using a series comma before the conjunction because it's never wrong to do so.

EXERCISE 3 Adding Commas to Sentences

Walter copied the quotations on the following page from a reference book. In his haste, he left out commas. Insert all necessary commas. If a sentence does not need a comma, write *C*.

1. There are three modes of bearing the ills of life: by indifference by philosophy and by religion. —Charles Caleb Colton

2. I sing of brooks of blossoms birds and bowers. —Robert Herrick

3. Some books are to be tasted others to be swallowed and some few to be chewed and digested. —Francis Bacon

4. You will find that deep place of silence right in your room your garden or even your bathtub. —Elisabeth Kübler-Ross

5. I reject get-it-done make-it-happen thinking. —Jerry Brown

6. Dancing is the loftiest the most moving the most beautiful of the arts. —Havelock Ellis

7. War's a brain-spattering windpipe-splitting art. —Lord Byron

8. What does education often do? It makes a straight-cut ditch of a free meandering brook. —Henry David Thoreau

9. Happy families are all alike; every unhappy family is unhappy in its own way. —Leo Tolstoy

10. For a while I thought history was something bitter old men wrote. —Jacqueline Kennedy Onassis

11. The four stages of man are infancy childhood adolescence and obsolescence. —Art Linkletter

12. Only in growth reform and change, paradoxically enough, is true security to be found. —Anne Morrow Lindbergh

13. There is nothing more enticing disenchanting and enslaving than the life at sea. —Joseph Conrad

14. My personal hobbies are reading listening to music and silence. —Edith Sitwell

15. Style is character. A good style cannot come from a bad undisciplined character. —Norman Mailer

EXERCISE 4 Checking a Paper for Punctuation

Take a paper you've written recently, and review it carefully. Focus particularly on end punctuation marks and commas. Check to see whether you have used these punctuation marks correctly. If you decide to make any changes in punctuation, be prepared to explain your decision.

Commas with Compound Sentences and Introductory Elements

▐▐▶ Use a comma before a coordinating conjunction that joins two independent clauses.

> Miguel wants to swim at the beach, and Sonia will sunbathe and read her book. [compound sentence with two declarative clauses]
> Does Miguel know how to swim, and will Sonia remember to bring her book? [compound sentence with two interrogative clauses]
> Sonia, keep an eye on Miguel in the water, and use sunblock on your skin. [compound sentence with two imperative clauses]

Generally, you do not need a comma between parts of a compound subject or a compound verb. The sentence below, however, uses a comma within the compound verb to prevent a misreading.

> I worry about his common sense, and am relying on you to guide him.

▐▐▶ Use a comma after an introductory adverb, participle, phrase, or clause.

> **Unfortunately,** the tennis star missed the ball. [introductory adverb]
> **Horrified,** the tennis star glared at the referee. [introductory participle]
> **Horrified by the call,** the tennis star glared at the referee. [introductory participial phrase]
> **In brief,** we won. [introductory prepositional phrase]
> **To the delight of our coach in her final year,** we won. [series of introductory prepositional phrases]
> **To help her with math,** Diane hired a tutor. [infinitive phrase]
> **His hair blowing in the wind,** the diver stood at the edge of the high cliff. [introductory absolute phrase]
> **As soon as we sat down to dinner,** the phone started ringing. [introductory adverb clause]

▐▐▶ Use a comma before a concluding adverb clause only if it expresses the idea of contrast or if the sentence might be misread without it.

> I watched quietly **as my brother put on his tie**. [no comma necessary before adverb clause]
> I watched quietly**, even though I could have helped him**. [comma before adverb clause expressing contrast]

See **Mechanics,** Lesson 13.5, for a discussion on using commas following introductory words such as *yes, no,* and *well.*

EDITING TIP

When the subject follows the verb, do not use a comma after one or more introductory prepositional phrases.

In the attic under a pile
of old clothes **are** the
paintings.

Exercise 5 Revising Sentences

On a separate piece of paper, revise each sentence so that it begins with an introductory phrase, adverb, or adverb clause. Add commas where necessary. **Hint:** You may need to add, drop, or change some words.

EXAMPLE   We will win the game if we practice diligently.
If we practice diligently, we will win the game.

1. Six American high school students astonished the judges at a world mathematics competition in Hong Kong.

2. All the students on the team achieved perfect scores on the exam for the first time in the history of the competition.

3. The American team claimed victory over sixty-eight other countries to bring home a win from the International Mathematical Olympics.

4. Every member of the American team answered all six questions correctly—a remarkable accomplishment.

5. The mathematics exam took a grueling nine hours to complete because of its difficulty.

6. The test was brief, consisting of only six questions.

7. Each question, however, was a complicated problem testing algebra, geometry, or numbers theory.

8. An American team has not won the competition since 1986, when Americans tied with Russian students.

9. Some teams, such as the one from China, train for the test by living together and studying year-round.

10. The Americans, hailing from New York, Massachusetts, Maryland, and Illinois, were coached by Walter Mientka, a professor of mathematics at the University of Nebraska.

CONNECTING
Writing & Grammar

Write What You Think

Successes like that of the math team in Hong Kong make Americans proud of our educational achievements. Write a brief essay explaining the academic successes of your school or the schools in your community. You may choose to focus on a particular club or on the successes of a specific individual.

Where possible, use examples and statistics to support your statements. When you've finished revising, edit your work to see if you've used commas and end punctuation correctly. Then share your work with your classmates.

Commas with Sentence Interrupters and Nonessential Elements

You learned about setting off an introductory element with a single comma in Lesson 13.3. Likewise, you must set off an **interrupter** that occurs within a sentence with a pair of commas.

▶ Use a pair of commas around a noun of direct address and around a parenthetical or transitional expression.

> Did you know**,** Orlando**,** that leather craft is a major industry in Morocco?
> Moroccan leather goods**,** by the way**,** make wonderful gifts.
> Tourists in Morocco**,** therefore**,** love to shop for leather goods.

▶ Use a pair of commas around a nonessential, or interrupting, phrase or clause.

An **essential**, or **restrictive**, phrase or clause is necessary to the meaning of the sentence. A **nonessential**, or **nonrestrictive**, phrase or clause adds information, but the sentence makes sense without it.

> My cousin **Zev** visited Morocco last summer. [no comma around essential appositive phrase; it tells *which* cousin]
> He saw leather goods in markets**, or souks,** throughout Morocco. [commas around nonessential appositive phrase]

> Some French teens **traveling with him** spent all their time in the souks. [no comma around essential participial phrase]
> Zev**, looking for the larger picture,** visited mosques**, or houses of worship**. [commas around nonessential participial phrase and comma before nonessential appositive phrase]

> The mosques **that are his favorite** are in Marrakech**, which is in the foothills of the Grand Atlas,** and in Rabat. [no commas around the essential adjective clause; commas around the nonessential adjective clause]

▶ Use commas to set off **contrasting expressions**.

> Leather bags and purses**, not book covers or desk accessories,** are the most popular Moroccan exports.

Do not, however, use commas with correlative conjunctions.

> While in Morocco, Zev ate **not only** couscous **but also** tajine.

Exercise 6 Adding Commas to Sentences

Review the following sentences, adding commas where they are needed. Write *C* if the sentence is correct.

1. Sumerian writing which developed about six thousand years ago involved cutting pictographs onto clay tablets.

2. A pictograph also called a hieroglyph is a picture representing a word or idea.

3. Ancient Egyptian calendars regulated by the sun and moon had 360 days.

4. Each month by the way had thirty days.

5. Sumerian wedge-shaped cuneiform writing appeared about 5,500 years ago.

6. Five thousand years ago, Egyptian musicians played not only lyres but also clarinets.

7. Wheeled vehicles incidentally first appeared in Sumeria more than five thousand years ago.

8. During the period from 3000 to 2500 B.C. the Phoenicians settled two cities Tyre and Sidon along the Mediterranean Sea.

9. The Great Wall of Uruk which had nine hundred towers was built by Sumerians between 3000 B.C. and 2500 B.C.

10. Rodney who loves dogs would be interested to know that Egyptians domesticated dogs nearly five thousand years ago.

11. The ancient Sumerians who also wrote poetry and knew about the healing qualities of mineral springs used oil-burning lamps.

12. The Sumerians developers of a numerical system based on six and twelve began using metal coins by 2500 B.C.

13. During the period between 2500 B.C. and 2000 B.C. Egyptians began using papyrus and moreover started their first libraries.

14. Bows and arrows were used as weapons in warfare for the first time during that same period.

15. The Egyptians not the Sumerians built pyramids.

Working Together

Exercise 7 Describing an Ancient Setting

Imagine yourself spending a day in an ancient civilization such as Egypt or Sumer. What do you think you'd see around you? Imagine what daily life might have looked like and sounded like. Think about what it might have smelled like and what the weather would have been like. Brainstorm ideas with others in a group. Then write two descriptive paragraphs filled with details of your imagined journey. Check your sentences for correct end marks and commas. Share your passages with classmates.

Other Comma Uses

▐▐▶ Use commas to set off interjections, such as *well*, *yes*, *no*, and single-word adjectives that begin a sentence.

> Well, have you seen *Microscopic*, the hit movie about the sinking of the world's smallest boat?
> Yes, I did.
> Ugh, I'll never see it.
> Curious, we stood in line for two hours to get in.
> Disappointed, we left even before the boat sank in the tub.

> See
> **Mechanics**,
> Lesson 14.1,
> for more on
> setting off
> long
> quotations.

▐▐▶ Use commas to separate parts of a reference, parts of an address, geographical terms, and parts of a date.

> The Beatles performed in Liverpool, England, at first.
> Turn to *The History of Art*, page 722, for more on that topic.
> Our favorite scene was Act I, scene 3, because of its humor.
> June 27, 1880, is the birth date of Helen Keller.

You do not need a comma between month and date or between month and year.

> Who else was born on June 27?
> Justice Thurgood Marshall resigned from the Supreme Court in late June 1991.

▐▐▶ Use commas following the greeting of a friendly letter and following the closing of both friendly and business letters.

> Dear Suki,   Sincerely,   Dear Aunt Thelma,   With love,

▐▐▶ Use commas to set off short, direct quotations.

> "I can't think of two TV shows that I like," Ralph complained.
> "Prime-time television," he claimed, "has gone down the tubes."

▐▐▶ Use a comma to set off tag questions.

> I told you that I scratched the new car, **didn't I**?
> You don't happen to have Theo's address, **do you**?

EDITING TIP

Don't use commas every time you see quotation marks. Quoted words or phrases that serve as subjects, predicate nominatives, or direct objects do not need commas.

"Yesterday" is her favorite Beatles song.

But my favorite is "In My Life."

Eddie sighs whenever he hears "While My Guitar Gently Weeps."

EXERCISE 8 Adding Commas to Sentences

Proofread the following sentences, adding commas where they are needed. **Hint:** A sentence may require the insertion of more than one comma. Write *C* if the sentence is correct.

1. Yes the play put all the students to sleep.

2. Well our class didn't have the background to appreciate this revival of the March 1938 comedy.

3. So do you think New York New York is the best place to see theater productions?

4. Michael Richards (Kramer on *Seinfeld*) was born on August 24 1950.

5. By Act III scene 2, of *Waiting to Nap* everyone in the audience was asleep.

6. "Wake up you dolts" Richard said. "You don't know what you're missing!"

7. I warned you not to attend didn't I?

8. We saw the same play in March 1999 and didn't like it then.

9. No I don't remember seeing it; I must have been asleep.

10. I read the *Playbill* page 14 to learn about the background of this theater.

EXERCISE 9 Editing a Friendly Letter

Review the friendly letter below. Add commas, periods, and other end punctuation marks where necessary. Remove unnecessary commas.

April 25, 2013

Dear Michelle

Well am I glad that you've decided on State U. Man are you going to love it here. I began a whole new life on September 4 2012 the first day of classes. You could say that the curtain went up on Act II scene 1 of my life on that day. "Let It Be," was the perfect song to wake up to that day.

Binghamton New York, is so different from Maplewood. It snows here every day in the winter. But in the spring, we have classes outside. That sounds great doesn't it?

I can't wait to see you next September, 3. I'll say "Hey welcome to campus."

As always

Karen

EXERCISE 10 Writing a Friendly E-mail

On a separate piece of paper, write a real or simulated e-mail to a friend you haven't seen or spoken to in a while. Tell him or her about what's been happening in your life. Share the details of some of your recent experiences. Inform your friend of some of the things you've been thinking about lately. Write about any plans you have. When you have finished your draft, edit it for the correct use of end punctuation and commas.

Correcting Run-on Sentences and Sentence Fragments

To correct a **run-on sentence**, use the following strategies.

▶ Add end punctuation and a capital letter to break up the run-on sentence.

RUN-ON	About four thousand years ago, Stonehenge was a center of worship, it was the Bronze Age.
CORRECTED	About four thousand years ago, Stonehenge was a center of worship. It was the Bronze Age.

▶ Change the run-on into a compound sentence.

RUN-ON	Most people in the ancient world lived in humble houses, the Minoan palace at Knossos had bathrooms.
CORRECTED	Most people in the ancient world lived in humble houses, **but** the Minoan palace at Knossos had bathrooms.
CORRECTED	Most people in the ancient world lived in humble houses; **however**, the Minoan palace at Knossos had bathrooms.

> **WRITING HINT**
>
> To keep your paragraphs engaging, aim for variety when you correct fragments or run-ons. Read your revised sentences in your head or quietly aloud. Listen to how they sound.

▶ Change one of the sentences into a subordinate clause.

CORRECTED	**Although most people in the ancient world lived in humble houses,** the Minoan palace at Knossos had bathrooms.

To correct a **sentence fragment**, use these strategies.

▶ Add the missing subject, verb, or both.

FRAGMENT	Spread from the Mediterranean through Europe.
CORRECTED	Trade routes spread from the Mediterranean through Europe.

▶ Attach the fragment to a complete sentence before or after it.

FRAGMENT	An obelisk from ancient Egypt. Cleopatra's Needle still stands in New York's Central Park.
CORRECTED	An obelisk from ancient Egypt, Cleopatra's Needle still stands in New York's Central Park.

▶ Drop a subordinating conjunction.

FRAGMENT	Because percussion instruments were added to Egyptian orchestral music nearly four thousand years ago.
CORRECTED	Percussion instruments were added to Egyptian orchestral music nearly four thousand years ago.

> **Enriching Your Vocabulary**
>
> The French words *em*, or "in," and *barca*, meaning "ship," form the roots of the word *embark*, which means "to go on board a ship or vehicle." As on page 278, it can also mean "to undertake an enterprise." You may *embark* on a career after high school.

EXERCISE 11 Editing a Paragraph

Review the following paragraphs to correct run-on sentences and sentence fragments. Read your edited version aloud to see that the sentences sound smooth together.

¹In about 2000 B.C., the Achaeans invaded. ²Invaded the Greek peninsula. ³Pushed farther south, conquering new territory throughout Greece. ⁴The Achaean kings ruled walled cities, through trading and looting, they built palaces and filled them with treasures. ⁵Outside the fortresses lived farmers, artisans, merchants, and traders. ⁶Paid tribute to the king.

⁷The Achaeans built on the achievements of the earlier Minoan civilization, their artisans reproduced Minoan designs on pottery and jewelry. ⁸And on their tools. ⁹From the Minoans, the Achaeans also learned writing, they adapted symbols from the Minoan alphabet.

¹⁰In about 1300 or 1250 B.C., Achaean kings banded together, they embarked on a war against the rival commercial power, Troy. ¹¹Troy which controlled key trade routes between the Aegean Sea and the Black Sea. ¹²The Achaeans emerged as the victors after a bloody war. ¹³The story of the fall of Troy and the aftermath is told in the *Iliad* and the *Odyssey*, two epic poems attributed to the poet Homer, he probably lived about five hundred years later. ¹⁴Composed these poems based on oral stories that had been passed along over many generations.

¹⁵Until nineteenth-century excavations proved the existence of Troy, historians had treated Homer's poems as fictions, now, although scholars do not look upon the *Iliad* and the *Odyssey* as pure history, they realize that the poems provide insights into the lives and values of ancient Greeks.

EXERCISE 12 Creating and Checking an Exercise

From a newspaper or magazine, copy a paragraph or two, removing all capital letters, end punctuation, and commas. Give the lowercased, unpunctuated text to a classmate, who will try to put in the missing capital letters and the punctuation. Then review your classmate's work against the original to see how the two are the same and how they are different.

Editing and Proofreading Worksheet 1

Edit the draft for errors in spelling, capitalization, punctuation, and usage. Write your edited version on a separate piece of paper. Compare your changes with those of a writing partner.

¹Three ancient civilizations arose in the fertile valleys of the Nile River, the Tigris River the Euphrates River and the Indus River. ²A fourth civilization developed along the Yellow River in northern China. ³Then between 5000 and 3000 BC. ⁴People in China began to form permanent villages and discovered effective ways to produce food. ⁵By about 1600 B.C. the Shang civilization arose. ⁶Lasting about five hundred years.

⁷Archaeologists unearthed more than 130 Shang sites. ⁸Which reveal a great deal about the Shang civilization. ⁹Like the Sumerians and the Egyptians the Shang developed a system of writing with pictographs! ¹⁰As time passed they introduced ideograms symbols that express ideas rather than objects. ¹¹They had ideograms for ideas such as unity or wisdom, all together the Shang written language contained more than three thousand characters.

¹²Within Shang society there was a strict class system although most of the people were poor peasants. ¹³The king his nobles and the priests assumed all political and religious responsibilities. ¹⁴In contrast with the lavish homes of the wealthy the farmers lived in simple small partially underground houses? ¹⁵These peasants as you might expect were called upon to serve as soldiers they also had to give a portion of their harvest to the king or to one of his local representatives.

Editing and Proofreading Worksheet 2

Edit the draft for errors in spelling, capitalization, punctuation, and usage. Write your edited version on a separate piece of paper. Compare your changes with those of a writing partner.

[1]King Arthur's Camelot has captured the imagination of one generation after the next, in fact tales of Arthur and his Knights of the Round Table have been enchanting people for more than a thousand years. [2]In dozens of languages and in many storytelling genres ranging from medieval epics to modern musicals movies and cartoons. [3]The legend's plot alone! [4]Which makes the story irresistible.

[5]According to the legend Arthur an ordinary boy pulls a sword which is named Excalibur from a stone. [6]Based on that deed Arthur becomes the king of England. [7]Subsequently he marries the beautiful Guinevere forms a brotherhood of chivalrous knights and undertakes a quest for the Holy Grail. [8]His realm is ultimately destroyed by passion evil and treachery. [9]With the end of Arthur's realm, comes the loss of loyalty and righteousness throughout the land. [10]Indeed there arises a civil war in which brother fights against brother?

[11]Did Arthur's court really exist and if it did exist where was it. [12]One site often cited is Cadbury Castle on a hill in Somerset England near the town of Cadbury which is in the southwestern part of the country. [13]Cadbury Castle was first identified as Camelot in 1542. [14]Excavations in the 1960s unearthed ruins from fifteen hundred years ago. [15]Archaeologists found evidence of a fortified gate tower and even a wood building, that might have been a great hall. [16]Do these ruins means King Arthur and Camelot existed. [17]Could these ruins be proof not just a coincidence.

Chapter Review

EXERCISE A Using Commas and End Marks Correctly

In the following sentences, insert all missing commas, periods for abbreviations, and other end punctuation marks. Correct run-on sentences.

1. Did you know that musical theater existed before Greek tragedy Roman comedy satire and mime?

2. Stone Age people used instruments they crafted from their surroundings to celebrate harvests births and successful hunts

3. A Stone Age painting dating from about 10,000 BC portrays a man wearing a buffalo mask dancing exuberantly and playing a stringed instrument

4. Although hardly a Broadway poster that cave painting from Ariège France is the oldest document of musical theater

5. What do you think of that?

6. Musical theater continued with the Greeks whose earliest dramas featured some music sung by a chorus

7. After Athens Greece fell in about 400 BC dramatists began theater groups that included professional musicians

8. The role of music in theater grew with Greek mime

9. By the sixth century AD the Christian church had suppressed theater which it thought to be sinful

10. But by the seventh and eighth centuries a new form of musical theater developed and that form in turn led to the mystery and miracle plays of the Middle Ages

11. In the sixteenth century music and dance were prominent in Florence Italy and in Paris France.

12. By the middle of the following century dance and singing theater split dance became ballet and singing theater became opera

13. The nineteenth century gave us Sir W S Gilbert and Sir A Sullivan and the light opera

14. Then the light opera evolved into what has become America's unique contribution to theater the musical comedy

15. Yes the heyday of American musical comedy was from the 1930s through the 1960s wasn't it?

EXERCISE B Editing Paragraphs

Edit the paragraphs below by inserting commas and end punctuation. Correct all run-on sentences and sentence fragments. Be sure to begin each sentence with a capital letter.

¹You know what a hula hoop is don't you. ²have you ever tried one!

³A hula hoop craze first swept the United States in 1958. ⁴As soon as the hoops arrived in stores the stores ran out of them. ⁵Within six months Americans bought twenty million plastic hoops ⁶Then there followed significant back injuries neck injuries and even heart failure ⁷However the hula hoop idea was not a new one nor were the related medical problems new. ⁸In ancient Egypt Greece and Rome kids made hoops from dried grape vines they rolled these toys tossed them and swung them around their waists ⁹In ancient England the center of the rolling toy formed a target for darts ¹⁰In some South American countries. ¹¹Kids used sugarcane plants to make hoops?

¹²Indeed children's hoop games have been around for a while ¹³In the fourteenth century England had another hoop craze? ¹⁴The hoops made of wood this time gave doctors fits. ¹⁵The attachment of the word *hula* to *hoop* dates to the eighteenth century movements of the hips needed to rotate the toy hoop match the movements in the beautiful traditional Hawaiian dance.

EXERCISE C Writing Rules of Thumb

Rules of thumb are easy-to-remember recipes for how to do everyday things—such as how to buy a computer or how to fend off a pushy salesclerk. Work with a group or a partner to come up with ten rules of thumb. Refer to your own experiences or to what parents or others have told you. When you've finished, check your sentences for the correct use of commas, periods for abbreviations, and end punctuation marks.

> EXAMPLE When taking a multiple-choice test, never change your first choice when you're not sure of your answer; your first choice is usually correct.

Punctuation: All the Other Marks

STUDENT WRITING
Movie Review

Godzilla
by Andrew Young
high school student, Yonkers, New York

Godzilla hit theaters with a seemingly weak punch. The movie had an enormous budget but came up short in the box office, which is why I didn't spend eight dollars to see it. I talked to people who saw it, and most reviews were extremely poor. It recently hit the stores, so I decided to pick it up. The movie is amazing. The special effects top those of *Jurassic Park* and *Independence Day*. The story line is a little weak, but still enjoyable. Matthew Broderick is funny and was an excellent choice.

The special effects seem so real that you will believe a giant monster is actually rampaging through Manhattan. Look for landmarks such as the Brooklyn Bridge and Madison Square Garden. The action scenes are well done, mixed with suspense and excitement. Just when you think the excitement has ended, it keeps going. This is true until the very end of the film. Watching this movie brings back memories of the old Japanese Godzilla movies. The thought of a man in a costume ravaging a homemade city makes me laugh when I see the computer-animated Godzilla of today.

I was extremely disappointed that I didn't see the movie in the theater. A thirty-five-inch screen with plain stereo does not do it justice. Like the *Star Wars Trilogy*, *Independence Day*, and the *Jurassic Park* movies, *Godzilla* must be viewed in the theater to truly appreciate its stunning effects.

For those who saw this movie already, see it again. If you are one of the unfortunate people who didn't see it in the theaters, I strongly suggest you rent this movie. Pop the popcorn, crank up the volume, sit back, and enjoy.

Andrew Young's movie review includes details about the movie's special effects, the setting, the plot, and the acting. His comparison of the recent movie to the original version of Godzilla gives his review both depth and perspective.

Did you notice that all the movies Andrew mentions are in italics? In this chapter, you'll learn when to use italics for titles and when to use quotation marks around titles. Make sure you punctuate titles correctly as you write your own movie and book reviews.

Colons

▶ Use a **colon** before a list of items, especially after the words *the following* or *the following items*.

> Among the after-school jobs some seniors hold are the following: video store clerk, sneaker salesperson, food service worker, and cashier.

▶ Use a colon before a formal statement or quotation and before a long quotation that is set off as a block (any quotation of more than three lines).

> One student, who works evenings at a family entertainment center, explains why her long hours don't bother her: "I don't sleep that much anyway. If I were home, I'd be watching TV or wasting time."

When a long quotation (more than three lines) is set off as a block, indent the quotation, and don't use quotation marks.

> Research shows that most often students work not to save money for college or to help support their families but to have spending money. Here is one student's view:
>> I'm not any good at saving. I earn about $700 a month, and each month I spend it all. My salary this month has paid for a cellular telephone, clothes, and an ear piercing. Whatever is left goes toward my prom.

▶ Use a colon between two independent clauses when the second restates or explains the first. Use a capital letter after the colon if what follows is a complete sentence.

> Some states restrict the number of hours that kids who are sixteen or seventeen can work per week during the school year: In New York, the limit is twenty-eight hours; Washington State's limit is twenty.

▶ Use a colon to set off a word or phrase you want to emphasize.

> Because she holds down an after-school job, Iris no longer has to do her two least favorite household chores: washing dishes and walking the dog.

▶ Use a colon in these situations: (1) between the hour and minutes, (2) between the chapter and verse in references to the Bible, (3) after the greeting of a business letter, (4) between a book's title and subtitle, and (5) in a bibliography, between the city and publisher.

> 9:42 P.M.   Luke 10:24–28   Dear Sir or Madam:
> Jobbs, Maya. *Kids at Work: Does it Pay?* New York: Carmel, 2000.

EDITING TIP

Don't use a colon between a verb and a subject complement or between a verb and a direct object (unless that object is a direct quotation). Don't use a colon between a preposition and its objects.

COMPLEMENT
Hannah's jobs were **salesperson and lifeguard**.

DIRECT OBJECT
Hannah threw **a ball and a beanbag**.

PREPOSITION
Hannah ran **to** the bridge, the track, and the school.

Don't use a colon after *such as*, *including*, and *especially*.

EXERCISE 1 Adding Colons to Sentences

Insert colons where they are needed in the following sentences. **Hint:** Not every sentence requires a colon. Write *C* if the sentence is correct without a colon.

1. The top two reasons teens give for working are to have spending money and to buy something expensive.

2. Of the many jobs Jake held, he enjoyed all but the following shoe salesperson, porter, busboy.

3. Jimea had to be at her job by 515 every day.

4. Youth employment boomed in the 1990s roughly one out of every four high school students had a job at any given time.

5. This trend has been fueled by the following conditions a plentiful supply of jobs in the service industry, a demand for teen workers, and the teens' desires for expensive clothes and other costly items.

6. Students are reading *After School Is Out Earn, Earn, Earn.*

7. Lia held four jobs in one two-year period video-rental worker, cashier, sneaker salesclerk, and dog walker.

8. The rise in student workers is a concern among safety experts, legislators, and educators.

9. These professionals cite the following as concerns health and safety risks and negative effects on schoolwork.

10. Studies have shown the following effects of working more than twenty hours each week doing less homework, getting lower grades, and skipping more classes.

11. Some observers think part-time work helps teens.

12. In fact, the president of one retailers' association claims that students learn valuable skills at work interpersonal communication and fluency with math.

13. Many educators strongly disagree they assert that the jobs lack challenge, impose time pressures, and create extra stress.

Write What You Think

Decide whether you agree or disagree with the following statement:

> Federal law should continue to put strict limitations on the numbers of hours teens can work each week during the school year.

Refer to **Composition,** Lesson 4.3 to find strategies for writing persuasively.

To respond to this issue, consider the advantages and disadvantages of after-school work as well as the financial needs students may have. Then state your opinion and support it with anecdotal evidence. Work at least two properly placed colons into your response. Revise and edit your work.

Semicolons

A **semicolon** can show that two or more ideas are closely related.

▶ Use a semicolon to join independent clauses in a compound sentence *without* a coordinating conjunction.

> Claude McKay was a great poet and essayist of the Harlem Renaissance; McKay did not write much after 1930. [Semicolon alone joins two independent clauses.]
> Claude McKay had few equals as a poet; **however**, his novels were not as well crafted. [Semicolon (before conjunctive adverb) joins two independent clauses.]
> Claude McKay had few equals as a poet; **as a result**, his poems still appear in textbooks. [Semicolon (before transitional expression) joins two independent clauses.]
> Claude McKay was a great poet and essayist of the Harlem Renaissance, **but** he did not write much after 1930. [With a coordinating conjunction, a comma joins two independent clauses.]

You may use a semicolon between independent clauses joined by coordinating conjunctions if either clause contains a comma. But you don't have to.

> She was the last one to read; but when she recited her poems, we were glad we'd stayed.

▶ Use a semicolon to separate items in a series when one or more of the items contain a comma.

> McKay was born in Upper Clarendon Parish, Jamaica; Langston Hughes was born in Joplin, Missouri, but grew up in Lawrence, Kansas; and Countee Cullen, born in Louisville, Kentucky, and adopted by a Methodist minister, grew up in New York City.

Common Conjunctive Adverbs

accordingly	meanwhile
also	moreover
besides	nevertheless
consequently	otherwise
furthermore	still
however	then
indeed	therefore

Common Transitional Expressions

as a result	in fact
for example	in other
for instance	words
from that	on the other
point on	hand
in addition	that is

EDITING TIP

Do not use a semicolon between an independent clause and a dependent clause or phrase.

We read poems by Langston Hughes, who is probably the best known of the Harlem Renaissance poets.

EXERCISE 2 Using Semicolons and Colons

Some of the following sentences need a semicolon; others require colons. Review the rules for colons in Lesson 14.1, and then add the proper punctuation marks below. If a sentence is correct, write *C*.

1. Khalilia says that the following are her favorite Harlem Renaissance poets Langston Hughes, Arna Bontemps, and Countee Cullen.

2. Jean Toomer wrote the groundbreaking novel *Cane* (1923) however, his later work never matched it.

3. Early in his writing life, Toomer wrote about African American themes however, his later work departed from those themes.

4. Toomer developed an interest in a Russian mystic from that point on, his production and fame dropped off considerably.

5. Toomer defined himself not as an African American, but as an American.

6. Bontemps and Hughes collected folklore, and they also wrote original works.

7. Zora Neale Hurston was also a folklorist she collected folktales, spirituals, sermons, blues, work songs, and children's games.

8. In her search for art from the Deep South, Hurston traveled through the following states Florida, Alabama, and Mississippi.

9. Her years of research led to the publication of *Mules and Men* it was the first volume of African American folklore by an African American.

10. Her most famous novel is *Their Eyes Were Watching God*, but some prefer *Dust Tracks on a Road*.

EXERCISE 3 Combining Sentences into Compound Sentences

On a separate piece of paper, combine each set of independent clauses into a compound sentence. Do *not* use coordinating conjunctions. You may introduce conjunctive adverbs and transitional expressions. Check your combined sentences for proper punctuation.

1. Zora Neale Hurston believed that folklore was priceless. It constitutes the art of the people, who never recognized it as art.

2. Hurston was a self-styled literary anthropologist. She used literary techniques to shape oral narratives.

3. She created a new literary language. The language reflected the poetry in the oral culture of blacks in the rural South.

4. Hurston wrote four novels, a memoir, and more than fifty shorter works. She was more prolific than any black woman writer had been before.

5. Hurston grew up in Eatonville, Florida. Eatonville was the first incorporated black community in the United States.

6. Hurston's mother was a teacher in Eatonville. Hurston's father served three terms as mayor there.

7. Hurston worked while in high school and college. She worked as a maid, waitress, and manicurist.

8. As an English major at Howard University, Hurston began writing short stories and poems. She joined the literary club there.

Underlining (Italics)

Italic type is the slanted type that looks like this. When you write by hand, use **underlining** to represent **italics**.

▭▶ Use underlining (or italics) for the following kinds of titles and names:

BOOKS	*Wuthering Heights* (novel) *The Republic* by Plato
	Songs of Jamaica (book of poems)
MAGAZINES	*The Nation* *TV Guide* *Smithsonian*
NEWSPAPERS	*The New York Times* *Denver Post*
PLAYS	*Hamlet* *Waiting for Godot* *A Streetcar Named Desire*
MOVIES	*Chariots of Fire* *It's a Wonderful Life* *Titanic*
TV/RADIO SERIES	*48 Hours* *The Lucy Show*
PAINTINGS, SCULPTURES	*Mona Lisa* *Three Musicians*
ALBUMS AND LONG PIECES OF MUSIC	the Beatles' *Abbey Road*
	Brahms's *German Requiem*
SHIPS, PLANES, SPACECRAFT	SS *United States* *The Spirit of '76*
	Apollo II

▭▶ Use italics for words and expressions from other languages and for words, letters, numbers, and symbols referred to as such.

OTHER LANGUAGES	*Bien entendu* means "well understood."
WORDS AS WORDS	Is *effect* or *affect* the correct word here?
LETTERS	How many *n*'s and *t*'s are there in *Cincinnati*?
NUMBERS, SYMBOLS	The *@* sign is above the *2*.

WRITING HINT

If a foreign word or expression has made it into an English-language dictionary, you don't have to italicize it.
Those tortillas were delicious.

EXERCISE 4 Underlining (Adding Italics)

Read the following anecdote. Add underlining to indicate italics.

[1]Last Tuesday afternoon, I went as usual to my teacher's house for my weekly piano lesson. [2]When I arrived, I learned that she'd been called away by an emergency involving her boat, Calypso. [3]I found myself with time on my hands, but it was beginning to rain.

[4]I had no umbrella but was carrying my music book, The Virtuoso Pianist in 60 Exercises, and a copy of the Tulsa Daily Journal. [5]To protect the book and me, I held the Journal over my head. [6]A block away, a theater was advertising two films, Godzilla and Godzilla Meets Titanic.

Enriching Your Vocabulary

The word *nausia* in Latin means "seasickness." The expression ad *nauseam*, on page 290, is Latin and is used to mean "to the point of disgust." Details of the horrors of war were repeated *ad nauseam* by the museum tour guide.

⁷I ducked under its awning to wait out the storm. ⁸I stood there for a while, humming the title tune from Gene Kelly's movie Singin' in the Rain. ⁹On the rains came, ad nauseam. ¹⁰Across the street was a bookstore with a small café. ¹¹I made a beeline for it.

¹²In the magazine section, I found a copy of SportsWeek, my favorite. ¹³I took it and Pop Music World with me to the café. ¹⁴There, under a copy of Grant Wood's painting American Gothic, I ordered a lemonade and sat down to read. ¹⁵Soon, the rain stopped, but I didn't. ¹⁶I was so thoroughly enjoying myself that when I finished my magazines, I read an article in Scientific Teens, which someone had left there, as well as the sports pages of America Today, which someone else had just finished. ¹⁷Sitting there in that bookstore, reading and also listening to Gershwin's opera Porgy and Bess playing in the background, I totally lost track of time. ¹⁸By the time I got home, dinner was cold, and The NewsHour was on TV.

Exercise 5 Writing Brief Reviews

Imagine that you are the culture critic for your school paper. On a separate piece of paper, write a brief review of (1) a magazine article you've read, (2) an album you've listened to, (3) a movie you've seen, or (4) a concert you've attended. Be brief, but be honest. Explain why you give the work or performance a thumbs-up or thumbs-down. Then swap papers with another class critic. Check each other's work for the correct use of italics (underlining).

You may wish to refer to the strategies for writing about literature in **Composition,** Lesson 4.7.

Quotation Marks

Lesson 14.3 shows italics (underlining) for certain works of art. This lesson tells when to use quotation marks for shorter works and for other purposes as well.

▮▶ Use **quotation marks** for titles of short works.

POEMS	"Ode to a Grecian Urn" "The Lake Isle of Innisfree"
SHORT STORIES	"Araby" "The Fall of the House of Usher"
ARTICLES	"Going Out of Our Gourds Over Pumpkins"
SONGS	"The Star-Spangled Banner" "Penny Lane"
SINGLE TV PROGRAMS	"Rescue at Sea" (an episode of *American Experience*)
PARTS OF BOOKS	Part I, "Essays and Memoirs"

▮▶ Use quotation marks at the beginning and end of a direct quotation but not with an indirect quotation.

Introduce a short, one-sentence quotation with a comma or a colon; introduce a quotation that is a long sentence or more than one sentence with a colon.

> Of T. S. Eliot, critics wrote**,** "Eliot was better equipped than any other poet to bring free verse into the twentieth century."

> **EDITING TIP**
>
> Don't use quotation marks for nicknames or slang.
> His nickname is ~~"~~Spike~~"~~; he's a ~~"~~yuppie.~~"~~

When only a word or two is quoted, use a lowercase letter if the quoted words do not begin the sentence.

> T. S. Eliot referred to W. B. Yeats as "the greatest poet."
> [no capital letter in quotation]

▮▶ Use single quotation marks for titles or quotes within a quotation.

> Brenda asked, "Have you read T. S. Eliot's poem 'Gerontion'?"

▮▶ The following rules apply to quotation marks with other marks.

Commas and periods These marks go inside a closing quotation mark.

> "Dinner is ready**,**" he announced.   The title of the story is "Araby**.**"

Semicolons and colons These marks go outside a closing quotation mark.

> Here are three reasons I like "Araby"**:** its characters, its plot, its poetry.

Question marks and exclamation points These go inside closing quotation marks if the quotation is a question or an exclamation; they go outside if the whole sentence is a question or an exclamation.

> "Did everyone read the poem**?**" she asked.
> Was she surprised when you said, "No"**?**

Exercise 6 Punctuating Sentences

Check the punctuation in the following sentences, and add or change punctuation marks or italics as needed. Some sentences may have more than one problem. If a sentence is punctuated correctly, write *C*.

1. Matthew Arnold's poem Dover Beach begins with The sea is calm tonight.

2. Virginia Woolf wrote the short work "The Lady in the Looking Glass."

3. In her introduction to her novel Frankenstein, Mary Shelley refers to Childe Harold's Pilgrimage, a poem by Lord Byron.

4. The Swedish Academy granted Derek Walcott the 1992 Nobel Prize for Literature and said, 'West Indian culture has found its great poet.'

5. James Berry, another leading Caribbean poet, wrote the poem Thoughts on My Mother.

6. In his short story, "The Rocking-Horse Winner," D. H. Lawrence explores the upper middle class.

7. E. M. Forster wrote many novels, including A Passage to India and A Room with a View.

8. Elizabeth Barrett Browning wrote, How do I love thee? Let me count the ways.

9. Browning's poem also contains these words, "I shall but love thee better after death.

10. Eavan Boland dedicated her 1967 book of poems, "New Territory," to her mother.

Exercise 7 Write Your Own Exercise

On a separate piece of paper, write one or more complete sentences for each item below. Mention actual titles wherever possible, but leave out all punctuation marks. Then exchange papers with a classmate. See if you agree on how to punctuate each sentence.

1. Your thoughts about an episode of a TV program you watched recently (Make up a name for the episode if you don't remember it.)

2. A song that you've heard recently

3. A direct quotation (actual or made up) at the beginning of a sentence

4. A quotation within a quotation

5. A short story or magazine article you've read and your thoughts about it

6. A poem you've read and your thoughts about it

7. A title of a chapter of a book you are reading and a summary of that chapter

More on Quotation Marks

Dialogue is the conversation between characters in a story or script. The best dialogue is natural sounding—the way real people actually talk. The part of the sentence that identifies the speaker is called the **dialogue tag**. Follow these accepted rules for punctuating dialogue when you write fiction or nonfiction.

▸ Begin a new paragraph every time the speaker changes.
> "Carl, let me hear your part from the beginning," Ms. Cronin said.
> "OK, here I go," Carl responded.

Note: The following rules also apply to punctuating other kinds of direct quotations, not only dialogue.

▸ When a direct quotation comes at the beginning of a sentence, use only one punctuation mark—a comma, question mark, or exclamation point (but *not* a period)—to separate it from the dialogue tag that follows.
> "Carl, try that line one more time and with feeling**,**" Ms. Cronin said.
> "Show us that you are angry and upset**!**" Mr. Tandy added emphatically.
> "How do I show that**?**" Carl ventured.

▸ When a dialogue tag interrupts a quoted sentence, begin the second part of the quotation with a lowercase letter.
> "I'll try again, Ms. Cronin," Carl replied, "**a**nd you'll see that I can do it better."

▸ Do not use a comma (or colon) and generally do not use a capital letter before a quotation that you introduce with the word *that*.
> The proverb says, "**A**ll good things must come to an end."
> The proverb says **that** "**a**ll good things must come to an end."

EXERCISE 8 Punctuating Dialogue

Add all the appropriate punctuation marks to the passage with dialogue below. Insert a paragraph symbol (¶) to show where a new paragraph should begin.

[1]It's Friday, and Zoe and Joseph are having lunch in the school cafeteria. [2]The new British group Ear Plugs is going to give a concert at the Imperial Theater next week Zoe tells Joseph. [3]When do tickets go on

sale? ⁴Joseph asks. ⁵They're on sale starting tomorrow Zoe replies. ⁶Well, why don't you go over there and get us a pair? ⁷I can't Zoe answers because tomorrow's a busy day for me. ⁸My cousins are in town, and I have to show them around all day. ⁹Why don't you go? ¹⁰I can't do it either says Joseph. ¹¹The two stare at each other across their food trays for what seems like hours. ¹²Are you talking to Nell again, Zoe? ¹³Joseph asks. ¹⁴Sort of she replies. ¹⁵Well, can you 'sort of' sit through a concert with her? he wonders aloud. ¹⁶I guess Zoe answers. ¹⁷Are you thinking what I think you're thinking? ¹⁸He nods. ¹⁹OK, she says. ²⁰I'll invite Nell to join us, and I'll ask her to go and pick up the tickets. ²¹Joseph beams. ²²Good thinking he says.

Exercise 9 Writing a Dialogue

Work with a partner or small group to create a passage with dialogue. Write the passage on a separate piece of paper, following the conventions for punctuating dialogue. When you write, try to make the dialogue as natural sounding as you can. You may use one of the following suggestions or an idea of your own.

1. Write a humorous conversation between two lions (or other animals) in a zoo.

2. Write a dialogue in which people are in conflict. The people can be friends, teammates, boyfriend and girlfriend, brother and sister, student and teacher, and so on.

Apostrophes

▸ Use an **apostrophe** to show where letters or numbers have been omitted.

I've   we're   they've   we've   doesn't   Class of '02   o'clock

▸ To show possession, add an apostrophe and -s ('s) to singular nouns. Add an apostrophe and -s ('s) to plural nouns that do not end in -s.

our cousin's house   a day's wait   Cass's skirt   Dickens's novels
bus's windshield   women's clothes   deer's trail   sheep's wool

▸ To show possession, add only an apostrophe (') to a plural noun that ends in -s.

students' addresses   five cents' worth   the Flores' pool

Use an apostrophe and -s ('s) to show the possessive form of indefinite pronouns.

everybody's favorite   anyone's guess   anyone else's father

▸ Add only an apostrophe to certain expressions that end in -s or have the sound of /s/.

for goodness' sake   for conscience' sake

▸ A few compound nouns have two correct possessive forms.

spider web *or* spider's web   rabbit foot *or* rabbit's foot

▸ To signal individual possession by two or more, make each noun possessive.

Erin's and Jenny's coats   Jess's and Talia's jobs

▸ To signal joint possession, make only the final noun possessive.

Lulu and Meg's dance class   Lewis and Clark's trip

▸ Use an apostrophe and an -s ('s) to form the plurals of letters, numbers, symbols, and words referred to as such.

The word *television* has two *e*'s and two *i*'s.
Her social security number has three *0*'s and two *4*'s.
Don't use &'s in your report.
The dialogue has too many *very*'s and *like*'s.

When you write about decades, both **1990s** and **1990's** are acceptable.

> **WRITING HINT**
>
> Some proper nouns made up of plural nouns do not take an apostrophe.
>
> Teachers College of Columbia University
>
> Boys and Girls High School

> **EDITING TIP**
>
> Don't use an apostrophe to form the plural of a common or proper noun.
> *pianos*
> Those piano's belong to the school.
>
> Never put an apostrophe in a possessive personal pronoun; it already shows possession.
> *hers*
> Don't touch that; it's her's.

EXERCISE 10 Using Apostrophes

Write the contraction or possessive for these words or expressions.

1. is not it ——————————

2. he would ——————————

3. they have ——————————

4. we are ——————————

5. will not ——————————

6. everybody ——————————

7. everybody else ——————————

8. another ——————————

9. each other ——————————

10. one another ——————————

EXERCISE 11 Correcting Apostrophes

Correct all errors in the use of apostrophes in the following sentences. If a sentence is punctuated correctly, write C.

1. Sophie said she couldnt get to the dance recital on time.

2. Should there be +'s in that equation?

3. How many ys are in *mystery*?

4. I prefer the music of the 1970s to the music of the 1980s.

5. Simones and Michels tickets are being held at the booth.

6. Chris choreography was too difficult for the young dancers.

7. Heres how to learn: study.

8. Its only five minutes work.

9. First we went to the womens' tournament, then the mens.

10. Hannahs parents new kitchen is a chefs kitchen.

11. Jacob applied to Teachers College of Columbia University.

12. I think the license plate had three 6s.

13. After a day's rest, Carmine went back to work.

14. Did you read about Hercules's labors?

15. At the poetry reading, we heard several poets works.

Hyphens, Dashes, Parentheses, Brackets, and Ellipsis Points

▶ Use a **hyphen** (-) in some compound nouns, in compound adjectives before a noun, and in fractions and numbers from twenty-one to ninety-nine.

president-elect   ice-cold soda
two-ton truck   two-thirds

P.S. Is it *highway* or *high-way*? Dictionaries show which compound nouns take hyphens.

▶ Use a **dash** (—) or a pair of dashes to highlight material; to show an abrupt break in thought or an interruption; or to mean "namely," "in other words," or "that is."

A World Series ring—a prized possession—was his goal.

TOM   Yesterday, you confiscated my books. You had the nerve to—

AMANDA   I did. I took that horrible novel back to the library—that awful book by that **dissident**, Mr. Lawrence.

▶ Use **parentheses**—( )—to enclose material of less importance.
The finals (a five-set series) start today.
The finals start today. (They can go for five matches.)
The finals (they can go for five sets) start today.

▶ Use **brackets**—[ ]—to enclose parenthetical material that is itself in parentheses and to enclose words that you insert as a comment or explanation into a quotation.

He retired from Harvard in 1999 (he did occasionally lecture at Boston University [BU]) and took up gardening.

Scott Turow said, "Michael Jordan [who retired in 1999] plays basketball better than anyone else in the world does anything else."

▶ Use three **ellipsis points** (. . .) to indicate omissions from quoted material. Use ellipsis points and a period at the end of quoted material.

I pledge allegiance to the flag . . . and to the Republic for which it stands. . . .

EDITING TIP

Adverbs that end in *-ly* do not need hyphens.
badlyhit ball

Compound adjectives that follow a linking verb should not be hyphenated.
The soda is no longer icecold.

Enriching Your Vocabulary

The Latin origins of *dissident* are the prefix *dis-*, meaning "apart," and the root *sidere*, meaning "sit." As someone who opposes the norm, a *dissident* might disagree with social standards.

EXERCISE 12 Punctuating Sentences

Check the punctuation in the following sentences, and add or change punctuation marks as needed. If a sentence is punctuated correctly, write *C*.

1. Edith Houghton was the first woman scout [1946] for a major baseball team.

2. Not many women, I can't think of any, scout for the major leagues today.

3. Mary H. Donlon was the first woman editor in chief of a law review.

4. Donlon was also the first woman from New York to become a federal judge.

   (see article on Genevieve Cline).

5. Cline was the first woman to be appointed as a federal judge 1928.

6. Jacqueline Cochran set a new altitude record for flying—55,253 feet—in 1961.

7. Bessie Coleman, the first licensed African American woman pilot, learned

   French [she was not allowed to take flying lessons in the United States] so

   that she could take flying lessons in Europe.

8. In Germany, Coleman flew a plane powered by a 220 horsepower engine.

9. Dorothy Fields was the first woman to win an Oscar for songwriting 1937.

10. Fields wrote song lyrics for forty one years.

EXERCISE 13 Using Ellipsis Points

Read the familiar passage from the Gettysburg Address by Abraham Lincoln below. Then copy over the passage with the three omissions specified below the passage. Use ellipsis points (three or four) to mark each omission you make.

[1]Now we are engaged in a great civil war, testing whether that nation, or any nation so conceived and so dedicated, can long endure. [2]We are met on a great battlefield of that war. [3]We have come to dedicate a portion of that field, as a final resting place for those who here gave their lives that that nation might live. [4]It is altogether fitting and proper that we should do this.

1. In sentence 1, delete the words *or any nation so conceived and so dedicated* and the commas around those words.

2. In sentence 3, delete the comma and the rest of the sentence.

3. In sentence 4, delete the words *altogether fitting and*.

Editing and Proofreading Worksheet 1

Edit the draft for errors in spelling, capitalization, punctuation, and usage. Write your edited version on a separate piece of paper. Compare your changes with those of a writing partner. **Hint:** Look for errors in verb usage.

[1]What do writers John Updike and Robert Penn Warren have in common. [2]Well: among other things each has written a poem about baseball. [3]John Updike who has wrote other sports:related literature wrote the poem Tao in the Yankee Stadium Bleachers and Robert Penn Warren wrote the poem *He Was Formidable*. [4]Both of these poems appear in the book "Hummers, Knucklers, and Slow Curves, Contemporary Baseball Poems" [University of Illinois Press; Urbana and Chicago, 1991.] an anthology. [5]The books' editor is Don Johnson.

[6]For people who thought that baseball and poetry were mutually exclusive, this is the book. [7]To change their minds. [8]Baseball poetry, they'll see, goes beyond the ballad Casey at the Bat, this volume including eighty four poems written by fifty seven poets in the 1950s through the 1980's. [9]Some of them first appeared in the baseball literary magazine, Spitfire. [10]The poems Johnson has included here are as "varied, evocative, and enigmatic as the game itself", he claims. [11]They are odes not to famous or legendary players but to the game. [12]From the major leagues to the minor leagues high school games Little League contests and pickup games in neighborhood fields or on the streets.

[13]The collection of poems in this book gets at the essence of the game of baseball. [14]For example: one poem, The Base Stealer, begins by describing the potential base thief as follows "taut like a tightrope walker." [15]Another, entitled Pitcher, starts with the sentence His art is eccentricity.

[16]In his foreward to the poems in the book, Johnson writes the following Baseball is poetry. [17]Baseball is ballet. [18]Baseball is chess. [19]Baseball is mystery.

Editing and Proofreading Worksheet 2

Edit the draft for errors in spelling, capitalization, punctuation, and usage. Write your edited version on a separate piece of paper. Compare your changes with those of a writing partner.

[1]The new department store that had opened in the mall was hiring. [2]Reggie and several of his classmates lined up: to fill out job applications in the hopes of getting an interview. [3]I certainly need this job Reggie said. [4]Not as much as I need it Irene replied. [5]But I need it more than either of you since I'm only $500 short on the car I have my eye on said Ben. [6]Irene laughed and said. [7]Ben, you'll never save $500? [8]Not by the time youre twenty one. [9]Not by the time your ninety nine! [10]You'll spend everything they pay you. [11]Now Reggie laughed and said Hey, none of us even has the job yet and there are fifty kids in line here for ten jobs. [12]What skills and qualities do you think they-ll be looking for asked Ben will they be impressed that I worked as a sales clerk. [13]Did you say a salesclerk? Irene asked. [14]You mean the time you worked at your uncle's bowling alley and handed out shoes? she continued. [15]Oh, I pointed out where the balls were, too and answered all the questions I was asked he replied. [16]Just as Ben was beginning to embellish his explanation, they came to the head of the line. [17]Reggie was the first to be spoken to. [18]Do you speak French fluently? [19]How about Russian? [20]Are you familiar with blinis, fois gras, and caviar. [21]We are looking for experienced sales help in the gourmet department. [22]Oh said Reggie. [23]Oh said Irene. [24]Bonjour answered Ben.

Chapter Review

EXERCISE A Using Colons and Semicolons

Insert colons and semicolons where they belong in the following sentences.
Hint: One sentence needs more than one punctuation mark.

1. The following appeared for the first time in the early 1950s the telephone-answering machine, 3-D film, and Mr. Potato Head.

2. The Russians launched *Sputnik* in 1957 consequently, the space race was off and running.

3. In 1958, the Brooklyn Dodgers moved to Los Angeles the Giants moved from New York to San Francisco that same year.

4. In 1960, the first fiber-tipped pens appeared it was also the year that halogen lamps first made their appearance.

5. Key historical events of the 1960s include three assassinations JFK's in Dallas, Texas RFK's in Los Angeles, California and Martin Luther King Jr.'s in Memphis, Tennessee.

EXERCISE B Using Italics and Quotation Marks

Insert underlining (to represent italics) and quotation marks as required in each of the following sentences. Make sure you place quotation marks in the right position in relation to other punctuation marks. If a sentence is correct as given, write *C*.

1. Joseph Conrad wrote the novel Lord Jim in 1900.

2. In that same year, Puccini's new opera Tosca was performed in Rome.

3. In 1900, the Daily Express first appeared on newsstands in London.

4. In 1899, John Dewey wrote the influential book School and Society.

5. The first trial flight of a *zeppelin* (a rigid airship) took place in 1900.

6. In 1897, Edwin Arlington Robinson composed the Realist poem Richard Cory.

7. In line 3, the character Richard Cory is described as "a gentleman from sole to crown.

8. William Dean Howells, who espoused Realism, said: Let fiction cease to lie about life; let it portray men and women as they are.

9. In 1899, Scott Joplin, the composer and pianist, released the tune titled Maple Leaf Rag.

10. Sigmund Freud's book The Interpretation of Dreams appeared in 1900.

EXERCISE C Adding Punctuation to Dialogue

Rewrite the following dialogue on a separate piece of paper. Use quotation marks and other punctuation marks correctly.

¹Their senior year has just ended, and Maya and Dan are talking about their summers. ²The college I got into has asked me to read several books during the next two months Maya complained, but I'll be traveling and then so busy working that I don't know when I'll find the time. ³How many books are we talking about? Dan asked. ⁴Eight! ⁵Really? ⁶Eight? ⁷Dan responded. ⁸My school wants me to read four novels, but I've already read two of them. ⁹Which ones Maya asked. ¹⁰Oh I read Ragtime by E. L. Doctorow and also Doris Lessing's The Golden Notebook, Dan replied. ¹¹Ragtime is on my list, too, Dan. ¹²Maybe I'll just see the play or rent the video. ¹³Don't do that, Dan answered. ¹⁴The book is far better than either one; you'll really like it. ¹⁵Well, Maya wondered aloud, what about the other seven on my list?

On a separate piece of paper, continue the dialogue between Maya and Dan for at least four more sentences. Avoid the use of *said* as much as possible.

EXERCISE D Using Other Punctuation Marks

Add punctuation to the following sentences. Decide whether to use apostrophes, hyphens, dashes, parentheses, brackets, quotation marks, or ellipsis points. **Hint:** Some sentences need more than one punctuation mark.

1. Hamlin Garland wrote in the late 1800s and early 1900s; his most famous story is "Under the Lions Paw."

2. The Wright brothers first successful flight occurred in 1903.

3. In 1904, Chicago [an American League team] beat Chicago [a National League team] to win the World Series.

4. France established the ten hour workday in 1904.

5. In 1906, the 12.5 mile Simplon Tunnel opened between Switzerland and Italy.

6. In 1906, African American poet Paul Laurence Dunbar died; he was thirty four.

7. Jack London 1876–1916 published the story *"To Build a Fire"* in 1908.

8. The U.S. population in 1910 92 million was less than half of what it is today.

Capitalization

15

Mechanics

STUDENT WRITING

Research Paper

Woodrow Wilson's "Peace Without Victory" Address, January 22, 1917
A Continuity of Thought
by Uthara Srinivasan
high school student, Flossmoor, Illinois

On January 22, 1917 [as European crises threatened to draw the United States into World War I], President Woodrow Wilson delivered a speech to the Senate titled "Peace Without Victory," in which he claimed America had "no concern with the 'causes or objects' of the war."[1] He did not reiterate this theme in his address on April 2. Rather, he asked Congress to recognize the state of war with Germany, and he urged the American people to give their "blood and treasure"[2] for democracy's sake. This dramatic shift from neutrality to belligerence has been presented as proof of Wilson's deceptiveness and his mastery of words. Former President Theodore Roosevelt charged that Wilson was part of a "nauseous hypocrisy."[3]

Yet, if one carefully scrutinizes a few lines of the "Peace Without Victory" speech, one detects a strong resemblance to the Fourteen Points and other [of President Wilson's] wartime speeches. This suggests that, despite the metamorphosis of America's policies, there was a goal that remained constant. This goal that drove Wilson tirelessly from one means to another was the hope for a liberal post war order. Regardless of what Wilson's critics allege, there is a powerful degree of continuity in his wartime speeches. An analysis of his "Peace Without Victory" speech and its striking similarities to previous and following speeches proves this point.

[1]"Peace Without Victory," in Henry Steele Commager, ed., *Documents of American History, Volume II: Since 1898,* 9th ed. (Englewood Cliffs, NJ: Prentice Hall, Inc., 1973), p. 125.

[2]Arthur S. Link, *Woodrow Wilson: A Brief Biography* (Cleveland: The World Publishing Company, 1963), p. 113.

[3]Patrick Devlin, *Too Proud to Fight: Woodrow Wilson's Neutrality* (New York: Oxford University Press, 1975), p. 684.

> Uthara Srinivasan's paragraphs make an effective introduction to her full research paper. In the first paragraph, the author introduces the problem that the paper will deal with and then states her claim in the second paragraph. The final sentence of the second paragraph tells the reader what to expect in the body of the paper.
>
> As you reread the introduction, notice the many different uses for capital letters. You'll review the rules for capital letters in the lessons and exercises in this chapter.

Proper Nouns and Proper Adjectives

Both **proper nouns**, which name particular places, persons, things, or ideas, and **proper adjectives**, which derive from proper nouns, begin with a capital letter.

▐▐▐➡ Capitalize the names of people.

   Emily Dickinson   Richard the Lion-Hearted   Martin Luther King Jr.

Some last names have more than one part. Find out whether the name is spelled with only one or with more than one capital letter; customs vary.

   MacNeill   O'Conner   Martin Van Buren
   Ludwig van Beethoven   Leonardo da Vinci   Miguel de la Torre y Díaz

▐▐▐➡ Capitalize geographic names.

PLANETS, CONSTELLATIONS	Mars the Milky Way the constellation Orion
CONTINENTS, DIVISIONS	Asia Africa Arctic Circle Tropic of Cancer
ISLANDS	Cuba Trinidad Staten Island Majorca
COUNTRIES	Egypt China Great Britain the Netherlands
STATES	Texas Utah Delaware South Dakota
CITIES	Detroit Salt Lake City Miami Dar es Salaam
BODIES OF WATER,	Aegean Sea the Great Lakes Hudson River
MOUNTAINS	Mount Everest Appalachian Mountains
LOCALITIES, REGIONS	Cape of Good Hope the Midwest
STREETS, HIGHWAYS	Broadway River Road Thirty-fourth Street
BUILDINGS, MONUMENTS	the Chrysler Building Buckingham Palace
PARKS, FORESTS	Yosemite St. Mary's Park Muir Woods

> **EDITING TIP**
>
> In these examples, articles and short prepositions that are part of a name are *not* capitalized—for example, *of* in *Tropic of Cancer*. Also, do not capitalize common nouns. Write *East River* but the *river*.

Do not capitalize compass directions. Capitalize directional words only when they refer to a region of the world or of a country.

   Drive east on Interstate 70.
   Gold was discovered in the American Southwest.

▐▐▐➡ Capitalize some nouns, verbs, and adjectives that derive from proper nouns.

   Persian rug   Elizabethan England   Stalinize   Stalinism

Some words that owe their existence to a proper noun have become so popular in English that they no longer take a capital letter. Again, use a dictionary to check when to capitalize and when not to.

SOURCE OF WORD	COMMON TERM
Louis Pasteur, microbiologist	pasteurize
John Montague, Earl of Sandwich	sandwich
James Watt, inventor	watt

> **WRITING HINT**
>
> Whenever you're not sure about whether to capitalize an adjective, check a dictionary, which sometimes gives two spellings, the preferred spelling first.
>
> french fry *or* French fry *but* French horn
>
> india rubber *or* India rubber *but* Indian pudding

ONLINE COMPONENTS   www.grammarforwriting.com

EXERCISE 1 Proofreading Sentences

Insert capital letters where they belong in the following sentences. To indicate a capital letter, write in the proofreading symbol of three underscores beneath the letter: (t). Use a dictionary or atlas for help if necessary.

1. Last night, we were able to see the constellation capricorn.

2. The potomac river forms the border between virginia and maryland.

3. Is captiva the name of an island off florida's west coast?

4. Did you know that monument valley is a tribal park in southern utah?

5. Gold was discovered on john augustus sutter's property in california.

6. Our hike up long's peak took us above the timberline.

7. Along seventy-fourth street, you'll see a series of townhouses.

8. The vietnam veterans memorial is a must for visitors to our nation's capital.

EXERCISE 2 Writing a Report

Work with a partner or small group to write a report based on the following notes. First, capitalize all the words on the note card that should be capitalized. Then, write your report on a separate piece of paper. Proofread it carefully to make sure you've written complete sentences and capitalized all the words that need to be capitalized

windsor castle—the patriarch of palaces

castle located on cliff along thames river, 25 miles from london, england

founded by william the conqueror in about 1070 as stronghold
became royal residence in 1110; replaced an ancient saxon palace

english kings and queens in residence at windsor castle for centuries
rooms remodeled in turn by edward III, charles II, george IV

george III liked it; wife (queen charlotte) had her private rooms moved to part called southeast tower

tower officially named queen's tower after coronation of elizabeth II

today Queen elizabeth: private weekends there

Copyright © 2014 by William H. Sadlier, Inc. All rights reserved.

306 *Chapter 15 • Capitalization*

Titles

▐▐▌➤ Capitalize titles and abbreviations of titles when they are used before names but not when they appear without a name. Also capitalize abbreviations of academic degrees after a name.

Senator Hiram Revels	a United States senator
Queen Christina	several kings and queens
Enid Lopez, **D.D.S.**	the dentist's office

▐▐▌➤ Capitalize a word that shows a family relationship only when it is used before a name but without a possessive pronoun.

Uncle Dan   Grandma Alice   my cousin Rosalie   her stepbrother

▐▐▌➤ Capitalize all the important words in the salutation of a business or friendly letter but only the first word of the closing.

Dear Sir or Madam: Dear Li,   Yours truly,   Your friend,

▐▐▌➤ Capitalize the first and last word and all important words in the titles and subtitles of works.

Note: Unless they are the first word in a title, do not capitalize the following small words: articles (*the, a, an*), coordinating conjunctions (such as *and, but*), and prepositions with fewer than five letters (such as *into, with, to*).

BOOKS	*Of Mice and Men* *Uncle Tom's Cabin*
PERIODICALS	*Chicago Tribune* *Smithsonian* magazine
STORIES, ESSAYS,	"A Mild Attack of Locusts"
	"The Night the Bed Fell"
HISTORICAL DOCUMENTS	the Gettysburg Address
POEMS	"Song of Myself" "The Raven"
PLAYS	*Pygmalion* *The Sound of Music*
	A View from the Bridge
TV SERIES	*Law and Order* *Cheers* *Live from Lincoln Center*
WORKS OF ART	Homer's *Breezing Up* Rodin's *The Thinker*
MUSICAL WORKS	Beethoven's *Fifth Symphony* "Singin' in the Rain"
MOVIES	*The Wizard of Oz* *The Graduate*
TRAINS, SHIPS, PLANES	the *Orient Express* the *Titanic* the *Enola Gay*
SPACECRAFT	*Apollo 11*

Enriching Your Vocabulary

The word *salutary* means "healthful" and comes from the Latin word for health, *salutaris*. The related word *salute* comes from the same root and is a type of greeting. Likewise, in a letter, the words of greeting at the beginning are called a *salutation*.

WRITING HINT

Remember that forms of *be* are verbs. They require capitals in titles and headlines.

Have you read John Updike's book *Rabbit is Rich*?

EXERCISE 3 Proofreading Sentences

Insert capital letters where they belong in the following sentences. To indicate a capital letter, use the proofreading symbol of three underscores beneath the letter: (n̲). If a sentence is correct, write C.

1. Graham Greene is my uncle John's favorite author.

2. Indeed, uncle John likes Greene's short story "across the bridge."

3. His favorite novel is Greene's *our man in havana*.

4. Marissa's favorite TV show is a soap opera, *the days of our lives*.

5. Ed wanted to watch both *meet the press* and *live from the met*.

EXERCISE 4 Proofreading a Letter

Work with a partner to insert capital letters where they belong in the letter of recommendation that follows. Use the proofreading symbol of three underscores beneath a letter to indicate that it should be capitalized: (f̲).

---

¹Dear professor Smith:

²I recommend my student Henry Harper for a part-time position at manassas national battlefield park. ³He is well read and self-motivated.

⁴While doing research for his term paper, "the immediate aftermath of the civil war," Henry developed a passion for that American tragedy. ⁵He began his study of the conflict by reading two general history books, *a people and a nation* and *the reader's companion to american history*. ⁶For a closer look at the mid-nineteenth century in america, he obtained James McPherson's book *battle cry of freedom*. ⁷For information on the causes of the war, he picked up Freehling's *the road to disunion*. ⁸He also obtained several books about military figures, including Freeman's biography of general Lee and Henry's own distant cousin pvt. James Harper's 1865 diary.

⁹I think you will find mr. Harper an impressive addition to your staff at the park.

¹⁰sincerely,

Pauline Esserman

Pauline Esserman, ph.d.

First Words, Organizations, Religions, School Subjects

Capitalize the first word in a direct quotation when the quotation either was originally a complete sentence or, as quoted, makes a complete sentence. But do not capitalize the first word in an indirect quotation, and do not capitalize a quotation if you precede it with *that*.

DIRECT	Julie said, "Your last move was sloppy. Do it again."
INDIRECT	Julie said that our move was sloppy.
DIRECT	The Declaration of Independence states, "All men are created equal." [Here, the *a* in *All* is capitalized even though it is not capitalized in the original.]
THAT + DIRECT	The document states that "all men are created equal."

If a quoted sentence is interrupted, begin the second part with a lowercase letter.

> "Now," she said firmly, "let's try it again."

▐▐▐▶ Use a capital letter after a colon if what follows is more than one sentence or if it is a formal statement or a quotation.

> The dean issued the following statement: No smoking.
> The new rule did not appeal to everyone: It bothered some faculty members who smoke as well as local tobacco shops.
> It didn't appeal to everyone: "We protest," said some faculty members.

▐▐▐▶ Capitalize the names of languages, nationalities, peoples, races, and religions.

> The national language of Iran is Farsi, and most Iranians are Muslim.
> The Seminoles were part of the Muskogee Confederacy.

▐▐▐▶ Generally, capitalize the names of groups, teams, businesses, institutions, government agencies, and organizations.

American Library Association	the U.S. Senate	William H. Sadlier, Inc.
Binghamton University	Greenpeace	Toronto Blue Jays

Some companies use capital letters unconventionally.

WordPerfect	PaineWebber	eWorld	aquaCorps

▐▐▐▶ Capitalize the names of school subjects that are followed by a number. Also capitalize the names of all languages and proper adjectives.

> Jonathan is taking French, Algebra 1, chemistry, and American history.

EDITING TIP

Capitalize a parenthetical sentence that stands on its own.

The test is on verbs. (Review irregular verbs.)

In general, do not capitalize a parenthetical sentence within another sentence.

The test is on verbs (review irregular verbs) and French culture.

EXERCISE 5 Proofreading Sentences

Insert capital letters where they belong. To indicate a capital letter, use the proofreading symbol of three underscores beneath the letter: (s).

1. do you know who it was who described Washington as "first in war, first in peace, and first in the hearts of his countrymen"?

2. She explained, "the baseball teams that play their preseason games in Arizona are part of the cactus league."

3. horses came to north america, thanks to europeans.

4. spanish explorers were the first europeans ever seen by the aztecs.

5. after he graduated from brown university, my uncle joined the organization called volunteers in service to america.

6. baseball teams recruit players from latin american countries. (currently, cuba is off-limits.)

7. he played in the national league and then coached for the orioles in the american league.

8. charles had to take algebra 2 in summer school.

9. he was the first jewish member of the house of representatives.

10. while he was there, the democratic party was in power.

EXERCISE 6 Create Your Own Exercise

On a separate piece of paper, write one or more complete sentences in response to each numbered item. When you've finished writing, exchange papers with a classmate. Proofread each other's sentences for the correct use of capital letters.

1. Tell what subjects you are taking this term.

2. Write a sentence in which you quote a writer, songwriter, or speaker.

3. Name two organizations you'd like to join in order to do volunteer work. Explain your choices.

4. Name two of your favorite sports teams, and compare their recent efforts.

5. Write a sentence about a religious holiday and how it is celebrated.

6. Name a country you'd like to visit and what you'd do once you got there.

7. Think of a quotation that has some meaning for you, and rewrite it in the form of an indirect quotation.

8. Name a company for which you'd never work. Give your reasons.

9. Name a club you'd consider joining and tell why.

10. Write a question that you think high schools should ask graduating seniors.

I and *O*; Historical Events, Documents and Periods; Calendar Items; Brand Names; Awards

▐▶ Capitalize the words *I* and *O*.

Always capitalize the first-person pronoun *I* and the rare interjection *O*. Capitalize the modern interjection *oh* only when it is the first word in a sentence.

> I used to want to be a firefighter; now I want to be a poet.
> She was running, oh, about five miles a day.
> "O valiant cousin! Worthy gentleman!"—*Macbeth*, Act I

P.S. You may quote a writer's use of *O*, but chances are, you won't be putting *O*'s into your own poetry or prose.

▐▶ Capitalize the names of historical and special events, documents, and periods.

HISTORICAL EVENTS	World War I Battle of Waterloo
SPECIAL EVENTS	Kentucky Derby the Special Olympics
	March Madness
DOCUMENTS	Declaration of Independence the Magna Carta
	Treaty of Paris
PERIODS	the Dark Ages the Industrial Revolution
	the Cenozoic Era

▐▶ Capitalize calendar items but not seasons.

CALENDAR ITEMS	Passover Palm Sunday Monday, June 4
SEASONS	autumn colors a hot summer fall semester

Do not use capital letters to refer to a century.

> twenty-first century   seventeenth-century painting

▐▶ Capitalize brand names for manufactured products.

> Microsoft Word for Windows   Honda Civic   Boeing 727

Do not capitalize the common noun that follows a brand name.

> Freshmouth mouthwash   Grovestand olives

▐▶ Capitalize the names of awards and prizes.

> the Pulitzer Prize   an Academy Award   the Newbery Medal

Enriching Your Vocabulary

The word *valiant* comes from the Latin word *valere*, which means "to be strong." It is also related to the word *value*. A *valiant* knight could be characterized by courage and bravery.

WRITING HINT

In general writing, you may spell a word in all capitals for emphasis.

STOP!

Avoid this practice in e-mail, where all capitals are interpreted as rude screaming. Instead, for emphasis in e-mail, use asterisks before and after a word or group of words.

You *must* meet me at 3 P.M.

You will also see the word **prize** or **award** lowercased as in "Pulitzer prize."

EXERCISE 7 Proofreading Sentences

Proofread the following sentences for the correct use of capital letters. Use the proofreading symbols of a slash to indicate lowercase and three underscores to indicate a capital.

     ⌿ummer = lowercase letter   the o̲lympics = capital letter

1. Barbara Tuchman's book, *A Distant Mirror*, is set in the Fourteenth Century.

2. When I was a kid, I loved Chocolate Chip Cookies by Chunky.

3. My uncle drives a buick century.

4. Early every Spring, Wallace takes out his baseball glove to oil it.

5. Pat prefers club soda to pepsi or sprite, two popular brands of flavored soda.

6. Sophie wrote, "When i read the gettysburg address, i was truly moved."

7. During the dig, the archaeologists discovered tools from the bronze age.

8. The wars of the roses were fought in the Fifteenth century between two English royal families.

9. She won an emmy for her performance on the sitcom.

10. In New Orleans, participants prepare year-round for mardi gras.

EXERCISE 8 Writing a Paragraph

Write one or more paragraphs based on the information in the table below. Mention names and figures from the table as well as other information you know about those movies or other successful ones. Include your opinions about the movies and their popularity. Check your paragraphs for the correct use of capital letters. Share your writing with classmates.

All Time Top 20 American Movies Through 2012			
RANK/TITLE/DATE	GROSS[1] (millions)	RANK/TITLE/DATE	GROSS[1] (millions)
1. Avatar (2009)	$760.5	11. The Lion King (1994)	$422.8
2. Titanic (1997)	$658.7	12. Toy Story 3 (2010)	$415.0
3. Marvel's The Avengers (2012)	$623.3	13. The Hunger Games (2012)	$408.0
4. The Dark Knight (2008)	$533.3	14. Spider-Man (2002)	$403.7
5. The Phantom Menace (1999)	$474.5	15. Transformers (2009)	$402.1
6. A New Hope (1977)	$461.0	16. Harry Potter and the Deathly Hallows (2011)	$381.0
7. The Dark Knight Rises (2012)	$446.9	17. Revenge of the Sith (2005)	$380.3
8. Shrek 2 (2004)	$441.2	18. Finding Nemo (2003)	$380.1
9. E.T. The Extra-Terrestrial (1982)	$435.1	19. The Return of the King (2003)	$377.8
10. Pirates of the Caribbean (2006)	$423.3	20. Spider-Man 2 (2004)	$373.5

[1]Gross is in absolute dollars based on box office sales in North America. SOURCE: Nash Information Services, LLC.

Editing and Proofreading Worksheet 1

Edit the draft for errors in spelling, capitalization, punctuation, and usage. Write your edited version on a separate piece of paper. Compare your changes with those of a writing partner. **Hint:** Watch out for spelling mistakes, too, although all place names are spelled correctly.

[1]Jane Austen, who was born near the town of basingstoke in the late Eighteenth Century and lived into the Nineteenth, was an english writer whose treatment of ordinary people gave the Novel its modern flavor. [2]Although her Formal Education was brief, she grew up within a loving network of family and friends, who provided a stimulating environment for her writing. [3](she would later populate her writing with these country people; in fact, austen once said, "three or four families in a country village is the very thing to work on")

[4]Austin's first serious work, which she wrote in 1793–1794. [5]Was a short novel entitled *lady susan*. [6]In 1801, when Jane was twenty six, the family moved West to the city of bath. [7]After that, the family moved a great deal, going to London, clifton, warwickshire, and southampton. [8]In 1809, Austen moved with her Mother and Sister to a cottage in the small village of clawton. [9]Their she wrote *sense and sensibility* and *pride And prejudice*. [10]which were published in 1811 and 1813, respectively. [11]*Pride and prejudice* begins with the famous statement that "A single man in possession of a good fortune must be in want of a wife." [12]austen wrote all her books anonymously; it was only after her death in 1817 that her brother Henry made publick her authorship.

[13]austen's focus on character and personality and on the tensions between her heroines and society makes her writing seem more like Modern Writing than that of the Eighteenth or early Nineteenth Centuries. [14]This modern feel, along with an abundance of wit and realism, makes Austen's novels appealing to readers today.

Editing and Proofreading Worksheet 2

Edit the draft for errors in spelling, capitalization, punctuation, and usage. Write your edited version on a separate piece of paper. Compare your changes with those of a writing partner. **Hints:** The word *sun* does not take a capital. Watch out for spelling mistakes, too.

[1]I knew that earth was the planet between venus and mars and the only one known too be inhabited by carbon-based Life Forms. [2]But i didn't know much more about my home planet, in fact, since my understanding belonged in the middle ages, so I did a bit of research. [3]I learned many things.

[4]First of all, I learned about the Theory that a gas cloud began to form about 10 to 15 billion years ago. [5]Later it cooled. [6]About 5 or 6 billion years ago, shock waves caused the collection of dust and gases to collapse and spin. [7]The spinning cloud flattened, and all its material started to drop toward its center. [8]This falling action was the beginning of today's sun.

[9]Turbulence at the outer edge of the cloud caused particles to clump together and form planetoids. which began acting like gravity collectors, that swept through space and gathered mass. [10]As they say, "a rolling stone gathers no mass; just planetoids do." [11]Meanwhile, the real action was at the center of the collapsing cloud; their it was getting hotter, and pressure was increasing. [12]Eventually, thermonuclear reactions ignited the sun. [13]Then the planets evolved. [14]there you have it; Now you know what I know. [15](for more information on Astronomy, read, as i did, the essay "a short history of the solar system" in our Science textbook.)

Chapter Review

EXERCISE A Proofreading Sentences

Insert capital letters where they belong in the following sentences. To indicate a capital letter, use the proofreading symbol of three underscores beneath the letter: (d).

1. who won the academy award for best actor in 2011?

2. Is seneca lake (near ithaca, new york) one of the finger lakes?

3. Robert e. lee lived in arlington, across the potomac river from washington, d.c.

4. humphreys peak (no apostrophe), home of the snow bowl, is the tallest mountain in arizona and one of the highest in the southwest.

5. Terry applied to universities in Georgia and alabama; her interest is archaeology.

6. Miguel moved to his aunt martha's apartment on twenty-sixth street in the neighborhood called chelsea.

7. Thanks to the invention by John McAdam, an engineer, we followed a macadamized road to hagerstown.

8. The board of directors of the continental oil company met with queen Elinor.

9. The mountains southeast of the sierras aren't nearly as high.

10. The gettysburg address is stored in the institution known as the library of congress.

EXERCISE B Proofreading Paragraphs

Proofread the following sentences for the correct use of capital letters. Use the proofreading symbol of three underscores to indicate a capital letter; use the proofreading symbol of a slash to indicate a lowercase letter. **Hint:** Names of chemical elements, such as zinc and plutonium, do not require capitals.

[1]marie Sklodowska and pierre curie met at the university of paris in the late

Nineteenth Century. [2]they married in 1895 and were among the pioneers of a

new field of study: The field of radioactivity.

[3]While the curies were at the University, a professor there, dr. henri

becquerel, discovered that the element uranium had unusual properties: It gave off something that darkened a photographic plate. [4]becquerel had discovered radioactivity. [5]After this discovery, marie curie, who was his student, began studying pitchblende, the mineral that contains uranium. [6]she concluded that there were other radioactive substances in pitchblende.

[7]Pierre put aside his own research and worked with his wife to study the pitchblende. [8]The work was tedious, difficult, smelly, and physically taxing. [9](they had to stir, for hours at a stretch, the boiling matter in a smelting basin.) [10]in 1898, their efforts resulted in a key finding.

[11]the curies discovered that, in addition to the uranium, the pitchblende contained two other radioactive elements: Polonium and Radium. [12]polonium was chosen as a name because marie was polish. [13]Radium, they found, was a hundred times more radioactive than uranium. [14]In 1903, the world recognized the efforts of becquerel and the curies: they were awarded the nobel prize in physics. [15]Marie Curie won another nobel prize in 1911, this time in chemistry, for her study of the chemical properties of radium.

[16]it wasn't until world war I that the disastrous effects of radioactive poisoning became known to the Public. [17]A number of workers who used a radioactive substance to illuminate dials had been wetting the points of their brushes on their lips. [18]in so doing, these workers had been accumulating significant amounts of radium internally. [19]Twenty-Four of them died of cancer within two Decades. [20]When marie curie died in 1934, she left her only property of value, a gram of pure radium, to her Daughter.

Spelling

STUDENT WRITING

Persuasive Essay

Student Parking Lot a Wild and Crazy Place
by Adam Andress
high school student, Clearwater, Florida

It's 2:40 P.M. at CCC. The crows are chirping, and the squirrels are happily look-ing for leftover lunch food in the trash cans. So far it has been a nice and quiet day. As the announcements come on, students hover near the classroom doors and get into position. The tension rises. The bell rings, aannd . . . "They're Off!!"

Students sprint to the parking lot with a speed only matched by the velocity they will achieve in their cars as they race to get out of school the fastest. Seniors usually get there first due to many advantages. They are closer to Haines Bayshore, and the juniors and sophomores have to swim to their cars after a rainy day.

"There is a drainage problem in the junior parking lot," said junior John Boni. "We have Lake Marauder in the parking lot, and my car is right in the center."

For lingering students on their way to their cars, it is now time to cross the road of death. If you have ever played the game Frogger, you know what it is like to cross the parking lot. As you wait to cross, the wind from the 50-mph cars blows your hair and slaps at your face. You then see a hole and run like you have never run before. You cross one lane in the parking lot successfully, but then a car pulling out of another lane almost gets you.

You jump into your car, but you drop your bag. Like Indiana Jones, you reach your hand out and grab it just in time to recoil before a car flies by and almost takes your hand with it. It is now time to pull out. Either there is a car heading in your direction at Mach 3, or the slowest-walking person is behind you. After about five minutes, you eventually succeed in pulling out on Haines Bayshore.

Wait a minute! Is that the sound of thunder? It's beginning to get louder. El Niño? Nope, it's the $3,000 stereo system installed in a car worth about half that. The volume is cranked up so that every single person on the campus can hear it. Who in his or her right mind can drive with such bass, one that makes the windows in your car rattle?

Some students might think that there needs to be more regulation during dis-missal, but what faculty member would go on a suicide mission like that? We need to just take our time and not rush, especially on Friday, or someone may get hurt.

We have made many requests to drive more safely, but the student body has not listened to a word of advice. So don't forget to buckle up, and please try to keep it under 20 mph.

> Adam Andress wrote this persuasive essay for an audience of his peers. His word choice is informal and friendly; he uses exaggeration and humor to make his point. In spite of his friendly style, however, he offers specific details and examples for his opinion.
>
> Can you find any misspelled words in Adam's essay? Look again. Adam's essay is effective partly because it is error free. In this chapter, you'll go over rules and advice to help you spell words correctly whenever you write.

Using a Dictionary

⫸ If you're in doubt about how to spell a word, use a dictionary.

In addition to verifying the spelling of an entry word, a dictionary helps with several other spelling issues related to the entry word. The call-outs on the entries below show the following information: how to spell an irregular plural of a noun; the comparative and superlative forms of an adjective; the past, past participle, and present participle of a verb; and words related to the entry word.

Entry word with syllable breaks

Past and present participle forms of verb

ac·cu·mu·late \ə-'kyü-m(y)ə-,lāt\ *vb* **-lat·ed; -lat·ing** [L *accumulatus*, pp. of *accumulare*, fr. *ad-* + *cumulare* to heap up — more at CUMULATE] *vt* (15c): to gather or pile up esp. little by little: AMASS <~ a fortune> ~ *vi*: to increase gradually in quantity or number.

Pronunciation

Part of speech

Etymology, or word history

ac·cu·rate \'a-kyə-rət\ *adj* [L *accuratus*, fr. pp. of *accurare* to take care of, fr. *ad-* + *cura* care] (1596) **1**: free from error esp. as the result of care <an ~ diagnosis> **2**: conforming exactly to truth or to a standard: EXACT <providing ~ color> **3**: able to give an accurate result <an ~ gauge> *syn* see CORRECT *adv* — **ac·cu·rate·ly** *n* — **ac·cu·rate·ness**

Related words

Irregular plural of noun

ac·cused *n, pl* **accused** (1567): one charged with criminal offense; *esp*: the defendant in a criminal case

Comparative and superlative forms of adjective

achy \āk'ē\ *adj* **ach·i·er; ach·i·est** (1875): afflicted with aches — **ach·i·ness** *n*

—from *Merriam-Webster's Collegiate Dictionary*, Eleventh Edition

In doing the following exercises, use a print or digital dictionary to find or check your answers.

Exercise 1 Using a Dictionary to Check Spelling

Write the letter of the correct spelling in the blank. If you're not sure of the correct spelling of a word, look up the item in a dictionary to check the correct spelling.

1. _____ (a) anilize   (b) analyze   (c) analize   (d) annalyze

2. _____ (a) compatant (b) competant (c) competent (d) compitent

3. _____ (a) cirkit   (b) cuircit   (c) cercuit   (d) circuit

WRITING HINT

If you can't find a word in a dictionary after trying a few possible spellings, ask someone for help, or use a computer spell-checker. The spell-checker may "guess" the word you're looking for.

4. ——— (a) contious   (b) consious   (c) conscious   (d) conscius

5. ——— (a) attendance   (b) attendence   (c) atendance   (d) atendence

6. ——— (a) elligible   (b) elegible   (c) eligible   (d) elidgible

7. ——— (a) hipocrisy   (b) hypocrisy   (c) hippocrisy   (d) hypacrisy

8. ——— (a) gratious   (b) gracius   (c) grashus   (d) gracious

9. ——— (a) morgige   (b) morgage   (c) mortgage   (d) moregage

10. ——— (a) intelligence (b) inteligence   (c) intellagence   (d) intellegence

Exercise 2 Using a Dictionary

Answer the following spelling-related questions. Use a college dictionary, as necessary, to answer the questions.

1. What are two plurals for the noun *index*? _____

2. What are all the points at which you can place a hyphen to hyphenate the word *possibility* at the end of a line? _____

3. How do you spell the past tense and the present participle of the verb *regret*? _____

4. What is an acceptable three-letter abbreviation for *phenylthiocarbamide*? _____

5. What is an adjective form of the noun *phlegm*? _____

6. What is an alternate spelling for *jujitsu*? _____

7. How do you spell the verb that means "to get off to a speedy start"?
   a. jump start b. jumpstart c. jump-start _____

8. What does your dictionary say about capitalizing (or not) geologic eras? Should you write *Precambrian* or *precambrian*? _____

9. How do you spell the word for the symbol for the medical profession? The word begins with the letters *cadu-*. ——— ———

10. What choices, if any, does your dictionary give you for spelling the past tense of the verb *program*? _____

Exercise 3 Create Your Own Exercise

Work with a partner to write two paragraphs. Your paragraphs can be the beginning of a personal anecdote, story, autobiographical incident, or letter to an editor at a newspaper or magazine. Then exchange papers with another pair of classmates to find and correct all misspellings.

Spelling Rules

In spite of the many irregularities in English spelling, there are some rules. There are also exceptions to the rules.

▐▌▶ Write *i* before *e* except after *c*.

Note that the words in the first line below have a long /ē/ sound. But *i* also comes before *e* in *friend* and *mischief*, which do not have a long /ē/ sound.

FOLLOW RULE	retrieve	relieve	niece	siege	
AFTER C	perceive	ceiling	conceit	receipt	deceive
EXCEPTIONS	seize	(n)either	leisure	weird	caffeine

P.S. If these rules and exceptions don't help, remember that you can always rely on your dictionary.

▐▌▶ Write *ei* when these letters are not pronounced with a long /ē/ sound, especially when the sound is a long /ā/, as in *neighbor* and *weigh*.

	height	their	foreign	forfeit		
SOUNDS LIKE AY	eight	freight	sleigh	reign	vein	veil

▐▌▶ Watch out for words with more than one syllable that end with the sound /seed/; only one word is spelled with *–sede*. Three words end in *–ceed*. All other words end in *–cede*.

-SEDE	supersede				
-CEED	exceed	proceed	succeed		
-CEDE	concede	intercede	precede	recede	secede

▐▌▶ Spell out numbers that can be expressed in one or two words. Rephrase a sentence so that you don't begin with a numeral.

The pool was twenty-five feet long.
The conference attendance was 9,782 students and 652 advisors.

250 people registered late. [rephrase sentence]
There were 250 late-registration attendees.

Some writers prefer not to mix numerals and spelled-out numbers in the same sentence. They'd recommend the following:

He began swimming only 25 meters at a time but worked up to 125.

Remember to use a hyphen when spelling out numbers from *twenty-one* to *ninety-nine*.

WRITING HINT

A good way to remember something is to make up a mnemonic, or memory, device. Here's a nonsense sentence to help you remember some of the exceptions to the *i*-before-*e* rule:

"**Either weird** sister can **seize** a lizard at **leisure**, but **neither** ever tries."

Enriching Your Vocabulary

The Latin verb *intercedere* comes from *inter,* or "between," and *cedere,* or "to move or go." It is the source of the English verb *intercede.* Have you ever tried to *intercede* in an argument between friends?

EXERCISE 4 Spelling Words with *ie* and *ei*

Fill in the blank in each of the following items with *ie* or *ei* to spell an English word correctly. Use a dictionary as necessary.

1. b——ge	6. s——ve	11. ch——f	16. sl——gh
2. conc——vable	7. s——ge	12. for——gn	17. counterf——t
3. financ——r	8. c——ling	13. p——r	18. sh——ld
4. gr——f	9. misch——vous	14. retr——ver	19. r——gn
5. p——ce	10. pr——st	15. br——f	20. r——n

EXERCISE 5 Spelling Words with the Sound /seed/

Fill in the blank in each of the following items with four letters to correctly spell an English word ending with the sound /*seed*/. Use a dictionary as necessary.

1. pro——	6. suc——
2. ac——	7. re——
3. con——	8. super——
4. pre——	9. se——
5. ex——	10. inter——

EXERCISE 6 Spelling and Placing Numbers

Decide if you should use numerals or spelled-out numbers in the following sentences, and, on a separate piece of paper, rewrite the sentences as necessary. Rearrange words or add words to a sentence as necessary to avoid starting with a numeral. Write *C* if a given sentence is correct.

1. In 2114, what do you think the United States will be like?
2. 2114 will probably hold some surprises.
3. Thinking one hundred years ahead is a challenge.
4. Thinking 99 years ahead is a challenge, too.
5. The guests ranged in age from twelve to 16.
6. Forty Four of the invited guests showed up.
7. 52 invitations had gone out.
8. The banquet room can hold up to one hundred twenty-two guests.
9. 122, in other words, is the maximum allowed for safety.
10. A gross of something is equal to twelve dozen things.

Prefixes and Suffixes

Prefixes and suffixes are groups of letters that change a word's meaning. A **prefix** (such as *de-*, *in-*, *mis-*, and *un-*) is added to the beginning of a word; a **suffix** (such as *-er*, *-ly*, *-ment*, and *-ness*) is added to the end.

▐▐▐▶ Adding a prefix does not change the spelling of the original word.

> **de**formed   **il**legal   **mis**spell   **un**necessary

▐▐▐▶ If a word ends in *-y* preceded by a consonant, change the *y* to *i* before adding any suffix except *-ing*.

pettiness	funnier	happiness
loneliest	hurrying	
EXCEPTIONS shyly	shyness	dryness

▐▐▐▶ If a word ends in *-y* preceded by a vowel, keep the *-y*.

joyous	buoyant	enjoyment	playful
EXCEPTIONS daily	said		

▐▐▐▶ Drop a word's final silent *-e* before a suffix that begins with a vowel.

> caring   likable   loving   creative   subtly

Note: American dictionaries give *likable*, *lovable*, *movable*, and *sizable* as preferred spellings but also include *likeable*, *loveable*, *moveable*, and *sizeable*.

▐▐▐▶ Keep the final silent *-e* if the word ends in *-ge* or *-ce* and the suffix begins with *a* or *o*.

> manageable   courageous   noticeable   outrageous   replaceable

▐▐▐▶ Keep the final silent *-e* before a suffix that begins with a consonant.

useful	boredom	resourceful	definitiveness
EXCEPTIONS argument	awful	ninth	truly wisdom

Note: American dictionaries give *judgment* and *acknowledgment* as the preferred spellings; *judgement* and *acknowledgement* are British spellings.

▐▐▐▶ Double the final consonant in some one-syllable words when the suffix begins with a vowel.

Doubling occurs when the word ends in a consonant preceded by a single vowel.

> grabbing   dropped   hottest   hitter

WRITING HINT

Sometimes, a word keeps the silent *-e* to distinguish it from another word that would otherwise be spelled the same. Examples include *dyeing* and *dying* and *singeing* and *singing*.

Some Prefixes and Their Meanings

Prefix	Meaning
circum-	around
dis-, un-	the opposite
il-, im-, in-, ir-	not
post-	after
pre-	before
re-	again
sub-	below
super-	above, beyond

Some Suffixes and Their Meanings

Suffix	Meaning
-able	capable of being
-ate, -en -fy	become, make
-dom, -hood	state of being
-er, -or	a person who
-less	without
-ment	state or condition of
-ous, -ful	full of

▥➡ Double the final consonant in some words of more than one syllable when the suffix begins with a vowel.

Doubling occurs if the root word ends in a single consonant preceded by a single vowel and the new word is accented on the next-to-last syllable. Do not double the final consonant when the new word is not accented on the next-to-last syllable.

DOUBLE CONSONANT	referred	submitted	occurrence	rerunning
SINGLE CONSONANT	reference	preference	preferable	

Note: Some words have two options for what happens when *-ed* and *-ing* suffixes are added. Dictionaries usually give the preferred option first. Examples include *traveled* and *travelled, canceled* and *cancelled,* and *programmed* and *programed.*

EXERCISE 7 Adding Prefixes and Suffixes

Write the word that results when the following prefixes or suffixes are added.

1. achieve + -able _____
2. argue + -ment _____
3. dis- + appearance _____
4. in- + consistency _____
5. un- + conscious _____
6. definite + -ly _____
7. fatal + -ity _____
8. excessive + -ness _____
9. conceive + -able _____
10. in- + frequent _____
11. grab + -ed _____
12. notice + -able _____
13. insure + -ance _____

14. natural + -ly _____
15. happy + -ness _____
16. un- + naturally _____
17. dis- + possess _____
18. in- + sensibility _____
19. use + -ful _____
20. sophomore + -ic _____
21. dis- + similar _____
22. tremendous + -ly _____
23. un- + specific _____
24. acknowledge + -ment _____
25. prefer + -able _____

EXERCISE 8 Writing New Words

Hold a competition. In a preestablished period of time (say, ten minutes), write as many words as you can that contain a given prefix or suffix (or both). Then get together with a group to compare lists. See if you can define all of the words you've listed. **Hint:** Use a dictionary throughout the competition.

Noun Plurals

For any noun, start with the singular form, and follow the directions below to form the plural.

Making Nouns Plural		
KINDS OF NOUNS	**WHAT TO DO**	**EXAMPLES**
Most nouns	Add -s to the singular.	amateur**s**, circuit**s**, benefit**s**
Nouns that end in -s, -x, -z, -ch, -sh	Add -es to the singular.	flourish**es**, box**es**, waltz**es**, kiss**es**, hunch**es**
Family names	Follow the two preceding rules.	the Lincoln**s**, the Koch**es**, the Lomax**es**, the Rabinowitz**es**
Nouns that end in -y preceded by a consonant	Change the -y to i, and add -es.	flurr**ies**, vacanc**ies** possibilit**ies**, personalit**ies**
Nouns that end in -y preceded by a vowel	Add -s.	survey**s**, delay**s**, buoy**s**, chimney**s**
Family names that end in -y	Add -s.	Kennedy**s**, Kolody**s**, May**s**, Carney**s**
Most nouns that end in -f	Add -s.	chief**s**, tariff**s**, sheriff**s**, belief**s**
A few nouns that end in -f or -fe	Change the f to v and add -s or -es.	kni**ves**, shel**ves**, lea**ves**, cal**ves**, li**ves**
Nouns ending in -o preceded by a vowel	Add -s.	kazoo**s**, patio**s**
Most nouns ending in -o preceded by a consonant	Add -es.	veto**es**, hero**es**, potato**es**, tornado**es**
Most musical terms ending in -o	Add -s.	alto**s**, soprano**s**, solo**s**, piano**s**, cello**s**
Compound nouns	Make the most important word plural.	surgeon**s** general, mother**s**-in-law, passer**s**by, **men** of straw, spoonful**s** or spoon**s**ful
Letters, numbers, and words referred to as words	Use an apostrophe (') + -s.	B**'s**, 5**'s**, &**'s** no if**'s**, and**'s**, or but**'s**
Irregular plurals, foreign plurals, and words that stay the same for both singular and plural	No rules apply! Memorize these forms.	children, mice, women, men, feet, teeth, data, geese, series, moose, oxen, trout, sheep, deer, species

EDITING TIP

Watch out for words that look misspelled but aren't. For example, sometimes *fishes* is the correct plural for *fish*.

Nouns with Two Acceptable Forms: hoo**fs** or hoo**ves**, scar**fs** or scar**ves**, dwar**fs** or dwar**ves**, volcano**s** or volcano**es**, mosquito**s** or mosquito**es**, flamingo**s** or flamingo**es**

Exceptions: *memos, silos*

Exercise 9 Forming Noun Plurals

Write the plural form of each noun. If you're unsure of the correct form, check a dictionary to see if it lists irregular plurals or alternate plural forms. If no plural form is listed, follow the rule in the preceding chart.

1. secretary-general _____
2. deer _____
3. Jones _____
4. focus _____
5. Tuesday _____
6. acquaintance _____
7. chief _____
8. committee _____
9. debtor _____
10. fraternity _____
11. glimpse _____
12. waltz _____
13. medium _____

14. sister-in-law _____
15. Berry (proper noun) _____
16. Martinez _____
17. grouse _____
18. judgment _____
19. piccolo _____
20. obstacle _____
21. woman _____
22. picnic _____
23. policy _____
24. square meter _____
25. cupful _____
26. stadium _____

Exercise 10 Writing with Noun Plurals

Imagine that there is a mission to another solar system and that you are in charge. You must bring two or more of everything. Write two or more paragraphs in which you tell what and whom you have decided to take. Be specific. When you've finished writing, check to see that all noun plurals are correctly spelled. Exchange papers with a classmate, and check for properly spelled noun plurals.

Editing and Proofreading Worksheet 1

Edit the draft for errors in spelling, capitalization, punctuation, and usage. Write your edited version on a separate piece of paper. Compare your changes with those of a writing partner.

[1]A sandwich is too or more slice of bread with a filling in between. [2]It's origin is interesting. [3]The first sandwich may have been the tidbit that the Jewish scolar Hillel ate about two thousand yeares ago and that is now a fixture at the Passover meal. [4]It consisted of bitter herbs and a flat bread. [5]The Romans also ate a form of sandwich which they called *offula*. [6]But the sandwich as we experience it today is a more recent invention.

[7]According to one vershion of the story, early in the morning of August 6, 1762, John Montagu, the fourth earl of Sandwich, was hungary. [8](Yes, there had been three earl of sandwiches before him.) [9]The problem was that he was busy gambleing away in one of his all-night sessiones of playing cards. [10]He didn't want to leave the table. [11]So he concieved of a solution by orderring his servant to toast two slices of bread and to bring them to him along with a couple of chunkes of roast beef. [12]When the man reappeared with the food. [13]The earl grabed the meat and stuck it between the toast and found it noticably tastyer than anything else he had eatten. [14]The first of moren quick lunchs had been created. [15]Within eighth years, the word *sandwich* became associated with the food item.

[16]In his life of liesure, Lord Sandwich acheived little else that was useful. [17]He had recieved a fine education at Eton and Cambridge. [18]He acquired at one point a high post in the navy. but [19]He was accused of mismanagment. [20]Then sandwich gave up on public service and proceded to devote himself to a life of gambleing. [21]But he had the approval of at least one of his acquaintances: Captain James Cook, the explorer whose journies Sandwich had outfited. [22]Cheifly to thank the earl for his finantial backing, Cook named the gorgous Sandwich Islands in the Pacific for him.

Editing and Proofreading Worksheet 2

Edit the draft for errors in spelling, capitalization, punctuation, and usage. Write your edited version on a separate piece of paper. Compare your changes with those of a writing partner.

[1]Paul Laurence Dunbar (1872–1906) was a poet and fiction writter. [2]He atended public schools in Dayton, Ohio. [3]His mother taught him to read, and his father taught him to tell storys.

[4]Dunbar was the only black student in his high school. [5]Their he was not only one of the outstanding editor in cheifs of the school newspaper but also class poet and president of the literery soceity. [6]After succeding in high school and graduateing, Dunbar worked as an elevator operator in a Dayton hotel. [7]He continued writting and finely was discovered. [8]He recieved the privalege of reading his poems at the 1892 meeting of the Western Association of Writers.

[9]Dunbar published his first volume of poetry in 1893. [10]He received encouragment from influential African Americans at that time. [11]Soon, however, he began sufferring from tuberculosis and dyed very young. [12]Still, he managed to write many essays and eleven volumes of poetry before he had to conceed to the illness. [13]33 was his age when he past away.

[14]Dunbar's parents were formerly enslaved. [15]Dunbar hisself acheived widespread recognition in his breif lifetime. [16]The journey from slavery to cultural hieghts seems great, but it was not without difficultys that embitterred Dunbar. [17]The poet's major unhappyness had to do with language. [18]He wrote some poems in dialect and some in gloryous and grand language. [19]He regreted that many people in his audience prefered the dialect poems. [20]Today, fortunately, both kinds of Dunbar's poems usualy appear in poetry anthologys.

Chapter Review

EXERCISE A Spelling with Prefixes and Suffixes

On a separate piece of paper, create as many words as you can from the
following lists of prefixes, suffixes, and words.

PREFIXES		WORDS		SUFFIXES	
dis-	re-	announce	copy	-ed	-ly
un-	in-	read	imagine	-ment	-able
mis-	pre-	appoint	taste	-ful	-ing

EXERCISE B Spelling Noun Plurals

Write the plural form of each noun in the space provided.

1. bench ——————————

2. monkey ————————

3. dormitory ——————

4. "at" sign (@) ——————

5. dolly ——————————

6. doily ——————————

7. dogcatcher ——————

8. dog day ——————————

9. emergency ——————

10. radio ——————————

11. mortgage ——————

12. Lipschultz ——————

13. Kenney ——————————

14. father-in-law ——————

15. flamingo ——————

16. silo ——————————

17. percentage ——————

18. survey ——————————

19. index ——————————

20. crisis ——————————

EXERCISE C Choosing the Correct Spelling

Look carefully at each choice and then choose the correct spelling of each word.
Write the letter of the correct spelling in the blank.

_____ 1. (a) alotment   (b) allottment   (c) allotment   (d) alottment

_____ 2. (a) refering   (b) reffering   (c) refferring   (d) referring

_____ 3. (a) misquito   (b) misquotoe   (c) mosquito   (d) mosquitoe

_____ 4. (a) disengenuous   (b) disingenuous
          (c) disingenous   (d) disinjenuous

_____ 5. (a) persperation   (b) perspiration
          (c) pirspiration   (d) perspirasion

_____ 6.	(a) tendency	(b) tendancy	(c) tendincy	(d) tendencey
_____ 7.	(a) shepard	(b) shepherd	(c) shephard	(d) sheperd
_____ 8.	(a) sherrif	(b) sherif	(c) sherriff	(d) sheriff
_____ 9.	(a) similar	(b) similer	(c) simmilar	(d) similiar
_____ 10.	(a) rhythm	(b) rythem	(c) rhythum	(d) rhythem

EXERCISE D Proofreading Paragraphs

Proofread the following paragraphs to correct all spelling mistakes. **Hint:** All proper nouns are spelled correctly.

[1]Today, scuba divers need a certificate verifieing their competance. [2]But people have been diving for centurys, allways fasinated by the idea of moving freely underwater. [3]In medeival Europe, people enjoyed romances in which Alexander the Great desended to the ocean bottom in a glass diving bell. [4]Alexander's acomplishment was complete fiction; the first real evedence of the use of technical aids to explore beneath water comes from the writings of Alexander's knowldgable tutor, Aristotle. [5]In one of his writen works, Aristotle mentions, in passing, that divers of his time used breatheing tubes. [6]He refered to them as "instruments for respiration, through which they can draw air from above the water."

[7]Subsequent descriptions of breathing tubes and masks occurr in German ballads of the twelth century and, later, in Chinese accounts of pearl divers off the southern coast of the mainland. [8]But the most detailed of these early accounts are those of the eleventh-century sientist al-Biruni. [9]He describes the peculier equipment worn by pearl divers in the Arabian gulf. [10]He writes that the divers wore leather hoods filled with air. [11]He explains that a long sealed tube attached to the hood was connected on it's other end to a dish with a hole in its center, through which air passed. [12]The dish, in turn, rested on the surface of the water, kept afloat by one or more inflated bags. [13]The diver, according to al-Biruni, could reasonabley expect to stay underwater for days useing this efficent devise.

Cumulative Review

EXERCISE A Punctuation Marks

Correct or add commas, end marks, and other punctuation marks in the following sentences. Correct errors in capitalization. You may add or rearrange words.

1. 1920 was the year that Eugene O'Neill wrote the play "Beyond the Horizon", for which he won the pulitzer prize.

2. In Paris France the organization called the League of nations came into being in 1920?

3. The movie *The Cabinet of Dr Caligari* was made in 1920.

4. In 1920; new Universities opened in Honolulu Hawaii and in Rio de Janeiro brazil.

5. In 1920 the United States produced 645 million tons of coal, Great Britain produced 229 million tons.

6. That year, Novelist Edith Wharton won a Pulitzer for her novel "The Age of Innocence."

7. When a bomb exploded in 1920 on wall street in New York City thirty five people were killed.

8. In 1920 Mohandas K Gandhi emerged as Indias leader in the struggle for independence from Great Britain.

9. In 1920 Harvard beat Oregon 7:6 in the Rose Bowl Sacco and Vanzetti were arrested and the Russian Civil War ended.

10. 1920 was the year of the boston red sox great mistake, they sold Babe Ruth to the New York yankees?

EXERCISE B Capitalization

Add capital letters where they are needed in the following expressions. If an item is correct, write *C*.

1. the phoenix gazette newspaper

2. the declaration of independence

3. the james river

4. the italian ambassador

5. the world's largest lake

6. the town of pine hill in the catskill Mountains

7. aunt mildred and uncle cal

8. the worst fast-food joint in town

9. the united nations

10. last year's winter vacation

11. the song "guys and dolls"

12. the nobel peace prize

13. renaissance art in italy

14. algebra 2 and physics

15. mike's submarines and soda shop

16. my favorite eatery

17. a clothing store on main street

18. dr. alan goldstein

19. valentine's day

20. arthur miller's play *a view from the bridge*

EXERCISE C Spelling

On a separate piece of paper, rewrite each sentence, correcting the misspelled words.

1. Niether Jared nor I will be able to compete on the paralel bars.

2. The lonely nieghbor was wierd.

3. The commitee was not competant or consistant.

4. The sign mispelled the word *procede*.

5. The liutenant was criticized for interceeding for the financeir.

6. The forgoten hero had been couragous.

7. There was practicaly no pressure on the psycology profesor.

8. When the sargent spoke officially, his persperation was particularly noticable.

9. Sophomores are not known for the qualitys of suabtlety and shareing.

10. The judgemental cheif surprised us when he mispoke.

EXERCISE D Proofreading a Passage

A block of words looks like a puzzle if it has no capital letters or punctuation marks. As you can see below, it's very hard to read such a block of words. On a separate piece of paper, rewrite the passage, adding all of the missing punctuation marks and capital letters.

doriot anthony dwyer the great grandniece of susan b anthony achieved a distinction of her own she was the first woman to be appointed to a first chair in a major symphony orchestra dwyer who began playing the flute at the age of eight was trained at the eastman school of music in rochester new york after getting her BS in music in 1943 she joined the washington national symphony two years later she joined the los angeles philharmonic as the second flutist then in 1952 she joined the boston symphony as the first chair flutist in 1974 dwyer was named to the womens hall of fame of the seneca falls historical society in seneca falls new york

Standardized Test Practice: Grammar and Usage

In addition to an essay component, standardized writing tests include a multiple-choice component that tests your understanding of standard written English. In this section of Level Gold, you will find four multiple-choice formats in four different sections. (For additional practice in standardized test formats with grammar feedback, go to www.grammarforwriting.com.) The four formats include:

- SAT Practice: Identifying Sentence Errors
- SAT Practice: Improving Sentences
- SAT Practice: Improving Paragraphs
- ACT Practice

Following these four sections is a practice test in which items from three formats are combined.

IDENTIFYING SENTENCE ERRORS

In this type of multiple-choice item, a sentence will have four words or phrases underlined and labeled **A** through **D**. Your task will be to identify an error, if there is one, and fill in the corresponding answer oval. If there is no error, your answer choice will be **E**, which is "No Error."

IMPROVING SENTENCES

In this section, your task will be not only to spot mistakes but fix them, too. In each test item, a sentence will be all or partly underlined. You must spot and fix an error, if there is one, within the underlined portion. Choices **B** through **E** each rephrase the underlined portion, serving as a possible replacement for it. Choice **A** repeats the underlined portion exactly as it is originally given. Choose **A** if you think the item is correct as is.

IMPROVING PARAGRAPHS

The test items in this section have the same structure as the ones in the Improving Sentences section but are keyed to a passage instead of an individual sentence. The items test your ability to revise and combine sentences within the context of an essay and improve its unity, organization and coherence, and word choice.

ACT PRACTICE

As its title suggests, this section is standardized test practice in ACT format. It includes two passages with grammar and usage items keyed to them. Like the Improving Paragraphs section, the test items ask you to revise and combine sentences within the context of an essay and improve its unity, organization and coherence, and word choice.

SAT Practice: Identifying Sentence Errors

Directions: In each item, one of the underlined words or phrases may contain an error in grammar, usage, word choice, or idiom. If there is an error, choose the underlined part that must be changed to make the sentence correct, and fill in the corresponding oval. If the sentence has no error, fill in oval E. In selecting answers, follow the requirements of standard written English.

Example

Although the sheltered harbor was deep, the huge sailing ship
    A   B

glided into it smoothly and without difficulty. No error   🅐 ⒷⒸⒹⒺ
         C   D   E

The correct choice is **A** because the subordinating conjunction, *Although*, is an illogical choice. It is because the harbor was deep that the ship was able to glide in smoothly.

1. Each member of the U.S. Exploring Expedition of 1838 reported on
   A   B

their experience to the government's investigator. No error   ⒶⒷⒸⒹⒺ
  C   D   E

2. Either a film by John Ford or one by Orson Welles are being shown
    A   B   C   D

at the local theater this weekend. No error   ⒶⒷⒸⒹⒺ
                       E

3. Who did President Jefferson select to lead the momentous expedition
   A   B   C

to explore the lands he recently had acquired through the
                        D

Louisiana Purchase? No error   ⒶⒷⒸⒹⒺ
       E

4. <u>Neither</u> repeated requests by the teacher <u>nor</u> frequent admonitions
    A   B

from the principal <u>convinces</u> the student to change <u>her</u>
                  C   D

behavior. <u>No error</u>   Ⓐ Ⓑ Ⓒ Ⓓ Ⓔ
        E

5. When Lenny <u>accidentally</u> kills the ranch owner's daughter-in-law in
                  A

John Steinbeck's *Of Mice and Men*, George <u>shot</u> his pal <u>rather than</u>
                                       B   C

allow the vengeful lynch mob <u>to capture</u> him. <u>No error</u>   Ⓐ Ⓑ Ⓒ Ⓓ Ⓔ
                            D   E

6. The <u>farther</u> I investigated the matter, the more convinced I <u>became</u>
       A   B

that we <u>had not been</u> on solid <u>footing</u> from the start. <u>No error</u>   Ⓐ Ⓑ Ⓒ Ⓓ Ⓔ
             C   D   E

7. I <u>certainly</u> appreciated the <u>twenty-nine</u> masterpieces of French <u>royal</u>
    A   B   C

furniture on display at the museum more <u>than Carlos</u>. <u>No error</u>   Ⓐ Ⓑ Ⓒ Ⓓ Ⓔ
                                  D   E

8. During our <u>recent</u> sail on the Aegean, we <u>visited</u> fishing villages,
            A   B

beach resorts, <u>idyllic</u> coves, and <u>we were exploring</u> ancient ruins.
                  C   D

<u>No error</u>   Ⓐ Ⓑ Ⓒ Ⓓ Ⓔ
  E

9. <u>Without scarcely</u> any worthwhile maps, Magellan led his small fleet
            A

around the world <u>although</u> <u>he himself</u> never completed the <u>pivotal</u>
                     B   C   D

voyage.   <u>No error</u>   Ⓐ Ⓑ Ⓒ Ⓓ Ⓔ
           E

10. Because the city of Cologne was famous in the Middle Ages for its
      A   B

great cathedral, later it became better known throughout Europe as
     C   D

the major producer of cologne. No error
                           E

Ⓐ Ⓑ Ⓒ Ⓓ Ⓔ

11. I have learned that longitude measured distances east and west of
     A   B   C

the Prime Meridian, a line running north to south through
                     D

Greenwich, England. No error
                 E

Ⓐ Ⓑ Ⓒ Ⓓ Ⓔ

12. Selecting the ideal spot for the photo shoot was no easy task; the
     A   B   C

photographer carefully examined several possible locales before
                               D

making a decision. No error
                E

Ⓐ Ⓑ Ⓒ Ⓓ Ⓔ

13. Throughout his life, John Brown failed at one business after another
      A

but finding his place in history with a brazen but doomed attempt to
     B   C

lead slaves in revolt against their owners. No error
                 D   E

Ⓐ Ⓑ Ⓒ Ⓓ Ⓔ

14. Participants are judged according to how well they sing, how
     A   B   C

gracefully they dance, and for their acting abilities. No error
                    D   E

Ⓐ Ⓑ Ⓒ Ⓓ Ⓔ

15. <u>Although</u> not <u>everyone</u> who reads <u>it</u> will agree, *Guns, Germs, and*
     A   B   C

Steel by Jared Diamond <u>will offer</u> a convincing explanation for the
                        D

differing developments of societies on different continents. <u>No error</u>   Ⓐ Ⓑ Ⓒ Ⓓ Ⓔ
                                                 E

16. Bartholdi's statue *Liberty Enlightening the World* <u>was given</u> as a gift
                           A   B

to the United States <u>from France</u> <u>near</u> 150 years ago. <u>No error</u>   Ⓐ Ⓑ Ⓒ Ⓓ Ⓔ
                     C   D   E

17. <u>Sculptors</u> need space <u>in which</u> to work on <u>their</u> craft, and <u>you</u> also
     A   B   C   D

need a variety of materials and tools. <u>No error</u>   Ⓐ Ⓑ Ⓒ Ⓓ Ⓔ
                             E

18. The concerned coach approached the pitcher <u>on the mound</u>
                                              A

<u>with a long face</u> and spoke <u>calmly</u> to him for a few minutes <u>while</u>
       B   C   D

another hurler warmed up in the bullpen. <u>No error</u>   Ⓐ Ⓑ Ⓒ Ⓓ Ⓔ
                                   E

19. The <u>members</u> of the group visited the Corcoran Museum <u>to see</u> the
        A   B

new Australian and American landscapes exhibit, and <u>they</u> loved
                                            C

<u>them</u>. <u>No error</u>   Ⓐ Ⓑ Ⓒ Ⓓ Ⓔ
  D   E

20. In New Guinea, <u>they</u> <u>have discovered</u> an island oasis untouched by
                   A   B

modern times <u>that</u> is home to several species found <u>nowhere else</u> on
               C   D

the planet. <u>No error</u>   Ⓐ Ⓑ Ⓒ Ⓓ Ⓔ
         E

SAT Practice: Improving Sentences

Directions: In each of the following items, all or part of the sentence is underlined. Beneath each sentence are five ways of phrasing the underlined part. Choice (A) is the same as the original; the other four choices are different. Select the answer choice that best expresses the meaning of the original sentence. Your goal is to produce the most effective sentence, one that is clear and not wordy. Choose (A) if the original sentence is better than any of the other answer choices.

Example

I wanted to take my cousins to the Museum of the Moving Image but didn't <u>because they had all ready been there.</u>

(A) because they had all ready been there

(B) since they have all ready been there

(C) because they had already been there

(D) since they, who had already been there

(E) because they will have already been there

The correct choice is **C**. The mistake in the original sentence has to do with two commonly confused words: *already*, an adverb meaning "previously," and *all ready*, an adjective meaning "completely ready." Choice **B** is incorrect because it leaves the incorrect word intact and incorrectly shifts to the present perfect tense. Choice **D** correctly uses *already* but creates a fragment by inserting *who*. Choice **E** incorrectly shifts to the future perfect tense.

1. Many people flock annually to Naples and Turin, but neither city <u>draw as many visitors as Rome does.</u>

   (A) draw as many visitors as Rome does

   (B) are drawing as many visitors as Rome is

   (C) draws as many visitors as Rome does

   (D) draws as many visitors as Rome will

   (E) is drawing the amount of visitors that Rome does

2. Ned Kelly was nothing more than a murderer and a criminal to the police, and to ordinary Australians he was a hero.

   (A) Ned Kelly was nothing more than a murderer and a criminal to the police, and to ordinary Australians he was a hero.

   (B) Ned Kelly was nothing more than a murderer and a criminal to the police and, in addition, to ordinary Australians he was a hero.

   (C) Because Ned Kelly was nothing more than a murderer and a criminal to the police, he was a hero to ordinary Australians.

   (D) To the police, Ned Kelly was nothing more than a murderer and a criminal, but to ordinary Australians, he was a hero.

   (E) Although Ned Kelly was nothing more than a murderer and a criminal to the police; on the contrary, to ordinary Australians he was a hero.

3. Anecdotal evidence show that hitting performance in minor league baseball is not necessarily a reliable indicator of how a player will hit in the major leagues.

   (A) show that hitting performance in minor league baseball

   (B) by showing how hitting performance in minor league baseball

   (C) shows that hitting performance in minor league baseball

   (D) which shows that hitting performance in minor league baseball

   (E) will have shown that hitting performance in minor league baseball

4. The authors *of Freakonomics* stating that conventional wisdom is often wrong, they claim that knowing what to measure and how to measure it is what is critical to understanding modern times.

   (A) stating that conventional wisdom is often wrong,

   (B) by stating that conventional wisdom is often wrong;

   (C) who state that, conventionally, wisdom is often wrong,

   (D) state that conventional wisdom is often wrong,

   (E) state that conventional wisdom is often wrong;

5. Like many crime novelists, Charles Willeford's books all take place in a particular region of the country.

   (A) Like many crime novelists, Charles Willeford's books all take place in a particular region of the country.

   (B) Like many crime novelists, Charles Willeford writes books that all take place in a particular region of the country.

   (C) Like many crime novels, Charles Willeford writes books that all take place in a particular region of the country.

   (D) Like many crime novels, Charles Willeford writes all his books while in a particular region of the country.

   (E) Like many crime novelists, Charles Willeford's books all take place in South Florida.

6. When President Lincoln and Frederick Douglass met, he told him all that was on his mind.

   (A) When President Lincoln and Frederick Douglass met, he told him all that was on his mind.

   (B) When President Lincoln and Frederick Douglass met, they told him all that was on his mind.

   (C) When President Lincoln and Frederick Douglass met, he told him all that was on their mind.

   (D) When President Lincoln and Frederick Douglass met, he told all that was on his mind.

   (E) When President Lincoln and Frederick Douglass met, the president told him all that was on his mind.

7. Wearing colorful shoes which is quite common today was once the exclusive privilege of the wealthy.

   (A) Wearing colorful shoes which is quite common today was

   (B) Wearing colorful shoes, which are quite common today, was

   (C) Wearing colorful shoes, which is quite common today, was

   (D) To wear colorful shoes, which is quite common today, were

   (E) Wearing colorful shoes, which is quite common today, were

8. Since the publication of her highly praised but controversial fourth novel, <u>the amount of requests she has received for speaking engagements has increased dramatically, week by week.</u>

(A) the amount of requests she has received for speaking engage-ments has increased dramatically, week by week

(B) the number of requests she has received for speaking engage-ments has increased dramatically, week by week

(C) the amount of requests she has received for speaking engage-ments will have increased dramatically, week by week

(D) the number of requests she will receive for speaking engage-ments has increased dramatically, week by week

(E) the amount of requests she receives for speaking engagements has increased dramatically, week by week

9. In addition to the many wonderful places I traveled to, <u>I should of visited Riga, Latvia, the "Paris of the Baltic,"</u> on my recent tour of former Soviet republics.

(A) I should of visited Riga, Latvia, the "Paris of the Baltic,"

(B) I should have visited Riga, located in Latvia, which is consid-ered home to the "Paris of the Baltic,"

(C) I should have visited Riga, Latvia, the "Paris of the Baltic,"

(D) I would of visited Riga, Latvia, the "Paris of the Baltic,"

(E) I could have visited Latvia, home of Riga, which is also known by many as the "Paris of the Baltic,"

10. <u>They believe that teachers can be good models for young children</u> if they themselves read something during class quiet-reading time.

(A) They believe that teachers can be good models for young chil-dren

(B) They believe that they can be good models for young children

(C) Many educators believe that a teacher can be a good model for young children

(D) Many educators believe that teachers can be good models for young children

(E) Many educators believe that they can be good models for young children

11. Famous people who lived in Arizona including politicians Barry Goldwater and Stuart Udall, writer Zane Grey, architect Frank Lloyd Wright, and Apache leaders Cochise and Geronimo lived there, too.

(A) Famous people who lived in Arizona including politicians Barry Goldwater and Stuart Udall, writer Zane Grey, architect Frank Lloyd Wright, and Apache leaders Cochise and Geronimo lived there, too.

(B) Famous people who lived in Arizona includes politicians Barry Goldwater and Stuart Udall, writer Zane Grey, architect Frank Lloyd Wright, and Apache leaders Cochise and Geronimo, who lived there, too.

(C) Famous people who lived in Arizona include politicians Barry Goldwater and Stuart Udall, writer Zane Grey, architect Frank Lloyd Wright, and Apache leaders Cochise and Geronimo.

(D) Famous people who lived in Arizona included politicians Barry Goldwater and Stuart Udall, writer Zane Grey, architect Frank Lloyd Wright, and Cochise and Geronimo.

(E) Famous people who lived in Arizona includes politicians Barry Goldwater and Stuart Udall, writer Zane Grey, architect Frank Lloyd Wright, and Apache leaders Cochise and Geronimo.

12. The competitive cyclist plans to train as rigorously if not more rigorously than she did for the last race.

(A) The competitive cyclist plans to train as rigorously if not more rigorously than she did for the last race.

(B) The competitive cyclist plans to train more rigorously than the last race.

(C) The competitive cyclist plans to train as rigorously as if not more rigorously than she did for the last race.

(D) The competitive cyclist plans to train as rigorously, if not more rigorously, than she did for the last race.

(E) The competitive cyclist plans to train as rigorously as, if not more rigorously than, she did for the last race.

13. Laura, who is only seven, likes playing tennis better than her brothers.

(A) Laura, who is only seven, likes playing tennis better than her brothers.

(B) Laura, who is only seven, likes playing tennis better than her brothers do.

(C) Laura, who is seven only, likes playing tennis better than her brothers.

(D) Laura, who is only seven, likes playing tennis better then her brothers.

(E) Laura, who likes playing tennis better than her brothers, is only seven.

14. Valued for their flavor and for their use as preservatives, some people in ancient civilizations prized and sought cloves, nutmeg, and other spices.

(A) Valued for their flavor and for their use as preservatives, some people in ancient civilizations prized and sought cloves, nutmeg, and other spices.

(B) Some people in ancient civilizations, valued for their flavor and for their use as preservatives, prized and sought cloves, nutmeg, and other spices.

(C) Some people in ancient civilizations prized and sought cloves, nutmeg, and other spices, which were valued for their flavor and for their use as preservatives.

(D) Valued for its flavor and for their use as preservatives, some people in ancient civilizations prized and sought cloves, nutmeg, and other spices.

(E) Prized for their flavor and valued for their use as preservatives, some people in ancient civilizations sought cloves, nutmeg, and other spices.

15. Because he is best known for his novels set in the West, Wallace Stegner also wrote several nonfiction books about exploration and settlement of the American West.

(A) Because he is best known for his novels set in the West

(B) Best known for his novels set in the West

(C) Because his best novels are set in the West

(D) Although he is best known for his novels set in the West

(E) Despite being better known for his novels set in the West

Ⓐ Ⓑ Ⓒ Ⓓ Ⓔ

SAT Practice: Improving Paragraphs

Directions: The passage that follows is an early draft of an essay. Some parts need to be rewritten. Read the passage carefully and answer the questions that follow. Choose the answer that most clearly and effectively expresses the writer's intended meaning. In making your decisions, follow the conventions of standard written English. After you have chosen your answer, fill in the corresponding oval.

(1) Does a writer have to experience things firsthand to be able to write about them convincingly? (2) For instance, can one write about outer space without ever having been an astronaut? (3) Anyways, I, who wish to be a writer one day, wonder about this issue.

(4) Consider John Steinbeck's poignant novels, *Of Mice and Men* and *The Grapes of Wrath*, about the migrant worker's experience in the 1930s. (5) Would these be as powerful and as moving as they were had the author not known manual labor and poverty? (6) Also, consider the terrific short story "To Build a Fire" by Jack London. (7) When I picture that scene where the dog warily keeps its distance from the freezing, dying man, one wonders whether it could have been written by someone who had never been in the wild and had never worked closely with sled dogs.

(8) Another writer, George Orwell, experienced the way of life he describes in several of his novels. (9) Although born into wealth, Orwell toiled as a dishwasher and for a time immersed himself in a life of poverty. (10) These experiences gave credibility to his writing about impoverished outcasts and society's attitudes toward them. (11) When you read his *Homage to Catalonia*, you can appreciate how Orwell's experiences as a volunteer fighting in the Spanish Civil War contributed greatly to his descriptions of soldiers' lives in battle.

(12) I'm sure that there are dozens more examples of how writers' personal experiences give verisimilitude to their writing. (13) However, I bet that there are an equal number of examples of how imagination and research have more than compensated for the lack of such firsthand experiences. (14) I mean, hey, let's face it. (15) If becoming a good writer has as prerequisites starving, freezing, or getting shot at, the writing trade will likely have few applicants. (16) As one of those applicants, I am on the fence about it at the moment.

1. In context, which of the following revisions is necessary in sentence 3 (reproduced below)?

   Anyways, I, who wish to be a writer one day, wonder about this issue.

   (A) Change "who" to "whom".

   (B) Change "wish" to "wishes".

   (C) Insert "often" before "wonder".

   (D) Change "Anyways" to "Anyway".

   (E) Delete "Anyways".

   Ⓐ Ⓑ Ⓒ Ⓓ Ⓔ

2. In context, which of the following is the best revision of sentence 5 (reproduced below)?

Would these be as powerful and as moving as they were had the author not known manual labor and poverty?

(A) (As it is now)

(B) Would these be as powerful and as moving as they were, had the author not known manual labor and poverty?

(C) Would these be as powerful and as moving as they had been had Steinbeck not known manual labor and poverty?

(D) Would these be as powerful and as moving as they are had Steinbeck himself not known manual labor and poverty?

(E) Would they be as powerful and as moving as they were had Steinbeck not himself known manual labor and poverty?

ⒶⒷⒸⒹⒺ

3. Which of the following is the best version of the underlined portion of sentence 7 (reproduced below)?

When I picture that scene where the dog warily keeps its distance from the freezing, dying man, one wonders whether it could have been written by someone who had never been in the wild and had never worked closely with sled dogs.

(A) where the dog warily keeps its distance from the freezing, dying man, one wonders that

(B) where the dog warily keeps its distance from the freezing and dying man, I wonder whether

(C) in which the dog warily keeps its distance from the freezing, dying man, one wonders whether

(D) where the dog warily keeps his distance from the freezing, dying man, I wonder if

(E) in which the dog warily keeps its distance from the freezing, dying man, I wonder whether

ⒶⒷⒸⒹⒺ

4. To what does the word "them" refer in sentence 10 (reproduced below)?

These experiences gave credibility to his writing about impoverished out-casts and society's attitudes toward them.

(A) his experiences

(B) the outcasts

(C) society

(D) the books he has written

(E) the experiences of the outcasts

5. In context, which is the best way to revise sentence 11 (reproduced below)?

When you read his Homage to Catalonia, *you can appreciate how Orwell's experiences as a volunteer fighting in the Spanish Civil War contributed greatly to his descriptions of soldiers' lives in battle.*

(A) Change "you can appreciate" to "one can appreciate".

(B) Insert "In contrast," at the beginning of the sentence.

(C) Delete "greatly".

(D) Insert "during his youth" after "War".

(E) Insert "For instance," at the beginning of the sentence.

6. In context, which is the best way to revise and combine sentences 14 and 15 (reproduced below)?

I mean, hey, let's face it. If becoming a good writer has as prerequisites starving, freezing, or getting shot at, the writing trade will likely have few applicants.

(A) I mean, let's face it though, because if becoming a good writer has as prerequisites starving, freezing, or getting shot at, the writing trade will likely have few applicants.

(B) I mean, hey, if to become a good writer has as prerequisites starving, freezing, or getting shot at, the writing trade will likely have few applicants.

(C) And let's face it; if becoming a good writer has as prerequisites starving, freezing, or getting shot at, the writing trade will likely have few applicants.

(D) But let's face it; if becoming a good writer has as prerequisites starving, freezing, or getting shot at, the writing trade will likely have few applicants.

(E) Let's face it: if becoming a good writer has as prerequisites starving, freezing, or getting shot at, the writing trade will likely have few applicants.

ACT Practice

Directions: You will find two reading passages in the left column and questions in the right column. In each of the passages, some words and phrases are underlined with a number underneath. The numbers refer to the questions at the right. Most questions ask you to choose the answer that best expresses the idea in standard written English or in the style of the passage. If you think the original wording is best, choose answer **A**, "NO CHANGE."

Other questions, indicated by a small number in a box, ask about the passage as a whole or about a particular section of the passage.

For each question, choose what you think is the best answer, and fill in the corresponding oval at the bottom of the page. Sometimes you will need to read several sentences beyond the numbered point in the passage to answer the question correctly. Begin by reading the entire passage before you start to answer the questions.

Passage I

The World's Oldest Game

[1]

Mancala a game of transfer may be the
₁
world's oldest board game. It has several
names, dozens of versions, and is popular
to this day throughout Africa, in parts of
Asia, in the Philippines, in the Caribbean,
and you can play it in South America. It
₂
has been played by kings and queens
using carved ivory boards adorned with
gold, it also has been played by elderly
₃
men in mourning and by children.

1. **A.** NO CHANGE
   B. Mancala: a game of transfer, may
   C. Mancala, a game of transfer, may
   D. Mancala, a game of transfer, can

2. **F.** NO CHANGE
   G. it is also played in
   H. in
   J. it is also in

3. **A.** NO CHANGE
   B. gold, but it also
   C. gold. It also
   D. gold and, in addition, it also

---

1. Ⓐ Ⓑ Ⓒ Ⓓ
2. Ⓕ Ⓖ Ⓗ Ⓙ
3. Ⓐ Ⓑ Ⓒ Ⓓ

[2]

There are three basic forms of the game, one that is played with two rows, one that uses three rows, and one that has four rows. One ancient version of the game, *wari*, is often played by children <u>only using</u> pebbles or seeds and holes
₄
they've scooped out of the dirt.

[3]

In Ghana, the Asanti people play *wari* using a board that has two rows of six cups. Two players face one another. Each places four seeds in each of the six cups in the row on <u>their</u> side of the board.
₅
6 Players lift the seeds from one of the cups on their side of the board and "sow" them, one by one, into other cups, moving in a counterclockwise direction. The object of <u>it</u> is to capture the most
₇
seeds; the player who has at least 25 seeds at the end, a majority of the total of 48 seeds on the board, is the winner.

[4]

If a player deposits his or her last seed into an "enemy" cup to make a final total of 2 or 3, <u>those seeds were captured</u> and
₈

4. F. NO CHANGE
   G. having
   H. using only
   J. also using

5. A. NO CHANGE
   B. his or her
   C. its
   D. one

6. Which of the following is the best phrase to insert at the beginning of this sentence?
   F. In addition,
   G. Before that,
   H. As one would expect,
   J. To play,

7. Which word best replaces "it" in this sentence?
   A. withdrawing seeds
   B. the game
   C. the victory
   D. moving seeds

8. F. NO CHANGE
   G. those seeds will be captured
   H. that seed is captured
   J. those seeds are captured

---

4. Ⓕ Ⓖ Ⓗ Ⓙ
5. Ⓐ Ⓑ Ⓒ Ⓓ
6. Ⓕ Ⓖ Ⓗ Ⓙ

7. Ⓐ Ⓑ Ⓒ Ⓓ
8. Ⓕ Ⓖ Ⓗ Ⓙ

the seeds of any unbroken sequence of 2's and 3's on the opponent's side of the board adjacent to and behind the looted cup are also taken. If a player finds the opponent's cups empty, he or she must attempt feeding seeds into enemy territory. <u>Also,</u>
9   10

<u>a player is not allowed to capture all the</u>
10

<u>opponent's seeds. This action would</u>
10

<u>prevent the opponent moving on the next</u>
10

<u>turn.</u> Instead, the player must leave one
10

cup intact.

Passage II

Naming Names

[1]

In our daily lives we see some names more than we see others. People need to go no <u>further</u> than their kitchen, bathroom,
11

pantry, or patio to see a host of products and <u>appliances whose familiar names or</u>
12

<u>brands were</u> the names of the family or
12

person who first patented or distributed

9. **A.** NO CHANGE
   B. to have fed
   C. the feeding of
   D. to feed

10. Which of the following is the best way to combine these two sentences?
   F. Also, a player is not allowed to capture all the opponent's seeds, although this action would prevent the opponent moving on the next turn.
   G. Also, a player is not allowed to capture all the opponent's seeds, being that this action would prevent the opponent moving on the next turn.
   H. Also, a player is not allowed to capture all the opponent's seeds; this action would prevent the opponent moving on the next turn.
   J. Also, a player is not allowed to capture all the opponent's seeds, because this action would prevent the opponent moving on the next turn.

11. **A.** NO CHANGE
   B. deeper
   C. closer to home
   D. farther

12. **F.** NO CHANGE
   G. appliances whose names or brands are
   H. appliances who's names or brands are
   J. appliances who's names or brands were

9. Ⓐ Ⓑ Ⓒ Ⓓ
10. Ⓕ Ⓖ Ⓗ Ⓙ

11. Ⓐ Ⓑ Ⓒ Ⓓ
12. Ⓕ Ⓖ Ⓗ Ⓙ

those items. In trips to the local mall or business district, we are likely to see a host of businesses whose names are the names of <u>their</u> original founders or founding

13

families. <u>Department store chains and car dealerships providing particularly good examples of this naming practice.</u>

14

14

14

[2]

Then there are the many inventions, common terms, and expressions named for their inventors or originators. Take, for instance, the Ferris wheel. George Washington Ferris Jr. was an <u>engineer, whom gave</u> Chicago's World's Columbian

15

15

Exhibition of 1893 an enormous wheel that could carry more than 2,000 screaming people, in 36 cars, more than 260 feet above the Midway and <u>brought</u> them

16

safely back down again. Ferris's wheel, which was as high as the tallest skyscraper in the city, was the sensation of the exposition. 17 Ferris was not alone in

13. To what does "their" refer to in this sentence?

   A. the local mall or business district

   B. the businesses

   C. the families

   D. the trips

14. Which of the following is the best version of this group of words?

   F. NO CHANGE

   G. Department store chains and car dealerships are provide examples of this naming practice, which is particularly good.

   H. Department store chains and car dealerships that are providing particularly good examples of this naming practice.

   J. Department store chains and car dealerships provide particularly good examples of this naming practice.

15. A. NO CHANGE

   B. engineer who gave

   C. engineer, that gave

   D. engineer, who, gave

16. F. NO CHANGE

   G. will bring

   H. bring

   J. had brought

---

13. Ⓐ Ⓑ Ⓒ Ⓓ

14. Ⓕ Ⓖ Ⓗ Ⓙ

15. Ⓐ Ⓑ Ⓒ Ⓓ

16. Ⓕ Ⓖ Ⓗ Ⓙ

contributing his name to the common lex-icon. With Henry Shrapnel, Charles Cunningham Boycott, Enoch Bartlett, R. J. L. Guppy, Joseph Guillotin, Jules Leotard, Thomas Bowdler, and John Duns Scotus (whose followers were known as dunces), he was in good company.
18

[3]

Thanks to the efforts of curious writers who have done the detective work, we know that many common words owe their origins to personalities of the past. The words *cardigan, hooligan,* and *lynch,* for instance, come from the real names of real people. Did you know that Clarence Bullwinkle was a used-car dealer in Berkeley, California, or that Charles Brown was a classmate of Charles Schultz when he was a student in Minneapolis? Did you
19
know that, when political operatives attempt to redistrict parts of a state for the purpose of creating favorable voting con-centrations, it is called *gerrymandering,*
20
which is precisely what Governor Elbridge
20
Gerry did in Massachusetts over 200 years ago? Over time, many people, accidentally

17. Which word or phrase can logically be inserted at the beginning of this sentence?
  A. However
  B. Nevertheless,
  C. But
  D. In addition,

18. Who or what is the antecedent of "he"?
  F. a person whose name is now the name of a common term
  G. the inventor of the exploding canister
  H. the inventor of the marvel of the Midway
  J. John Duns Scotus

19. A. NO CHANGE
  B. they were students
  C. Brown was a student
  D. Schultz was a student

20. F. NO CHANGE
  G. the practice is called *gerrymander-ing;* which is precisely
  H. it is called *gerrymandering.* Which is precisely
  J. they call it *gerrymandering,* which is precisely

17. (A) (B) (C) (D)
18. (F) (G) (H) (J)

19. (A) (B) (C) (D)
20. (F) (G) (H) (J)

or not, have contributed their names to political science, literature, and other disciplines. Just about every field has been effected.
21

[4]

22 It is in the sciences where one finds the greatest connection between peoples' names and key terms associated with biology, chemistry, physics, and astronomy. Anders Celsius was an astronomer; Gabriel Daniel Fahrenheit, a physicist; and Louis Pasteur, a chemist. Georg Simon Ohm was a physicist and mathematician, and Allesandro Volta was a physics professor. Andre Marie Ampere studied magnetism. Most likely, that was not why he was guillotined during the French Revolution.

21. A. NO CHANGE
    B. altered
    C. affected
    D. afflicted

22. Which word or phrase can logically be inserted at the beginning of this sentence to link ideas in paragraphs 3 and 4?
    F. Nonetheless,
    G. In contrast,
    H. However,
    J. Because

21. Ⓐ Ⓑ Ⓒ Ⓓ

22. Ⓕ Ⓖ Ⓗ Ⓙ

Practice Test

PART A

Time—25 Minutes (1 question)

You have 25 minutes to write an essay on the topic below.

DO NOT WRITE AN ESSAY THAT ADDRESSES ANY OTHER TOPIC. AN ESSAY ON A DIFFERENT TOPIC WILL NOT BE ACCEPTED.

Plan and write an essay on the assigned topic. Present your thoughts clearly and effectively. Include specific examples to support your views. The quality of your essay is more important than its length, but to express your ideas on the topic adequately, you will probably want to write more than one paragraph. Be sure to make your handwriting legible.

Consider the following statement. Then write an essay as directed.

"In a real sense, people who have read good literature have lived more than people who cannot or will not read."

—from S. I. Hayakawa, *Language in Thought and Action*

Assignment: Write an essay in which you agree or disagree with the statement above, using examples from history, current events, science, art, music, or your own experience to support your position.

WRITE YOUR ESSAY ON A SEPARATE SHEET OF PAPER.

Time—35 Minutes (46 questions)

Directions: In each item, one of the underlined words or phrases may contain an error in grammar, usage, word choice, or idiom. If there is an error, choose the underlined part that must be changed to make the sentence correct, and fill in the corresponding oval. If the sentence has no error, fill in oval E. In selecting answers, follow the requirements of standard written English.

Example

As his father did before <u>him</u>, the talented young filmmaker
A   B

<u>will have made</u> one acclaimed film after <u>another</u>. <u>No error</u>   Ⓐ Ⓑ Ⓒ Ⓓ Ⓔ
C   D   E

1. <u>Every</u> astronaut on the team described <u>their</u> dream mission to the
     A   B

paper's science reporter <u>who had accompanied</u> <u>them</u> on a training
                             C   D

exercise. <u>No error</u>   Ⓐ Ⓑ Ⓒ Ⓓ Ⓔ
         E

2. <u>Either</u> a musical <u>or</u> a drama will be among the entertainments
     A   B

<u>planned</u> for this <u>year's</u> summer arts festival. <u>No error</u>   Ⓐ Ⓑ Ⓒ Ⓓ Ⓔ
    C   D   E

3. <u>Whomever</u> is picked to be the next Secretary of State will face a
       A

variety of sensitive issues, <u>many</u> of <u>which</u> <u>promise</u> to be quite
                         B   C   D

challenging. <u>No error</u>   Ⓐ Ⓑ Ⓒ Ⓓ Ⓔ
           E

STANDARDIZED TEST PRACTICE

4. Although she had <u>neither</u> fine <u>stationery</u> nor quality writing
                  A   B

instruments, the <u>girl's first efforts</u> at letter writing <u>is</u> admirable by
                    C   D

any standards. <u>No error</u>   Ⓐ Ⓑ Ⓒ Ⓓ Ⓔ
               E

5. <u>Regarded</u> as the foremost <u>exponent</u> of French realist literature,
      A   B

Gustave Flaubert wrote *Madame Bovary*, his masterpiece; *Trois*

contes; and <u>he also wrote</u> a few plays <u>and short stories</u>. <u>No error</u> Ⓐ Ⓑ Ⓒ Ⓓ Ⓔ
             C   D   E

6. A <u>new and poignant</u> memorial on the West Side of <u>lower</u> Manhattan
          A   B

<u>honors</u> the many Irish who <u>immigrated</u> from Ireland in the
 C   D

nineteenth century. <u>No error</u>   Ⓐ Ⓑ Ⓒ Ⓓ Ⓔ
                 E

7. Singapore, <u>which</u> is a city-state, a republic, and an island off the
              A

<u>southern</u> tip of the Malay Peninsula, is smaller <u>than</u> <u>any</u> Pacific Rim
  B   C   D

<u>state</u>. <u>No error</u>   Ⓐ Ⓑ Ⓒ Ⓓ Ⓔ
 D   E

8. On <u>their</u> last excursion to the Galapagos, the Explorers Club
       A

<u>members</u> photographed marine iguanas, giant tortoises, fur seals,
  B

and <u>they took pictures of</u> <u>hawks</u>. <u>No error</u>   Ⓐ Ⓑ Ⓒ Ⓓ Ⓔ
          C   D   E

9. During the McCarthy "witch hunts" of the 1950s, the junior senator

from Wisconsin accused <u>several</u> members of the Hollywood
                      A

community <u>of being</u> Communists, without <u>having</u> <u>scarcely</u> any hard
         B   C   D

evidence. <u>No error</u>   Ⓐ Ⓑ Ⓒ Ⓓ Ⓔ
        E

10. The explorers during Europe's Age of Discovery <u>had to thank</u>
                                    A

<u>who</u> invented the compass for <u>providing</u> that invaluable
 B   C

navigational <u>aid</u>. <u>No error</u>   Ⓐ Ⓑ Ⓒ Ⓓ Ⓔ
          D   E

11. I <u>have read</u> that Athens is a classic example of what geographers
     A

<u>will call</u> a *primate city* <u>because</u> of <u>its</u> cultural and historical
   B   C   D

significance. <u>No error</u>   Ⓐ Ⓑ Ⓒ Ⓓ Ⓔ
          E

12. <u>Selecting</u> the movies that <u>would be screened</u> in the festival was
    A   B

challenging for the committee members who <u>had to choose</u> from
                                  C

<u>between</u> many fine films. <u>No error</u>   Ⓐ Ⓑ Ⓒ Ⓓ Ⓔ
  D   E

13. Desdemona, a character in Shakespeare's tragedy *Othello*, <u>was</u> the
                                    A

Moorish general's <u>beloved</u> wife and the <u>object</u> of <u>his</u> unwarranted
            B   C   D

jealousy. <u>No error</u>   Ⓐ Ⓑ Ⓒ Ⓓ Ⓔ
    E

14. Interior <u>monologues, which</u> may be direct <u>first-person</u> expressions or
                  A   B

third-person <u>treatments, encompasses</u> several forms, including
                C   D

dramatized inner conflicts, self-analysis, imagined dialogue, and

rationalization. <u>No error</u>   Ⓐ Ⓑ Ⓒ Ⓓ Ⓔ
                E

15. I <u>first</u> read Jack London's short story "To Build a Fire" <u>near</u> twenty
      A   B

years ago and have reread <u>it</u> several times since, always <u>immensely</u>
                          C   D

enjoying the experience. <u>No error</u>   Ⓐ Ⓑ Ⓒ Ⓓ Ⓔ
                        E

16. The house was <u>only</u> half full for opening night, <u>which</u> was
                        A   B

disappointing <u>not only</u> for the producers <u>but also</u> for the director
                   C   D

and actors. <u>No error</u>   Ⓐ Ⓑ Ⓒ Ⓓ Ⓔ
             E

17. <u>Although</u> it was <u>initially</u> treasured as a precious metal, aluminum
      A   B

soon lost its <u>luster; vigorous</u> mining, coupled with new extraction
                  C

techniques, <u>caused</u> its price per pound to plummet. <u>No error</u>   Ⓐ Ⓑ Ⓒ Ⓓ Ⓔ
              D   E

18. Originally intended as a cheap replacement for rubber, Silly Putty,

<u>formerly</u> <u>known</u> as "nutty putty," racked up huge sales when <u>it</u> was
  A   B   C

packaged in small plastic eggs and <u>is sold</u> to toy stores in the '50s
                                   D

and '60s. <u>No error</u>   Ⓐ Ⓑ Ⓒ Ⓓ Ⓔ
       E

Directions: In each of the following items, all or part of the sentence is underlined. Beneath each sentence are five ways of phrasing the underlined part. Choice (A) is the same as the original; the other four choices are different. Select the answer choice that best expresses the meaning of the original sentence. Your goal is to produce the most effective sentence, one that is clear and not wordy. Choose (A) if the original sentence is better than any of the other answer choices.

Example

My friends and I often go to the movies in the <u>afternoon, the tickets cost less than,</u> and the theaters are not as crowded as they are at night.

(A) afternoon, the tickets cost less than,

(B) afternoon the tickets cost less than

(C) afternoon; the tickets cost less then,

(D) afternoon; because the tickets cost less than,

(E) afternoon, so the tickets cost less then

19. *Smiley's People* and *The Perfect Spy* are two fine, taut espionage novels; but neither, many believe, <u>are as good as</u> Le Carre's best work, *Tinker, Tailor, Soldier, Spy.*

(A) are as good as

(B) of the two are as good as

(C) is as good as

(D) of them are as good as

(E) is

20. <u>Australia is the world's sixth-largest country; it is the world's smallest continent.</u>

(A) Australia is the world's sixth-largest country; it is the world's smallest continent.

(B) Because Australia is the world's sixth-largest country, it is the world's smallest continent.

(C) Australia is the world's sixth-largest country; this is due to the fact that it is the world's smallest continent.

(D) Although Australia is the world's sixth-largest country, it is the world's smallest continent.

(E) Australia is the world's sixth-largest country and is the world's smallest continent.   Ⓐ Ⓑ Ⓒ Ⓓ Ⓔ

21. As Huckleberry Finn and a runaway slave, Jim, journey down the Mississippi, Huck, who is good-natured, <u>overcame conventional racial prejudices</u>.

(A) overcame conventional racial prejudices

(B) will overcome conventional racial prejudices

(C) overcomes conventional racial prejudices

(D) overcomes, conventionally, racial prejudices

(E) has overcome conventional racial prejudices   Ⓐ Ⓑ Ⓒ Ⓓ Ⓔ

22. For some park rangers, answering questions about the future of federal funding for our national parks may be <u>as common as to give information</u> about park features, trails, and trail safety.

(A) as common as to give information

(B) as common as to answer questions

(C) as common as to give answers

(D) as common as giving information

(E) as common as information   Ⓐ Ⓑ Ⓒ Ⓓ Ⓔ

23. <u>Found guilty of extortion, the judge sent the mobster to prison.</u>

(A) Found guilty of extortion, the judge sent the mobster to prison.

(B) The judge sent the mobster, who was found guilty of extortion, to prison.

(C) The mobster was sent to prison by the judge whom he found guilty of extortion.

(D) The judge, found guilty of extortion, sent the mobster to prison.

(E) The mobster, found guilty of extortion by the judge, sent him to prison.   Ⓐ Ⓑ Ⓒ Ⓓ Ⓔ

24. <u>Unlike many athletes at the trials, Kuo's running times caught</u>
<u>the attention of several scouts, including two he wished greatly to</u>
<u>impress.</u>

(A) Unlike many athletes at the trials, Kuo's running times caught
the attention of several scouts, including two he wished
greatly to impress.

(B) Unlike those of many athletes at the trials, Kuo's running
times caught the attention of several scouts, including two he
wished greatly to impress.

(C) Unlike many athletes at the trials, Kuo caught the attention of
several scouts with his running times, including two he
wished greatly to impress.

(D) Kuo's running times, unlike many athletes at the trials,
caught the attention of several scouts, including two he
wished greatly to impress.

(E) Kuo's running times, unlike many other athletes at the trials,
caught the attention of several scouts, including two he
wished greatly to impress.   Ⓐ Ⓑ Ⓒ Ⓓ Ⓔ

25. <u>Not many students were among the people who volunteered to help</u>
<u>clean up the park after the free concert, which was unfortunate.</u>

(A) Not many students were among the people who volunteered
to help clean up the park after the free concert, which was
unfortunate.

(B) Not many students were among the people who volunteered
in cleaning up the park after the free concert, which was
unfortunate.

(C) After the free concert, which was unfortunate, not many students were among the people who volunteered to help clean
up the park.

(D) Among the many people who volunteered to help clean up
the park after the free concert, there were few students, which
was unfortunate.

(E) It was unfortunate that not many students were among the
people who volunteered to help clean up the park after the
free concert.

26. In Barbara Tuchman's *The Guns of August*, she illuminates, step by step, the way in which the fateful decision to go to war was reached.

(A) In Barbara Tuchman's *The Guns of August*, she illuminates, step by step, the way in which the fateful decision to go to war was reached.

(B) In Barbara Tuchman's *The Guns of August*, she illuminates the way in which the fateful decision to go to war was reached, step by step.

(C) In her book, *The Guns of August*, Barbara Tuchman illuminates, step by step, the way in which the fateful decision to go to war was reached.

(D) The way in which the fateful decision to go to war was reached in Barbara Tuchman's *The Guns of August* was illuminated by her, step by step.

(E) In *The Guns of August*, she illuminates, step by step, the way in which the fateful decision to go to war was reached.

Ⓐ Ⓑ Ⓒ Ⓓ Ⓔ

27. I moved slow and steadily when I first spotted the bear; then I turned and ran away as fast as my feet would carry me.

(A) I moved slow and steadily when I first spotted the bear

(B) I moved slow and steady when I first spotted the bear

(C) Moving slowly and steadily when I first spotted the bear

(D) I moved slowly and steadily when I first spotted the bear

(E) I moved, slow and steadily, when I first spotted the bear

Ⓐ Ⓑ Ⓒ Ⓓ Ⓔ

28. Physiatrists have backgrounds in physical therapy, and you also need a medical degree, too.

(A) , and you also need a medical degree

(B) , and they also have medical degrees

(C) , and you also have medical degrees

(D) and physiatrists also need a medical degree

(E) , and they also need a medical degree

Ⓐ Ⓑ Ⓒ Ⓓ Ⓔ

29. Had I known how long the first movie was going to be, I would not of planned to see two that day.

(A) I would not of planned to see two that day

(B) I wouldn't of planned to see two that day

(C) I would not have planned to see two that day

(D) I would not plan to see two that day

(E) I could not of planned to see two that day

30. At the Wigwam in Chicago, not everyone in Lincoln's future cabinet <u>had their hopes of winning the presidency dashed</u>, but Chase, Seward, Blair, and Bates certainly did.

(A) had their hopes of winning the presidency dashed

(B) had their own hopes of winning the presidency dashed

(C) had hopes themselves of winning the presidency dashed

(D) had his hopes of winning the presidency dashed

(E) had their hope of winning the presidency dashed

31. <u>The Scandinavian countries—Norway, Sweden, Denmark, and Finland—share a similar heritage and culture, a harsh climate, and a long and close relationship with one another.</u>

(A) The Scandinavian countries—Norway, Sweden, Denmark, and Finland—share a similar heritage and culture, a harsh climate, and a long and close relationship with one another.

(B) The Scandinavian countries—Norway, Sweden, Denmark, and Finland—share a similar heritage and culture, a harsh climate, and they share a long and close relationship with one another.

(C) The Scandinavian countries: Norway, Sweden, Denmark, and Finland, share a similar heritage and culture, a harsh climate, and a long and close relationship with one another.

(D) Because they share a harsh climate, the Scandinavian countries—Norway, Sweden, Denmark, and Finland—share a similar heritage and culture, and have had a long and close relationship with one another.

(E) The Scandinavian countries—Norway, Sweden, Denmark, and Finland—share a similar heritage and culture because they have a harsh climate and have had a long and close relationship with one another.

32. <u>Upon entering the stage of the packed theater, the audience gave the respected conductor a standing ovation.</u>

(A) Upon entering the stage of the packed theater, the audience gave the respected conductor a standing ovation.

(B) Upon entrance to the stage of the packed theater, the audience gave the respected conductor a standing ovation.

(C) The audience, upon entering the stage of the packed theater, gave the respected conductor a standing ovation.

(D) The audience in the packed theater, upon his entrance to the stage, gave the respected conductor a standing ovation.

(E) The audience gave the respected conductor a standing ovation when he entered the stage of the packed theater.

33. NATO was established in 1949, with a principal tenet: <u>an attack upon any one member had been regarded as an attack on all.</u>

(A) an attack upon any one member had been regarded as an attack on all

(B) attacks upon any one member were regarded as an attack on all

(C) an attack upon any one member would be regarded as an attack on all

(D) an attack upon any one member had been regarded as an attack on all members

(E) an attack upon any one member was an attack on all members

34. <u>I couldn't hardly believe it when I learned</u> that the first person to propose the idea of contact lenses was none other than Leonardo da Vinci.

(A) I couldn't hardly believe it when I learned

(B) I couldn't scarcely believe it when I learned

(C) I couldn't believe learning

(D) I couldn't believe it when I learned

(E) I couldn't scarcely believe learning

35. In the first Olympic Games of modern times, held in Athens in 1896, Thomas Burke of the United States <u>had a faster time in the 100-meter dash than anyone.</u>

(A) had a faster time in the 100-meter dash than anyone

(B) had a faster time in the 100-meter dash than anyone else

(C) had a faster time in the 100-meter dash than everyone

(D) had a time that was faster than anyone's

(E) had a faster time in the 100-meter dash then anyone else there

36. Michigan's Marvin's Marvelous Mechanical Museum has the world's largest slot machine, an original spotlight from Alcatraz, several nickelodeons, <u>and it also boasts a conveyer chain from which forty remote-controlled airplanes hang</u>.

(A) and it also boasts a conveyer chain from which forty remote-controlled airplanes hang

(B) but it also boasts a conveyer chain from which forty remote-controlled airplanes hang

(C) and a conveyer chain from which forty remote-controlled airplanes hang

(D) and, in addition, it also boasts a conveyer chain from which forty remote-controlled airplanes hang

(E) and forty remote-controlled hanging airplanes from a conveyor chain

37. <u>Because I have taken an interest in the construction of Hoover Dam, an amazing achievement by any standard, I am fascinated by large-scale engineering projects.</u>

(A) Because I have taken an interest in the construction of Hoover Dam, an amazing achievement by any standard, I am fascinated by large-scale engineering projects.

(B) After I took an interest in the construction of Hoover Dam, an amazing achievement by any standard, I am fascinated by large-scale engineering projects.

(C) When I took an interest in the construction of Hoover Dam, an amazing achievement by any standard, I was fascinated by large-scale engineering projects.

(D) Although I was fascinated by large-scale engineering projects, I took an interest in the construction of Hoover Dam, an amazing achievement by any standard.

(E) Because I am fascinated by large-scale engineering projects, I have taken an interest in the construction of Hoover Dam, an amazing achievement by any standard.

38. John Wesley Powell knew that, by exploring the Colorado River and the Grand Canyon, <u>he was making history; therefore, he kept a daily journal</u> of the expedition's progress and discoveries.

(A) he was making history; therefore, he kept a daily journal

(B) he was making history; therefore, he keeps a daily journal

(C) he was making history, therefore, he kept a daily journal

(D) he was making history and kept a daily journal

(E) he was making history by keeping a daily journal

39. Although we knew that the Cahokia Mounds, the remains of what was once a large city, were located just east of St. Louis, <u>we had never drove by them on our visits to the area.</u>

(A) we had never drove by them on our visits to the area

(B) but we had never driven by them on our visits to the area

(C) we had never driven by them on our visits to the area

(D) we had never driven by it on our visits to the area

(E) we never had been driving by them on our visits to the area

ⒶⒷⒸⒹⒺ

Directions: The passage that follows is an early draft of an essay. Some parts need to be rewritten. Read the passage carefully and answer the questions that follow. Choose the answer that most clearly and effectively expresses the writer's intended meaning. In making your decisions, follow the conventions of standard written English. After you have chosen your answer, fill in the corresponding oval.

(1) It's easy to name places that have had meaning for me in my life. **(2)** But to name the single most significant place—now that is more challenging. **(3)** My home and my bedroom there are both very special places for me, as they would be for anybody. **(4)** My school, where I spend so much time and where my friends and teachers are, is also a reasonable choice. **(5)** And I'd have to consider, too, the quarter-mile track at the school, where I've spent countless hours training, running, and competing in meets.

(6) But when I dig deeper, the answer comes to me: a small porch of a small mountain cottage. **(7)** Several years ago, I spent a few summers at that cottage with my sister and my grandmother. **(8)** On most days, we would all sit on that porch for hours. **(9)** She told us all about her parents, who immigrated from South America. **(10)** And while we listened intently, she'd rattle off the names of all eight of her brothers and sisters and their spouses, too, and would tell us something about each of them, such as where they lived and what kind of work they did. **(11)** We loved every minute of it. **(12)** When Grandma finished, she tested us. **(13)** My sister and I recited the names (as many as we could, anyway) as Grandma smiled at us and nodded approvingly.

(14) Sadly, Grandma has been gone for some years now. **(15)** But I often think back fondly to those summers and to those memorable conversations on that porch. **(16)** I can recall them vividly, as if they had taken place only yesterday. **(17)** For it was on that porch I learned for the first time that I was part of something, I learned where I came from and with who I came. **(18)** I don't recall growing any taller during those summers; but on that lopsided, peeling old porch of that old, weather-beaten bungalow, I began to feel a little bigger.

40. In context, which of the following is the best word or phrase to insert at the beginning of sentence 3?

(A) Certainly,

(B) Nonetheless,

(C) On the one hand,

(D) Therefore,

(E) Surprisingly,

41. Sentence 5 in the passage is best described as

    (A) presenting the author's viewpoint

    (B) providing an additional example

    (C) emphasizing a key point

    (D) summarizing the main points in the paragraph

    (E) introducing a new topic   Ⓐ Ⓑ Ⓒ Ⓓ Ⓔ

42. In context, which of the following revisions is necessary in sentence 9 (reproduced below)?

She told us all about her parents, who immigrated from South America.

    (A) Change "who" to "whom".

    (B) Delete "South America".

    (C) Insert "in the late 1800s" after "South America".

    (D) Change "immigrated" to "emigrated".

    (E) Delete "all" and insert "whom we'd never met" after "parents".   Ⓐ Ⓑ Ⓒ Ⓓ Ⓔ

43. In context, which of the following is the best revision of sentence 10 (reproduced below)?

And while we listened intently, she'd rattle off the names of all eight of her brothers and sisters and their spouses, too, and would tell us something about each of them, such as where they lived and what kind of work they did.

    (A) (As it is now)

    (B) And while we listened intently, she'd rattle off the names of all eight of her brothers and sisters and their spouses, too; and would tell us something about each of them, such as where he or she lived and what kind of work he or she did.

    (C) And while we listened intently, she'd rattle off the names of all eight of her brothers and sisters and their spouses, too; she would tell us something about all of them, such as where they lived or what kind of work they did.

    (D) And while we listened intently, she'd rattle off the names of all eight of her brothers and sisters and their spouses, too, and would tell us something about each of them: where they lived or what kind of work they did.

    (E) And while we listened intently, she'd rattle off the names of all eight of her brothers and sisters and their spouses, too; by telling us something about all of them, such as where they lived or what kind of work they did.   Ⓐ Ⓑ Ⓒ Ⓓ Ⓔ

44. In context, which of the following most logically replaces "it" in sentence 11 (reproduced below)?

We loved every minute of it.

(A) them

(B) those summers

(C) Grandma's tales

(D) our relatives' lives

(E) talking

45. In context, which of the following is the best revision of the underlined portion of sentence 17?

For it was on that porch that I learned for the first time that I was part of something, I learned where I came from and with who I came.

(A) (As it is now)

(B) that because I was part of something, I learned where I came from and with whom I came

(C) that I was part of something, I learned where I came from and with whom I came

(D) that I was part of something; I learned where I came from and with whom I came

(E) that I was part of something—I learned where and with who I came from

46. Which of the following would make the most logical final sentence for the essay?

(A) I owe so much to my grandmother.

(B) I imagine that my sister feels the same way I do.

(C) That porch was truly a very special place for me.

(D) Then I truly began a growth spurt.

(E) I'll never find another porch like it.

Commonly Confused Words

➠ **accept, except** *Accept* is a verb that means "to receive willingly" or "to agree to." *Except* is a preposition that means "but."

> The school agreed to **accept** the company's offer of used computers.
> All students **except** ninth graders will have access to them.

➠ **advice, advise** *Advice*, a noun, means "a recommendation" or "an opinion." *Advise*, a verb, means "to offer advice."

> My **advice** is to speak up for yourself.
> I **advise** you to speak to the boss about the promotion.

➠ **affect, effect** *Affect* is a verb that means "to influence." The noun *effect* means "the result of an action"; the verb *effect* means "to cause" or "to bring about."

> Lack of sleep may **affect** your grades.
> What are the **effects** of the cutbacks in service?
> Time-outs are meant to **effect** a change in the way a team performs.

➠ **all ready, already** *All ready*, an adjective, means "completely ready." *Already*, an adverb, means "previously."

> I have **already** packed my suitcase and am **all ready** to leave.

➠ **all right** *All right* is always two words. The word *alright* is not acceptable in formal written English.

> Is it **all right** to invite her?

➠ **all together, altogether** *All together* means "in a group." *Altogether* is an adverb that means "completely" or "in all."

> I worked on the school newspaper for four years **altogether**.
> I kept the papers **all together** in my drawer.

➠ **amount, number** Both words refer to a quantity. Use *amount* with nouns that cannot be counted (for example, *water* or *sand*). Use *number* with nouns that can be counted (for example, *books* or *calories*).

> The **amount** of junk mail that we receive is staggering.
> The **number** of people at the party kept increasing.

➠ **anyway, anyways** The word *anyway* does not end with an -s.

> I didn't make the team, but I went to the games **anyway**.

▐▌▶ **anywheres, everywheres, nowwheres, somewheres** These words are spelled incorrectly. *Anywhere, everywhere, nowhere,* and *somewhere* have no *-s* at the end

> We saw palm trees **everywhere**. I couldn't see snow **anywhere**.

▐▌▶ **bad, badly** Use *bad,* which is always an adjective, after a linking verb. Use *badly,* an adverb, to modify an action verb.

> He plays **badly**. I feel **bad** about his poor playing.

▐▌▶ **beside, besides** *Beside* means "by the side of." *Besides* as a preposition means "in addition to." *Besides* as an adverb means "moreover."

> We rested **beside** the falls. **Besides** me, John and Dolores were there.
> We were hungry; **besides**, we were tired of lugging our packs.

▐▌▶ **between, among** Use *between* to refer to two people or things. You can also use *between* when discussing three or more items if you think that only two will be compared at a time. Use *among* to refer either to a group of people or things or to three or more people or things.

> **Between** you and me, we'll get the job done in an hour.
> Can you tell the difference **between** a saguaro, a cholla, and a prickly pear?
> We chose from **among** several routes.

▐▌▶ **bring, take** *Bring* refers to a movement toward or with the speaker. *Take* refers to a movement away from the speaker.

> Karl **brought** me a souvenir. Please **take** this package to him.

▐▌▶ **complement, compliment** *Complement* means "something that completes or makes perfect." *Compliment* means "to praise."

> She **complimented** me by saying that my tie **complemented** my jacket.

▐▌▶ **different from** When comparing two nouns, use *from,* not *than,* after *different.*

> Mars is **different from** Earth.

▐▌▶ **emigrate, immigrate** To *emigrate* means "to move away" from one country to settle in another. To *immigrate* means "to come into a country to settle there."

> When the famine hit Ireland, many people **emigrated** from that country.
> Many Irish **immigrated** to the United States after the famine began.

farther, further *Farther* refers to physical distance. *Further* refers to additional degree or time.

> Which is **farther** from Boston—Springfield or Providence?
> They said that nothing could be **further** from the truth.

fewer, less *Fewer* refers to nouns that can be counted. *Less* refers to nouns that can't be counted.

> I eat **fewer** donuts than I used to but not **less** meat.

good, well *Good* is always an adjective, never an adverb; *good* after *feel* often means "happy" or "content." *Well*, however, can be both an adjective and an adverb. The adverb *well* means "done in a satisfactory way." The adjective *well* means "in good health."

> It felt **good** to feel **well** after two weeks with a fever.
> Now he will work to play **well** again.

had ought, hadn't ought Drop the *had*. Use just plain *ought* and *ought not*.

> They ~~**had**~~ **ought** to start early to miss the rush hour traffic

irregardless, regardless Always use *regardless*; *irregardless* isn't a word.

> Will the manager be fired, **regardless** of his track record?

learn, teach Don't use *learn* when you mean *teach* or *instruct*. *Learn* is what a student does; *teach* is what a teacher does.

> I **learned** how to embroider from a Hmong woman who **taught** our class.

lay, lie *Lay*, which means "to set something down," always takes a direct object. *Lie*, which means "to place oneself down" or "to stay at rest in a horizontal position," does not take a direct object.

> **Lie** on the blanket, and I will **lay** the sunblock, books, and drinks beside you.

loose, lose *Loose* means "not tight." *Lose* means "to misplace."

> You may **lose** your earring because it is too **loose**.

off, off of Don't use *of* after the prepositions *inside, outside,* and *off*. Also, use *from*, not *off* or *off of*, when you're referring to the source of something.

> I took the apples **off** ~~**of**~~ the table and put them **inside** ~~**of**~~ the cabinet. I got the car keys **from** my father.

▐▌▶ **passed, past** *Passed* is the past tense of *pass* and means "went or gone by." *Past*, as a noun, means "a former time." As a preposition, it means "beyond."

Driving **past** the mall, we **passed** our friends in their car.

▐▌▶ **raise, rise** *Raise*, which means "to lift up," always takes a direct object. *Rise*, which means "to go up" or "to get up," does not take a direct object.

At camp, we **raise** the flag right after we **rise** each morning.

▐▌▶ **real, really** *Real* is an adjective that means "actual." *Really* is an adverb that means "actually" or "genuinely."

The election results were a **real** surprise. We were **really** excited.

▐▌▶ **set, sit** *Set* means "to place" or "to put." *Set* takes a direct object except when it refers to the sun. *Sit*, which means "to occupy a seat," does not take a direct object.

Let's **set** the beach chairs down and **sit** for a while as the sun **sets**.

▐▌▶ **some, somewhat** *Some* is an adjective. *Somewhat* is an adverb meaning "slightly." Don't use *some* as an adverb.

Let's think about cooking **some** food.

The rain has let up **somewhat**.

▐▌▶ **stationary, stationery** *Stationary* is an adjective meaning "fixed," "still," or "in one place." *Stationery* is a noun that means "letter paper."

The word processor was **stationary** on the desk. The **stationery** was in the printer.

▐▌▶ **than, then** *Than* is a conjunction that introduces a subordinate clause, the second part of a comparison. *Then* is an adverb meaning "therefore" or "next in order or time."

I study harder **than** she does. **Then** why don't I get higher test scores? I'll watch how she takes notes in class; **then** I'll adopt her system.

▐▌▶ **this here, that there** In standard written English, *this* and *that* are used alone. Drop the word *here* or *there*.

I'm trying to fix **this ~~here~~** chair. Please hand me **that ~~there~~** screwdriver.

Index

bibliographies
    colon between city and
      publisher in, 285
    punctuation in, 267
bibliography source card, 102–3
block method in organizing
  compare and contrast essay, 72
block quotations, 90
    colon to introduce, 285
    indenting, 285
bodies of water. *See* geographical
  terms
body, in essay, 34–35
books
    capitalizing titles of, 307
    colon between title and subtitle
      of, 285
    italics for titles of, 289
    quotation marks for parts of,
      291
    and subject-verb agreement, 223
brackets, 297
brainstorming in prewriting, 9–10,
  60, 84
brand names, capitalization of, 311
bring, take, 370
buildings, capitalization of names
  of, 305
businesses
    capitalization of names of, 309
    capitalization of officers' titles,
      307
business letters. *See also* letters
    capitalization of salutation and
      closing of, 307
    colon after greeting of, 285
    commas following closing of,
      275
    cover letters as, 112–13
    editing, 199
    full-block style, 109, 112
    modified-block style, 109

C

calendar items, capitalization of,
  311
call to action in persuasive writing,
  32, 66
capitalization
    of abbreviations, 307
    of artworks, 307
    of *be* in titles, 307
    of brand names, 311
    in business letters, 307
    of calendar items, 311
    of centuries, 311
    after colon, 309

    of compass direction words, 305
    and dictionary rules, 305
    of first words of quotations,
      293, 309
    of first words of sentences, 141
    of geographic names, 305
    of interjection *O*, 311
    of names of awards and prizes,
      311
    of names of family members,
      307
    of names of groups, teams,
      businesses, institutions,
      government agencies, and
      organizations, 309
    of names of historical and
      special events, documents, and
      periods, 311
    of names of languages,
      nationalities, peoples, races,
      and religions, 309
    of names of people, 305
    of names of planes, ships,
      spacecraft, and trains, 307
    of names of school subjects, 309
    in outlines, 34
    of parenthetical sentence, 309
    of prepositions and articles that
      are part of names or titles, 305
    of pronoun *I*, 311
    proofreading for, 19
    of proper adjectives, 127, 311
    of proper nouns, 121, 311
    of short words in titles, 307
    of titles, 307
    of titles of school courses, 309
    unconventional use of, 309
    and use with quotation marks,
      293
    of words derived from proper
      nouns, 305
cause, 76
cause and effect, transitional words
  and expressions showing, 28, 39,
  78, 79
cause-effect chain, 78, 79
cause-effect essay in expository
  writing, 76–81
-cede, spelling rules for, 321
-ceed, spelling rules for, 321
centuries, capitalization of, 311
characters
    in literary analysis, 90
    in narrative writing, 55, 56
charts in prewriting, 71–72
chronological order, 27
    in narrative writing, 30, 56

chronological relationship,
  transitional words showing, 39
cities, capitalizing names of, 305
claim, 33
    as part of argument, 63
    as part of informative/
      explanatory writing, 74, 80
    as part of literary analysis, 89
    as part of research papers, 104
    as part of timed essay, 117
    See also thesis statement
clarity, 68
clauses
    adjective, 39, 179, 223
    adverb, 39, 181
    elliptical, 181
    essential, 179, 273
    if, 207
    independent (or main), 177, 285
      in compound and
        compound-complex
        sentences, 185
    intervening, 215
    nonessential, 179, 273
    noun, 183
    subordinate (dependent), 39,
      149, 177, 277
      choosing between *who/whom*
        in, 235
      in complex sentences, 185
      words to introduce, 123
clincher sentence, 22
closing, in friendly and business
  letters
    capitalization of words in, 307
    commas following, 275
closure in narrative writing, 61
clustering in prewriting, 10–11
coherence, 68
    defined, 27
    importance of, 34–35
    strategies for, 27–28
collective nouns, 121
    listing of, 221
    subject-verb agreement with,
      221
colon(s), 285
    in bibliography between city
      and publisher, 285
    capitalization of words
      following, 309
    between chapter and verse in
      references to Bible, 285
    before formal statement or
      quotation, 285
    after greeting of business letter,
      285

colon(s) (*continued*)

    between hour and minute, 285

    between independent clauses, 285

    to introduce long (block) quotation, 285

    before list of items, 285

    with quotation marks, 291

    to set off word or phrase for emphasis, 285

    between title and subtitle of book, 285

combination paper, 93

combining sentences, 45. *See also* complex sentences; compound-complex sentences; compound sentences

    appositives/appositive phrases in, 163

    commas in, 37, 39, 147

    compound subjects and verbs in, 37

    conjunctions in, 37

    conjunctive adverbs in, 37, 147

    correcting run-on sentences in, 149–50

    correcting sentence fragments in, 141, 147

    phrases in, 161

    semicolons in, 37, 149

    single-word modifiers in, 45

    subordinate clauses in, 39

comma(s)

    after abbreviations, 267

    after closing of friendly and business letters, 275

    in combining sentences, 37, 39, 149

    with compound sentences, 271

    before concluding adverb clauses, 271

    after conjunctive adverbs, 149

    with coordinating conjunctions, 269

    with direct address, 273

    after greeting of friendly letters, 275

    and independent clauses, 37, 149, 271

    with introductory elements, 271

    after introductory prepositional phrases, 161

    with quotation marks, 275, 291

    with semicolons, 287

    to separate geographical terms, 275

    to separate parts of a date, 275

    to separate parts of an address, 275

    to separate parts of a reference, 275

    to separate quotation from dialogue tag, 293

    to separate two or more adjectives before a noun, 269

    in a series, 269

    to set off absolute phrases, 165

    to set off contrasting expressions, 273

    to set off direct quotations, 275

    to set off interjections, 113, 275

    to set off introductory adverb clauses, 181, 271

    to set off nonessential appositives and appositive phrases, 163

    to set off nonessential clauses, 39, 179

    to set off nonessential elements, 179, 273

    to set off nonessential participial phrases, 165

    to set off nouns of direct address, 273

    to set off parenthetical or transitional expressions, 273

    to set off sentence interrupters, 273

    to set off short direct quotations, 275

    to set off tag questions, 275

    in use with dates, 275

commands. *See* imperative sentences

comma splice, 149

common nouns, 121

    comparative as degree of comparison, 249, 251

compare and contrast essay in expository writing, 69–75

comparisons, 24

    degrees of, 249, 251

    double, 249

    illogical, 251

    irregular, 249

    in narrative writing, 61

    transitional words and expressions to show, 28

    unclear, 251

complement, compliment, 370

complements

    defined, 151

    object, 155

    subject, 153, 285

    and linking verbs, 153

complete predicate, 143

complete sentences, 17, 147

complete subjects, 143

complex sentences, 185

    independent clause in, 185

    subordinate clauses in, 185

compliment, complement, 370

compound adjectives, hyphens in, 297

compound-complex sentences, 185

    independent clause in, 185

    subordinate clauses in, 185

compound direct objects, 151

compound indirect objects, 151

compound nouns, 121, 271, 295

    hyphens in, 297

    showing possession with, 295

    spelling plurals of, 325

compound numbers, hyphens in, 297, 321

compound predicate nominative, 231

compound predicates, 37

compound prepositions, 131

compound sentences, 37, 177, 185

    changing run-on sentences into, 277

    commas in forming, 271

    independent clauses in, 185

    semicolons to join independent clauses in, 287

compound subjects, 37, 219

    subject-verb agreement with, 219

compound verbs, 37, 271

    and commas with, 271

computer spell checker, 319

conclusion in essays, 35, 75

concrete nouns, 121

conditions contrary to fact, subjunctive mood to express, 207

conjunction(s)

    in combining sentences, 37, 149

    coordinating, 37, 133, 149, 269

    correlative, 37, 133, 149, 273

    defined, 133

    subordinating, 39, 133, 181, 277

        listing of, 181

conjunctive adverbs, 149

    in combining sentences, 37, 149, 287

    in correcting run-on sentences, 149

    listing of, 37, 149, 287

constellations. *See* planets

construction, incomplete, 237
content in revising, 16
continents, capitalizing names of, 305
contractions, 125, 253, 295
    apostrophes in, 295
    in dialogue, 293
contrast, transitional words and expressions showing, 28
contrasting expressions, commas to set off, 273
controlling idea in essay, 33
coordinating conjunctions, 133
    in combining sentences, 37, 149
    and commas in series, 269
    and commas when combining independent clauses, 269
    and compound sentences, 287
    in correcting run-on sentences, 149
    in forming compound subject or predicate agreement, 37, 219
    and pronoun-antecedent agreement, 239
    and subject-verb agreement, 219
correlative conjunctions, 133, 273
    in combining sentences, 37, 149
    in correcting run-on sentences, 149
    in forming compound subject or predicate, 37, 219
    and pronoun-antecedent agreement, 239
    and subject-verb agreement, 219
correlative constructions, parallel structure in, 187
counterarguments
    in persuasive essays, 66
countries, capitalizing names of, 305
cover letter, 109
    drafting, 114
    example of, 111
    prewriting in, 113–14
    proofreading in, 114
    publishing in, 114
    revising and editing, 114, 199
    skills for writing, 112–13
critical thinking
    in expository writing, 70, 77, 83
    in literary analysis, 89
    in narrative writing, 55–56, 60
    in persuasive writing, 65
    in writing résumé and cover letter, 112

D

dangling modifiers, 257
dash, 297
data, 221
dates, commas to separate parts of, 275
decades, apostrophes in writing about, 295
declarative sentences, 141
    punctuation with, 141, 267
decreasing degrees of comparison, 249
definite articles, 127
definitions, 24
    in persuasive writing, 65
degrees of comparison, 249, 251
    decreasing, 249
    illogical, 251
    irregular, 249
    unclear, 251
demonstrative pronouns, 123
    listing of, 123
dependent clauses, 177. *See also* subordinate clauses
descriptive writing
    sensory details in, 30
    spatial order in, 30
details, 60
    elaborating with supporting, 24
    sensory, 30, 56
development, 24
dialogue
    in narrative writing, 56
    quotation marks with, 293
    and slang in, 293
dialogue tag, 293
dictionaries
    capitalization rules in, 305
    degrees of comparison in, 249
    hyphens in, 297
    preferred spellings in, 323
    prefixes in, 323
    singular/plural status for problematic nouns in, 223
    suffixes in, 323
different from, 370
direct address, noun of, 145
direct commands, imperative mood to express, 207
directional words, capitalizing, 305
direct objects, 151, 153, 155, 201, 233, 235
direct object test for irregular verbs, 201
direct questions, 267
direct quotations, 291, 293

capitalizing first words of, 309
    commas to set off, 275
do, in forming the emphatic form of verbs, 203
documents, capitalization of names of, 311
doesn't/don't as singular and plural verbs, 215
double comparison, 249
double negative, 253
drafting
    and a cover letter, 114
    defined, 14
    in expository writing, 74–75, 81, 85, 107
    in literary analysis, 91–92
    in narrative writing, 57, 62
    outline in, 13
    in persuasive writing, 68
    research paper, 107
    for résumé and cover letter, 114
    strategies in, 14–15

E

editing, 9
    of business letters, 199
Editing and Proofreading Worksheets, 279, 280, 299, 300, 313, 314, 327, 328
Editing Tip, 125, 129, 151, 153, 161, 167, 183, 187, 197, 201, 203, 207, 215, 217, 219, 233, 237, 249, 251, 253, 267, 271, 275, 285, 287, 291, 295, 297, 305, 309, 325
effect, affect, 369
effect, cause and, 76
ei, spelling rules for, 321
elaboration, 24
ellipsis point(s), 90, 297
elliptical adverb clause, 181
elliptical construction, 237
e-mail, showing emphasis in, 311
emigrate, immigrate, 370
emphasis
    colon to set off word or phrase for, 285
    showing in e-mail, 311
    transitional words and expressions showing, 28
emphatic form of verb, 203
English, standard, 199, 215, 251, 253
essays, 33–35
    body in, 34–35
    capitalizing titles of, 307
    cause-effect, 76–81